First-Time Europe

written and researched by

Doug Lansky

ROUGH
GUIDES

www.roughguides.com

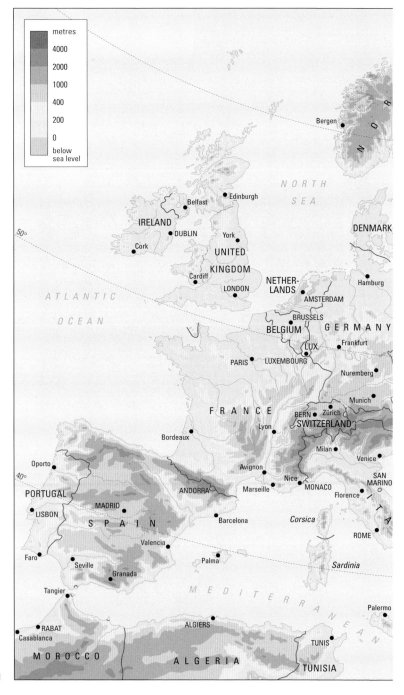

metres
4000
2000
1000
400
200
0
below
sea level

NORTH

Bergen

NORTH
SEA

Belfast ● Edinburgh

IRELAND

DUBLIN

York

Cork

UNITED
KINGDOM

DENMARK

Hamburg

ATLANTIC

OCEAN

Cardiff
LONDON

NETHER-
LANDS

AMSTERDAM

BRUSSELS

BELGIUM

GERMANY

Frankfurt

LUX.

PARIS ●   LUXEMBOURG

Nuremberg

Munich

FRANCE

BERN ● Zürich

SWITZERLAND

Bordeaux

Lyon

Milan ●

Venice

Oporto

Avignon

Nice

SAN
MARINO

PORTUGAL

MADRID

ANDORRA

Marseille

MONACO

Florence

I
T
A

LISBON

SPAIN

Barcelona

Corsica

ROME

Faro

Valencia

Seville
Granada

Palma

Sardinia

Tangier

MEDITERRANEAN

Palermo

● RABAT
Casablanca

ALGIERS

MOROCCO

ALGERIA

TUNIS

TUNISIA

50°

40°

II

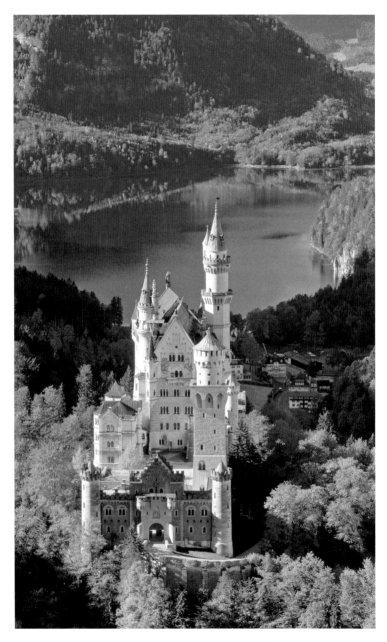

△ Neuschwanstein Castle, Germany

First-Time **Europe** | **INTRODUCTION**

Introduction to

First-Time
Europe

Italians don't serve "deep pan" pizza. Swedes aren't all blonds. And the French probably won't French-kiss you when you first greet. But none of these little cultural realities is reason enough to put off your trip to Europe – the "Old World" offers more architecture, wine, music, fashion, theatre and gastronomy per square kilometre than any other continent. Which means heading off the main routes will still land you waist-deep in cultural treasures. The continent boasts over seven hundred million people (including Russia), in excess of three hundred World Heritage Sites and more legendary paintings than you can point your camera at. And it's usually just a matter of a short bus or train ride to get from one place to the next – though even a bicycle will often suffice.

 Europe stretches 4200km from the southern tip of Portugal to the northeastern coast of Norway, and just as far from Iceland to Athens. But with the reunification of East and West at the end of the 1980s leading to widespread improvements in roads and rail, Europe is more accessible than ever. The introduction of the euro makes spending easier and means you're no longer giving away fistfuls of commission to the moneychangers every time you cross a border. What you put this little saving towards is quite limit-less: climbing a Swiss Alp, tasting wine at a French chateau, renting a surfboard in Portugal, having tea and scones in England, chilling out in Sweden's *Ice Hotel* or soaking your toes in the Adriatic off the Croatian coast. You'll almost be able to kid yourself that one of these will be achieved with the savings you'll reap from a common currency, especially if you're using clever budgeting tricks and strategies (see p.65) to cut costs along the way.

Europe's riches are waiting; the decision to find them is yours. In other words, this book is not going to try to persuade you to travel, nor try to convince you that stomping around with a backpack will fulfil whatever may be missing from your life. Travel is an urge best cultivated from within. In fact, one of the biggest favours you can do for yourself is to travel when you want to, not when someone else thinks you should. The more eager you are to open yourself up to life on the road, the more willing you'll be to shrug off the pre-packed experience and reap real rewards.

Of course, that first trip overseas can be intimidating, and few people ever feel completely ready. You'll invariably

▽ Street market, Madrid, Spain

△ The Matterhorn, Switzerland

make some mistakes along the way – we all have – but with this book you'll be able to sidestep the major pitfalls. It will walk you through some of the more baffling bits of the planning process that tend to trip up many travellers, and will also show how to enrich parts of your travels that commonly get glossed over, make sure you have your gear and documents in order before leaving, and help bring the entire overseas experience together well within your budget. You might start by cracking open the map on pp.ii–iii and let your mind ponder the possibilities. Then flip to p.5 and learn how to start customizing your journey.

The country profiles in the second part of the book provide a glimpse into each country to assist with your preparation, highlighting landmarks and festivals, providing more detailed weather info and letting you know if there are any bus or train passes you should consider buying before your arrival. Of course, you'll want more specific information eventually, either from websites or publications listed in the Basics section at the end of the book or from your guidebook once you arrive, but at this point such facts and figures would bog down the planning process rather than help it along. And you'd barely be able to lift this book. Besides, there is such a thing as too much planning. One of the greatest thrills of travel is making your trip up as you go.

FAQ

Will I manage travelling around Europe only speaking English?

Better than you'll manage only eating at *McDonald's*. English and, when necessary, a few hand gestures will get you by just fine in most situations. Remember to keep your speech slow and basic, skip the slang, and don't take a puzzled look as a sign to speak louder. That said, if you make the effort to pick up a language, you'll enrich your experience tenfold. At the very least, take twenty minutes to learn "please", "thank you", "excuse me", "where?", "toilet", "how much?", and "eight euros for a beer?! You must be out of your mind!" in the local languages. For more info on language schools, see p.102.

I've got €3500 saved up. Will that be enough?

No problem. The question is: for what kind of trip and for how long? To figure out a daily budget that fits your comfort level and to discover which countries offer the best value, turn to the "Costs and savings" chapter (see p.65). You'll pick up savings tips there as well.

How do I figure out where to sleep each night and what to see during the day?

Easy. Carry a guidebook. There are extensive lists of places to stay at various price ranges in each city, with short descriptions to help you narrow down your selection. They even have maps to help you navigate your way there – often to places within walking distance from the central train station. In peak periods such as summer, you may want to find an Internet café and book a few days or weeks in advance for central hostels in popular cities. At most tourist offices (often conveniently located at the train station), they'll call around and find an available room for you once

you've arrived. Of course, you can always just show up at the front door with your pack. For more, see p.157.

I'm thinking of going with my best friend. Is that a good idea?

Possibly not. Travelling with a partner or two should be a

Why even the rich travel cheap

There's a trend shift under way, a return to the old-fashioned style of travelling where people actually seek out the foreignness of a place. A few of the world's premium hotels now charge over €20,000 for a single night in their top suite, but no matter how nice the room, many are waking up to the fact that no four walls make up a complete (or very real) travel experience. It's what happens outside the hotel, your connection with

△ Cave hotel, Cappadocia, Turkey

your immediate surrounds and your interaction with the local people that enables you to embrace travel with the intensity it deserves. Even the most exclusive bespoke tour operators are starting to send some of their clients to more rough-and-tumble digs in remote destinations in an effort to help them unearth unique cultural experiences that tap into the essence of a place. If you're travelling on a minuscule budget, you might keep this in mind and look at those pensions and hostels with a new light: you're not letting cushy funding insulate you from the elements of cultural travel.

carefully weighed decision. Turn to p.58 to make sure you know what you're getting into and how to minimize the potential pitfalls.

There's just two weeks left before my trip and I haven't done a thing. I don't even have a passport. Am I too late?

Nope, but you've got your work cut out. Step 1: sort out your passport. You'll need expedited service (see p.108). Step 2: get some credit cards. You'll probably want two. Or at least one credit card and one cash card. Step 3: get hold of a budget card like ISIC or another you qualify for. Step four: buy your plane ticket. Step 5: organize rail and bus passes. There are a few other things you'll need, and you can find all that on p.122.

I've heard there are bus and train passes you can use to get around. Which is better?

The typical bus pass is a bit cheaper, but comes with more hand-holding (it drops you right off at a specific hostel). On board there are only other travellers (and videos playing on the TV), so there's not as much local cultural interaction, but some people love it as you do meet loads of other travellers. You can also travel on regular long-distance buses, but one of Europe's real treats is the incredible rail system, and it's nice to be able to get up and take a stroll to the dining car during a long journey.

I was thinking of going for a month. Is that too little time?

One month in Spain is more realistic than two months in Spain, France, Germany, Holland, Italy, England and Austria. You get the idea. To figure out a manageable amount to try and conquer on your trip, see p.5.

What if everything gets stolen, even my passport?

Go to the local police and report it. Have them call your nearest embassy. Call your parents collect and get some funds wired. There are a few other important things to do (see p.188), but the message is this: you'll be OK. To prevent this from happening in the first place, check out the "Carrying valuables" chapter (see p.139).

Is there one thing I should take that I probably haven't thought of?

Earplugs. Many hostels are located next to busy intersections and night-clubs. Some cabins on night trains don't have great ventilation and you need to keep the window open, which lets in plenty of air but more decibels than you'd care for. And then there's the ubiquitous snoring roommate. There are several more practical things you'll want to bring as well, though. For a complete list, check out p.132.

Is there anything I should leave at home?

Yep, several things. Starting with your "going out" shoes. If you find you need a pair of dress shoes for a night or two, you can pick up a hip pair (retro-hip, anyway) for €4 at a secondhand store. Textbooks are a popular pack-along with well-intentioned students, but the cumbersome tomes rarely get opened. For more items better left behind, see p.136.

Do I really need travel insurance?

Only if you get injured. Or very sick. Or sued for some driving accident. If this happens and you don't have insurance, you're screwed. Well, not just you. Possibly your parents and employer as well, depending on how shrewd and aggressive their lawyers are and how much you owe. The question is which

△ Trevi Fountain, Rome, Italy

insurance to get. Turn to p.113 to find out what to look for and why you shouldn't just buy the one your travel agent tries to sell you on the spot. For European citizens, if you've got the right forms (E111 – see p.113 for when and where this is being phased out – or E128), you've got your medical expenses covered, at least for emergency services.

things to enrich your journey

Adventure and cultural insights can be found almost anywhere. How you decide to travel and what you decide to do is far more important than where you decide to go and what you intend to see. Thinking in terms of "doing" rather than "seeing" will enhance that most vital and often elusive dimension to your travels: depth.

01 **Climb a mountain** Mont Blanc, France

02 **Try the local specialities wherever you go**
Chestnuts in İstanbul, Turkey

03 **Make friends with other travellers**

04 **View attractions early** St Mark's Square, Venice, Italy

05 **Hunt for bargains at the local market** Grand
Bazaar, İstanbul, Turkey

06 **Try the local firewater**
Oktoberfest, Munich, Germany

07 **Take in at least one great local meal** Mýkonos, Greece

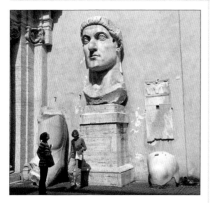

08 **Learn some art history** Capitoline Museum, Rome, Italy

09 **Take a painting course** Luxembourg Gardens, Paris, France

10 **Grab tickets online to avoid queues** The Louvre, Paris, France

11 Rent a bike and explore
Amsterdam, the Netherlands

12 Kayak through a fjord
Nordfjord, Norway

13 Check out a sporting event Italian fans at King Baudouin Stadium, Brussels, Belgium

14 Volunteer Cleaning up a beach in Brittany, France

16 Read a novel set in the place you're travelling through Reading *The Old Curiosity Shop*, London, England

15 Jump in the ocean

ACTIVITIES | CONSUME | EVENTS | NATURE | SIGHTS

17 **Learn a foreign language** Studying a sign for the Acropolis, Athens, Greece

18 **Taste some wine at a chateau** Burgundy, France

19 **Take in the cultural scene** Minack Theatre, Land's End, England

20 **Experience a new sport** Hurling, Dublin, Ireland

21 Try a family stay Provence, France

23 Participate in a festival
Running of the Bulls, Pamplona, Spain

24 Explore a place not in the guidebook

25 Float down a river on a barge Grand Union Canal, England

Contents

Colour section

The big adventure

Country profiles

Basics

small print and Index

First-Time Europe

The big adventure

Planning your big trip

Deciding where to go, how to get there, what to do and how long to stay is a lot easier than it sounds. In this chapter, the planning process is chopped into smaller, easier-to-chew pieces that will get you under way, from figuring out what activities are available in each place to avoiding troublesome weather and catching the festivals you don't want to miss. Because prices change from year to year, sometimes peak season to low season, and exchange rates fluctuate on a daily basis, many guides are reluctant to list specific prices. That's an easy way out, but doesn't make it easy to calculate your budget or get a sense of prices as you read. In this guide, you'll find prices listed in euros (€) in nearly all cases. At the time of research, the rates were approximately €1: $1.25 and £0.70 ($1: €0.80; £1: €1.45.)

How much time do you need?

Here's a better question: how much time can you spare? You could easily spend a lifetime hopping around Europe and not see or experience all it has to offer. So, carve out whatever time you can and worry later about what you'll do with it. Besides, it's easier to come home early than try to push back deadlines once you're on the move.

I don't have much money – should I travel cheap or wait until I've got the funds to do it in style?

Independent budget travel in Europe isn't for everyone. Especially if you're not thrilled about eating most of your meals picnic-style on park benches or in youth hostel kitchens, or spending the night in a place that considers the urine stain on the mattress all the decoration the room needs. If this doesn't seem like it would faze you, you're in luck; the cultural and social payoff of budget travel is enormous, the experience invaluable. As nice as it may sound to travel in comfort, a thick wallet has a tendency to insulate you from the very culture you're trying to experience. That is, you don't want the only locals you meet to be the ones carrying your bags and serving you drinks. You don't want the places you stay to be identical to the places you can stay back at home. And a tight budget helps in this regard, whether you want it to or not.

If you're not ready to travel on the cheap, you'll still find plenty of essential information and itinerary ideas from the ensuing pages, but you may have to limit your time on the road, or knock off a bank. Three months of air-conditioned tours, meals served on real tablecloths, and comfortable hotel rooms could set you back €24,500, whereas it can be done for €4900 or even less with a few tips from the "Costs and savings" chapter (see p.65).

The truth is, you won't know how long you'll want to go for until you get out there. You may meet someone who will invite you along on a camping trip, or you might stumble across a great course that lasts two months, or suddenly have a burning desire to sketch Italy's most famous frescoes. The trick at this point is to structure your trip so that those unforeseen experiences can happen.

If you already know how long you've got, you should be thinking about the pace of your trip. How many countries, cities and activities should you try to tackle in that amount of time? A good guideline is this: don't plan more than four major activities per month in advance. (Sorry, visiting Spain doesn't count as a single activity, but things like a two-day cooking class, a short stay with a relative, a few days exploring a major city and a hiking trip do.) Less than four is even better. If you plan to see, say, Paris and Rome in June, that doesn't necessarily mean you're only going to see these two cities. It means you get to make up the rest of your plans on the move as you travel between. This approach allows for ample flexibility, plus any transport delays you may encounter (when it comes to transportation strikes, the French and Italians are in a league of their own).

If the length of your trip is largely dictated by budget, check out the "Costs and savings" chapter (see p.65) to help calculate your time on the road and maximize the funds you have. However, you don't need to let your initial funds shorten your trip. "Working, volunteering and studying" (see p.82) covers jobs and volunteer projects, so you can leave home with minimal money or stretch your trip for years.

Any amount of time is better than none, but less than a month doesn't give you much of a chance to get into the rhythm of travel. You may get accused by "hard-core" travellers of not getting a real taste of the road on a short trip, but don't be put off by their comments; if you concentrate your trip in one area and take some type of course or stay with some locals, you'll get a more culturally enriching experience than most of them ever do. A year off has a nice ring to it, but that's not a realistic time frame for those with jobs to return to or student loans that need paying off. Travel over a year and people back home may start to think you've completely lost it. Two to six months is a reasonable target. It will give you a chance to do some exploring and even allow you to dig a little deeper with one or more cultures. The best option is to have a flexible ticket so you can return when you're ready.

How much time do you need in each place?

Two days. That is, two days longer than you think. Maybe even two weeks. The faster you go and the more ground you cover, tempting though it may be, the less you'll see. According to the author Wendell Berry, "Our senses…were developed to function at foot speeds." The same way that slowing down improves your peripheral vision when driving, reducing your speed enables you to take more in while you travel. Or take the advice of travel author Peter Moore: "If you're having a good time – stay. If you've met someone you fancy and who fancies you – stay. If you're too buggered to move – stay. If the police are closing in on you – go." If you're not pressed to press on, you might forge a friendship with the traveller you met over breakfast or find out your favourite musician is giving a concert in an ancient amphitheatre nearby, or that the local cultural centre is offering free palm-tree-climbing lessons. With enough time and curiosity, something interesting is bound to happen.

Why you need a pit stop and when you should take it

Travel can be romantic and adventurous, but finding your way around a city, coordinating train schedules, locating a place to stay, taking the stairs up every tall structure for a scenic overview, using perplexing toilets, sampling palate-numbing foods and testing each country's unique beers – the things that give independent travel its bite – combine to form an exhausting experience. Give yourself a chance to relax.

To some extent, taking a break is going to happen on its own. You might stumble upon a place you can't resist, get stuck waiting for a ferry that's not running due to inclement weather, find a fun person or group of travellers to hang out with or just hit the sensory-overload wall.

The last one will occur if the first four don't. This exhaustion – think of it as cultural burnout – typically occurs after two to four months of continuous, fairly fast-paced travel, but you'll need to find your own threshold. It may creep up on you, or it may just descend on you all at once but there's always one main symptom: you spend more and more time in cafés and hostel lounges and less time out exploring towns and museums. There's a simple remedy for recharging your wanderlust: stay put. Give yourself a chance to absorb and process what you've seen. Write some long letters. Get to know a few locals. Take the opportunity to earn some money. Who knows, stay in one place long enough and you might even fall in love.

On a long trip, allow yourself the flexibility to stop when you need it, or plan ahead so you end up at your dream hangout. If you hope to work or volunteer, or take a course (see p.000), or pay a relative an extended visit, you might try to plan some of that ahead of time as well. Whether or not you schedule a pit stop in advance, you should factor in some "down time": at least two weeks for every three months on the road. On a two-month trip, try to give yourself at least a week in one spot.

Where to go

Here's the good news: you can't miss. That is, there's no wrong place to go. It's what you decide to do there that makes the real difference. Want to spend two weeks in France? Two weeks at a homestay learning French, two weeks visiting the tourist attractions in Paris, and two weeks at an intensive cooking school are so different they can hardly be summed up as "spending two weeks in France". Even on that same farm, at those same attractions and at that same cooking school, you'd have a hard time replicating the experience of someone else who did those things. There are simply too many variables. Forget about trying to find the "Top 10" this and the "best-of" that

– you *can* find a magical experience, but if you don't push yourself off the tourist trail and do something that moves you, there will be very little "top" or "best" or "magical" of anything, unless you count "best staged photo in front of famous architecture." And remember: what might seem awful at the time may, in retrospect, prove to be the most life-changing event of your journey.

To find the best places, the only person to consult is yourself. Grab a pencil, take a look at the four points below, and start jotting down places, sights and activities that sound appealing. You can figure out how to connect them later.

Go where you speak the language

No, not English. A second language (although an English-speaking country is a fine place to begin your travels). Even if you can just read a menu and a few street signs, you're off to a good start. Europe is a great place for the lingual novice; you can almost always find an English speaker when you need one. Tapping into these ubiquitous translators should be your safety net, however, not your crutch. The idea is that, once you start using a language, once you start looking around and trying to decipher the words or communicate where you need to go, the learning curve becomes nearly vertical and you're taking a big step into the culture you've come to experience.

Go where you have family or friends

Don't be afraid to look up that childhood pen pal in Estonia or your third cousin once removed in Portugal. To cover your bets, bring along some kind of document or a snapshot to help bridge any gaps. Despite any present-day politics, you'll find Europeans have a special place in their hearts for relatives and old friends that have been separated by oceans for years. With a little luck, you'll find you've got yourself a cultural guide. You'll almost certainly get a free place to stay and, if nothing else, an inside look at the way they live, from food and interior decor to lawn bowling and nude beaches, or whatever your relatives happen to do for fun.

Go somewhere you've longed to see

A little wanderlust goes a long way. If there's some place you've read about, heard people talk about for ages, or had some sort of child-hood fascination with, then that's not a bad reason to go – at the very worst, it's a decent starting point. Let James Joyce's *Ulysses* be your tour guide through Dublin or jumpstart your wandering in Paris by retracing a few scenes from *Amélie*. If it sounds too trivial, keep in mind that many of the travellers who end up in Transylvania are there just because they like the sound of it.

Attractions of the world

When you start travelling, you hear a lot about "attractions" and "must-sees" and "wonders". Is it tourist-bureau hype or is there something to it? In reality, it's a bit of both. When the hype is old enough, it seems to become legend, or even fact. The classic is the "Wonders of the World". For the record, Europe had three of the original Seven Wonders of the Ancient World: the Statue of Zeus in Olympia, Greece; the Temple of Artemis at Ephesus, Turkey; and the Colossus of Rhodes, Greece. Unfortunately, they've all been destroyed.

None of the twelve Natural Wonders are located in Europe, only five of the nineteen so-called Forgotten Wonders and just three Modern Wonders. What's left? Plenty – Europe has 306 of UNESCO's 754 World Heritage Sites, more than any other two continents combined. These are the world's architectural and archeological treasures, as defined by this special United Nations body. There's a wide range of sites. Many, like the Cathedral of Notre-Dame in Paris or the archeological areas of Pompeí, you're familiar with. Others, like France's fortified city of Carcassonne or Italy's Botanical Garden in Padua, you may have never heard of. Are they less impressive than the more famous sights? Perhaps, but there are almost certainly fewer crowds. To find out where they are and their historical significance, visit Ⓦhttp://whc.unesco.org.

Forgotten Wonders
The Colosseum, Rome, Italy
The Leaning Tower of Pisa, Italy
Mont-Saint-Michel, Normandy, France
The Parthenon, Athens, Greece
Stonehenge, England

Modern Wonders
The Eiffel Tower, Paris, France
The Channel Tunnel, under the English Channel
Big Ben, England

Follow your interests

This is perhaps the best tool to use to start picking your destinations. The concept is simple enough: instead of thinking about what you'd like to see, think about what you'd like to do. Approach the trip as a chance to collect unique experiences, not passport

Museum heavyweights

Louvre
Where: Paris, France
What: Classics, sculptures and artefacts
Most famous pieces: *The Mona Lisa*, *Winged Victory* and *Venus de Milo*
Cost: €8.50, €6 after 6pm
Website: ⓦ www.louvre.fr

Hermitage Museum
Where: St Petersburg, Russia
What: Classics, sculptures and artefacts
Most famous piece: Possibly Cézanne's *Girl at the Piano*
Cost: €13
Website: ⓦ www.hermitagemuseum.org

British Museum
Where: London, England
What: Artefacts, architecture and other items uprooted by the British Empire
Most famous pieces: Its mummy collection and the Rosetta Stone
Cost: Free, donation requested
Website: ⓦ www.thebritishmuseum.ac.uk

Kremlin and Armoury
Where: Moscow, Russia
What: Royal carriages, guns and tsars' clothing
Most famous pieces: Fabergé eggs, Orlov Diamond and Tsar cannon and bell
Cost: €16

Kunsthistorisches Museum
Where: Vienna, Austria
What: Classics
Most famous pieces: Its Titian and Giorgiones collections
Cost: €10
Website: ⓦ www.khm.at

Prado
Where: Madrid, Spain
What: Classics
Most famous piece: *Las Meninas* by Velázquez
(Picasso's *Guernica* has been moved to Museo Reina Sofia)

stamps, postcards and snapshots in front of famous monuments. If you're a golfer, you might pursue the sport to its roots with a round at the Old Course in St Andrews in Scotland. Or try a twist, and stop for a game of ice golf in Finland, where you can play with a bright-orange ball, tee it up on an ice cube you hack out of the

Cost: €3
Website: ⊛http://museoprado.mcu.es

Vatican Museums
Where: Rome, Italy
What: Maps, frescoes and classics
Most famous piece: The Sistine Chapel
Cost €19.50
Website: ⊛www.vatican.va/phome_en.htm

Tate Modern
Where: London, England
What: Modern art
Most famous piece: Whatever's in the Turbine Hall (the collection changes every six months)
Cost: Free, donations encouraged
Website: ⊛www.tate.org.uk

Uffizi
Where: Florence, Italy
What: Frescoes and sculptures
Most famous piece: Any number of masterpieces, from Botticelli's *Primavera* to Titian's *Urbino Venus*
Cost: €8
Website: ⊛www.uffizi.firenze.it

Deutsches Museum
Where: Munich, Germany
What: Natural sciences, technology and industry
Most famous piece: Its aeroplane collection
Cost: €7.50
Website: ⊛www.deutsches-museum.de

City of Science and Industry
Where: Paris, France
What: Astronomy and science
Most famous piece: Its chrome ball-styled planetarium
Cost: €7.50
Website: ⊛www.cite-sciences.fr

fairway, and putt on icy "whites". If you like to cook, you might take a pastry course at the world-famous Cordon Bleu school in Paris or try a day of pasta preparation at a villa in Tuscany. The more original your approach, the more unique your experience is likely to be.

When to go

On a long trip, you can't be everywhere at just the ideal time. Don't knock yourself out trying. Usually, if it's too hot inland, you can head for the coast. And if it's too hot on the coast you can move to higher elevations, where temperatures are milder. Sweating it out in Rome? It's only 25km from the beaches of Fregene and Ostia in the costal town of Fiumicino. Or take an overnight train into the Alps and hike around Lugano. It's pretty impossible to avoid a day or two of rain, but finding good weather typically requires just two things: keeping your eye on the weather reports, and a flexible schedule. What you need to investigate, therefore, is not the ideal time to be in each location, but if there are any dates you should absolutely avoid (see p.18). Much of this depends on what you plan to do. Southern Italy in January may be chilly but it's fine for city exploring, especially if you plan to be inside museums and churches, whereas the weather in Chamonix in January may render mountain biking impossible. If you plan to hitch sections of your journey on boats, make sure you check out the seasonal schedule. Similarly, you'll want to know if there are any dates not to miss. If you're applying for a seasonal job, there's usually a tight window. And it's a pity to unwittingly arrive in Venice a day after Carnevale has ended; you're stuck with the crowds but have missed the event. See the individual country profiles for more specific information on local weather and events.

Off-season travel

It's not all gravy during the off-season. Some places just never quiet down. I was in Florence, Italy one November and it felt as if I had taken a bus to Chicago, but for the old buildings and marble statues of pantless men. English, not Italian, was by far the dominant language on the streets, and the people walking around without a camera were in the minority. Florence (and Venice) aside, I found off-season travel to be hugely rewarding. I got into sights faster, my pictures weren't spoiled by people resting their behemoth bums on the 2000-year-old ruins and, above all, a surprising amount of local flavour surfaced, even in places like Paris.

Leif Pettersen

Travel seasons

Travelling in the peak season is climatically favourable, but the advantages of touring Europe out of season are numerous: low-cost and less crowded flights, better chances of finding a room at the cheapest hostels, shorter queues at museums, less need for reservations, and – best of all – fewer visitors to distract you from the culture you came to observe. However, you may be looking at a few hidden expenses. Some of the cheapest hotels shut down in the off-season, so you may be forced into more expensive digs. If it's cold enough to rattle your teeth loose at night, expect to pay extra for a room with heat. If you've arrived in the hot and sweaty season, be prepared to pay more for air conditioning. Sure, you can combat these with a good sleeping bag or a cold, wet sarong wrap, but you

European festivals and events

Cities and towns come alive during festivals. The locals are more upbeat, more welcoming and the experience is often more interactive. It's a pity to miss a festival by a day or two, and arrive just in time to watch the streets get cleaned while you pay for the still-inflated hotel prices. Festival planning usually takes some advance legwork, though, as cities and towns can get booked up over a year in advance. Last-minute accommodation, if indeed there is any, gets snatched up several days before the event, but the extra effort it takes to attend a festival is almost always worthwhile. There are hundreds to choose from around Europe. In some you can participate, in some the spectators become part of the spectacle whether they want to or not, but the exuberance is nearly always palpable.

Here are a few of the major events around the continent. To find some of the lesser-known festivals, turn to the country profiles at the back of the book and see ⊛www.festivals.com and ⊛www.world-party.com.

Carnevale, Venice, Italy. A decadent renaissance festival, pyjama party, and three-day rager played out against the backdrop of the world's most picturesque sinking city. The costumes are as elaborate as they are expensive. And guess what? They're for sale. Feb–March (the week prior to Ash Wednesday); ⊛www.venice-carnival.com

St Patrick's Day, Dublin, Ireland. If you're not in green, you better have a good excuse. And a hangover that makes you feel green doesn't count. There's everything from Skyfest, an enormous fireworks display, to a treasure hunt that has families scurrying around the city. The full week of "craic" culminates with 500,000 lining the streets for Ireland's biggest parade. March 11–17. ⊛www.stpatricksday.ie

Las Fallas, Valencia, Spain. Two million people unite in Valencia to honour St Joseph by building six-metre-high papier-mâché effigies of local or national celebrities, parading them through town, then stuffing them with fireworks and explosives and setting them ablaze. Sound like fun? Grab some earplugs and join the riot. March 15–19; ⊛www.fallas.com

Cooper's Hill Cheese Roll, Brockworth, England. Maybe the hospital was running low on patients but, for whatever reason, people have been chasing a cheese down a sixty-degree slope here for over 200 years. Most tumble in a blur of legs, hands and dislocated shoulders all the way to the bottom. Don't worry; there are plenty of ambulances standing by. Last Mon in May; ⊛www.cheese-rolling.co.uk

Paris Air Show, Paris, France. You don't need to be on the market for your own private F-15 to attend. The public, all 300,000 of them, turn out to see new models take off from the spot Charles Lindbergh first landed. It's the biggest air show going. June (odd numbered years only); ⊛www.paris-air-show.com

World Cup 2006, Germany. If you want to time your trip to coincide with the biggest event in Europe, this would be the one. Football is often called the world's largest religion, and when you see the costumes, face paint, praying and chanting, you'll know why. When the high altar comes to

Deutschland, the entire country will turn into one big footballing frenzy. June–July 2006; ⓦ www.fifaworldcup.com

Royal Ascot, Ascot, England. You can bet on the horses, but keep your eyes on the pomp on parade; morning suits for men and formal dresses for women, not to mention hats of all sorts, from those with the shade coverage of a patio parasol to dainty little numbers not much bigger than a cinnamon roll. Tues–Sat; third week in June ⓦ www.royalascot.co.uk

Glastonbury Music Festival, Glastonbury, England. The biggest, baddest jam-fest in the UK. Performers on the three main stages have included Oasis, Paul McCartney, James Brown, and a full cast of platinum-selling album-holders. On the fringe of the concert you'll find market stalls (over 600 of them) offering everything from goat meat to henna tattoos. Not enough? Check out the freak show or help make a giant rhino out of mud. June 25–27; ⓦ www.glastonburyfestivals.co.uk

Montreux Jazz Festival, Geneva, Switzerland. Expanding from its jazz roots, this world-famous music event now bursts with blues, rock and pop acts as well. Each summer around 200,000 people congregate on the eastern shore of Lake Geneva to watch some of the best musicians on the planet jam in the Alps. The festival has its own currency, so be sure to exchange your euros for "Jazz" when entering. First two weeks of July; ⓦ www.montreuxjazz.com

Il Palio, Siena, Italy. Combining bribes, religion and dirty tricks, this horse race is straight out of the Middle Ages. To be precise, 1147. Riders representing Siena's different neighbourhoods battle and race around the town square for three laps. The party starts for days before each of the two big races. Early July & mid-Aug; ⓦ www.ilpaliodisiena.com

Running of the Bulls, Pamplona, Spain. People have been testing out their insurance polices at this event for years. Eight days of drinking, revelling in the streets and, oh yes, attempting to avoid stampeding bulls on a narrow, winding, cobblestoned street armed with nothing more than a pair of running shoes, a rolled-up newspaper and a hangover. July; ⓦ www.sanfermin.com

Love Parade, Berlin, Germany. At the world's largest rave, you'll see mosaic tattoos, blinding hair colours, and more body piercings than you can shake a ... well, you better think twice before you shake anything at them. Millions of technophiles dance nonstop as they squirm through the über-fest, exchanging sweat, drugs and exotic diseases. July; ⓦ www.loveparade.de

La Tomatina, Buñol, Spain. Take one small town that produces cement, one town plaza, 30,000 mostly drunk lunatics and 40,000 kg of tomatoes. Mix aggressively for one hour or until town is sufficiently red, then rinse at a local watering hole. Last Wed in Aug; ⓦ www.lahoya.net/tomatina

Oktoberfest, Munich, Germany. Just grab a seat and a frothy *mas* and start slidin' back the brew. The atmosphere (over 5000 buzzing, swaying, happy drinkers per tent) makes the beer taste even better. But don't let the name fool you; most of the event takes place in September. Sept–Oct; ⓦ www.muenchen-tourist.de

might not always be in the mood. As a general rule, the best times to visit are at the beginning and end of the tourist cycles, the so-called shoulder seasons (March 1–June 1 and Sept 1–Nov 1 for southern Europe; April 15–June 1 and Sept 1–Oct 1 for northern Europe), when you get the good weather without the crowds.

When not to go

Rather than aiming for the perfect time to go, focus on avoiding the wrong time, bearing in mind that there are degrees of right and wrong to consider as well. For example, you might want to steer clear of Rome in August – all the Italians have left on vacation and the country is invaded by scores of tourists and sweltering temperatures. It's not a great time to be there, but it's hardly a catastrophe. However, if you plan on cycling across Scandinavia, you absolutely don't want to be doing it between November and March.

In general, winter (Nov–Feb) in northern Europe is cold and rainy, and snowstorms are common. Southern Europe can get chilly, but is typically quite mild. Summer (June–Aug) is pleasant in northern Europe and very hot in southern Europe.

△ It's hard to avoid the rain at the Wimbledon Tennis Championships, London

Planning around local holidays and events

Your overnight train pulls into the station, you stagger over to the tourist information bureau and say you're looking for some budget accommodation for a night or two. The person behind the counter is nodding their head like a paint shaker before you even finish your sentence. There's a Rotary Club convention and a national youth volleyball competition in town and they've taken up all the rooms. The best the tourist office can do is a double room at the *Ritz* for €285. Or you can stay an hour out of town at a little hostel situated next to a minimum-security psychiatric ward.

Occasionally, scheduling conflicts occur. A rock concert, business convention or sporting event unexpectedly disrupts your travel plans. So what do you do? First, try to avoid the situation by keeping an eye on your guidebook for national holidays or other events that might cause a hotel-booking frenzy. Then, if you expect the city's accommodation to fill up, email ahead for a reservation (websites to hostels can be found in your guidebook), or try a site like ⓦwww.hostelworld.com or delay your arrival until a more auspicious day. If you're already there, the easiest thing to do is to simply move on to the next town. For this, the tourist office can be quite helpful. It's the perfect time to head somewhere not mentioned in a guidebook, but before you do, ask for a list of accommodation the tourist office represents and a phone book. Cross-check their list with the one in the *Yellow Pages*. Often, there are several hotels, especially the cheaper digs, not on the list. Give those places a call first; they're the most likely to have a room. Or look for less conventional places to stay, such as university dormitories or campgrounds that rent tents. Don't forget to ask about rooftop sleeping at hostels if the weather is favourable.

Researching your trip

The Internet works a treat for trip planning. Let's say you speak Spanish and you like scuba diving: start at your favourite Web search engine, type in "scuba" and "Spanish" and see what pops up, then narrow the search with words like "shark" or "tequila" or whatever diving aspects you deem essential. You can often find reviews and references online as well just by adding the words "reviews" or "references" to the search.

For specific activities, look in specialized magazines and newsletters. For a cooking course or fine dining, for example, you might look in *Gourmet Magazine*; for photography trips, *Outdoor Photographer*. If you're looking for general ideas, major-city newspaper travel sections are invaluable. A similar assortment, often with more edgy writing, can be found in adventure magazines, with some of the best ideas located among the tour advertisements listed in the back. That doesn't necessarily mean you ought to sign up for their tours – many of those things you can do on your own for a fraction of the price.

For information directly from other travellers, try ⓦwww.roughguides.com's Travel Talk, where you can post and read messages on thousands of specific travel topics. Other sites, such as ⓦwww.virtualtourist.com and ⓦwww.lonelyplanet.com's Thorn Tree, offer similar discussion boards.

Preparing your parents and employers

Not everyone may be as excited about your big trip as you are. Some parents might need a bit of convincing on the merits of such an endeavour, especially if you're making a large request for funding. Some employers will wonder what they'll gain by keeping your position available. So here's a little ammunition to help fight your corner.

Dear Mom and Dad,

I know you want what's best for me. I know you want me to be safe. And I know you want me to (earn a living/attend university/stop moonlighting as an erotic dancer). We both want those things. But as I see it, life isn't about racing to the finish line. I'll get a (job/degree) eventually, but I want to appreciate life first. Just now, I have a few things I need to work out, and there's no better place to get a taste of life's options than the world's biggest classroom. This is the perfect time in my life for free-spirited travel. I don't have kids. This may be the one chance in my life to do it on my own terms. And Europe is one of the world's safest destinations. Besides, plan B is to move back in with you.

Pre-talk

Start by softening them up with some early hints. Weeks, months or years before you reveal your plans, try to let it slip during conversation that you've always wanted to travel to Europe, see a bit of the world. Or, if you have specific interests like learning a language or taking a cooking course, drop that in as well. Keep it casual and speculative. You don't want a conversation about it at this point; you just want to plant a few seeds.

Passion

Let your enthusiasm shine through. Few people like to get in the way of someone pursuing their dreams. Often, it's infectious, and you'll find parents and employers wishing they could take a journey of their own.

Educational value

Europe is the world's largest cultural classroom. Travelling through it will help instil many of the essentials you just don't get at university: self-reliance, confidence navigating through new surroundings, a chance to experience paintings and architecture and develop new language skills. If you have any specific courses you're considering, mention them as well.

You won't be the first

The strongest examples you can find may be friends of your parents who have taken such trips, and still went on to successful careers. Do some research into some of your parents' favourite authors, cooks and TV personalities. Chances are more than one of them has taken such a trip in their youth and has probably brought it up during an interview you'll be able to find archived on the Internet.

Tie it to a university programme

If you can find a study-abroad programme that enables you to transfer credit, you may find you have a better argument for staying in Europe over the summer after the programme ends or going a few months before it begins. For many

Dear boss,

I value my job and hope I'll be working here for years to come. But just now, I can feel I need an educational break. Some companies send employees to business school or to various workshops and courses. I'd like the education that comes from travel – an edification investment I plan to pay for myself on an upcoming extended trip to Europe. I will make sure all pressing projects are completed before departing and help train any transition personnel you'd care to bring in. However, if you would take me back upon my return, I believe the company will benefit from my experience. I know I can bring new value to the job: an international perspective, a familiarity with meeting people, more confidence and street smarts. And I think you'll find I'll have more focus and renewed energy for the tasks. On paper, it may not look as tidy as sending me to business school, but in real terms it will be more practical. And it will come at just a fraction of the cost with far less time away from the company.

parents, the university connection cements the educational value of the entire experience overseas.

Know what you're talking about

Read through this book and you'll have all the background info you'll need to answer your parents' questions about how you're going to get around, what you're going to do and how you can make it the safest possible experience. If you can demonstrate that you've done your homework, then they'll be able to see this is something you've put time and thought into, not just your heart.

Talking money

When asking parents for money, borrow a tactic from the politicians. First sell the concept, then worry about the funding. If they ask what it will cost, tell them you're not sure, still looking into it, but that you'll take all steps to keep it as cheap as possible. Even with generous parents, as a show of good faith, you may offer to put your own money into it to the extent that you can.

Prepare for your return

Some parents may worry that you won't come back for years. Or will become some sort of vagabond, drifting back overseas and never taking what they might consider a "real job" (for my parents, this turned out to be a legitimate concern). Put them at ease by talking about what you'll do when you return. Explain that the trip will help focus your plans for the future. Of course, this will require the daunting task of coming up with some plans. Remember: nothing is set in stone, so if there are some career buzz words you know they like to hear (such as "medical school"), this would be the time to toss them around.

Your itinerary

OK, you've got a few places in mind, some weather you want to miss and a few dates you want to hit for festivals or seasonal activities. Before you start stringing it together, there are a few more things to consider.

If it's your first big trip, start out gently. If you're going to Turkey, Germany and England, for example, Turkey is the most challenging of the three and won't make the best starting point.

Ease of travel

Very easy (strong traveller infrastructure, no language barrier):
England, Northern Ireland, Republic of Ireland, Scotland, Wales

Easy (strong traveller infrastructure, nearly all locals speak English):
Denmark, Holland, Norway, Sweden, Switzerland

Moderate (fair to good traveller infrastructure, some language barriers):
Austria, France, Germany, Italy, Spain

Tougher (mixed traveller infrastructure, considerable language barrier):
Bulgaria, Hungary, Romania, Russia, Turkey

Besides, after Turkey, Germany and England won't seem nearly as exciting. If you start in England, it'll still be exhilarating, but much easier. Once you get a feel of getting around on your own, move on to a more challenging country like Germany, where there's a solid infrastructure, but a language barrier. After that, navigating the bus stations and markets of Turkey will be significantly easier to handle.

Take a moment and consider the balance of your trip. You want a good mix of attractions, adventure, a course or two, a little wandering, a break, maybe a ferry or canal passage, a measure of hiking, and possibly even a dose of meditation. Chances are your trip may be thin in a few of these areas. Look back at the activity list on p.14 for some ideas on how you might round out your experiences. Just remember to space them out. You don't want to feel like you're trapped in an adventure race, trying to tick a slew of attractions off your list before jumping on your flight back home.

To find out how to connect the dots with the best-suited transportation, see the "Getting there and around chapter" p.26.

Checking political stability

Europe is extremely stable, but there's no shortage of strikes and – depending on how you feel about watching protesters put cobblestones through a *McDonald's* window – you might not want to be in a city during a G8 meeting or World Bank gathering. Try to get into the habit of picking up an international newspaper and scanning the headlines. America's State Department tends to play up the dangers, which may help prevent lawsuits but can also scare people away from a reasonably safe destination. Instead, or at least as a comparison, try the UK's foreign office (⊛www.fco.gov.uk), Australia's advisories (⊛www.dfat.gov.au) or Canada's department of foreign affairs (⊛http://voyage.dfait-maeci.gc.ca), for a more sensible assessment.

Activity booking

Just because you find the ideal activity, that doesn't mean you have to book it there and then. In fact, you can often save more than fifty percent of the cost by foregoing the middlemen and making arrangements once you arrive. However, there are some courses and tours that fill up well in advance. You can't always tell which these are, but it's possible to make a decent guess. You could reason, for example, that there's a steady stream of overnight hiking trips heading out in the Alps so, if you're not too particular about which peak, you'll find a tour that fits your level, even last-minute. If you're after something a bit more famous, and something specific, such as a short pastry course at Le Cordon Bleu cooking school (⊛www.lcbparis.com), it's worth booking ahead. You can always call or email, say you're not sure about your arrival dates just yet and ask if they antici-pate a problem booking a week or two ahead of time.

Sample itineraries

1 One month
Start in Dublin; bus to Limerick; bus to Doolin, ferry to Aran Islands; ferry to Galway, horseback riding tour; bus to Belfast; bus to Dublin.

2 One month
Start in Zürich; train to Interlachen, adventure activities; train to Montreux Jazz Festival; train to Zermatt, climbing course and hik-ing; back to Zürich.

3 Two months
Start in London; fly to Barcelona; train to Marseille; train to Florence, take cooking course; train to Venice; train to Italian Alps, mountain-biking tour; train to Vienna, visit relative; fly back to London.

4 Two months

Start in Amsterdam; train to Bruges; train to Paris, pantomime lessons; train to Bordeaux, wine tasting; train to Pamplona, Running of the Bulls; train to Barcelona; ferry to Ibiza, disco hopping; fly to London; hitchhike to Edinburgh, single-malt Scotch tour; ferry to Amsterdam.

5 Four months

Start in Berlin; train and ferry to Copenhagen, rent bicycle and ride and take trains to Fredrikshavn; ferry to Oslo; train to fjords, hiking and white-water rafting; train to Stockholm, kayak in archipelago; ferry to Helsinki, train to St Petersburg; train to Vilnius; train to Kraków, visit Auschwitz; train to Prague, beer tasting; train to Berlin.

6 Four months

Start in Rome, study Italian; train to Brindisi, Greek island hopping around the Aegean Sea; ferry to Athens, cooking class; train to Belgrade; train to Budapest; train to Vienna, take photography course; train to Salzburg, *Sound of Music* tour; train to Munich, Oktoberfest; train to Venice; train to Rome.

Not planning at all

Here's another way to go about it: get a passport, rustle up some cash and hop on the next plane to Europe and head in whichever direction cries out. If you need a visa to get into a country, no worries; just pick somewhere else. Or fill out a visa application, find a cheap hotel and wait for the visa to be processed. While you're waiting, you might study the language and meet a few locals. Or don't. Go with the wind and your whims.

The drawback to planning your trip, free spirits claim, is that, to a large extent, you decide in advance what you're looking for. So, while you'll probably find "it", you'll likely miss many of the unpredictable things that are subtly trying to find you.

Getting there and around

Y
ou can get a consolidated flight to Europe, buy a motorcycle in London, ride around Britain, sell it, take a ferry to Ireland and then buy a horse. Ride down the coast, sell it, take a ferry over to the European continent, zip along the Mediterranean with a one-month rail pass, then hitchhike to Paris and catch the Eurostar under the Channel to London for your return flight. The price, length of journey, reliability of arrival and comfort vary enormously with each. This chapter will help you compare the most popular choices so you can find the one that best fits your budget and itinerary (or lack thereof).

Getting to Europe

There's some truth to the famed airline axiom that savings come with restrictions, discomfort and stopovers. But only some truth. You can get reduced prices on tickets on reputable airlines with direct flights as well.

If you're not tied to one particular destination, you should check prices on flights to the cheapest gateways in Europe. Start with London, Amsterdam and Paris, then try Rome, Milan, Madrid and

Frankfurt. Trying to begin your journey with a flight into, say, the Swiss Alps, isn't going to do much more than make your travel agent light up with dollar signs.

If prices are relatively equal, book with a well-informed travel agent and get their email address and phone number. They can point out things you never thought of (eg a flight that leaves at 6am, before there's any cheap transport running to the airport) and provide access to consolidator fares. Besides, it's nice to have someone to contact in case you're in a jam.

> If I'm flying into Europe with a one-way ticket, I always get a flight to Amsterdam. You may want to buy a train, bus or plane ticket out of the country in advance, just in case the immigration officials ask. Don't fly into the UK (especially Heathrow or Gatwick airports) without a return ticket. If you are going to be working or studying in Europe (and therefore spending a year or longer) you'll probably want to get a one-way ticket and then take advantage of the cheap tickets out of London to come home.
>
> Tim Uden,
> Editor, @www.bugeurope.com

But before you call an agent, do a little online checking on your own, so you'll know a good price when you see one. Start looking on the major online booking engines (@www.expedia.com, @www.orbitz.com, @www.travelocity.com and Europe's @www.opodo.com) and check out the lowest published fares for a particular flight. Here are a few tips that will help keep down the costs:

- Take an hour or two and try combinations of dates into different cities (Amsterdam, London, Madrid, Paris, Frankfurt and Milan are good hubs) at one or more of the online booking engines mentioned above. Sometimes, just leaving a day later or flying into a different city can make a difference of €125. In this sense, a little flexibility can translate into substantial savings.
- Often, the cheapest tickets are sold far in advance. Call a trusted travel agent and ask him/her to book the cheapest fully refundable ticket available. Then keep looking. If you find something cheaper, simply cancel the first ticket.
- For Internet bookings, consider purchasing the ticket on a Wednesday (when airlines offer special promotions), not on a weekend (when the prices shoot back up).
- Once you find a good deal, go directly to that airline's site to see if they're offering any other special promotions to places nearby that are even cheaper. Or any frequent-flier bonuses. Strange as it may seem, flights and prices can differ between the airlines' sites and the site where you originally spotted the flight. You might, for

example, find a great fare on a Virgin Airways flight though Expedia that Virgin doesn't offer on its own site.

- Keep in mind the cheapest fares are often less direct, less conveniently scheduled and may involve an airline you've never even heard of. If you have more time than money, this is a fine way to grab a deal.
- Don't let your "frequent-flier" plan get in the way of finding the best ticket. First, look for the best deal, then if two or three offer similar fares, pick the one that fits with your mileage plan.
- If you don't live in a hub city (eg Los Angeles, New York, Toronto, Sydney), look for ads in the mainstream press in the nearest one to you (*New York Times*, *San Francisco Chronicle Travel*, *LA Times*, *Washington Post*, *Toronto Star*, *Melbourne Age*, *Sydney Morning Herald*), plus any student newspapers or the free and alternative newspapers such as *Village Voice*, *Montreal Mirror* and *San Francisco Bay Guardian*. If you find a great price, but you've never heard of the company, buy with a credit card so you can stop payment if need be.
- Consider an open-jaw ticket (see box opposite). If you know your itinerary, you may be able to save by not backtracking.

Travel agents

Don't assume, just because you're speaking with a "discounter" or "consolidator" (including those listed below), that you're getting the best deal. And don't assume all will spend a lot of time with your questions – many deal in bulk and are looking for a quick booking. Do a good deal of searching before you speak with an agent so you can ask better questions and act quickly (if there are limited seats left). Don't pay with cash or deal with a company that doesn't take credit cards.

- **Adventure World** Based in Australia (☎02 8913 0755) with an office in New Zealand (☎09 524 5118). ⓦwww .adventureworld.com.au.
- **Air Brokers** International consolidator. ⓦwww.airbrokers.com.
- **AirTreks** Multi-stop international low-price ticket seller based in the US (☎1 877 247 8735). ⓦwww.airtreks.com.
- **Flight Centre** Discount flight specialist with offices in Australia (☎133 133), Canada (☎1 888 967 5355), New Zealand (☎0800 243 544), South Africa (☎0860 400 727), the UK (☎0870 499 0400) and the US (☎1 866 967 5351). ⓦwww.flightcentre.com.

What's what

APEX: Advance Purchase Excursion Fare. This standard budget ticket usually needs to be purchased 7–21 days before departure and you stay between seven and ninety days at your destination before returning. Changes come with penalty fees.

Bucket shops: these travel agencies are unbonded (ie uninsured) discount ticket sellers that operate mainly in large gateway cities like Singapore, Bangkok, San Francisco, New York and London. Many bucket shops are small-time operators that may go out of business overnight or try to pull a fast one. Insist on a receipt that lists complete restrictions and refunds and – just in case – purchase by credit card so you can stop payment if the ticket never materializes. How do you find them? Try the newspaper travel sections of the major cities mentioned above. Just look for the smallest ads with the lowest prices. The insured version is called a "consolidator" (see below).

Charter flights: some agents can make arrangements on charter flights at incredible savings. However, changing plans can mean high penalties.

Consolidator: these travel agents buy blocks of tickets from the airlines at a reduced rate (on certain popular flights), and pass on that saving to you.

Discount clubs: a fee-based membership service that offers discounts in the range of twenty to sixty percent. Just check to make sure they offer discounts on the types of services you are likely to use. For example, great deals on four-star hotel suites may not be for you.

Discounter: they work with special student and youth fares and often deal in consolidated tickets as well. Many offer related services like rail passes and ID cards. STA Travel and Travel Cuts are typical examples.

Open-jaw ticket: these are two one-way flights sold for half their round-trip value, with an overland connection in between that you provide. For example, if you fly into London and then travel around southern Europe by train, instead of using two travel days to zip back to London to catch your flight home you can buy an open-jaw ticket and fly back from, say, Rome.

Super APEX: not an action figure with unlimited powers. Like APEX but a bit cheaper and limits the stay to 7 to 21 days at your destination. Sometimes, also called "Eurosaver".

• **Moment's Notice** Discount travel club based in the US (☎1 212 486 0500). ⓦwww.moments-notice.com.

• **STA Travel** UK-based agent with hundreds of offices in the US (☎1 800 777 0112) and coverage in Canada as well (☎888 427 5639). Specializes in student and independent travel. Also sells ID cards, insurance and rail passes. ⓦwww.sta.com.

• **Student Universe** US-based (☎1 800 272 9676). Also sells insurance and rail passes. ⓦwww.studentuniverse.com.

- **Trailfinders** UK-based all-round travel agent (☎020 7937 1234) with offices in Australia (☎1300 780 212). ⓦwww.trailfinders .co.uk.
- **Travel Cuts** Canada-based (☎866 246 9762) with offices in the US (☎1 800 592 2887). Specializes in student and independent travel. Also sells ID cards, insurance and rail passes. ⓦwww.travelcuts.com.
- **YHA Travel** The same people that sell YHA membership cards also book budget travel. Offices around Australia. ⓦwww.yha.com.au.

Courier flights

Courier travel can make for some bargain getaway trips. Especially if you're single, live near (or can very easily get to at a moment's notice) a major international gateway airport (Vancouver, San Francisco, Los Angeles, New York, Sydney) and have a schedule looser than a yoga master on Valium.

Serving as an air courier – for a company, not for an independent guy with a leather jacket and a gold tooth – is a completely legal arrangement in which you give up your check-in luggage space (leaving you carry-on only) to transport goods for a courier service. You carry an invoice (plus as many layers as you can wear), they handle all the actual carrying – and they give you a heavily discounted (typically 40–85 percent off) or free ticket in return. They get their freight delivered quickly and you get a good deal. In other words, you become a one-person FedEx. Now, here's the fine print:

- You can put in requests for times and destinations, but for the most discounted tickets you may be asked to leave on a day's or week's notice.
- You get a round-trip ticket that brings you back home within one or two weeks – this can be stretched up to several months, but don't count on it.
- You have to be over 18 or 21.
- There may be a lot of competition to "work" as a courier, especially to popular destinations and during popular times of year, so even if you get a flight the discount may not be substantial.
- You often have to join a courier service (that is, pay a membership fee of about €40 in the US, for example) before you can start getting transport assignments. If you're not deterred by the restrictions, the membership fee can be well worth it.

Air Courier Services:

Air Courier Association Ⓦwww.aircourier.org
Air Courier Travel Ⓦwww.aircouriertravel.com

Standby services

Standby services – such as Airhitch (Ⓦwww.airhitch.org) and AirTech (Ⓦwww.airtech.com) – are a bit like the arrangement that flight personnel have. (They fly for ten percent of the cost of a ticket, but they're on standby.) If there's no room, they aren't flying. With standby services, you pick the flight you want (there are one-way and return flights to choose from), pay a fraction of the price of a regular ticket (about €200 for a round-trip to Europe from the US or Canada), and then either go standby or get an email 24 hours in advance. You either need to be able to get to a departure city in a particular region to catch your flight or be very patient and wait for a flight from your city to come up. And they may not take you exactly where you want to go. So, if you're very flexible, it's great. If you're trying to plan a trip in advance and need dates to correspond with certain planned events, it's less than ideal. They regularly fly to Europe from New York, Los Angeles, Boston and Washington, DC. There are some flights from Minneapolis, Orlando and other cities in the US, but not many.

Air travel within Europe

The "Costs and savings" chapter (see p.65) explains why augmenting your rail or bus pass with a cheap flight within Europe can be a great idea. This section will tell you how to get that cheap air flight. With cut-throat budget airlines battling it out in the skies, your biggest cost for a flight within Europe is likely to be getting yourself out to the airport. Really. It's not uncommon to find flights for €4–30, except for certain routes at certain times of the year, when demand is particularly high

Many of these start-up "no-frills" carriers use minor airports located a little further from the city centre, but honestly, who cares? You'll probably save the time back immediately, since the gates of these small airports tend to be no more than 100m from the check-in. When they say "no frills", they generally aren't kidding, but since the flights are almost never more than three hours, it doesn't matter that it feels more like a bus. Pack a meal and something to drink and you'll be fine. You might even pack some cheap earphones so you don't need to buy the feeble ones they try to flog you on the plane. No need to worry about safety. Whatever corners they need to cut to streamline their company, there's no getting around the strict EU regulations that govern the flight industry.

Zipping around on flights, no matter how cheap, is probably not the best way to see Europe (it's hard to make cultural inroads and experience the country at 30,000 feet), but it offers a great chance to connect two or three spots that might otherwise be out of range. For example, you might want to spend the bulk of your trip travelling in Spain and Portugal, but you can hop on a plane in Barcelona and get to Rome or Dublin for a long weekend without breaking your budget.

Ryan Air is the biggest player and London's Stansted Airport the budget epicentre. But if you're in Stockholm, Copenhagen, Birmingham, Venice, Rome, Milan, Stuttgart, Leeds, Cologne, Bonn, Bratislava, Vienna, Budapest, Dublin, Amsterdam, Rotterdam, Glasgow, Brussels, Barcelona, Frankfurt and more … you've got yourself a hub and a range of cheap destinations to choose from.

These new budget start-ups haven't been a big hit with travel agents, though. Many agents won't have anything to do with them (there's no commission). And some of the carriers have bypassed agents altogether to save money through more direct sales. There's not one agent or website that has access to all the fares offered (at least not at the moment), so to check rates you need to contact these carriers directly, best by website.

- **Cheap Flights** This engine will scour the Web for the best deals offered by other discount brokers and consolidators and then point you there. If one booker keeps popping up during your searches, jump directly to their homepage. Ⓦ www.cheapflights.co.uk.
- **Last Minute** Mostly for holiday spots and charter flights, but with destinations around the continent, this bargain sale site even has last-second deals you can jump on. Ⓦwww.lastminute.com.
- **Open Jet** After you take a quick look at the major carriers' prices (for example, on Ⓦwww.opodo.com, as many major players have cut fares to try to compete with these budget airlines), try this

site. One search on openjet.com will query the following budget airlines: easyJet, MyTravelLite, bmibaby, Volareweb, Basiq Air, Hapag-Lloyd Express and Germanwings. Then look through the budget airline list below and check out any sites applicable to your departure or destination cities. Ⓦwww.openjet.com.

- **Aer Arann** You read right. And it's pronounced just like it looks – I think. Ireland-based, with flights around the UK. Ⓦwww.aerarann.com.
- **Air Berlin** While everyone else is taking out the frills, Air Berlin is sticking them back in (and raising the budget rates slightly). If you want entertainment, snacks, reductions for under-21s, no charge for kids, and bikini-clad women dancing around in their ads, this is it. Ⓦwww.airberlin.com.
- **Air Scotland** For the budget ride out of Edinburgh or Glasgow in the middle of winter, and whenever else you need a bit of Mediterranean climate. Ⓦwww.air-scotland.com.
- **Air Wales** The Welsh budget airline flying to spots around the UK and further afield. Ⓦwww.airwales.com.
- **Basiq Air** Ah, finally a complicated way to spell "basic". Transavia airlines operates this service out of the Netherlands. Its main hubs are in Amsterdam and Rotterdam. Ⓦwww.basiqair.com.
- **bmibaby** British Midland's budget start-up is pronounced "B-M-I Baby" (which saves trying to say "Be My Baby" over the phone with a straight face). Main hubs are in Manchester, East Midlands and Cardiff. Ⓦwww.bmibaby.com.
- **easyJet** The airline that sounds like a cheap laser printer is one of the most popular budget carriers in Europe, with destinations linking almost everywhere with everywhere else. The main hubs are Luton, Bristol, Gatwick and Stansted in the UK. Ⓦwww.easyjet.co.uk.
- **Excel Airways** Departing from airports around the UK and flying further south than most – Greece and Egypt – in addition to the western European beaches. Plus meals, leather chairs and entertainment without paying extra. Ⓦwww.excelairways.com.
- **Flybe** No, it's not a high-tech Frisbee. Short for "Fly British European," it has bargains to popular summer destinations. Ⓦwww2.flybe.com.
- **Fly Globespan** A Scottish carrier operating out of Edinburgh, Glasgow and Prestwick, and heading to warm spots in southern Europe. Ⓦwww.flyglobespan.com.
- **Fly Zoom** Canadians throw in meals with their budget carriers, so it's hard to fault this airline even if the name makes it sound like the planes are made of Lego. Ⓦwww.flyzoom.com.

- **Germanwings** Perhaps the easiest German company to spell after BMW. The website has a clever click-on-map function to choose your destination. Main hubs are in Cologne/Bonn and Stuttgart. ⓦwww.germanwings.com.
- **Hapag–Lloyd Express** Odd name, cheap flights. Main hubs are in Dublin, Newcastle and Manchester. ⓦwww.hlx.com.
- **Iceland Express** If you want to fly to Keflavik, this is your airline. It does get you close to Reykjavik for a shamefully good deal, and almost makes the country seem affordable. ⓦwww.icelandexpress.com.
- **Jet 2** Not to be confused with a B-movie action sequel. It's a budget airline based in the UK (Leeds and Bradford) that flies to major hubs in mostly sunny spots. ⓦwww.jet2.com.
- **Maersk Air** A Copenhagen-based carrier that flies around Denmark and to spots around Europe, including all the popular beaches down south. ⓦwww.maerskair.com.
- **MyTravelLite** No, it's not a fad diet drink for people on the move, but a UK airline that flies, mainly, from Birmingham to sunny cities around Europe. ⓦwww.mytravellite.com.
- **Norwegian Airlines** It's not easy to get around Norway on the cheap. Keep your fjords crossed this will help ease the travel expenses. ⓦwww.norwegian.no.
- **Ryan Air** Ryan Air is like the wacky Irish uncle that came up with the whole low-fare, anti-perk concept and somehow got it off the ground. Main hubs are in Dublin, London, Stockholm, Brussels, Milan, Barcelona and Rome. Flies to sixteen countries and 88 airports around Europe. ⓦwww.ryanair.com.
- **Sky Europe Airlines** The low-cost carrier of central Europe. Main hubs are in Budapest, Vienna and Bratislava. ⓦwww.skyeurope.com.
- **Snowflake** This budget branch of Scandinavian Airlines is even more popular than the SAS mother ship. Main hubs are in Stockholm and Copenhagen. ⓦhttp://snowflake.airkiosk.com.
- **Sterling Airlines** Flying from Denmark, Sweden and Norway to central and southern Europe for great rates. ⓦwww.sterlingticket.com.
- **Thompson Flights** Operating from airports around the UK, Thompson flies sun worshippers to European hot spots for some of the best rates going – especially with last-minute deals. You can even purchase extra legroom. ⓦwww.thomsonflights.com.
- **Volareweb.com** An Italian company that sounds more like a URL than a budget airline. Main hubs are in Venice, Milan and Rome. ⓦhttp://buy.volareweb.com.

- **Wizz Air** If you can get past the dopey name, you may be in for a bargain. This eastern European carrier brings budget flights to "Polish and Hungarian Euro-freshers". Ⓦhttp://wizzair.com /index.shtml.

Flight passes

Discover Europe with the Star Alliance (Ⓦwww.staralliance.com). Choose among 41 countries with this air pass of three to ten distance-priced coupons (€54–165+). To qualify, your travels to and from Europe have to be on a Star Alliance carrier. You can change your reservation at any time so long as the routing isn't changed, but you can't visit the same place twice.

Or else, you can try europebyair (Ⓦwww.europebyair.com). Travellers heading to Europe can fly on 26 different airlines to more than 150 cities within Europe at the flat rate of €82 per flight plus airport taxes. Each €82 coupon is valid for 120 days on nonstop flights between any two cities within the system. You can buy as few as one, and there are no blackout dates. But – here's the catch – you have to buy the tickets before you enter Europe and you don't get refunds for the ones you don't use. Reservations (and reservation changes) can be made at any time.

By train

If you don't set foot on a train at least once while you're in Europe, you're missing something. Besides the overpriced stale food they like to serve onboard. Europe is train country. How else would you describe a rail network totalling 240,000km? (By comparison, there's 45,000km of rail in the US and Canada, an area more than twice as big.) It's not necessarily the cheapest way to get around; it's simply the preferred way. And not because the rail routes are often more scenic – the facing

Seasoned travellers know all the easy ways to cut corners. The first time I went Eurailing, I learned this trick from a road warrior.

To use a day of the Eurail Flexi Pass, you need to write – in pen – the date in the space provided on the ticket. Veterans knew that by travelling on the first of the month, and writing a slanted "1", they could later turn it into a "2" or a "7". They'd travel on the fifth of the month, and make a rounded "5" that could later become an "8". A "9", a "6" and a "3" could become an "8" as well.

You'd think the conductors would have caught on by now.

Sean Keener,
Director Ⓦwww.bootsnall.com

JOURNEY TIMES BY PLANE

▲ Tromsø

Rovaniemi

900km
1hr 20min

Joensuu

508km,
55min

Turku
194km
40min

350km
2hr

St Petersburg

Helsinki

Stockholm

Tallinn

686km
1hr 30min

1030km
2hr 45min

Moscow

282km

580km

Riga
1hr 10min

205km
55min

Vilnius

BALTIC SEA

Minsk

Warsaw

293km
55min

Kiev

1hr
Ostrava

Kraków

Bratislava

197km,
40min

Suceava

459km
1hr 35min

Timişoara
533km
1hr 15min

225km
35min

Constanţa

BLACK SEA

T'bilisi

Belgrade

Bucharest

400km,
1hr

Varna

571km
55min

Sarajevo

Sofia

370km
1hr 25min

Burgas

Yerevan

Dubrovnik

150km
Plovdiv

İstanbul

445km
1hr

Ankara

S
e
a

Thessaloniki

453km
1hr

553km
1hr 5min

Corfu
511km
55min

Aegean
Sea

327km
1hr

İzmir

470km

Antalya

Athens
435km 1 hr

349km
50min

1hr

Kós

Rhodes

288km
55min

S E A

Crete

| 0 | 500 km |

Europe rail and bus passes

Rail passes

Eurail Pass
(first class)
Fifteen days €486
One month €782
Two months €1106
Three months €1368

Eurail Youth Pass (under-26),
(second class)
Fifteen days €342
One month €549
Two months €776
Three months €960

Eurail Flexi Pass
(first class)
Any ten days in two months €574
Any fifteen days in two months €756

Eurail Youth Flexi Pass (under-26),
(second class)
Any ten days in two months €404
Any fifteen days in two months €530

Eurail Select Pass
(first class)
(up to five adjoining countries)
Any ten days in two months €516
Any fifteen days in two
months €657

Eurail Youth Select Pass
(under-26, second class)
(up to five adjoining countries)
Any ten days in two months €361
Any fifteen days in two
months €500

Eurail countries:
Austria, Belgium, Denmark, Finland, France, Germany, Greece, Hungary, Ireland, Italy, Luxembourg, Netherlands, Norway, Portugal, Spain, Sweden, Switzerland.

InterRail Pass
Sixteen days in one zone €332
Twenty-two days in two zones €451
One month in all zones €618

InterRail Youth Pass (under-26)
Sixteen days in one zone €236
Twenty-two days in two zones €320
One month in all zones €439

InterRail zones:
Zone A Ireland; *Zone B* Finland, Norway, Sweden; *Zone C* Austria, Denmark, Germany, Switzerland; *Zone D* Croatia, Czech Republic, Hungary, Poland, Slovakia; *Zone E* Belgium, France, Luxembourg, Netherlands; *Zone F* Portugal, Spain; *Zone G* Italy, Greece, Slovenia, Turkey; *Zone H* Bulgaria, Romania.

seats provide an opportunity to meet locals or chat with friends, the aisles allow you to stretch your legs, some carriages allow full reclining at night and the train's chug-chug adds an authentic travel beat to any conversation.

Buying a train ticket is as simple as walking up to the ticket window, saying the name of the town you want to go to and handing over a credit card or cash. The biggest problem is that, in most European countries, this is a painfully expensive way to get around.

Bus passes

Busabout Pass

Two weeks unlimited travel €346
Six weeks unlimited travel €686
Twelve weeks unlimited
    travel €1008

Busabout Youth Pass (under-26)

Two weeks unlimited travel €313
Six weeks unlimited travel €619
Twelve weeks unlimited
    travel €892

Busabout Flexi Pass

Any twelve days in two
    months €561
Any sixteen days in two
    months €685

Busabout Youth Flexi Pass
    (under-26)
Any twelve days in two
    months €487
Any sixteen days in two
    months €619

Busabout countries:

Austria, Belgium, Czech Republic, England, France, Germany, Italy,
Netherlands, Portugal, Spain, Switzerland.

Eurolines Pass
    (1 June–15 Sept)
Fifteen days unlimited
    travel €285
Thirty days unlimited travel €425
Sixty days unlimited travel €490

Eurolines Youth Pass (under-26)
    (1 June–15 Sept)
Fifteen days unlimited
    travel €240
Thirty days unlimited travel €345
Sixty days unlimited travel €380

Eurolines Pass
    (16 Sept–31 May)
Fifteen days unlimited
    travel €220
Thirty days unlimited travel €310
Sixty days unlimited travel €390

Eurolines Youth Pass (under-26)
    (16 Sept–31 May)
Fifteen days unlimited
    travel €185
Thirty days unlimited travel €250
Sixty days unlimited travel €310

Eurolines serves major cities in:

Austria, Belgium, Britain, Croatia, Czech Republic, Denmark, Estonia,
Finland, Hungary, Ireland, Italy, Latvia, Norway, Poland, Romania, Russia,
Slovakia, Spain, Sweden, Switzerland.

Enter the rail pass (Eurail for North Americans and those Down
Under; InterRail and Eurodomino for Europeans). There are
scores of options. You can buy a pass that allows either unlimited
travel during a set period or a fixed number of days during a set
period. Some allow travel in multiple countries, some limit travel
to just one country.

Prices change, but the box on p.38 should give you a
good idea. There are several more passes available online

Sitting on a train

It's not quite as straightforward as it sounds. On most regular trains, you can just hop on board with your rail pass, grab a second-class seat (the train cars are marked as such on the outside, and the conductors are typically guarding the first-class entrances) and relax. But like a subway ticket, individual train tickets and rail passes don't guarantee a seat, just passage on the train. On some particularly popular journeys you may end up hopping from one free seat to the next at every stop, or get stuck standing in the aisles or in the noisy passageway between train carriages when the seats completely fill up. You can avoid that by paying to reserve a seat (about €9) or getting to the station early (or the day before) and asking at the ticket window how crowded the train will be.

All high-speed trains – crowded or not – require a seat reservation, which is going to cost about €9–12 per ride, even if you have a rail pass. You also have to pay extra for a sleeper car or couchette on overnight journeys. The sleeper is luxury train travel – at least, some of it is. It covers the range from a semi-soft bunk bed in a shared room to a real bed with a washstand and fresh sheets and towels. Prices for one night range from about €33 to €125, depending on the comfort level. The couchette is like a small cabin where the seats fold flat and you can sleep side by side with a few fellow passengers. Some turn into double-decker bunk beds with the sort of padding normally found in dental waiting-room furniture. A couchette costs about €25 a night. Some trains also have special reclining seats ("sleeperettes") like you might find in business class on a plane, which can also be reserved. You can find a place to sleep without a reservation, and many do, but you're taking your chances spending a night in an upright seat or getting bumped from your recliner in the middle of the night by someone who boards with a reservation. It could make the difference between a full day of sightseeing and spending your day passed out on a park bench for a four-hour nap.

at ⓦwww.raileurope.com and ⓦwww.raileurope.co.uk; see p.38 to compare prices and p.72 to best take advantage of your pass.

By bus

There are two bus passes worth looking into, and they both under-cut the train fares: Eurolines (ⓦwww.eurolines.com) and Busabout (ⓦwww.busabout.com) – see box on p.39 for a price guide. Eurolines is cheaper and functions as Europe's standard long-distance bus line, connecting 35 cities across Europe, while

Border crossings

There are border crossings in Europe, but chances are you won't notice them on a train or bus. Perhaps you'll spot names on road signs, or the train conductor may start speaking a different language. There won't be any sort of announcement or blinking lights. Few, if anyone, will actually ask to see your passport. And, unless you ask kindly, they won't put a stamp in it.

Busabout is aimed specifically at budget travellers – taking you not just around Europe but right to a hostel (one they hope you'll stay at) – and provides onboard movies and a guide. That gives you less reason to look out the window and less opportunity to meet locals, but it will save you the hassle of finding a hostel and will put you in touch with more travellers.

By car

Driving offers the chance to take control of your itinerary, get to places you can't easily reach (or reach at all) with public transport, and (with enough people) even save money. Whether you decide to buy or rent a car (both covered in this section), there are some basic tips that will make the experience more enjoyable:

- **Drive defensively** In France, Greece, Italy and several other countries it may seem like most drivers are making up new traffic laws as they go. Stay cool and follow the law, even if those around you aren't.
- **Learn the metric system** To roughly figure out miles when you see kilometres, divide the number by two and add ten percent (ie 150km would be 75 + 15 = 90 miles). It's not exact, but close enough. And it's about four litres of gasoline to a gallon – yes, it is about as expensive as twelve-year-old Scotch. If you're in Germany, Italy or France and near the Austria or Luxembourg border, cross over to fill up and save about €0.90 per gallon.
- **Don't use the car for city sightseeing** It's usually a lot cheaper and easier to find free parking well outside of the city, and use public transport to get into town. (For more on parking, see p.47.) It's quicker, better and more environmental to get out and wander cities on foot, especially since most European cities have more curves than a bag of pretzels and half of them are one-way streets.

JOURNEY TIMES
BY TRAIN & BUS

Driving in Italy

"Okay," Renato explained, as I adjusted the rear-view mirror of my red Ford Fiesta, "driving in Napoli is like a video game. You just have to relax, stop thinking, and feel it in your stomach."

I fastened my seat belt.

"What are you doing?!" he reprimanded. "No one in Napoli wears seatbelts. You want to look like a tourist?"

I unbuckled. Then Renato told me that about a decade ago when the mandatory seatbelt law was passed and briefly enforced, people started wearing t-shirts with a black stripe painted across the chest.

We came to the first traffic light, but cars were only stopping if there was faster traffic coming from the other direction. It seems red, yellow and green lights are, in the eyes of Napolitano drivers, just colours, and should be obeyed no more than Christmas decorations.

I asked Renato why the drivers ignored them. "If they followed rules," he explained, "they'd be stuck in traffic for hours."

"But they are stuck in traffic for hours," I pointed out.

"Well, yes," he admitted, "that's true."

My lesson also had an acoustic component. In Napoli, the horn is not just a warning device, but a musical instrument, and Renato played it beautifully. When we passed a voluptuous woman walking on the sidewalk, he reached over and hit the side of the horn, delivering three short, cute squeaks. No one looked over at us except the woman he was honking at, as if everyone knew only she was the object of the honk. Later, five machine-gun-style honks got the attention of his friend on the other side of the street. One quick blast warned a driver not to cut us off. When we were in a crowd of people, Renato reached over and honked with a short double-tap to the centre of the horn, and people moved. A few were slow to get out of our way, and a two-second blast was required. This longer honk was quite effective, but protocol dictated that they shoot us a nasty look as they stepped aside.

Watching some Napolitano drivers squeeze past me on the right, drive up on the curb, and triple-park, I wondered aloud how they ever passed their driver's tests. "They probably didn't," Renato answered. "Up until a few years ago, anyone could buy a black market license for around €500."

Now that I was getting the hang of it, it was time for a little sightseeing. Renato gave me the three-second tour: "University there, church there, blond there! (honk)"

D L

- **Know where you're heading** You'll rarely see north, south, east and west signs to point you in the right direction; just directions to specific towns. Before pushing off, take a good look at the next town's name and the next big city's name.

- **Stick to the back roads** Highways are fast, but boring. Take advantage of your mobility and go places rail and bus travellers can't. Most back roads are in excellent shape and offer much cheaper and more interesting food, and far more scenery.

- **Be aware of hidden expenses** Special super-freeways in France and Italy have tolls (about €5 per hour), and you may be spending up to €17 a day for parking in major cities. With new regulations, you now have to pay to drive in downtown London (€7 a day). The "congestion charge" (⃝www .cclondon.com) isn't the only fee you'll have to consider.

Oslo also has one. And driving in Norway in winter without proper winter tyres is fineable. Two countries require drivers to get a sticker to use their national motorways (sold at border crossings): €25 for the Swiss highway permit, €5 a week for Austria's. And tax on your rental is typically 18–25 percent (zero in Switzerland, but their rates are higher).

- **Know the signs** Thanks to EU regulations, road signs have been standardized. There are only a few you really need to know, so take five minutes to learn them. To get to the centre of town, you can typically find signs pointing you to *Centre-ville*, *Zentrum* or *Stadtmitte*, while the tourist office is designated by "i", "VVV" or *turismo*.

- **Don't speed** Many European countries take speeding seriously: Germany, because you can go as fast as you like, and other countries, because they seem to be financing their government with the fines. An €85 ticket is not uncommon. Some places have speed cameras mounted on the side of the road. If one flashes when you go by, just smile. You'll pay the fine later when the rental company tacks it on to your credit card account.

Renting a car

This is probably the most hassle-free way to drive. But then, you're paying for that convenience. If you can put together a group of travellers, however, you may not be paying much. It depends on how much you drive. With two people in a rented compact car with unlimited kilometres driving five hours every other day, a month is going to cost about €850 per person. Driving five hours every fourth day will set you back about €550 each, or roughly the same as a rail pass. With four people driving a slightly larger car five hours every third day, this will bring the costs down to just under €425 per person.

Weekly rentals with unlimited kilometres are the most economical short-term solutions and can be booked over the Web, via a travel agent or directly with the company. It's usually cheaper to book from home. Having said that, it's worth taking a look at the pricing of some rental consolidators (ⓦwww.autoeurope.com and ⓦwww.kemwel.com). As with flights, these agents buy in bulk and pass on the savings. If you're travelling for more than three weeks, a lease (sometimes called a "buy-back") is going to be the best option. You get a new car and unlimited kilometres, plus breakdown cover and zero-deductible (zero-excess) insurance for a great

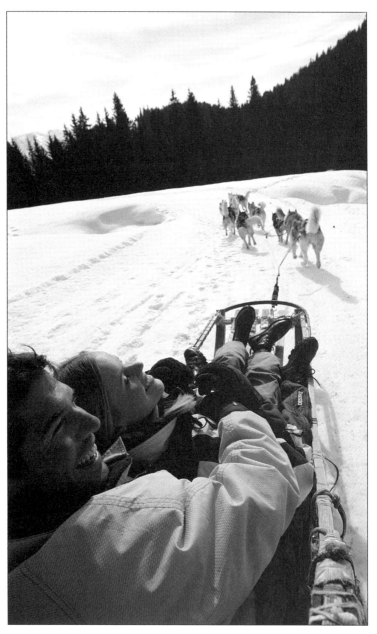

△ Try a new way of getting from A to B

rate. In addition to the sites above, try ⓦwww.europebycar.com and ⓦwww.renaultusa.com.

Remember, when you rent a car, you're liable for the whole shebang. There's a Collision Damage Waiver (CDW) supplement, which covers the car (usually with a deductible fee of a few hundred dollars – roof, tyres and windshield aren't usually covered) and costs €8–20 a day, depending on the country, the car and the rental company. There are two ways to do it cheaper. The first is to call your credit card company and ask if they offer coverage for free with your card if you use it to pay for the rental. Some do, some don't, but always ask them to spell out exactly what happens in case of an accident. Plan B is to buy the CDW elsewhere: Travel Guard (ⓦwww.travelguard.com), for example, sells it for €6 a day, though check validity for Italy and Ireland, as they may not allow it.

Most rental companies won't hand over the keys if you're under 21. Many want to you be 25, or will stick you with under-age insurance fees. If you're considered too young, leasing may be a better option, as the leasing companies are more relaxed with age limitations. STA Travel (ⓦwww.statravel.com) may also be able to help with rentals for the under-25 set.

A valid driver's licence is all you need in most European countries to rent a car. In Bulgaria, the Czech Republic, Hungary, Italy, Poland, Romania, Slovenia and Spain, you'll need an international driver's permit (IDP), which is simply a translation of your licence. It feels better to hand to a police officer if you get pulled over, but it just makes it easier for him to write out the ticket. It's simple enough to get (about €17, plus two passport-size photos at your national auto association – Australia ⓦwww.rac.com.au; Canada ⓦwww.caa.ca; New Zealand ⓦwww.nzaa.co.nz; UK ⓦwww.theaa.co.uk; US ⓦwww.aaa.com or ⓦwww.nationalautoclub.com).

The surest way of saving money with your rental car is to make sure you don't pick it up at the airport when you land, if you plan to start your trip by exploring a city for a few days. Paying €30–50 a day for the car plus another €17 to park it safely is a quick way to flush around €250 down the drain. Instead, pick up your car after your initial city sightseeing and plan to return it before sightseeing at the end of the trip. And if you're not picking up the car at the airport when you arrive, don't bother to go back there to get it. Pick up in town (away from the train station, as well), and you

Hitchhiking

In many countries around Europe, hitchhiking is an accepted way of getting around and drivers are sympathetic to your roadside plight (as many have done some hitching themselves). In others, such as parts of Scandinavia, you're something of a pariah, although it's still very much possible to thumb your way around. Bear in mind though that there are dangers inherent to hitchhiking beyond the normal traffic risks. The driver who seemed nice enough to stop for you may not in fact be very nice at all. And, once you're in the car with such a person, you're at a serious disadvantage. Female travellers in particular are at a higher risk; it's advisable for women never to hitch alone. Rough Guides doesn't recommend hitching as a safe means of getting around, but if you do choose to hitch, be aware of the risks and check out the "Security" section opposite for tips on making hitchhiking as safe as possible.

Presentation

☐ Start by dressing well. You've only got a few seconds to make an impression. This is the time (in case it's been a while) to wash your clothes and tuck in your shirt. A jacket and tie is out of place – you should look like a budget traveller; just a clean and trustworthy one. Leave the black and camo colours in your pack.

☐ Remove the hat and sunglasses. They need to be able to see your face clearly, see that you're not hiding anything.

☐ Don't smoke while waiting for a ride.

☐ Minimize the luggage. The four-piece custom luggage set with a windsurfer isn't going to get you far. One bag – a midsize backpack – is ideal.

☐ If you're standing on the side of the road, place your pack neatly in front of you to show that you're a backpacker travelling their country on a budget. Some (not Americans, typically) like to put a flag patch of their home country on their pack to highlight the foreign-traveller angle.

☐ Hold up a sign. Not a necessity, but it can help. Carry a permanent marker and then just look for an old pizza box or chunk of cardboard. Try to pick a place that's not more than two hours away so you've got an excuse to get out if nine hours with this driver seems intolerable. Similarly, they may be intimidated about spending a full day giving you a ride. If it goes well, you can explain that you're actually going a bit further. Some people use a sign with a giant smile on it. Or "Student traveller". Or "I don't smell funny". If you're standing at or near a stoplight, you might try something funny on the back, so you can flip over if you've got someone's eye for a few seconds.

☐ Hitching is easiest for a single guy, a single woman, a couple or two women. Three of anybody is too many – it's hard to find anyone with enough room – and intimidating. Two guys can be intimidating to many drivers as well. If hitching as a single woman, see the security section below.

☐ The typical age range is 18–30. If you're over 30 and look young, you can pull it off, but drivers tend to shy away from people who aren't in this group.

Location

☐ Usually the best place to hitch is at a gas station near the motorway. This means getting directions from the tourist office or a website (🌐 www.autostopguide.com has all the best places in Europe to hitch) and taking a bus or subway there. Simply ask people who are at the pump (ah, a captive audience). Say you're a student trying to see their country cheaply and you'd appreciate a ride. Offer to chip in for some petrol as well. Or buy a coffee/Coke for the journey. With this method, it should take five to thirty minutes to get a ride. Besides, you have plenty to eat and someplace to stay warm/cool while you hitch.

☐ If you need to stand on the side of the road, make sure there's plenty of room for the driver to stop; that they're going slowly and don't need to concentrate on merging or accelerating; and that you can be seen from a distance.

Security

☐ Safety starts with your appearance. You're going to likely get safer rides if you look the part. Kind drivers (and owners of nice cars) are far less likely to pick up travellers who look like street urchins, or smoke, or seem even remotely like they might be a threat to their safety.

☐ If you're hitching on the side of the road and a car pulls over, don't just run after it and jump in. Take a moment to go to the passenger side window (open the door if the driver doesn't put down the electric window) and ask where he/she is going. Use those precious few seconds to see if the driver looks dangerous in any way; if there are other potentially dangerous people in the car; or if there's any smell of alcohol or open bottles.

☐ Women are not advised to hitch alone. If you do chose to do it, you should only consider hitching at gas stations. If anyone looks mildly suspicious, don't even ask them for a ride. In fact, try to restrict your hitching requests to families with young kids and single women drivers who look presentable. Also, non-hitch hitching can be an option (see p.50).

Strategy

☐ If you're going further down the highway and the driver needs to let you off, ask him to stop at a well-positioned gas station *before* the city he's living in. If he takes you into the city, you'll still need to take a bus back out to a gas station on the other side of town.

- ☐ If there's a chance it might rain, buy a cheap umbrella. No one wants a soaking-wet person in the car.
- ☐ Bring enough food and drink to last you for several hours.
- ☐ As a rule of thumb, give a place two hours before you give up. You'll normally find a ride well before that.
- ☐ Learn the local signs. It's not always a question of putting your thumb out. That's just the standard. In Latvia, you use an open hand instead; in parts of eastern Europe you flap your arm like a bird with a dislocated wing.

Be a good hitcher

- ☐ You represent the hitchhiking community when you accept a ride. If the driver has a good experience, they may stop for more hitchers later so be a good ambassador.
- ☐ Don't smoke unless you get permission first.
- ☐ If they picked you up because they wanted some company on a long ride and feel like talking, talk back. If you must sit silently and don't feel like making conversation, come up with a good excuse or stop hitching.
- ☐ If you arrive at a spot where there are already one or more hitchers, the etiquette is that you head down traffic (the direction cars are headed) and stay 20–100m away. Sometimes drivers zip past the first person, then get a bad conscience and see you and stop (or slow down for the first person but don't like the look of him), so it's not the worst place to be.

Non-hitch hitching

- ☐ Put up a notice in your hostel saying that you're looking for a ride and you don't mind sharing petrol expenses. Put up notices in other hostels as well. Often groups of travellers will have rented or bought a car and are looking for some help with the costs.
- ☐ Contact a rideshare or lift centre (in Switzerland, for example, many cities offer a ride service called *Mitfahrzentrale*). Some are paid (a small fee both for membership and per kilometre driven) while others request a donation. See ⓦ www.hitchhikers.org for more info.

may skip an ugly tax (possibly as much as seventeen percent) on the total rental fee.

If you can get a good deal, try renting a car with a built-in GPS system. These are incredible inventions and may never serve you better than they can in Europe. The digital map shows exactly where to go and can even give voice prompts like "Take the second left one hundred metres ahead." Miss a turn and it will recalibrate your route.

It can even tap into the public traffic system and automatically replan your route to avoid traffic jams. But it's not as fun as looking at a map.

Buying a car

The UK seems like a good place to buy a car because there's a great market for them aimed at travellers; everything is in English, so contracts aren't so intimidating; it's a common point of entry; and if you're going to buy a car, doing it at the beginning of your trip makes the most sense. The problem is European driving can be tricky enough without having to worry about being on the left-hand side of the road. Taking the vehicle over to mainland Europe (and back if you plan to sell it) gets expensive as well; and you don't really want a right-hand drive car on mainland Europe where they drive on the left. Naturally, if you plan to do your driving exclusively in the UK, buy your car there. If not, you might consider picking it up on mainland Europe. If you have a friend or relative who is willing to help you register the vehicle, let them help. Frankfurt, Amsterdam and Paris are particularly good car-buying cities for travellers. Look on the Web (Netherlands ⊛www.viavia .nl; France ⊛www.jannonce.com), classified papers and on notice boards at hostels. You should be able to find a car for under €850 that will get you around. Even if you sell it for €425 after two months, it'll still be cheaper than a rental.

But if you buy a car you should insure it. And this is the tricky bit. Talk to the sellers and see what they did and if they'll help you. Otherwise, consider buying the car in a place where you have local friends or relatives.

By ferry

Obviously, you can't realistically travel the whole of Europe by ferry, but the services on offer (see map on pp.52–53 for route information) do provide handy little short cuts here and there.

By bicycle

This is a continent that deserves to be seen from a bike. The hamlets that tour buses and cars roll past regularly are some of the

JOURNEY TIMES BY FERRY

Lerwick (Shetland) ▲ Bergen (Norway) Gothenburg (Sweden) ▲

Aberdeen — 12hr 30min; NF

DENMARK

Esbjerg

SCOTLAND

1hr 44min–3hr 15min; StenL

N. IRELAND

Stranraer

Belfast — 2hr 45min; SC

Isle of Man Douglas

Newcastle

NORTH SEA

NETHER-LANDS

Amsterdam

Dublin — 2hr 45min; SC — 10hr; NM

5hr; SC

3hr; StenL — Holyhead — Liverpool

Hull

REP. OF IRELAND

IRISH SEA

UNITED KINGDOM

Rosslare

Cork

3hr 40min–3hr 45min; StenL

WALES

Fishguard

ENGLAND

Harwich — 3hr 40min; StenL

Hoek van Holland

Rotterdam

GERMANY

London

Dover — 2hr; HS/P&O/SF

Zeebrugge

Brussels

BELGIUM

N

Portsmouth

Newhaven

Calais

Plymouth

9hr 30min; 1hr 30min; P&O

1hr 15min; HS

3hr; P&O

LUXEM-BOURG

ENGLISH

8hr 45min; BF

Dieppe

CHANNEL

Cherbourg

Le Havre

Caen

FRANCE

0   200 km

Roscoff

St-Malo

Paris

Santander (Spain) ▼▼ Bilbao (Spain)   Larvik (Norway) ▲▲ Oslo (Norway)

SPAIN

Barcelona

N

5hr 30min; B/TM

8hr 30min; B/TM

3hr 45min; TM

Menorca

Ciudadela

Valencia

3hr; B/TM

5hr; TM

Palma

Mallorca

Ibiza

2hr; B

Denia

4hr; B

Ibiza Town

Formentera

MEDITERRANEAN SEA

0   50 km

Oslo/Gothenburg – Kiel line

0   50 km

6hr; CL

12hr; StenL

8–12hr 30min; CL

7hr; DS

Gothenburg

6hr; CL

Hirtshals

Frederikshaven

2–3hr; StenL

13hr 30min; StenL

Varberg

SWEDEN

20hr; CL

16hr; DS

Grenå — 4hr; StenL

20min; HHF/S (Helsingør–Helsingborg)

Karlshamn

Helsingør

Helsingborg

1hr 10min; BHS

Copenhagen

Malmö

Ystad — 7hr; BHS

DENMARK

Trelleborg

Rønne — 4hr; P

3hr 45min; S

Sassnitz

7–9hr; P/UL

Kiel

9hr; NL

5hr 30min–7hr 30min; S/TTL

7–11hr; P

Travemünde

Rostock

7hr 30min–9hr 30min; TTL

Swinoujście

AdL: Adriatica Lines ⓦwww.adriatica.it
AgL: Agoudimos Lines
  ⓦwww.agoudimos-lines.com
AnL: Anek Lines ⓦwww.anek.gr
B: Baleària ⓦwww.balearia.net
BF: Brittany Ferries
  ⓦwww.brittany-ferries.com

BHS: Bornholmstrafikken
  ⓦwww.bornholmstrafikken.dk
CL: Color Line ⓦwww.colorline.no
DS: DFDS Seaways
  ⓦwww.dfdsseaways.se
E: Eckerölinjen
  ⓦwww.eckerolinjen.fi

F: Finnlink ⓦwww.finnlink.se
FF: Fragline Ferries
  ⓦwww.fraglineferries.gr
FL: Fjord Line ⓦwww.fjordline.no
HF: Hellas Ferries
  ⓦwww.hellasferries.gr
HHF: HH Ferries ⓦwww.hhferries.se

Umeå
0   200 km
FINLAND
3–5hr; RGL
Vaasa
NORWAY
SWEDEN
Gulf of Bothnia
Nådendal   Turku   Helsinki   St Petersburg
3hr 30min; EL/SeaL/SilL/T/VL
7hr 30min; F
12hr; SeaL/SilL/VL
3hr; E Eckerö   Mariehamn
Grisslehamn
5–7hr; SilL/T/VL
13hr; SilL/T
Oslo
Kappelskär
11hr; F
Tallinn   Paldiski
RUSSIA
Sandefjord   Larvik
Strömstad
2hr 30min; CL
Stockholm
Nynäshamn
27hr 30min; RS
ESTONIA
11hr; SAL
Kristiansand
For detail see inset below left
BALTIC SEA   Ventspils   Riga   LATVIA
Hirtshals
Frederikshaven
Gothenburg
Varberg
18hr; S/SAL
Liepāja
Grenå
Karlshamn   Karlskrona
15hr; LBS
Klaipeda   LITHUANIA
Helsingør
Helsingborg
Copenhagen   Malmö
10hr Stnrl
Vilnius
Minsk
DENMARK   Trelleborg   Ystad
Rønne
Kiel   GERMANY   Sassnitz
Rostock   Gdynia
Travemünde   Swinoujście   Gdańsk
POLAND   BELARUS

Venice   Trieste (both Italy)

CROATIA   Split
8hr 30min; AdL
Ancona (Italy)
15hr; AnL/ML/SF
24hr; AnL (to Igoumenitsa)
34hr; AnL (to Patra)

NL: Nordö Link www.nordoe-link.se	RS: Riga Sealine www.rigasealine.lv
NM: Norse Merchant www.norsemerchant.com	S: Scandlines www.scandlines.se
P: Polferries www.polferries.se	SAL: Scandlines Amber Line www.scandlines.dk
P&O: P & O Ferries www.poferries.com	SC: Seacat www.seacat.co.uk
RGL: RG Line www.rgline.com	SeaL: Seawind Line www.seawind.fi

23hr 30min; ML (to Corfu),
22hr; ML (to Igoumenitsa),
19–29hr; AnL/ML/SF (to Patra)

ADRIATIC SEA
27hr; AnL

9hr; VF (to Corfu),
9hr 30min; SF/VF (to Igoumenitsa),
15hr 30min; SF (to Patra)
Tiranë
Bari
5hr 30min–7hr; AgL/FF/HML/MLL/MWF
Brindisi
ALBANIA

N
ITALY
6hr 30min; AgL/FF/HML (to Igoumenitsa)
Corfu

| SF: Sea France www.seafrance.fr |
| SFF: Superfast Ferries www.superfast.com |
| SilL: Silja Line www.siljaline.se |
| SmyL: Smyril Line www.smyril-line.com |
| StenL: Stena Line www.stenaline.se |
| T: Tallink www.tallink.se |
| TM: Trasmediterránea www.trasmediterranea.es |
| TTL: TT Line www.ttline.se |
| UL: Unity Line www.unityline.pl |
| VL: Viking Line www.vikingline.se |
| VTL: Ventouris Lines www.ventouris.gr |
| VT: Ven Trafiken www.ventrafiken.se |

HML: Hellenic Mediterranean Lines www.hml.gr
HS: HoverSpeed www.hoverspeed.com
IF: Iscomar Ferries www.iscomarferrys.com
L: LatLines www.latlines.lv
LBS: Lisco Baltic Services www.lisco.se
ML: Minoan Lines www.minoan.gr
MLL: Med Link Lines www.mll.gr
MWF: MyWay Ferries www.hellasferries.gr/myway
NF: Northlink Ferries www.northlinkferries.co.uk

Igoumenitsa   GREECE
Paxos
10hr; HML
12hr; HML/MLL   Kefallonia   Patra
16hr 30min; HML/MLL/MWF
17hr; HML   Zakynthos
0   200 km

Why to travel by bike

Modern transportation, especially in Europe, is reliable. That's the problem. It's so easy, and rather tempting, to book your way as you go. Biking doesn't quite let you get away with that. Bad weather, fatigue and punctures force flexibility into your trip and make you stop where you never thought you would. Okay, you look a bit silly interacting with the locals while wearing black spandex shorts with a built-in sweaty maxi-pad. But if you take that next step and shave your legs, it somehow looks more natural. Some countries, like France, have great respect for this type of travel. There's a historical precedent for it – the concept was sold to them long ago as the horse that needs no hay. Trucks make room for you on narrow roads, and the locals cheer you along. Even if, like me, you don't feel that sporty when you start, you'll be in incredible condition by the time it's over. And at the end of a 100-mile day, when you pull into a pub or café and see the people who've just been sitting around, there's a tremendous feeling of accomplishment, and a touch of arrogance. You almost want sit down next to someone and ask, "So, what did you do today?"

Tim Moore

Author, *French Revolutions: Cycling the Tour de France* and *Travels with My Donkey: One Man and His Ass on the Pilgrimage Way to Santiago*

greatest treasures. With the great road races ripping by at one point or another (Giro d'Italia, Vuelta de Espana, Tour de France), you find a great respect for cyclists (though not always much actual room on the road). In fact, taking a bike around Norway or Sweden and camping for free among the fjords or on the coast is quite possibly the single cheapest way to see Europe. You just pay for your plane ticket, plus some of Norway and Sweden's overpriced food, and out on the back roads expensive restaurants aren't even an option. Denmark offers some of the best biking, with 10,000km of bike trails packed into a country that's not more than 300km wide and 500km long. The Netherlands also has excellent bike trails.

Europe's larger cities all have daily and weekly rentals. Or you can buy a local bike when you arrive. They have everything from €40 rusty wrecks that work to the very same top-of-the-line Treks, Cannondales, Giants, Bianchis and the like you can find at home.

And just because your bike holds four saddlebags, that doesn't mean you should bring all four. You'll probably need them all if you're camping. But if you're planning to stay at hostels or pensions (and there are plenty along the way to keep you from camping if you'd rather have a comfortable bed after a long ride), two saddlebags should be sufficient. The reduced weight is a godsend going up hills. But, more importantly, it makes security less of an issue. If you want to head into a market or restaurant, or up a flight of stairs to check the availability of a hostel (something you'll be doing daily), it's easy to lock up the bike and carry your two bags along. With four bags (or five, including a front bag), that's not much of an option, so someone will get stuck guarding the gear – or you'll need one impressive security system.

Bringing your bike on a plane can be an issue. That is, a cost issue. Some carriers will provide you with a bike box, some won't. You'll need to find out in advance. The easiest thing to do is to get a bike box for free at your local cycle shop and then buy a pedal wrench to remove the pedals yourself (even if they do it for you, you'll still need the wrench to put the pedals back on when you arrive). Take off the handlebars and tape them to the frame of the bike, lower or move the seat as well. And then make sure the whole thing is well padded. Another option, if it's OK with your airline, is to simply put it on board without a box. Just leave it as is, with a huge "Fragile" note on it. Chances are, handlers will be gentler with it if they can see what it is.

When biking around Europe, you can put up a tent in a campground or free camp (if legal) more easily than if travelling by train or bus, since you'll be passing through the rural areas anyway. You can also easily make hotel reservations by carrying a mobile phone and a guidebook; just call ahead to a hostel or B&B once you get a sense of how far you'll get that day. A phone is also particularly handy to have along in case of any falls in fairly remote areas.

With a tour

If you'd rather follow a leader than a map, guidebook or your nose, then taking a tour will certainly provide some peace of mind and remove any worry of planning. Or maybe you think you'd like to go it alone but want a bit of hand-holding to start out your trip and boost your confidence. There are plenty of tour operators happy to take your money. The tougher part is just deciding on a tour.

Regional tours

These include everything from four-star luxury tours to local packages that can be arranged in almost any midsize city. There are thousands of tour companies to choose from at any number of levels, and it certainly helps to get a personal recommendation or find some favourable reviews before you sign up to one. In many areas, hostels team up with local tour operators (or allow tour operators to leave posters around, for which the hostel may get a commission); the operators typically offer off-road budget trips to scenic spots in the area that are hard to access by local transport. Often, these tours are good fun, but try to get a sense of what the guide is like beforehand and trust your instincts.

Bicycle tours

A support vehicle and leader provide a good deal of assistance on a long bike trip. However, this turns one of the cheapest ways of seeing Europe into a rather expensive one.

- **BackRoads** Classic upscale tours; about €2480 for one week. ⓦwww.backroads.com.
- **Bicycle Beano Tours** Vegetarian bike tours in Wales; about €620 for one week. ⓦwww.bicycle-beano.co.uk.

- **Bike Rider Tours** Upscale tours; €2050–2480 for one week. ⓦwww.bikeriderstours.com.
- **Butterfield and Robinson** Luxury tours; €3300–4135 for one week. ⓦwww.butterfield.com.
- **Euro-Bike Tours** Mid-range tours with thirty years of experience; €1650–2060 for one week. ⓦwww.eurobike.com.
- **Pack and Pedal Europe** Among the cheaper tours; €850–1240 for one week. ⓦwww.tripsite.com.

Europe-wide tours

You can get everything from fourteen cities in six days on a bus ("on your right, the blur of lights out the window is Paris") to a speciality tour that visits the best restaurants in one tiny region for over a week. For speciality travel, take a look at "Planning your big trip" (p.5).

The three main bus tour companies shuttling travellers (often at breakneck speed) around Europe are Contiki (ⓦwww.contiki .com), Trafalgar (ⓦwww.trafalgar.com) and Cosmos (ⓦwww .cosmos.com). All three typically start and end in London. One of the main differences is the age of passengers (Trafalgar's and Cosmos' are older). However, Trafalgar has a special "break-away" tour aimed at 21- to 38-year-olds. Contiki seems to attract that range on its normal buses, with a slightly more party atmosphere. All companies run more than a dozen tours within Europe, but here's a little snapshot of the sort of tours they provide:

Sample Contiki tour: London – Amsterdam – Rhine Valley – Munich – Hopfgarten (Austrian Tyrol) – Venice – Lauterbrunnen (Swiss Alps) – Paris – London. Ten days, €565.

Sample Trafalgar tour: London – Amsterdam – Rhineland – Innsbruck – Venice – Florence – Italian lakes – lucerne – Paris – London. Ten days, €990.

Sample Cosmos tour: London – Brussels – Heidelberg – Black Forest – Lake Titisee – Rhine Falls – Liechtenstein – Lake Lucerne – Interlaken – Lausanne – Paris – London. Eleven days, €874.

Travelling alone
and with others

F or many, this is one of the most difficult decisions of the trip. And understandably so. There are several factors to consider before making this choice, with sizeable pros and cons for each. All things being equal, you'll probably want to travel solo, at least for some portion of your trip. Even if all things aren't equal and there's someone you'd really like to travel with, read through this chapter so you know the risks you'll be taking and how to minimize them.

Travelling alone

Obviously, this is the more intimidating path. It's also the most potentially rewarding. And it's not nearly as frightening as it may sound. First, travelling alone does not necessarily mean you'll be travelling alone for the bulk of your trip. Quite the opposite, in fact. Most solo travellers just end up travelling with different people for different legs of their journey. Everywhere you go, from museums to hostels to cafés, you'll run into other solo travellers who'll be delighted to travel with someone and, because there are often significant price breaks on rooms for pairs and in dormitories, there's a good chance you'll be sharing accommodation. Even shy travellers find the dialogue easy to start; you already have your travel destination and independent spirit in common, not to mention doubtless shared frustrating experiences. At times, it can almost be more difficult to find periods to be on your own. For those who are still uncertain about their ability to meet travel partners on the trail, you can, virtually everywhere, sign up for a group tour along the way and surround yourself with an entire platoon of companions.

The benefits of travelling solo

You learn about yourself. You'll find out what your likes and dis-likes are. And you'll be able to act on them. Often travellers spur each other on to check off a "to-do" list. With no one looking, maybe you'll give that famous museum a miss and rent a bike and head for the countryside instead. You'll be less distracted and more likely to notice the small things happening around you. With more time to reflect, you'll get better writing in your journal, more thoughtfully composed photos, additional reading time and greater insights from studying the culture – in short, you'll absorb more of the country you're travelling in. Your hair, skin colour, clothes and height may make you stand out to varying degrees depending on the location, but as a single traveller it's easier to blend in. Plus, you're less likely to be attracting attention by speaking English with your partner. Instead, you'll be approached by more locals and other travellers eager to make conversation. They're often anxious to meet foreigners but can be intimidated by couples, not wanting to interrupt your conversation or intrude. This means solo travellers are much more likely to return home with an address book filled with

I first went to Europe just after I graduated from college. I bought a Volkswagen right from the factory in Germany and drove around the continent – drank wine in Pamplona during San Fermin and downed beers in Munich's Hofbrau Haus. But the stronger memories are meeting up with friends from college and doing things I could have done at home. I wasn't in a tour group, but might as well have been.

I learned that you learn far more during your travels if you go alone. Or as a couple. Or with children. When I travel with a film crew, for example, there are typically two campfires: one with me and the film crew and one with the locals. When you're alone, there's just one campfire. You sit with the locals and find out what's important to them. It's moments like that that provide the reason for travel.

Tim Cahill,
Author of *Lost in My Own Backyard,*
Hold the Enlightenment, and *Jaguars*
Ripped My Flesh

great contacts from all over Europe and from travellers from around the world.

Women travelling alone

Women can and do travel solo throughout Europe. Some countries, such as Norway, Sweden, Denmark, Finland and the Netherlands, make this quite easy and provide a better starting point. In southern Europe, you'll rarely feel threatened (for safety tips, see p.185), but you may be perceived as something of an oddity, so expect numerous enquiries. It's helpful to have a story for the men (you're meeting up with your husband in the next town, for example), but many questions will come from women, which is a great conversation starter and can often offer interesting insights.

The possibility of rape and robbery should be taken seriously, but can be minimized (see p.190). Most likely, the harassment you get will be a mild irritant: an admirer on a long train ride who thinks he can charm you with a six-hour story or a whistle on the street. But it can be more offensive as well: an anonymous hand brushing your breasts or bum in a crowded market. The trick is being able to distinguish between a tactless man and a dangerous one. Always trust your instinct. If any man makes you feel at risk, simply move to a train compartment where there are safer-looking people (preferably women or other travellers), head to a more crowded street, pop into a busy store or stop a police officer.

If you're heading overland into a country or region that you're a little unsure of, you can almost always find a trustworthy travel companion (even a male companion, if limiting the sexual harassment is more important) to accompany you for at least a few days, if not longer, provided you're going in the same direction. It may take a day or three to find the right person, but in places where the hassle factor is high, such as crossing into Morocco or heading to Turkey, a male companion can make things much easier (especially if you tell people you're married).

Travelling with others

Travelling with a companion isn't all bad. In fact, there are some nice benefits: minimized culture shock, medical security (they can help get you to a doctor if you get sick or carry you back to the hostel after you've passed out in a bar), money saved when staying in double rooms and taking taxis. For many, though, a travel partner's most important role is offering moral support for the never-ending onslaught of new situations to face. And helping avoid the fairly frequent party-of-one meals or having your ear bent by some garrulous locals.

△ Social adventure or logistical nightmare?

The risks of bringing a friend

Just because you're the best of friends, there's no guarantee you'll travel well together. Twenty-four hours a day of reassurance and sharing for weeks or months on end can put a serious strain on even the best of friendships. In fact, you're putting that friendship at risk. Having to make constant decisions – often with little sleep, a hangover, or a faulty air-conditioning system on a long train ride – can test the tightest bonds. And here's something else to keep in mind: if you think it would be nice to stumble upon some romance on the road, you better pray you meet twins going in the same direction, because your friend isn't going to want to hang around while you fall in love.

Maintaining your travel relationship

If you do decide to go with another person, there are a few things you can do to increase the chance that you'll still be friends at the end of the journey. For starters, give yourselves the option of separating for a while. You may even want to plan ahead for it ("After the Running of the Bulls, we'll head our own way, then meet up in Barcelona"). Even just a morning or afternoon apart every few days can be enough breathing room to sustain a travel relationship. A better bet, however, is to build some solo time into the trip. Perhaps a week or two apart every other month: sign up for different courses or adventure activities in the same region or tackle a city separately. Pick a meeting time and figure out a few ways to get in touch in case one person can't make it, such as email or by leaving a note at a certain hostel.

What to look for in a travel partner

First, you want someone with the same budget. If you don't see eye to eye (or wallet to wallet), it's going to be a straining trip. If one person is going down the comfort route while the other is on a tight budget, you won't be staying at the same places, eating at the same restaurants or doing as many activities together. Or, more likely, you will, but neither of you will be having a good time doing it. The one on a tight budget will feel like a Scrooge, always getting their budget pushed too far, having to eat plain rice at a nice restaurant or sit outside while the other goes to a string of expensive museums. The one on the bigger budget will be roughing it more than they'd like, yet feel they're shamelessly indulging in front of their companion the entire time.

If your budgets are in alignment, then check if your itineraries are. Talk about what you hope to do during a typical day. Will you get up early and aggressively pound the pavement of a city or sleep until noon, then linger in a café and read a book? Will you be pursuing cultural activities or beaches? Are you keeping things flexible or planning all the details? These are not the sort of things you want to discover after you've started travelling.

Finding a travel partner

Many people find the prospect of travelling alone so daunting they try to line up a travel partner before leaving. They place personal ads in travel magazines, newspapers and on websites. These correspondence-arranged partnerships may work out, but all too often they don't: heading out on the road together is like getting married after one blind date. There's no need to do this, especially without taking at least one short local trip together

Snowballing into large groups

When I arrived at the train station in Madrid, I sat down at a bench beside two Australians. We started talking and decided we'd buy some beer while we waited for our train to Lisbon. One of the Aussies did the buying, so we still had plenty left over when we got on the train and were joined in the couchette by a Dutch couple and two Danish women. The night train turned into something of a night party and by the time our train pulled into Lisbon there was some sort of unwritten rule that we weren't going to split up.

First, we waited for the Aussies to find a bank machine, then the Dutch wanted to buy some stamps and send off a few postcards, while one of the Danes went in search of water. We waited. The Danes had already picked out a hotel they liked from the guidebook, but no one else thought it sounded that appealing, especially since it was on the other side of town and getting there would be a minor logistical hassle, short of chartering our own bus. So, we kept walking and making suggestions and the only ones we could agree on didn't have place for all seven of us. Meanwhile, it felt like I was part of some kind of tourist platoon walking down the street in V-formation with large backpacks. We'd been in Lisbon for well over two hours and at this rate it didn't seem like we'd ever be able to shed our packs, much less find a place to stay without renting an entire floor at the *Hilton*. I half-heartedly suggested we abandon the group lodging idea, find our own hostels and meet up for drinks later. The quick consensus had us all in rooms within twenty minutes.

D L

first. You'll meet so many travellers during your travels, it's much more natural and sensible to make friends first, travel for a while without commitment and only continue together as long as it's working out.

Travelling with a crowd

With more than two people, you're going to find yourself taking votes, which is a fine way to run a democracy but a maddening way to set an itinerary. Whether you leave with a group or simply snowball into an international party on the move, beware: you're going to be about as subtle as a Hare Krishna tambourine parade dancing through a public library. Another potential problem is getting anything done. It's nice to find a social group. But instead of corralling yourself into a tour group, a better idea is to pick a bar or restaurant in the next town and say you'll meet them there at a certain time. Then everyone can break up and go their own way.

Travelling on a long organized tour

This locks you in with a group for the duration of the tour, for good and bad. Such trips tend to bring out the best in some people and worst in others. Lifelong friendships are common, but so are group conflicts, and you won't likely see much about the latter in the brochure. So make sure you ask about the time available away from the group, then take advantage of it when you get the chance. You might actually want to make substantial independent time part of your criteria when selecting a tour.

4

Costs and savings

hat does it cost to travel around Europe? Seems like a reasonable question, but it's a bit like asking what a car costs. It depends very much on the type of car. Or, in this case, the type of trip. A personalized, independent journey doesn't come with a standard price tag, so you're going to have to make some fundamental calculations based on your level of travel comfort, the activities you want to do, where you want to go and the length of your trip – and this chapter will show you how.

Without narrowing down these factors, you'll have a hard time getting within €2000 of an accurate figure on a three-month-long trip. Why? Take a typical European budget of €50 per day, plus €605 for a plane ticket (if you're flying from the US), €960 for a three-month youth Eurail ticket, €230 for insurance and €350 worth of gear, and you get a total of around €6650. If you stop and work at, say, an ecological farm for two weeks, you're down to €5900, plus whatever you manage to earn. If you stay with relatives/pen pals for a week and spend a week in a cheap hangout collecting your thoughts (and a tan), you're down to €5500. If you confine your travels exclusively to cheaper countries and use other budgeting tricks to bring your daily rate down by €10, and you use a two-month Flexi Rail pass coupled with additional local transport that you pay for along the way, that will cut your costs down to €4500. Conversely, if you decide to have two nice meals a week, stay in two decent hotels a week and take two courses during your trip, you might be looking at a daily budget of €100, which would bump that original trip plan from €6650 to nearly €10,000.

Daily costs on the road

Even with a rail or bus pass, it's possible to spend anywhere between €2500 and €25,000 on a three-month trip. It all depends on how you want to live while you're there. So, you can either make do with what you have or gather more funds before you depart. See the box on pp.68–69 for help calculating your daily budget.

How do you travel cheaper?

Without a number of budget tricks, you may end up travelling on a high-end budget while only getting mid-range value. The key to saving money on the road is not to concentrate exclusively on the big expenditures, but to find small savings along every step of the way. Beyond picking countries where your funds will

Where you can stretch your money

The five most expensive (overall) countries

1. Norway   2. Switzerland   3. Finland   4. Sweden   5. France

The five cheapest (overall) countries

1. Romania   2. Bulgaria   3. Poland   4. Turkey   5. Slovakia

Typical cheapest hostel (dorm room bed) costs per country

Most expensive:	Mid-range:	Budget:
Finland €21	Britain €17	Estonia €12
France €21	Spain €15	Czech Republic
Norway €21	Austria €14	€10
Russia €21	Germany €14	Hungary €10
Sweden €21	Ireland €14	Latvia €10
Switzerland €21	Slovenia €14	Turkey €10
Denmark €19	Belgium €13	Slovakia €9
Greece €19		Bulgaria €8
Netherlands €19		Poland €8
Italy €18		Romania €8

Consumables index (food, drinks and alcohol) per country

(100 = euro zone average)

Most expensive:	Mid-range:	Budget:
Norway 172	Italy 109	Turkey 70
Ireland 144	Austria 106	Estonia 65
Denmark 139	Belgium 104	Slovenia 65
Switzerland 139	Germany 104	Hungary 63
Finland 130	Netherlands 103	Czech Republic 61
Sweden 127	Luxembourg 102	Latvia 60
Britain 121	Portugal 90	Slovakia 59
France 111	Spain 81	Lithuania 57
		Poland 55
		Romania 50
		Bulgaria 49

A few things to consider: Sweden and Norway have free camping rights. France and Italy have more museums you're likely to pay for (at around €7 each). And, in the summer, you'll likely be buying more drinks and ice cream in southern Europe's sweltering heat. Just as you might even be more likely to splash out for an air-conditioned room. Also, in the Scandinavian countries, alcohol is very expensive (helping push up the consumables index) so if you don't drink, or don't drink much, they're more affordable. Since there's not a huge difference in the range of the cheapest supermarket food, these things just mentioned can make a significant difference.

Select your level of comfort from the list below, then figure out how many weeks or months you plan to travel and which countries you plan to spend the most time in, then add up the costs. For example, using the info below, if you plan to spend one month in Norway on a low-end budget (€1050), one month in Spain on a medium budget (€1500) and one month in Romania on an upper budget (€1950), it will tally up to a total of €4500.

Low-end budget

Accommodation: sleeping in hostel dormitory rooms, sharing rooms in the very cheapest hotels (no matter how bad the guidebook description), camping or renting a tent at campgrounds, sleeping on trains and buses.

Transport: your rail or bus pass can be supplemented with some hitchhiking or very short local bus rides, plus a flight or two under €25.

Food: eating cheap food purchased at supermarkets, and the lowest-priced side dishes at budget restaurants or at street stalls.

Lifestyle: no clubbing and nothing more than the occasional beer. Limited museum visits and no lingering drinks at nice cafés.

Low-end budget expenses:
Expensive country: daily €35; monthly €1050
Mid-range country: daily €30; monthly €900
Cheap country: daily €20; monthly €600

Middle budget

Accommodation: cheapest digs, occasionally sharing a two-person room and sleeping on a train or bus without reserved bed.

Transport: bus or rail pass can be supplemented by occasional hitching, but more often side-trips just under one hour by train or bus, plus one or two flights under €50.

Food: eating cheap food purchased at supermarkets and at budget restaurants.

Lifestyle: a few coffees a week at nice cafés. Museums are not limited but

last longer, savvy saving is about a combination of tricks and a deliberate lifestyle adjustment that rations out the creature comforts, or drops them altogether. People love to spend countless hours surfing the Web and calling around to find the cheapest ticket to Europe. Of course, you don't want to end up paying more than the guy sitting next to you on the plane, but don't adventure activities are. The occasional night on the town, but not more than one reasonably priced drink per day.

Midde budget expenses:
Expensive country: daily €65; monthly €1950
Mid-range country: daily €50; monthly €1500
Cheap country: daily €40; monthly €1200

Upper budget

Accommodation: occasional splurge on decent budget hotel; otherwise, private rooms in hostels.
Transport: rail or bus pass can be supplemented by a few additional days of travel. Train beds on overnight journeys.
Food: one decent restaurant meal per day.
Lifestyle: unlimited coffee, liberal drinking, two nights out per week and several adventure activities during the trip.

Upper budget expenses:
Expensive country: daily €100; monthly €3000
Mid-range country: daily €85; monthly €2550
Cheap country: daily €65; monthly €1950

High-end budget

Accommodation: quaint hotels and B&Bs.
Transport: comfortable sleepers on night trains; high-speed trains with mandatory reservation supplements; some taxis in cities; plane travel for short trips to other parts of Europe.
Food: eating out two meals a day at moderately priced restaurants; inexpensive wine with dinner and occasional beer or wine with lunch.
Lifestyle: concerts and clubbing three nights a week, accompanied by moderate drinking; almost daily stops in cafés for coffee and snacks; no limit on museums and occasional adventure activities.

High-end budget expenses:
Expensive country: daily €200; monthly €6000
Mid-range country: daily €175; monthly €5250
Cheap country: daily €125; monthly €3750

knock yourself out in a massive effort that will not likely save you more than €50–200. Why? That's not where the real savings are found. With some self-discipline and a few budget tips, you can reduce your daily budget by as much as €12. Over a three-month-long trip, that's a saving of €1080. Even on a one-month trip, that's €360 you can leave in the bank.

Budgetitis syndrome

When you first start travelling, spending comes naturally. Almost too naturally. A beer here, a T-shirt there, a few museum passes, a nice meal. Maybe you're too caught up in the excitement of arriving or spending to cushion your landing into a new culture. Whatever the case, after a few days or weeks, many realize they're over budget and begin to feel the stress of a money belt getting thinner. The natural response to this relentless stream of expenditure is an attempt to stem the outflow. And when travellers meet and compare notes, boasting rights go to the one surviving on the lowest funds. When it gets competitive, that's when budgetitis really sets in. Symptoms include: walking an extra twenty minutes to find a bread shop whose loaves are three cents cheaper; full-blown arguments with taxi drivers over the equivalent of 25 cents; and skipping a meal because the local supermarket prices seem a little high. In extreme cases, travellers might party all night (without drinking... well, not much), then sleep in a park during the day. They'll only travel by hitchhiking and show up at soup kitchens for food, paying with the minimum donation. This is one of the most common budget travel afflictions (followed closely by exaggerated storytelling), and at some point during a long trip you'll likely suffer from it yourself.

If you can sense this happening, you have to take a step back and remember why you're travelling. It's fine to save money while you're on the road, but you need to balance this with the fact that you're not travelling in order to save money. Better to come home a week or two early and suffer a little less.

Discount cards

There's no magic wand to wave and get guarantee savings everywhere you go, but for €18 an International Student Identity Card (ISIC) comes close (๏www.isic.org). There are also youth cards (for under-26s) and teacher cards issued by the same organization that offer similar discounts. They provide significant deals for museums, local transport cards, plane tickets and more. You may very well make up the €18 on the flight over. The trick is remembering to ask for the discount. It won't help you much in restaurants, but nearly anywhere a ticket is required be sure to ask. Also, use it as a backup ID card you can leave behind when renting bikes and so on.

Another popular card is the Hostelling International Card (€21; ๏www.hiayh.org; see p.159 to find out if you like the sound of hostelling). If you want to get this card, you'll need to do so in your home country before leaving. With it, you get discounts on about 2000 affiliated hostels around Europe, plus reductions on transport, including discount car rental, bus and train travel. The card will pay for itself within four nights. The downside is that you can get many of the transport discounts with an ISIC or youth card, and these official hostels don't pack the party atmosphere of the private hotels and are often not centrally located.

If you find you're staying at a number of VIP-affiliated private hostels (there are about five hundred in Europe, mostly concentrated in Scandinavia and Ireland), you might as well pick up a €17 VIP Backpackers membership card (ⓦwww.vipbackpackers .com) while you're on the road and start getting the roughly five percent discounts per night – that is, if you think you'll use it more than 21 nights, which is what it takes to earn back the card's value.

Flights

The "Getting there and around" chapter (see p.26) has more details on how to get the cheapest flight, but a good basic guideline to follow before booking any flights is to do a little checking on your own so you'll know a good price when you see one. Start looking around on the Web (ⓦwww.expedia.com, ⓦwww.orbitz.com, ⓦwww.travelocity.com and Europe's ⓦwww.opodo.com are among the major online booking engines), and check out the lowest published fares for a particular flight. Then, all things being relatively equal, book with a well-informed travel agent and get their email address and phone number. The advantages of using an experienced travel agent are two fold: they are aware of the finer points that most travellers overlook, such as ease of airport connections and they are able to access considerably cheaper fares.

Rail passes

Most Europe rail passes can only be purchased in your home country, but with the Internet this isn't such a problem. If you're already in Europe, or on your way there, you can order it online, have it sent to your parents or friends and then get them to forward it to you. The more difficult task is selecting the right rail pass. You can't bargain your way to a cheaper rail pass, but there are several ways to get more for your money:

- If you plan to stay in one spot for a while, try to time it at the beginning or end of your journey so your active pass isn't sitting idle more than it need be.
- Consider a Flexi Pass (certain number of travel days allowed within a fixed time period) instead of an unlimited travel pass. You don't want to spend every day on the train anyway.
- Supplement a Flexi Pass with cheap, shorter trips. If you calculate the per-day value of a Flexi Pass, it's around €25. If you're travelling, say, the 97km from Florence to Siena in Italy, a second-class ticket costs €17. Typically, if the journey is less than an hour and you're not on a high-speed train, it's going to be cheaper to buy a ticket at the window and save travel days on your pass.
- Check for weekend deals before using your Flexi Pass. In Germany, for example, you can land bargains with Deutsche Bahn's "Happy Weekend" ticket.
- Don't be afraid to use flights just because you have a rail ticket. You'd spend a few days of your trip on the train (and use up a few days of your rail pass) to get from London to Portugal

△ Using your rail pass efficiently will cut down your transport costs considerably.

or Greece. With cut-throat budget airlines practically giving tickets away, chances are you can find a one-way flight for less than €100, possibly even less than €40. That will save you time and roughly €50–75 worth of your Flexi Pass, plus overnight and reserved-seating supplements that will push the total over €85.

- As a rule of thumb, the less flexible the rail pass, the cheaper it is. In other words, if you know more or less where you plan to go (and you don't feel obligated to hit every single region or country), you can get a much better deal. However, sometimes it's not much of a bargain. For example, a youth traveller can get ten travel days in two months in five adjoining countries for €361 with the Select Pass. To access all seventeen countries with the same number of travel days, it's just €404. Forty euros seems like good value for the extra flexibility. If you're on a shorter trip or know you're not going to visit more than three adjoining countries, the €313 Three-Country Pass offers a more significant saving.

- If you only want to travel in one country and can't decide which, know that some single-country passes cost more than others. In Portugal, you get four travel days within fifteen days for €87 (first class); France, four days within one month for €180 (second class); and Norway, three days within one month for €173 (second class).

Buses

Buses are going to be cheaper than trains almost every time. In England (home of Europe's most expensive trains), they'll be roughly one third of the cost. So, it's a good way to save some money. However, you can't get up and stretch your legs the same way. And, if you're using Busabout, you won't be rubbing elbows with the locals. If you're looking for travel or party partners, however, that can be a good thing. For bus passes, follow the same basic strategy listed on p.72.

Accommodation

Europe is equipped with some of the world's best hotels, and you could blow a month's budget (and then some) on a single night in any one of them. (One Swiss hostel has a suite that goes for over €20,500).

Your guidebook will steer you to the type of place you're after, but at this planning stage one of the best things you can do to save money on the road is prepare yourself for sleeping in no-star accommodation. That means sleeping in dorm rooms when available, trying to share a room with another traveller if there are doubles with lower rates, and not letting yourself be put off by places described in your guidebook as basic, or even grungy. If you're armed with earplugs and a good sleep sheet, you'll be fine. Other money-saving ideas for bottom-end digs are:

- Stay in small towns and rural areas – hostels and pensions in large cities pay the most rent, and pass the costs on to travellers.
- Make a point of getting addresses of travellers you meet, then stay with them if you're heading to their home town or city. Try to give a few days' or weeks' notice with an email. Taking a digital camera is good in this respect – it's nice to attach a photo of you together when you request a place to stay. They might have offered their address to dozens of travellers or had a bit too much to drink and have trouble remembering your name when you make contact.
- Cram the rooms full. Go for a quad and find three other travellers to take up the extra beds so you all get a better deal than sleeping in a single or double room.
- Head to campgrounds just out of town and rent their walk-in tents (with real beds).
- Check out housing at universities over the summer. Empty dorm rooms are often rented out at cut-rate prices.
- Hang out around the students' union and look for a friendly group. Introduce yourself and ask if you can crash on someone's floor or sofa in exchange for a beer or two, plus free accommodation at your parents' home if they ever get there. Women can do this safely as well (and will likely have an easier time of it) by approaching a group of women.
- A few places may offer sleeping on the roof for half the price if you have a mat and sleeping bag. It doesn't hurt to ask.
- If staying in private rooms, accepting one without a private WC and shower can save you €17–34 per night.

Museums

Europe is chock-full of some of the world's best museums, and chances are you're going to be visiting several. Look into multi-museum passes when you know you'll be visiting a few in the same town. The Paris Museum pass for example, pays for itself in just a few visits and lets you stroll by the snaking queues. Even a single pass to the Louvre is worth picking up in advance, not just to avoid the long queues during peak season, but to save. Tickets are a few euros cheaper when purchased from local vendors, such as a Fnac store (ⓦwww.fnac.com) in Paris.

Food

Cosy restaurants and old-world cafés are tempting places to relax, socialize with other travellers and people-watch. They're also nice places to run down your budget: those double café lattés add up in a hurry. And fleeing to *McDonald's* isn't always going to help. Switzerland has, on average, the world's most expensive *McDonald's* – over €4 for a Big Mac. Minimizing these little luxuries is going to be the first unpleasant step. Here are a few others:

- Find the little restaurants that don't have English menus. Places smart enough to put a few languages on the menu are usually savvy enough to jack up their prices as well. Another approach is to look for places where you don't see any other foreigners.
- Look for restaurants near universities. Students worldwide have little money for eating, and there's almost always a cottage industry set up to serve them.
- Sample the street food, find a few favourites and make meals out of them. Two full days of street-vendor-bought meals costs the equivalent of one decent restaurant-meal.
- Think pizza. In Italy and elsewhere, pizzas come in just one size, which more than covers a typical plate. These single servings provide some of the best deals in Europe and can typically be had for €4–6. If you've got a small appetite, they're enough for two.

- If you want a recommendation, ask a construction worker. They're often on a limited budget and know where to find a nearby filling meal.
- Cook in hostels. Check your guidebook for hostels with kitchen access. It's always cheaper to cook as a group, so don't be afraid to stick your head into the lounge and ask if anyone wants to pitch in and make a communal dinner.
- Single-portion supermarket dining works. You'll soon learn how to survive on fruit, yoghurt, sandwiches and crisps.
- Try the samples at supermarkets. During weekends and busy shopping times in large supermarkets in big cities, you can often find a tremendous range of free samples available. With a little luck, you can get an entire meal, as long as you don't mind getting it in fifteen separate servings.
- Bring food onto trains. Trains throughout the world are united by one common theme: bad food at ridiculous prices. Bring more than you think you'll need, plus water.
- Hit the buffets and salad bars: look for a cheap salad bar or buffet and then stack your plate about 1m high. This may require some advanced engineering skills.
- Pizza gathering – not officially recommended, but it works. Travellers have been known to hang out in franchise pizza joints, order a small salad, then grab the untouched slices from other tables when groups get up to leave.
- Order economically. A restaurant is a great place to rest your feet and socialize, but to keep the bill down consider ordering one

Watch for cons and extra fees

At restaurants, waiters may play more tricks than just serving warm soft drinks and seeming to squeeze in a round of golf before getting the food to your table. They may also incorrectly add up the bill, conveniently in their favour. Always double-check it.

One popular gambit in tourist areas is to place a bread roll on your table right when you sit down, then charge a whopping fee for it if you so much as breathe on it. If you're not interested, have them take it away. It may be as tasty as a stone, but it's difficult to stare at when hungry.

If you're trying to have an inexpensive meal, make sure you don't pick a place with a cover charge – a fee for just sitting down at the table. Feel free to ask if there is such a fee (sometimes called a "service fee"). If there isn't, make sure it doesn't magically appear on the bill.

If the menu says that tax is included in the prices, they shouldn't be adding the tax fee on top of the total price.

appetizer and complementing it with a few filling side dishes instead of a main meal.

- Eat seasonal. Fruits and veggies getting shipped in out of season aren't as fresh, taste worse and cost more.

Saving on restrooms

There are savings to be had here, and not just from trying to hold on to it. It's not often you'll encounter a squatter, or hole in the floor where the toilet is supposed to be, but you'll run into restroom attendants everywhere who'll charge for use of their facilities, or automatic WCs that require coin activation.

At some point you'll need to use one, so carry change. Tipping the attendant is often optional, but if you can splash a few small coins in the cup it at least sounds generous. Some have specific fees for things like toilet paper or hand towels and some have outrageous admission rates, as much as €1, no matter what you plan to do.

It's best to find free toilets, though they're not always easy to come by. *McDonald's*, traditionally one of the most popular free bathroom options, have more recently set up security measures – typically, keypad locks with codes only available to paying customers. If you're reasonably presentable and not toting a large backpack that denotes you as a budget traveller, you might be able to pop into a nice hotel. If questioned by the doorman, you can say that you're scouting the place for your parents or checking out the restaurant's menu as a possible dining option that evening. One of the best options, especially while waiting in train stations where you almost always have to pay for toilet services, is to spot a train that isn't due to depart for a while, then hop aboard, use the restroom and hop back off.

Tipping

If you can figure out a formula that works for tipping across Europe, you should probably be working at NASA or cracking codes for MI6. Tipping in Europe is a confusing affair. In some upscale environments, you might be giving a waiter ten to fifteen percent, while in that same country it would be perfectly fine to leave nothing at a lower-end café.

To generalize, tipping in Europe at the lower levels of service is more about rounding up and token tips than straight percentages. For instance, if your lunch tab comes to €5.60, you might leave an even €6. With a tab of €9.80, round up to €10 for service you could have just as easily done without. In some places, it's just as appropriate to leave a fifty cent or €1 coin, even if that works out to be a two percent tip. The same basic concept applies for taxi rides. If the ride comes to exactly €5, you're fine without a tip (unless carrying bags or other service was provided). If it's €5.70, you should probably just pay €6 and tell the driver to keep the change. In a crunch, you can always ask a fellow diner (especially if you're treating yourself to a meal in a swanky restaurant, where the tip will more likely be ten to twelve percent) or your hotel concierge for some guidance. But the final decision is up to you. Give what you feel is appropriate and leave the restaurant or cab with confidence.

Changing money

Changing money isn't as straightforward as money changers would like you to believe. In fact, in many cases it's a mathematical mind-twister and, like in Vegas, the house has you by the short and curlies. There are a few tips that will help keep more money in your pocket after the transaction is over:

- Avoid changing money at hotels, hostels and bureaux de change. They're well situated, have great opening hours and charge you a fortune for all that convenience.
- Always compare before changing money. The rates can differ even on the same street. Check banks or the post office.

- When you shop around, don't be fooled by nice rates. Money changers specialize in fee juggling. They use a few mechanisms to make sure they get your money. They either use a flat fee (as a minimum) or a percentage of the total amount changed. Which one you use often depends on the amount you're changing. Typically, if you're exchanging a lot of money (say €500), the minimum fee will be irrelevant so you can look at rates and commissions. If it's a small amount, you'll want to pay closer attention to the minimum fee and rate.
- Look for the buy rate and sell rate. The difference (their profit) is probably around five percent. If it's more or they don't show it, something may be fishy.
- Minimize transactions. Take a moment to calculate what you'll need, because every time you change cash, travellers' cheques or withdraw money from a bank machine, you're paying for the transaction (see p.141).

Bargaining

You can't walk into a shopping centre and start bargaining for food, just as you can't back home. But there are a number of excellent handicraft and knick-knack markets across the continent where you can bargain, and these provide some of the best shopping in Europe. You can also bargain your hostel/hotel room down during off-season and negotiate book swaps – the basic bargaining concept is the same for all of these.

The golden rule of bargaining is to keep a smile on your face. It's OK to be firm with your offer, even walk away at an impasse, but if you think of it as a game and keep the atmosphere light and friendly, it's hard to go wrong.

Getting an excellent price on an item, however, is another story. The sellers are the experts, but you hold the cash, so you're in control. The first thing to do is find out from a local or fellow traveller who's familiar with the market what the real going rate is. In Europe, there typically isn't a special price for locals, so you have one less barrier to hurdle. Now you've got a goal. More importantly, this little bit of research will help you recognize any serious price gouging. That is, sometimes vendors, just for sport, like to see how much they can get for an item and may throw out a completely outlandish price and see if you'll take the bait.

The next step is to take a look at what you're wearing.

It's hard to haggle a price down with a ring on every other finger or a watch on your wrist that will tell you the time 300m under water. Leave the expensive camera, jewellery and the €200 Gore-Tex jacket in the hotel room (or in your daypack) if you know you're heading to a market to do some bargaining. Then go early. Many vendors share the belief that a sale early in the day will bring them good fortune, so they may be more likely to lower their prices than they would otherwise. This also increases your chances that you'll be alone with the vendor, which works to your advantage. With other potential customers browsing within earshot, the vendor may feel pressure to keep prices high.

The next step may be the most difficult: hide the true extent of your interest. That is, you don't want to hold something up to show your travel partner and say: "Look at this. It's perfect!" The vendors may not be fluent in English, but this exchange won't escape them. You might start out by lifting the item you're interested in for a moment and casually asking how much it costs. They'll either respond with an inflated price, a decent price or this question: "How much will you give me for it?" If you've done your research, you're in good shape for any of these. If you get an inflated price, make an offer that's equally below your target price. The vendor will immediately dismiss it as unfair, and you – here's where that smile really comes in handy – can say: "Maybe we could start the bargaining over again, but this time at a more realistic level." Your next offer should be just under your target price. On the other hand, if the vendor starts the bargaining at a very reasonable level, don't expect it to go down much. Pick a price just under your target and be prepared to come up in price fairly quickly. Finally, if you're asked to start the bidding, you might say: "Actually, I spoke to a few people who bought these as gifts, and they told me I shouldn't pay more than $X". The vendor will immediately know that you've been doing your homework, but may not be ready to give it up to you at that price. If that's the sense you get, you can say: "Perhaps that's the local price I heard about. As a visitor to your country, I'd be willing to give you a little more." Then offer a price that's one or two percent higher.

Another more businesslike approach is to introduce yourself to the vendor and tell them that you're considering doing all of your shopping in their boutique and try to get a bulk discount. After some small talk, the vendor will probably let you steer the conversation to prices. If you're still not close by the second round, let them know that you're sorry it doesn't sound like it's working out and thank them for their time. They've already put some time into the deal and won't want to lose a fairly substantial customer, so chances are they probably won't let you go that easily.

In the end, it should be a win–win experience. And if you keep the negotiation friendly, keep your cool and only buy at a price you feel good about, it will be. Despite any dramatic claims of losing money, a vendor will never sell you merchandise at a loss, so you shouldn't leave feeling guilty that you obtained an unjustly low price.

5

Working, volunteering and studying

I f you're European, your passport is a ticket to landing jobs around the continent. If you don't have an EU passport, you might find yourself in this typical scenario: you've finished a semester of studies in Europe, you've got two months to bounce around before you need to return home, and you've got some kind of rail or bus pass burning a hole in your pocket with sixteen major cities, twelve beaches and fourteen museums on your wish list. Here are two reasonable questions to ask: is there really time to find a job, volunteer or pick up a new skill? And why should I bother?

You should at least consider making the time. Especially if you want a truly unique, enriching travel experience. Because, no matter how many museums and handicraft markets you hit, no matter how many kilometres you log on buses, trains and ferries, no matter how little you pay for your night's accommodation, you're not likely to get under the skin of a place until you stop and engage yourself. It doesn't matter if you're working, volunteering or studying; all it takes is some ongoing interaction with locals to develop a connection and make some friends. If you've studied, consider the relationship you've had with your closer classmates compared to the one you've had with people you've shared a bus ride with. It's a different level entirely. Some jobs, volunteer projects and courses immerse you in the culture more than others, and it's not always easy to tell in advance which will and which won't, but at least you'll still be earning money, helping others or learning a skill – not a bad way to pass your time in Europe.

Note to EU passport holders: you may wish to skip ahead to the section on choosing and finding a job.

Working

Travellers have been running out of money before they've exhausted their wanderlust for years. Every day, travellers hit the road with just a few months' or weeks' worth of cash in their pockets. Depending on your age, nationality and professional skills, there are countless options available to keep yourself financially afloat.

Bad news first: the European Union doesn't really want non-EU passport holders to waltz over and land a job. Especially Americans. For New Zealanders, Canadians and Aussies, there are some special visas called "working holiday visas" that make things quite convenient (see p.85 for a list of "working holiday" countries). Without such agreements, even a very short-term job can come with Himalayan hurdles. Now the good news: you can still get a job almost anywhere.

For a legal job, the most important thing to remember is that you need to enter the European country you'll be working in with the proper stamps and papers to be eligible for work, so even if you find a job after arriving you would still need to return home, fix the paperwork, and then re-enter the country with all your documents in order. Some organizations can help you with the application forms, especially if you're a student or recent graduate.

Work placements for students and recent grads

Several agencies have popped up to help students and recent graduates (those who received a degree within the last four months) get special visas. These agencies apply mostly to Americans, but they can help just about anyone if the country you want to work in doesn't have some sort of holiday work-visa arrangement with your country. In which case, they provide the easiest way of taking care of the paperwork. You still have to pound the pavement and find your own job (one where the employer doesn't mind taking you on for just a few months), but at least you can show the employer you've got a work permit. The drawback is that this handy red-tape-cutting service doesn't come free. In fact, it may run you about a month's wages: €450. Typically, the short-term jobs you'll be able to find aren't going to come with meaty pay cheques or bonuses. And you've still got to pay for accommodation and food. In other words, you'll be paying to wait tables full-time in Paris for two months, even if you speak fluent French. Other common jobs include au pair work and teaching English. If the pay cheque isn't as important, some of these organizations offer help arranging interesting internships. You should probably think twice about handing over funds for this. You can call up the companies direct-ly, say you're a student and that you want to work for free to get some firsthand experience, and no paperwork should be necessary.

- **American Scandinavian Foundation** Ⓦwww.amscan.org. Two- to three-month summer placements for Americans aged 21 and over. Particularly for those studying Engineering, Chemistry, Business and Computer Science.
- **Bunac Working Adventures Worldwide** Ⓦwww.bunac .org. Exactly what the name says (except, perhaps, the "Bunac" part). European programmes are only offered in Britain and Ireland.
- **CDS International** Ⓦwww.cdsintl.org. Programmes in Germany and Switzerland aimed at young professionals seeking international experience.
- **Council Exchanges** Ⓦwww.ciee.org. Offers programmes in Germany, France and Ireland.
- **International Cooperative Education Programme** Ⓦwww.ciemenlo.com. Eight- to twelve-week paid internships in Belgium, England, Germany and Switzerland, for those with for-eign language skills.
- **InterExchange Work Abroad Programmes** Ⓦwww .interexchange.org. Programmes for Americans and Canadians 18 and older in Belgium and Norway.

The "working holiday"

If you're between 17 and 30 years old and not American, you are eligible to seek employment while "on holiday" in the UK and several other countries. In the UK, you Commonwealth citizens (those from Australia, Canada, New Zealand, Antigua and Barbuda, Bahamas, Barbados, Belize, Grenada, Jamaica, New Grenadines, Solomon Islands and Tuvalu) can work for up to two years. Here's the fine print: you have to leave immediately when your two years is up (and the clock starts ticking the moment your visa is issued); you can't have children with you over the age of 5 (or you must leave before they turn 5); you can't apply for public funds if you can't support yourself; if you're married, your spouse must meet all of the "working holiday" criteria. Also, if you have any criminal convictions you may be denied a visa. In other EU countries, you 17- to 30-year-olds without kids typically get a year for your working holiday, though depending on the particular agreement you may only be allowed to work for six months of that. Much depends on your nationality. See below for details.

"Working holidays" for Australians

For a UK visa, contact the UK embassy in Australia (🌐www.uk .emb.gov.au). Cost: AUS$94 for a six-month visa, AUS$195 for any 6- to 24-month one. It takes about two to three months to process. In the EU, you have "working holiday" arrangements with: Denmark, France, Germany, Ireland, Italy, the Netherlands, Norway and Sweden. Surf to their embassy websites in your country for application info.

"Working holidays" for New Zealanders

For a UK visa, contact the UK embassy in New Zealand (🌐www.britain.org.nz). Cost: NZ$101 for a 24-month visa. It takes about two to three months to process. In the EU, you have "working holiday" arrangements with: Belgium, Denmark, Finland, France, Germany, Ireland, Italy, the Netherlands and Sweden. Surf to their embassy websites in your country for application info.

"Working holidays" for Canadians

For a UK visa, contact the UK embassy in Canada (ⓦwww.britain incanada.org). Cost: CAN$94 for a 24-month visa. It takes about two to three months to process. In the EU, you have working holiday arrangements with: France, Germany, Ireland and the Netherlands. Surf to their embassy websites in your country for application info.

Britain's ancestry clause

In you're a Commonwealth citizen and you want to work in Britain and have a grandparent who was born in Britain or Northern Ireland (and you can prove it), you can apply for a special UK Ancestry visa that enables you to live and work in Britain for an initial period of four years. Visit the website of your nearest British embassy for details.

Starting your job search online

It's not just au pair gigs and private English lessons. You can find IT jobs, translation positions, adventure-guiding jobs, fruit-picking jobs, wine jobs, ski resort jobs and more. Your best starting points on the Web are probably ⓦwww.jobs-in-europe.net and ⓦwww.workanywhere.com. Even though most travel jobs involve pavement pounding upon arrival, the Web can still be of some help. Once you learn the basics below, you'll be able to fine-tune your Web searching. For tips on landing the job, see p.97.

Direct employment

The hardest jobs to get are the ones that you set up on your own by applying directly to European companies before you leave. To get a job offer without an interview takes some serious legwork, luck or great connections – typically, all three, plus a low-budget miracle. That may mean starting with a bulk mailing of your CV (résumé) and cover letter followed by hours of overseas follow-up calls. Let's say you get a job offer. In order for the company to arrange a work visa for you, they need to be able to show the government that someone from their country or elsewhere in the EU couldn't do the job. Once you understand this position, you can better focus your job search to fit your unique skills. Say, for example, you've got Web-programmer skills and have been doing campus promotions at your university. You'd have a good shot landing a job with a European company trying to target English-speaking university-age customers with a new website. And they'd have a good shot at getting you a work visa. Some creative thinking is in order to figure out what marketable skills (in addition to your English speaking and writing) will make you an appealing candidate and also make you an easy sell to the immigration bureau. At any rate, all such permissions must be arranged long before your arrival, so this is one of the first things you'll want to do when planning your trip.

Illegal work

If you do illegal work, you could very well – depending on the laws of that country, which are certainly worth looking into – find yourself slapped with a fine, thrown out of the country (guess who gets to pay for the ticket home?) or landed behind bars (picking up free language lessons from your cellmates!). With that little disclaimer out of the way, there are scores of employers who don't mind hiring unregistered foreign help and, from experience, know that the authorities will turn a blind eye. In fact, you may go to great lengths to secure a work permit only to be paid under the table. They often just like knowing you have a permit in case the police show up requesting documents.

Seasonal work

One of your best chances of turning up and landing a decent-paying job with no previous skills (or a work permit) is going to be taking advantage of the seasonal openings. It's largely a matter of being in the right place at the right time, and if you know what you're looking for it's easy to coordinate.

Ski jobs

Working in the Alps or Pyrenees can be a fantastic experience, especially if you find a job that allows you to put your skis on regularly. Unfortunately, those aren't as common as you'd think. For a job, either apply in writing for work with a tour company in your country six to eight months in advance or arrive at your desired resort around November and start walking the streets. Be especially careful about hiring yourself out as a freelance ski instructor – most resorts keep a keen eye out for unofficial lessons on the slopes and prosecute. Possible jobs include: ski tuning, rental-shop fittings, ski guiding, lift operator, bartender, dishwasher, table waiter, restaurant cook, chalet cook/housekeeping, childcare, singer/guitar player at bars, reception staff, maintenance staff, sales clerk, supply driver, bouncer and DJ. Countries with ski resorts include: Andorra, Austria, Bulgaria, France, Germany, Italy, Norway, Scotland, Slovakia, Slovenia, Spain, Sweden and Switzerland. If you want to find out a bit more on the Web first, try ⓦwww .skiconnection.co.uk, ⓦwww.nomadicjobs.com or look up the resort you want to go to and send out your CV to shops around town. The largest ski resorts include:

- **Chamonix** ⓦwww.chamonix.net
- **Les Trois Vallées** (Courchevel, Meribel, Val Thorens, all inter-connected) ⓦwww.les3vallees.com
- **Val d'Isere** ⓦwww.valdisere.com

For other ski areas, try ⓦwww.resortsonline.com.

Summer-resort work

For summer resorts, you may want to turn up two months before the season begins (March–May) to beat the rush for jobs, then go travelling regionally and return when the job starts. On the hotel/bar/restaurant side, women tend to have an easier time finding work. Possible jobs include: camp counsellor for kids, bartender, waiter, hotel receptionist, hotel housekeeper, cook, baker, sales clerk, supply driver, singer/guitar player at bars, DJ, rental-shop clerk, cleaner, bouncer, guide, sports instructor, lifeguard, scuba instructor and campground maintainer.

Harvest-season work

If you can eat it, you can probably find work picking it if you turn up at the right place in the right season – from strawberries to dates to apples. Most harvesting jobs are in the fall, but they can be found all summer long. The best place for pre-trip research is the Internet: try ⓦwww.pickingjobs.com. Pay is often based on the amount you pick, and it may take a few days to get up to speed. No one is going to remind you when to drink water or that you should protect yourself from the sun, so take care of that yourself. Bring a good hat, sun cream, and drink throughout the day. And remember to ask for adequate protection when pesticides and other noxious chemicals are sprayed.

Manual labour

Construction jobs tend to be underpaid and overworked. There's often a spot or two in cities where labourers show up each morning and get selected by employers. If no such place exists, or the competition is too fierce, look for large construction sites and ask for work directly from the foreman. There's also plenty of factory work; the nastier tasks usually come with a higher wage. If they don't, don't do them. Possible jobs include: house renovation, road building, landscaping, shrimp peeling and fish packing.

Working independently

Money-making opportunities for the creative entrepreneur are almost endless. You could discreetly sell cool drinks on a hot beach or cheap umbrellas on a busy street when it rains. And if you have a trade that allows you to work independently, even better. But unless you have a work permit, find out about the penalties, assess the risk and keep a low profile. If you're looking for a street to perform on, think about good acoustics, an original act and a place where the police are kind (northern Europe tends to be popular in this regard). Often, small towns, with many pedestrian streets and few buskers (street performers), bring good fortune. Also, keep an eye out for festivals, which attract crowds with ample pocket change and time to stick around until the end of your act, when the hat gets passed. A clever performance with showmanship and a dose of humour will out-earn a talented musician nine out of ten days. Other possible jobs include: masseur, private cook, private music instructor, street juggler, house cleaner, window washer, gardener, language tutor, jewellery street-seller, T-shirt designer and

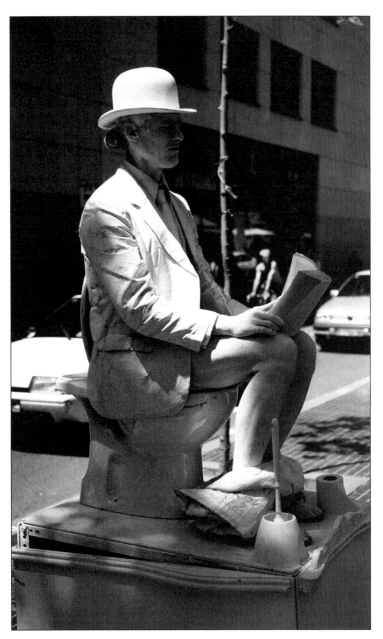

△ A bit of creativity will go a long way towards making money in Europe peddler, and promotional pamphlet distributor (to other travellers for local bars/hostels).

Teaching English

If English is your mother tongue, you have a university degree of some kind, can dress smartly and carry yourself with confidence, you have a decent shot at landing a job without a TEFL or similar certificate. You can certainly hire yourself out as a private tutor. But there's a lot more to teaching a language than just being able to speak it, and any amount of instruction will be helpful. The problem is, the instruction isn't that cheap (about €1250) or quick (roughly 100hr of coursework), and not all programmes are created equal. In Europe, the British-based CELTA (Certificate in English Language Teaching to Adults) is probably the most recognized brand of TEFL/TESOL certificates, and you can take them just about anywhere. (Quick decoder: TEFL is "Teaching English as a Foreign Language" and TESOL is "Teaching English for Speakers of Other Languages" – basically the same thing.) If you decide you want to go after a TEFL certificate, you have a few options:

- **Get it near where you live** – search ⓦwww.cambridge-efl.org for the closest location.
- **Get a certificate online** – a bit shady and probably not as useful in terms of practice and feedback.
- **Take a CELTA or other reliable course in the city or country you want to work in** – you can find out the reputable courses by asking local employers or checking out a TEFL forum like the one at Dave's ESL Café ⓦwww .eslcafe.com, a good source for general job searching and classroom teaching tips and lessons. This is probably the best option because it means spending more time in the country and the local language schools have the best job-placement connections. In addition to CELTA, Trinity College London programmes (ⓦwww.windsorschools.co.uk) are also well known.
- **Go some place where it's a bit cheaper to get a TEFL degree** – in places such as Thailand or Egypt, you may get accommodation thrown in for that €1250. (If you're paying €20 a night for six weeks in Europe, that's €840. And you can probably buy a return ticket from London to Bangkok for less than that. Try ⓦwww.teflinternational.com.)

In Europe, most of the jobs these days can be found in Eastern and Central Europe, where the TEFL isn't quite as critical. If you do have a TEFL certificate, though, you'll probably land a better job or beat unqualified competition, and find it easier in the classroom than if you were winging it. Is it worth the money and time to make that "livable wage"? That's your call. But you probably needn't bother with the €250 weekend introductory course; those who require a real certificate won't be impressed. Most of the best jobs require a six- to twelve-month contract to prevent you from skipping out and leaving their students with verbs unconjugated and participles dangling.

Teaching diving

Europe may not be anyone's top pick for an exciting dive, but Europeans still want to get certified, and often before they go on holiday. With a Divemaster certification (®www.padi.com), you may be able to find some work, especially in large cities, provided you speak the language. Unlike resorts, schools prefer people for longer stretches, so that may make things a bit more challenging on a traveller's schedule. There are a number of good wreck dives around the Med and even some coastal resort areas with decent visibility if sun and sand is more important. Try ®www.scubayellowpages.com for a listing of diving companies at destinations around Europe. In terms of landing a job, most certified instructors have success making personal contact with dive shops and get paid under the table for their work. Or they return later, once the proper work visa has been processed back home. You might try applying directly to some of the larger, more professional resorts (those destinations with multiple dive shops on ®www.scubayellowpages.com, for example).

Journalism and photography

Travel writing and travel photography are very competitive fields, and in both cases your chances of supplementing your income or supporting yourself while travelling will be greatly enhanced with well-honed skills from a course or formal education, but no matter how much natural ability or number of course certificates you may have, selling your material without an established track record is extremely tough.

That means, if you're serious about writing or camera-clicking your way around Europe, you'll want to give yourself a head start by making inroads in the industry: get some articles or photos published (no matter what the subject), build a relationship with editors and start putting your portfolio together.

Once you have a solid client list of people willing to buy your prose or pictures, you can actually make money during your travels. Unfortunately, it can take months or, more likely, years to develop such contacts. The other, and far more popular approach, is to document your trip (photographers should use slide film, the industry standard) and try to sell it upon your return. This can certainly bring in some money, but you're not likely to get it until long after you return. Cold-calling an editor just before you leave and asking if you can, despite your complete lack of experience, report your way around Europe, is a textbook example of how not to go about it.

Otherwise, you might apply to work directly with the large wire services (such as Associated Press or Reuters) or, if you plan to stay put for a while, try small English-speaking newspapers overseas (Ⓦwww.world-newspapers.com/europe.html).

Multinational jobs

If you happen to live near the headquarters of an international company, surf their website and find out where their overseas offices are located and what they do. If you've got some language skills or other marketable training that may interest them, try to arrange for an interview. If you don't live near the headquarters, that doesn't mean you need to give up just yet. Not all require you to interview at their central command centre.

Wine jobs

There's everything from tasting to sales to grape picking to estate management to biology work. Try Ⓦwww.agriseek.com, Ⓦwww .vinexchange.com and Ⓦwww.winecountryjobs.com. Or go to Ⓦwww.wineweb.com/mapeuro.html and get the contact info for European wineries and contact them directly yourself.

IT jobs

There are hundreds of IT recruitment firms in just about every European country. If you want to go down that route, you might do an Internet search with the name of the country you want to work in plus "IT jobs" or "IT recruitment" or "computer jobs". Otherwise, you might take a look at ⓦwww.dice.com, ⓦwww .professionalpeople.com (for placements in eastern Europe), and ⓦwww.eurosearch.net.

Au pair jobs

Assisting with children can, depending on the family, be a good arrangement. Live-in au pairs typically earn less in Europe than in the US, but rates are often adjusted if you have a college degree, childcare education, special language skills and great letters of recommendation. And, of course, if you work more hours or care for more children (for more than three children, wages should go up roughly ten percent for each child). Wages may also be slightly higher in major cities, where there's more competition. The work-load varies from one family to the next, but for €65 a week you might expect about five hours of work per day for five days a week, with two or three babysitting evenings – more for live-out au pairs. Keep in mind that by staying with the family you'll be saving €5000–15,000 in annual rental costs. Typically, you get your own room, about €300 a month, and perhaps use of a car and a chance to accompany the family on vacations. So much depends on the family, so ask lots of questions before taking the job. Start your research with these websites:

- ⓦwww.aupair-agency.com
- ⓦwww.greataupair.com
- ⓦwww.aupair.com
- ⓦwww.perfectaupair.com

Government and NGO jobs

Landing work for a government isn't as intimidating as it might sound. In fact, governments may even offer more opportunities for people to start their careers overseas than any company, and you don't necessarily have to carry a gun, classified microfilm or a pen that doubles as a rocket launcher to get your pay cheque. The US government alone has 50,000 employees working overseas. Non-Governmental Organizations (NGOs) are typically major charities, environmental groups or human rights organizations, and they need willing overseas workers – some are volunteers, but most offer paid positions. For a solid listing of NGOs, check out NGO Watch, at ⊛www.ngowatch.org.

Australian government jobs

- **Australian Public Service Gazette** ⊛www.psgazetteonline .gov.au

Canadian government jobs

- **Canadian International Development Agency** ⊛http://w3 .acdi-cida.gc.ca/internships
- **Department of Foreign Affairs and International Trade** ⊛www.dfait-maeci.gc.ca/ypi-jpi/web_guide-en.asp

New Zealand government jobs

- **New Zealand's International Aid and Development Agency** ⊛www.nzaid.govt.nz
- **Overseas diplomatic posts** ⊛www.mfat.govt.nz/about/careers /posts/oseas.html

UK government jobs

- **Department for International Development** ⊛www.dfid .gov.uk
- **Foreign and Commonwealth Office** ⊛www.fco.gov.uk

US government jobs

- **Central Intelligence Agency** ⊛www.cia.gov
- **Department of State** ⊛www.state.gov
- **Peace Corp** ⊛www.peacecorp.gov
- **US Agency for International Development** ⊛www .info.usaid.gov
- **US Information Agency** ⊛www.usia.gov

United Nations Development Programme

Eight to ten weeks of on-the-job training for enrolled graduate students fluent in two of United Nations' official languages (see ❀ www.undp.org).

United Nations Young Professional programmes

Junior professional posts are given for assignments of four to eight months. Send enquiries to:
World Bank
1818 H Street NW
Washington, DC 20433

Can you spot a bad travel job?

So many travellers who head abroad end up in the worst travel jobs. The reason isn't so surprising. They can't tell a great travel job from a lemon. A great job, they think, is any one they can get. So, they take the first one that comes along without ever checking if it fits with the travel experience they're after.

Let's take a typical job search. Say you want to work in a ski resort. You go to the French Alps, search frantically for a job and land one washing dishes, realizing you were lucky to get anything with your dodgy language skills. You're thrilled to have work, but the minimum wage doesn't get you very far in a pricey resort. After working eight-hour days six days a week (fairly standard), you notice you've only put your skis on a few times and, as the lone washer, you've been kept too busy to meet anyone at the restaurant. Eventually, you'll wonder what the point is. It took me about three weeks.

The fact is, very few jobs in ski resorts pay well (considering the high cost of living) and many don't allow you much time to ski. Savvy ski bums now prefer to work overtime at a better-paying job elsewhere, then head to a ski resort, find some cheap accommodation and ski their asses off for a month.

Contrast this with picking grapes in France. Even if you can't arrange to get paid, you can probably get your room and board covered. Let's say you work a week at a small chateau, meet loads of people, drink as much wine as your liver will permit and leave with a memorable experience that didn't bankrupt you.

Still not sure what a bad job is? If you can't answer "yes" to at least one of the following questions, you'd do well to look for a different job. Factoring in living costs, does the job bring in enough money to cover future travel? Does it make for an interesting experience or provide you with a valued skill? Is it a relatively easy workload and/or does it offer a lenient schedule that allows you to partake in local activities you enjoy?

Landing a job while in the country

OK, let's say you've splashed out for a work permit organized by a student work-permit agency (or taken advantage of a "working holiday" visa – see p.85), you still have to find a job... yourself.

Wake up early, check the classified ads in the paper, check notice boards, put up your own messages, dress smartly, don't wear sunglasses, take off that hat, lose the body piercings, cover any tattoos that may frighten small children, dye your hair back to a colour that could at least pass for real hair, leave your shorts in the hostel as well as the loose-fitting jeans that expose your designer underwear, double-check your letters for typos and return calls promptly. In short, don't give them a reason to dismiss you.

No potential employer wants to read over a sampling of your term papers. Let's face it, you probably don't want to look at them again, either. Nor are they going to read through a stack of recommendation letters. What you should bring is some appropriate clothing. Or enough money to pick some up when you arrive. If you think a suit is appropriate for the job, you may wish to cart one along. A current CV (résumé) will come in handy. As will a few official copies of your diploma.

If you are rejected, take it with a smile, thank them for their consideration and always take the opportunity to ask them where you might find work. If you've made a good impression, most people won't mind providing a few leads.

Furthermore, don't cross off a potential employer just because they said no a few days or a week earlier. Things change. One of their employees may quit or get sacked. Or perhaps someone they were expecting never showed up. They might even realize that they needed more help than they thought. And as long as your approach is polite, your perseverance will be respected.

If you're going after a more corporate-type job, the best thing you can do once you've arrived is arrange for an interview. Buy yourself a phone card and start making calls. If you know you really want to work in a certain field, try to arrange a quick meeting even if you've heard they don't have any openings. You might start by saying something like "I expected there weren't any openings at the moment, but as part of my foreign study experience I need to at least do a short interview to get an insider perspective. If you could spare, say, ten minutes in the next day or three I'd be grateful." Or figure out your own way in. Then, when you get the meeting, ask a few questions, see if a free internship might be possible. Before you accept an offer for free work, though, say you just need to explore a few other leads. If you like the place, at least you'll have a fall-back opportunity. Or ask if this person knows anyone else in the industry worth contacting. Who knows: if you make a good impression, you might at least get a good referral.

If you're going after a restaurant/bar/resort job, just show up and ask for the manager or owner. They'll want to take a look at you, check that your brain processor can handle the tasks required and test out your language skills.

If nothing comes along, you'll need some imagination. And funds – a good month's worth, or longer if you're prepared to accept a position that doesn't pay. See p.89 for entrepreneurial jobs.

For more info on landing a job, try one or more of the following books or websites:

- *International Jobs* by Erich Kocher
- *International Jobs Directory: 1001 Employers and Great Tips for Success!* by Drs. Ron & Caryl Krannich
- *International Job Finder: Where the Jobs Are Worldwide* by Daniel Lauber
- *Live and Work Abroad: A Guide for Modern Nomads* by Huw Francis, Michelyne Callan
- *Work Abroad: The Complete Guide to Finding a Job Overseas* by Clayton A. Hubbs
- *Work Your Way Around the World* by Susan Griffith

- **Job Monkey** ⓦwww.jobmonkey.com
- **Monster** ⓦwww.monster.com
- **Transitions Abroad** ⓦwww.transitionsabroad.com

You got the job

Once you get a job offer you plan to accept, ask for a few days to fix housing arrangements. Look into family stays, university-room rentals, and enquire at various hostels to see if they'll offer you a long-term deal.

If you work abroad and declare your earnings there, knowing that the amount is too small to be taxed in that country, bear in mind that you might be taxed for the amount in your home country, depending upon reciprocal agreements and any other income sources.

Volunteering

It may not seem like Europe needs saving. There's certainly not the level of poverty and disease you'd find in Africa, but there are people, parks, political groups in need of help and absolutely no shortage of organizations that would like you to come and volunteer for them.

Donating your time can be a tremendously fulfilling experience, but picking a good programme is not as straightforward as you'd imagine. If you don't select carefully, your time contributed may feel like time wasted. Or it may be fulfilling for you, but little benefit, if any, to the community. The fact is that some organizations' definitions of efficiency and utility will differ substantially from your own, or the flashy review quotes dotted about their website.

And many of the volunteer ventures are almost identical to English-teaching and labour-intensive work projects that you could be getting paid for. You might be moving boxes, doing dishes or shovelling cow dung, which is fine, provided you know what you're getting into. So, before you sign up, make sure you get an exact description of what you'll be doing and what they expect you to accomplish during your visit. You'll want some local orientation before you're dropped off with your project and a reliable local contact for emergency support, supplies and advice. You can ask for these things because you're not just going to be working there for free; you're almost certainly helping finance it. And perhaps the most surprising thing about volunteering is that it isn't as cheap as it sounds. First, there's the air fare or rail/bus transport. Then you often need to pay a fee that covers your lodging, food, insurance and the entire screening and orientation process. It's not uncommon to be shelling out more than €350 a month. As a guideline, the more exotic the project (eg studying dolphins in Europe's aquariums), the more you pay to assist.

Most projects have specific dates for training and transporting new volunteers. Plus, the organizations prefer to screen applicants, so showing up to lend a hand, though well intentioned, can actually backfire. Your best bet is to make arrangements long before you

Volunteer projects

Projects change all the time, but here are a few ideas:

Build a school or clinic, help staff an "eco-house", renovate hiking paths in parks and nature reserves, track animals, assist at a camp for children with learning disabilities, develop ecotourism, promote health-care, work with a women's cooperative, practise sustainable agriculture, teach English, join an archeological dig, help renovate a castle or monastery, develop a small business enterprise or support human rights efforts.

leave. If you're already on the road, your time will be well spent making contact at a nearby Internet café. With a more Web-advanced organization, you may be able take care of all the details before you arrive.

Rewards of volunteering

- Feel that you're striving to leave the world in a better condition than when you arrived.
- Live and work in a community where it's easy to make friends.
- Learn customs and language skills.
- Get to know volunteers from around the world.
- Get hands-on practical experience.
- Put your professional skills to use to make a tangible difference in people's lives.

Types of volunteer projects

Some organizations want strong backs, others strong minds. All want good attitudes and your financial support. As you begin your search, you'll find some of the projects are seasonal, some go year-round and some are unique ones that pop up when a university professor has received a major research grant. If possible, try to take advantage of the time of year you'll be volunteering (ie you don't want to be volunteering indoors in Portugal in spring-time when the weather is great). If you know where you want to be and what you want to do, try typing some keywords into your favourite search engine. Start with the location, then the type of work, plus "volunteer", "help" or "assist". Meanwhile, here are a few volunteer sites to get you started:

- **Idealist** ⓦwww.idealist.org
- **Taking It Global** ⓦwww.takingitglobal.org
- **Volunteer Abroad** ⓦwww.volunteerabroad.com
- **Volunteer International** ⓦwww.volunteerinternational.org

Studying

If you don't have time to work or get involved with a volunteer project during your trip, it's always possible to find time for a course; some take just half a day. Jumping into a course is one of the most enriching things you can do on your trip: it's a chance to learn a new skill that will remain with you long after you've returned home. Education aside, many offer a nice break from the travel scene and provide a chance for you to meet up with some locals or other foreigners with similar interests.

Many courses can be arranged at the last minute, but most often the better programmes require some advance booking. Look into this well before you arrive; in some cases, well before you arrange any flights. Unless you're absolutely sure about the soundness of a programme, don't pay the entire fee in advance. And pay with a credit card to help protect yourself. The courses listed below are by no means a definitive list, they are meant to provide a sample of some of the activities out there, and are only intended to be used as a starting point.

Learning to cook

Want a great souvenir? Learn how to make one amazing local dish. You'll be impressing friends and family with it for ages, provided you don't keep serving it to the same people. France, Italy and Spain are the most popular destinations for the gastronomically inclined, but cooking schools can be found almost anywhere. If you find you're really enjoying a local cuisine, talk to the local tourist office about courses available. Most last from a half-day to a month, with widely varying prices. As well as the listings below, try ⓦhttp://cookforfun.shawguides.com or *The Guide to Cooking Schools* by Dorlene Kaplan.

- **APICIUS Cooking School** Florence, Italy ⓦwww.apicius .itclasses. Taught in Italian (recipes can be translated, individual courses can be held in English). One-day wine class (in group) €41; one-class individual course €182; one-week summer workshop €1240.

- **Cooking in Turkey** Kalkan, Turkey Ⓦwww.owlsland .com/cooking.htm. Emphasis on making bread, grape molasses, yoghurt and ethnic courses. The price of €992 for a week includes lodging, meals and excursions. May, June, September and October.
- **Glorious Greek Kitchen** Athens, Greece Ⓦwww .cuisineinternational.com. Indoor/outdoor kitchen and class size can vary from five to forty. The price of €1400 for a week includes lodging and meals. One-day culinary walking tours with lunch are available for €70. Closed January, July and December.
- **Le Cordon Bleu French Cooking** Paris, France Ⓦwww .cordonbleu.com. The Grande Dame of cooking schools. You can take a single-day intro course for €145 on nearly any subject. Or a four-day elective course for €745. Or a one-month intensive certificate-level course for €5780.

Learning a language

Learning a language isn't as difficult as you might think, even if you've taken a language in school for years, hated it, learned next to nothing and vowed you'd never bother with it again – as I did.

Taking that step back towards language learning can be a humbling experience. And if you get a headache for the first couple of weeks, it just means your brain is working overtime – a sign that you'll have things figured out soon.

One thing you can say about intensive language schools is that they work. The combination of small groups or even one-on-one tutoring plus a family stay, or simply living in the country, has become some sort of magic formula, and you walk away with a better grasp of the language than you might get in years of regular schooling. And often without the brain-crushing boredom you associate with learning the past imperfect subjunctive gerund form of exceptions to masculine nouns. Again, that doesn't mean it's easy and that you'll be able to down beers at the local pub while you suck up linguistic nuances (unless you count pronouncing the beverages correctly). That bit comes later, after you've picked up the basics.

Credit crisis

OK, you've found the perfect foreign language school and plan to study for about three weeks, all the while enjoying horseback riding and beach parties with your new-found classroom friends. For North Americans, the only thing stopping you now is transferring the classes so your university knows it's actually an educational experience and not just a pseudo-academic vacation.

Attaining credit for studying in a language school takes persistence, though. Make the effort to find the language school that's right for you, with professional courses and a certified staff, referrals and contacts – basically, anyone that can sell the point that this language school is not one big fiesta, and that you learn more words than just "guacamole" and "cerveza".

These programmes can have significant value, even if you don't get academic credit for them. Consider the economics: the average student spends an average of two years studying another language in college. At the University of California, for example, it takes three consecutive classes for two years to fulfil requirements. These classes are an hour a day, four days a week. Two years of this instruction will cost over $3000 in the public system (well over $6000 at a private college), and often students (like myself) still feel unskilled in the language. Look at it that way and the intensive programmes start to look like a bargain. You can actually become proficient in the language and the average cost for two months (about 120hr) of classroom instruction, room, board and travel excursions runs to about $1500. After one of these intensive courses, it's not unusual for students to test out of language requirements with less time, less money and more fun.

Eric Tiettmeyer,
Ⓦ www.studenttraveler.com

"Hello", "please" and "thank you" won't take more than five minutes to learn, no matter what the language. If you want to move beyond a few words, a language course is a great way to start your travels in a new country. Aside from tools that will help you unlock the cultural codes of the country, you'll meet more locals, be able to get assistance when needed, keep your grey matter active and make your travels far more meaningful. You'll need at least three weeks to make real progress, no matter how intensive the course is. Two months should provide good conversational skills, depending on your study habits.

Many of the better-known language courses take place in towns loaded with English-speaking students – great for your social life, but lousy for language discipline. It's better (and cheaper) to select a smaller or less popular town where you'll get an experience far more intensive than the more expensive "intensive" courses offered in major language-learning centres.

If you're set on a specific course, you may need to sign up in advance. Otherwise, you can walk in off the street and usually start the same day. And, naturally, you can find inexpensive private tutors to teach you in nearly any city. Put up a notice near a university and you'll have a few offers within hours.

Studying photography

Even if you're just taking a pocket camera, learning how to compose your photographs is going to get you a lot further than expensive film and an overpriced lens. You may not learn anything more valuable than the tips on p.224, but you'll need to practise them and develop an eye for what works and what doesn't. That means taking oodles of photos, getting them developed immediately and having them critiqued. You can find community photography workshops for less than €100, but the upper-end instruction doesn't come cheap. It does, however, often include a trip to Europe, which may be how you'd like to begin your journey, getting comfortable with a group before venturing out on your own.

- **Close Up Expeditions** Ⓦwww.cuephoto.com. Workshops concentrating on nature, landscape and traditional cultures; 7–21 days. Figure on about €200 per day, including lodging, meals and ground transport.
- **National Geographic Expeditions Photo Journey to Tuscany** Ⓦhttp://nationalgeographic.com. Several prominent National Geographic photographers and photo editors come along to hand-deliver personal tips and tricks to budding photographers. Seven days for €2865 (not including flights, plus €207 for singles who want a private room).
- **Traveller's Eye Photo Tours** Ⓦwww.phototours.info. Lisl Dennis, one of the world's top travel photographers, takes groups to Provence for eleven-day tours. Other tours include trips to international locales selected for their architecture, culture, customs and cuisine. On-location demos, one-on-one sessions and evening photo discussions. Tours cost €3886 (plus €518 for single travellers who want a private room), including lodging and meals but not air fare.

Wilderness survival and alpine courses

You hardly need one of these to get by in Europe, but you never know when survival skills will suddenly come in handy. Most survival schools are run by – here's a real shocker – Americans, but many of the programmes take place outside the US. And some of the best alpine schools are located in the heart of the Alps. Some, such as NOLS and Outward Bound, place more emphasis on the group experience, while others are more technically oriented. If you already speak French, German or Italian, you might feel comfortable jumping right into a European course in the Alps. Make sure you ask plenty of questions (see p.56) before making your decision.

- **NOLS** ⓦwww.nols.edu. Roughly €662–992 per week, with courses typically lasting two weeks to one month. Transferable educational credit is possible with some universities.
- **Outward Bound** ⓦwww.outwardbound.org. Roughly €830 per week, with courses of one to eleven weeks. Focuses on wilderness training and team building.
- **Survival School** ⓦwww.survivalschool.co.uk. This UK-based school charges about €75 for a one-day course and €970 for a five-day course. Several specialized hands-on classes are available.

If you're more interested in staying alive in the mountains and ticking off summits in the process, check out the list of international mountaineering courses at ⓦhttp://dmoz.org/Recreation/Climbing/Guides_and_Schools, or one of the two listed below:

- **Bob Culp Climbing School** ⓦwww.bobculp.com. Rock- and ice-climbing trips in Chamonix and the Italian Dolomites; five days or more at €165 per day per person (air fare not included).
- **Swiss Association of Mountaineering Schools** ⓦwww.bergsportschulen.ch. Select schools by speciality (ice-climbing, high-altitude skiing, etc) or region, and the links will put you in touch with professional Swiss guides.

Meditation

If the fast pace of life on the road starts taking its toll on your nerves, the regular pub visits aren't helping and your Valium prescription has run out, consider taking a personal time-out. That might mean a couple of yoga classes or a week in silent seclusion. No matter. Getting back in touch with your mind and body, however you decide to go about it, can be an invigorating pit stop – just what you need to continue on your physical and inner journey. Many courses are offered in English and the ones that aren't are easy enough to follow by looking at the instructor's movements. Just keep an eye out for local yoga, qi gong and meditation centres as you go. Here are a few links to a variety of yoga schools in Europe to get you started:

- **Ashtanga** Ⓦwww.ashtanga.com/html/europe.html
- **Blue Mountain Center Meditation Centres** (UK and Holland) Ⓦwww.nilgiri.org
- **Iyengar** Ⓦwww.iyengar-yoga.com/yoga_centers/europe
- **Shambhala** Ⓦhttp://db.shambhala.org/db/index.html
- **Sivananda** Ⓦwww.sivananda.org

6

Documents and insurance

Getting your documents in order for a big trip to Europe isn't nearly as much of a hassle as it sounds – just a case of sorting out your passport, any necessary visas and some travel insurance. Hardly any European countries require visas (or they make it easy for you to pick them up upon arrival). But take a look below to see which apply to your nationality and then be sure to check out the box on p.122 for the all-important departure countdown.

Passports

A passport is a document issued by your country of citizenship that establishes your identity and enables you to exit and re-enter your country of citizenship. That is to say, without a passport you're looking at a short trip. Probably to the airport and back. See the box on p.108 for how you get one.

Two or more passports

The important thing for dual or triple passport holders is that you pick one passport to use during your trip – the one that grants you

Australia

Regular service 32-page passport AUS$150, 64-page passport AUS$226; ten working days; can be done online or at post office, but you must be interviewed.

Expedited Additional fee of AUS$60 to process in two working days (case-by-case basis ☎131 232).

Photo info There are various guidelines and restrictions on Australian passport photos. See ⊛www.passports.gov.au/Web/newppt/index for details.

Valid For ten years.

Canada

Regular service 24-page passport CAN$85, 48-page passport CAN$90; processing time: 27 days by mail (not including mailing time), ten days in person; no renewal available, new passport must be purchased, photocopies of identity documents (eg driver's licence) must be signed by a guarantor.

Expedited Express: two to nine days an additional fee of CAN$30. Urgent: same day or next day (only available on case-by-case emergency basis) an additional fee of CAN$70.

Photo info There are various guidelines and restrictions on Canadian passport photos. See ⊛www.dfait-maeci.gc.ca/passport for details.

Valid For five years.

New Zealand

Regular service Ten working days NZ$71.

Expedited Three working days NZ$146. Call-out service, when urgent delivery falls out of working hours, NZ$401; ☎0800 225 050.

the most visa-free access or work privileges – and only use the other for emergencies (leave the third one at home with your document copies so it can be mailed to you if a crisis should arise). It may be tempting to swap when you can save a little money on a visa, but if you get questioned by a customs official you need to be able to demonstrate a clear travel history. Any gaps will raise suspicions. To keep the customs process at borders moving smoothly, don't bring up your multiple citizenship unless asked.

Visas

Visas are essentially stamps (but sometimes stickers or entire documents) inserted into your passport by immigration officials

Photo info There are various guidelines and restrictions on New Zealand passport photos. See ⓦwww.passports.govt.nz for details.

Valid For ten years.

UK

Regular service Three-week service at post offices and select travel agents £42; about two weeks if applying at certain post office branches and Worldchoice travel agents.

Expedited One-week service at passport offices £70. Same-day premium service is technically not available for standard passports, but you can try calling ☏0870 521 0410 if you think your situation merits special consideration.

Photo info There are various guidelines and restrictions on British passport photos. See ⓦwww.ukpa.gov.uk for details.

Valid For ten years.

US

Regular service Six weeks $85; $55 for renewal.

Expedited "About two weeks" expedited service $145 plus overnight shipping both ways. Or make an appointment to visit one of the twelve regional passport agencies (if near you) for $95. At ⓦwww.americanpassport.com and similar sites, one- to three-business-day service $264. Emergency same-day service $294.

Photo info There are various guidelines and restrictions on US passport photos. See ⓦhttp://state.gov/travel for details.

Valid For ten years.

or embassies or consulates acting on their behalf, and grant you permission to enter their country for a specified period of time. There are other conditions that can be included as well – such as the right to work, the right to re-enter the country multiple times and the right to extend your visa – which may require special approval. Much of this depends on which passport you hold. Each country has its own set of agreements with other countries, with fees yo-yoing (with diplomacy) in the region of €20–50.

In Europe, they're not an issue for most passport holders, and once you're on the continent you'll rarely have to show your passport while crossing borders.

Many countries don't require any visas for some passport holders, or simply hand them out at the airport or border crossing for free or a small fee (Turkey's is about €20–50, for example). Otherwise, they can take anywhere between a day and a few weeks to process, but they can usually be taken care of within a few days if you opt to pay an additional fee to expedite the application.

The mysterious thirty-day Russian tourist visa

This is the old-school method of tourism – make visitors jump through daunting loops of red tape.

You need a passport that's valid for six months. Easy. A photo or two. Easy. A *podtverzdeniye* (standard tourist invitation) from an authorized hosting Russian travel agency, registered with the Russian Ministry of Foreign Affairs (MID RF). Huh?! A tour voucher or its copy, attested by said authorized Russian travel agency. Yuck. And a cover letter from your travel agency at home containing dates and points of arrival and departure to and from Russia; means of transport; itinerary in Russia; the name of the hosting Russian agency and its reference number. Double yuck. Plus, the visas aren't cheap: €85 for a basic one that's ready in six business days and good for single entry, quickly escalating to €290 for a double-entry visa processed the same day. Think the Mafia has gotten into the visa office?

What the tourist bureau wants is for you to book everything in advance – preferably an expensive tour. The traditional way around this is to get an invitation from a hotel or hostel (who can offer invitations for any length of time, provided you spend one night with them) – typically, a youth hostel in St Petersburg (⊛www.ryh.ru). When contacting any hotel or agency in Russia regarding visas, ask about their recent experience with the particular consulate to which you intend to apply. Also – watch out for this – when contacting the consulates, some like to charge you €8 to reply with information by fax or email. For additional general info on obtaining a Russian visa, see ⊛www.visatorussia.com.

Americans

Russian consulates now require a new two-page application. You should, in theory, contact the consulate nearest you, but they all have their own quirky ways and the word on the Web is to try to avoid the one in Washington, DC. Most prefer the one in San Francisco:

New York: ⊛www.ruscon.org
San Francisco: ⊛www.consulrussia.org
Seattle: ⊛www.netconsul.org

Costs range from $100 for a single-entry visa that takes six or more working days to process, to $450 for the same-day processing of a multiple-entry visa.

Austria, Belgium, Denmark, Finland, France, Germany, Greece, Iceland, Italy, Luxembourg, the Netherlands, Norway, Portugal, Spain and Sweden have joint visas that allow you to spend three months in total in the entire group of countries, known as the Schengen Area. The ten new members of the European Union (Cyprus, Czech Republic, Estonia, Hungary, Latvia, Lithuania,

Australians

You need to apply at the consulate assigned to the state where you live. The basic fee is AUS$85 for twelve business days' processing. It costs AUS$140 for the issue of a visa after office hours and AUS$160 during weekends or holidays. But, as they like to say on their website (Ⓦwww.sydneyrussianconsulate.com/visa.htm), "processing times, requirements and fees are subject to change without notice".

Canadians

Canadians can apply at consulates in Ottawa, Toronto and Montreal, though you might consider sending your application to the San Francisco consulate. Contact the Canadian consulate first at Ⓦwww.rusembcanada.mid.ru. Costs range from CAN$75 for a single-entry visa that takes fourteen days to process to CAN$300 for the same-day processing. Toronto does not issue double- or multiple-entry visas:

    Toronto: Ⓦwww.toronto.mid.ru
    Montreal: Ⓦwww.montreal.mid.ru
    Ottawa: Ⓔruscon@rogers.com

British citizens

You can show up at the consulate in London in person, but get there very early if you want to avoid the queues. If there are already about twenty people waiting, you may not get processed before closing (though if you wait around long enough, you'll probably get approached by people offering visa services for £30 – they'll queue up for you). Better yet, mail it in and wait three weeks. Or go to Edinburgh. But don't mail your application there without contacting them first (visa@edconsul.co.uk). Costs range from £30 for a single-entry visa that takes eight or more working days to process to £150 for the same-day processing of a multiple-entry visa:

    London: Ⓦwww.rusemblon.org

The Finnish option

St Petersburg is just a four-and-a-half-hour train ride from Helsinki. Pick up a Russian visa in town when you book a short, on-the-spot tour (try Finnsov Travel at Ⓦwww.finnsov.fi). Pay the typically outrageous application fees and away you go.

Malta, Poland, Slovakia and Slovenia) are also members of the Schengen Area in terms of visas. The UK and Ireland are not.

Americans, Canadians, New Zealanders and UK citizens do not need a visa to enter Europe for less than ninety days. There are, however, a few exceptions, noted below.

- **Americans** require visas for Russia (get in advance) and Turkey (can be obtained at any point of entry).
- **Canadians** require visas for Russia (in advance) and Turkey (at any point of entry).
- **New Zealanders** require visas for Romania (at any point of entry), Russia (in advance) and Turkey (at any point of entry).
- **UK citizens** require visas for Russia (in advance) and Turkey (at any point of entry).

If you plan to stay more than ninety days in any one country, check the website of its embassy in your country (Ⓦwww .embassyworld lists all embassies). New Zealanders, for example, have a special deal: the right to spend three months separately (not just three months in total) in each of the following countries: Austria, Belgium, Czech Republic, Denmark, Finland, France, Germany, Hungary, Greece, Iceland, Italy, Luxembourg, Malta, the Netherlands, Norway, Portugal, Slovenia, Spain and Sweden.

Getting visas at home

If you're planning to work legally in a country, apply for that visa first, since it must be arranged from your home country. (For more details on working abroad, see p.83.) Also, if you're planning to stay more than three months, you'll need a visa before you arrive. For instance, Australians heading to France must pay AUS$170 for a visa allowing them a stay of more than three months without a work permit. Getting such a visa is a two-month minimum wait, and also requires a certificate of Police Record, proof of medical coverage while in France, proof that you can support yourself financially, and a signed declaration that you will not take up employment during your stay.

Entry for students on study programmes

If you're arriving in Europe to study for a semester or more, you should have all your study abroad documentation (eg an official

Other considerations

Be aware of local holidays, as visa-issuing offices at home are likely to be closed on these days.

paper stating where and when you'll be studying and living) with you to present to the customs officer. Your study abroad programme will tell you if you require a special visa and how to obtain it if you do, but it will be your responsibility to make sure it's processed and ready in time.

Insurance

Here's the most important thing you need to know about travel insurance for an extended trip: get some. To find out why, what makes a good policy and what it costs, read on.

Why get insurance?

Just as experienced drivers still need to get car insurance, experienced travellers know that travel insurance is a necessity. All it takes is one mishap – a drowsy bus driver, a patch of sand when you try to brake your rented scooter, a knee twist during a mountain hike – and your family might be stuck selling their home to cover your rescue by helicopter, air-ambulance ride home, surgery, plus ongoing treatment (which may not be covered by your home insurance policy). Any of these things could happen to you in your own country, but at home you're probably covered. Overseas, where your coverage is unlikely to apply, this could easily top €100,000, not including any long-term medical expenses. A comprehensive health-insurance plan may cover some of your medical expenses, even those incurred overseas, but it's unlikely to pick up some of the major rescue and repatriation costs. Even among countries that have reciprocal health agreements (such as those with European passports travelling within the EU, who need to carry an E111 form, which will be replaced with electronic medical insurance cards by 2008, starting with France and Spain in June 2004 and Britain in September 2005), you will not be fully covered, and certainly not for repatriation.

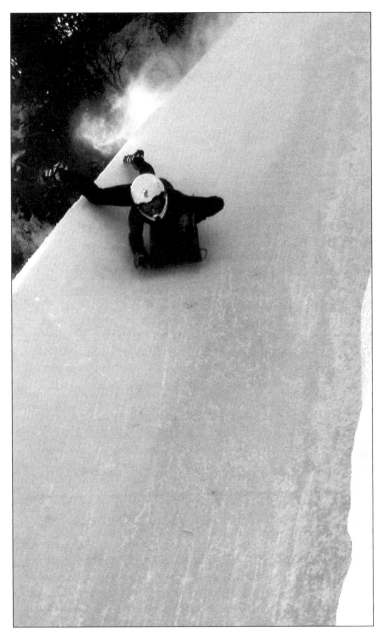

△ You never know when you might need cover – the Cresta Run, St Morritz

If, at the last moment before your trip, you get terribly sick, called up for jury duty, robbed or whatever, you don't want to get stuck with cancellation fees on top of it. A good policy will cover this, but for this service to kick in you need to get insurance about the time you buy your ticket (not the day you get called up for jury duty). Also, if your trip is disrupted for an emergency, your insurance company should assist with arrangements to continue your trip once you're ready.

No one plans on legally defending themselves while abroad. But if it happens, it's unlikely to be cheap. Say you hit a local cyclist while driving a rented car on a difficult-to-navigate road. Or scuff the entire length of a new Mercedes with the rusty pedal of your rented bicycle. Travel insurance is about the only way to prepare for such an unfortunate event.

Finding an insurance policy

First, you need to find out what you're insured for already, so you can pick out a policy that covers the gaps. Without this knowledge, you'll likely be wasting your money on double coverage. Unfortunately, this means sifting through the fine print. You might start with your homeowner's insurance policy to see if it covers lost luggage (even your parents' policy, if their home is still your official residence, may have you covered).

Second, check to see what kind of travel insurance your credit card company offers, and whether it is solely for tickets or goods purchased using the card. Some credit cards offer flight insurance in the event of a plane crash or other transportation accidents. Then take a look at your medical policy. Will it cover you for illnesses or accidents incurred overseas? If so, photocopy the list of activities it will cover you for (or ask your insurer to send you the list). Finally, check out your life insurance policy. Will it still pay out if you die bungy jumping in France or mountain climbing in Switzerland?

For lost luggage, it's worth noting that airlines generally reimburse travellers up to €16 per kilo, but the process is time-consuming and potentially exasperating.

Not all travel insurance is created equal. Most of the best policies aren't cheap, but that doesn't mean the most expensive policies are the best. One sign of a good insurer is a featured list of what they will and won't cover – most prefer to bury this information,

Insurance for Europe

A basic insurance policy (using the same international student travel agency) for a trip around Europe costs:

For Australians (bought in Australia)
AUS$203 for a one-month trip
AUS$297 for a two-month trip
AUS$399 for a three-month trip

For Canadians (bought in Canada)
CAN$60 for a one-month trip
CAN$98 for a two-month trip
CAN$122 for a three-month trip

For New Zealanders (bought in New Zealand)
NZ$259 for a one-month trip
NZ$385 for a two-month trip
NZ$457 for a three-month trip

For Brits (bought in the UK)
£31 for a one-month trip
£51 for a two-month trip
£66 for a three-month trip

For Americans (bought in the US)
$150 for a one-month trip
$180 for a two-month trip
$230 for a three-month trip

More expensive policies will normally cover some of the more "risky" activities or pay out larger amounts.

knowing you'd rather hack off your arm with an old butter knife than dig through the fine print of their policy. Especially since it can be rather gruesome at times – with payouts listed for things like dismemberment or loss of an eye. But it's important to know exactly what you're getting.

No two lists of activities seem to be the same. Some policies will require a supplement for an activity that other policies include in the most basic package. And some won't cover you if you get hurt or injured in countries that appear on your foreign office's travel-warning list. Some give you extra money if you're taken hostage on a plane and some won't cough up a cent. Some provide excellent emergency assistance, but little medical coverage. And many pad their list of benefits with things like "money transfer referrals" and "embassy referrals" – which is nothing more than a referral that you could find in half the time with a search on the Internet, or in this book.

It's best to scan through a few brochures or websites and compare (start with ⓦwww.insuremytrip.com or ⓦwww.worldtravelcenter.com). If you're checking the Web, be aware that some policies only apply to certain nationalities. STA Travel's insurance, for example, has a nice package for UK citizens, but their policies for Americans and Australians are rather feeble and more expensive by comparison. Find out who the underwriter of the insurance is (it's almost never the travel agency issuing it), and try to contact that company direct to see if they're offering a deal. Again, check what you're covered for already.

Many policies provide 24-hour emergency assistance – a collect-call phone number you can ring from anywhere and get access to an English-speaking operator, who will keep you on the line while you sort out your troubles. With standard, inexpensive travel gear, you needn't bother with protection against theft unless it's either already included in the policy you want or you're carrying something expensive (a swanky camera, watch, etc). But such items may be covered in your homeowner's insurance. Besides, in the event of a theft, replacing your backpack, some clothes, toiletries and a pair of sandals with items available locally is going to be quite cheap and a lot less hassle than trying to get reimbursed for every little well-worn item. (If you do have theft insurance, take a photo of all your gear, save the receipts and store them in a safe place at home.) Find out if your insurance provider will pay your expenses directly or reimburse you. In either case (but especially the latter), ask for and hang on to receipts for everything.

Another common insurance perk is cancellation and trip interruption coverage. However, when they say that you have coverage for this, it doesn't mean you get your money back if you suddenly decide not to go. Such expenses are only covered if the reason for cancelling or interrupting your trip is stated in your insurance policy. Typically, it applies if you or your travel partner gets sick or injured, or if there's a death in your immediate family. There are other reasons as well, but you need to read the fine print to discover what they are.

In addition to the comparison sites above, Rough Guides is now offering travel insurance. It actually has one of the easiest policies to understand and offers an upgrade for more adventurous types. Pithy endorsement aside, before deciding, check the coverage and fine print (see ⓦwww.roughguidesinsurance.com) to see if it makes the most sense for you.

Insurance for specific activities

It's hard to anticipate what opportunities may come your way while you're travelling. Even timid travellers work up considerable nerve to try new things after a few months on the road. Remember to check the fine print for the activities you hope to do, but also try to give yourself as much leeway as possible, in terms of your policy, to try new things. In fact, a quick way to find the relevant section of your policy is to scan through the fine print until you see a list of activities grouped together. There's a good chance you'll have to call and enquire about some specific activities they've left out.

Before you leave home

Assuming you can't squeeze everything into your backpack, you'll need a place to store the possessions you don't take with you to Europe; preferably, somewhere they'll remain until you return. Keeping your plants green while you're away is another nifty trick. This chapter will help you think through the arrangements you'll need to make before departing. (To get your finances squared away for the big trip, see p.141.)

Renting out your property

If you want to make money while you're away, consider renting your flat out to a company. They'll probably be willing to pay a decent sum, provide a guarantee of payments and ensure the safekeeping of your property (of course, not everyone has an apartment that would appeal to an executive). The second choice is renting to a trusted friend. You'll have to give them the customary "trusted friend" discount, but you'll prosper in other ways: it's nice to have someone who can take care of things for you while you're away and handle any problems that may arise. And not change the locks on you.

To avoid the hassles of dealing with tenants, you may wish to work out an arrangement with an estate agent or property manager, who will not only lease your place but also collect the rent and handle any difficulties. This service isn't cheap, but if you're less worried about turning a profit than having to deal with day-to-day hassles, this could be the way to go. Otherwise, you can take out an ad. And ask around before ringing your favourite newspaper – often, there are much cheaper alternative publications that attract a much better targeted group.

If you do rent your flat to previously unknown tenants, take a few precautions:

- While you are with your tenants, take a video camera and walk around the property, video-taping everything with running commentary. ("There's a little hole in the wall I made while practising my approach shot with an 8-iron. There are eight wineglasses in the cupboard.") This will help protect them against minor damage you may forget about during your trip, and keep you protected against anything new that appears. Plus, it's a nice reminder that you've got the evidence and they should be on good behaviour. If you're going with an estate agent, you may wish to do this before you leave anyway, so you can prove any damage upon returning.

- Agree on anything that requires maintenance, such as plant watering or garden care.

- Show the tenants that things are in working order (refrigerator, washing machine and so on), and make sure as many of these points as possible are listed in the contract, if this doesn't fall under a landlord's purview.

- Remove and store personal treasures and anything that would cause the slightest emotional stir were it to break or grow legs and walk off.

- Have some family member or friend keep an eye on the tenants and deal with any emergency situations that may arise. And let your tenants know that someone will be watching them.

- For minor issues, let them know you should be emailed. Bring the number and email address of a trusted electrician and plumber with you, so you can take care of things that pop up with minimal effort.

- Arrange for your mail to be forwarded to parents or friends, who can sort out the junk and send on what you need to your next port of call.

Leaving an empty flat

If you're leaving your flat empty, unplug appliances, cancel your newspaper subscription, cancel the cable TV, have your phone turned off, clean out the fridge and make sure someone is coming by every so often to check on the property. If you do leave your phone on, change the message on your answering machine. Note that "Hi, I'm in Europe for the rest of the month. Leave a message and I'll return your call when I get back in August," is not a great idea.

Plants

Don't just hand over your plants to a friend, unless you happen to know their horticultural survival record. It's more important to pick someone who's good with plants than pick a good friend. Just about anyone with a green thumb will be happy to find some space for your flora, and possibly take better care of them than you would.

Pets

It's not always easy to find someone who will love your pet as much as you do. Your best bet is going to be leaving your canine, feline or fish with a friend or family member, which may involve some carefully chosen endearment opportunities. There's a lot of effort involved, so think of your pet's most attractive qualities and try to coordinate those with visits from prospective pet guardians. If you have a dog who can catch a Frisbee, play catch with the friend who would find that most appealing. If the pet is cute and friendly and successfully helps you line up dates, let your desperate friend see this in action. If it cuddles up on your bed and keeps you warm, ring your pals with poor heating. If it's sweet, but looks menacing, perhaps some security-minded woman living alone might find this useful. A creative solution may be in order; think outside the litter box.

Departure countdown

You could theoretically get everything together in less than a week. You might pick up an ulcer in the process, but you could do it. You'd also pay more and miss out on valuable pre-trip research. Better to start two to four months in advance.

Three to four months before departure

☐ Get a passport (see p.107). If you have a passport, make sure it has several blank pages left.

☐ Figure out what sort of jobs, volunteer programmes or courses you'd like to do (see p.82). Gather applications and apply to those that require advance submissions.

☐ Consider your budget (see p.65). If you don't have the funds for the trip you want, perhaps you should think about picking up some extra work before you leave.

☐ Start surfing the Web for plane tickets (see p.26).

☐ Start looking around for the right insurance policy (see p.113). If you're going to try to reach Europe by yacht or cargo ship, check ideal times and places to start your trip (see p.8).

Two to three months before departure

☐ If you're flying, book a plane ticket and try to get insurance at the same time to cover you in the event of cancellation.

☐ Start thinking about the things you'd like to do and see.

☐ Arrange visas (see p.108) for any extended stays due to work, volunteering or study, plus the first country of entry (if necessary) and any countries with complex visa requirements.

☐ Make arrangements for your apartment rental (see p.119).

One to two months before departure

☐ Get a medical and dental checkup if you haven't had one for a while.

☐ Get credit cards and bank cards (see p.140), and meet with your banker to set up your finances (see p.141) so they can be handled while you're away, either with help from your parents or via Internet banking. Try to set up a line of credit.

☐ Get any discount cards (ISIC, teacher card, youth card, HI card) you need (see p.170).

Two to four weeks before departure

☐ Buy your travel gear. If you're bringing or sending ahead new hiking boots, start breaking them in (see p.137).

☐ Arrange for a communication card or kit (see p.171) if you plan to use one, and a mobile phone, if you plan to take one (see p.176).

☐ If you need to get more rugged glasses, order additional contact lenses or determine your prescription, visit an optician.

One to two weeks before departure

☐ Leave parents or friends an envelope with photocopies of your documents (credit cards, passport, etc) that can be sent to you in case of an emergency. Take photo of your travel gear to leave behind.

☐ Take care of any veterinary needs your pet may have before dropping it off with a caretaker.

☐ Arrange for your mail to be forwarded/held if your parents or roommate isn't willing to handle it.

☐ Check the CDC website (🌐 www.cdc.org) for any medical outbreaks you should be aware of.

☐ Check the websites of one or two state departments for updated security issues.

Two to three days before departure

☐ Pack.
☐ Test your pack (see p.125).
☐ Reconfirm flight.

Day of departure

☐ Run over check list one last time.

Packing

A sk a dozen "packing experts" for a list of what to take and you'll get a dozen different lists. Packing is neither an art nor a science; it's a combination of practicality and personal preference. And the only list that really matters is yours. The problem is it will take you a good six months on the road in various conditions to get a solid grasp of what you actually use and what you can do without. Until then, it's better to bring less and pick up any additional items you need along the way. This may sound like twisted logic,

What travellers are carrying

In the middle of the summer, I spent a few days walking around Stockholm's central train station with a notepad and a scale to see what (and how much) backpackers take with them. I spoke to every traveller I managed to stop, and weighed their packs. The average weight was just over 20kg. Some of the heaviest packs (over 25kg) belonged to women who weighed less than 55kg. It looked like they were going to be crushed at any second, Wile E. Coyote-like, under their packs. Everyone I asked had something they wished they hadn't brought. I asked several of them to open up their packs so I could peek inside. If you're wondering what people with huge packs are carrying around, here's what's taking up about seventy percent of their load: shoes, a sleeping bag, souvenirs and a full load of dirty laundry.

Least used items: formal shoes for going out, textbooks, and extra novels
Most used items: sandals and rain jacket

but throwing things away is actually far more difficult – at least, nobody seems willing to do it. In this chapter, you'll get the skinny on selecting a pack, which things you can leave at home, what to do with souvenirs, how to handle your film developing and how to put together your own medical kit.

Why take less

The pros of a large pack seem obvious: you have more stuff you might need, more clothes for the right occasion, plenty of toothpaste, and a few creature comforts from home. The cons are perhaps less obvious, but very much worth noting. A big pack comes with:

- a bigger risk of getting robbed – you're easier to spot, have more stuff to steal, and it's harder to run away.
- bigger locker fees – it's harder to walk around with a large pack so you're more desperate to find a place to leave all your stuff, and you'll need a bigger, more expensive locker each time.
- big sweat stains – the more odour you emit, the more often you have to wash. Spend five minutes walking in summer weather with an eight-kilo pack on your back and five minutes with a twenty-kilo pack and you can see for yourself.
- transport problems – it's more difficult to run for a train or bus (and you will have to run at some point), and it's harder to lift the pack over your head into a luggage rack without disturbing the people around you.
- more gear to lose or forget to pack, and more time spent packing things up each day.

The backpack test

You should be able to pack it in five minutes. You should be able to easily lift it over your head and you should be able to wear it for two hours without suffering minor back spasms. The last step is to toss your pack across the room and then step on it. Someone (maybe even you) is going to sit on it, step on it or drop it at some point, so you may as well get it over and done with now. So don't pack breakables – or make sure you pack them well. And even if the odds are that it won't get stolen, prepare as if it will. Which means leaving your mother's pearls, your snakeskin cowboy boots and your collector's-edition silver-plated backgammon set at home.

Picking a pack

Newton's law for backpacks would have read something like this: no matter what size pack you bring along, you'll always manage to fill it. No one travels with a half empty pack. At least, I've never seen a traveller with a partially empty pack. Therefore, the single best thing you can do is start off by buying a small rucksack: 40–55 litres – slightly bigger than your average day bag. Once you do this, it's pretty hard to go wrong. The stuff you don't need simply won't fit in. I managed for nine years with that size just fine, and thousands of others have as well.

But be forewarned: that's not likely to be the advice you'll get from the travel shop employees. Just remember where they're coming from: the bigger the pack, the more it costs and the more stuff they can sell you to put in it.

A pack is not the place to try to save money. Take an internal-frame model for support. Couple that with a major brand name (you don't want it coming apart at the seams) and you're looking at prices in the range of €75–150. There are a few bells and whistles that are nice to have, but you'd do well to skip the zip-off daypack; they don't make the best daypacks and, when attached, tend to unbalance the main pack and keep your valuables furthest from your body. Instead, check out the rucksacks used by climbers. They keep the gear closer to your torso for a fuller range of motion and better balance. Packs that extend wide with side pockets make it extremely difficult when you're getting on and off trains and buses. Packs that extend straight back (such as those with attached packs) force you to lean forward to counter the weight. There should be some kind of alternative opening that allows you quick access to the inside or bottom of the pack for things like a rain jacket or first-aid kit. Make sure there are compression straps on the outside (usually, the sides) to keep the stuff inside from jiggling about while you walk and to make the pack smaller. Look for a top compartment that's completely detachable, because if you can raise and lower that you can stuff things under it more easily, like a rain jacket during a hike or a damp towel on the way back from the beach. If you need to carry a bag of souvenirs to the post office, for example, the pack can "grow" to accommodate the extra gear temporarily. Also, you could detach it completely, clip on a camera strap, and you've got a shoulder bag that makes an ideal daypack.

The most important feature is that it fits comfortably. This is not something you should buy over the Internet, unless you've tried it on first. The waist strap should not dig into your hips and the straps should be easily adjustable when you're on the move. Sometimes, there's one strap that's meant to be sized to the wearer, and it's not that simple to find or adjust. Have the salesperson do it for you. Every pack feels great when there's nothing in it. Drop something heavy in before you try it out. (Good shops have weighted inserts for this very purpose.) There are now a number of special packs for women that are worth checking out, especially if you have a more curvy or petite body type. These packs feature narrower shoulder straps, a shorter frame, more cant on the waist strap and a pack mounted lower on the frame.

Think twice about packs with wheels. They weren't built to contend with European cobblestones. You can, of course, roll them in some places, but in just as many you can't. And in most airports (where they work best) you can find free trolleys. For hiking trips, the extra weight of the wheels coupled with a less flexible plastic suspension isn't worth it. At the risk of sounding like a drill sergeant, if you can't carry it, you don't need it.

Organizing your pack

To facilitate the almost daily packing ritual, make things easier to find and minimize the damage of a sudden rain shower or a broken shampoo bottle on the rest of your gear, keep things in separate bags, one for each of the following: clothes, toiletries, first aid, miscellaneous items, plus an extra plastic bag for wet clothes.

All of your clothes, minus what you need to wear, should fit nicely into a compression sack; one that holds a midweight sleeping bag will do nicely. With a few yanks on the cords, your clothes will be compressed to the size of a rugby ball. Crumpling is unavoidable unless the clothes are wrinkleproof, and even then they won't look perfect. To minimize creases, try rolling your clothes first.

Clothes

If you've gone on a short, family vacation to a resort with white beaches or ski slopes, you're familiar with the luggage situation:

Just one outfit?

There are two basic approaches to dressing: stay in the same town and change clothes every day, or wear the same clothes and just change towns. When you travel, you just have to accept that your general standard of cleanliness is going to be lower than you're used to. Also, you're going to have to wash your clothes daily, or tri-weekly – if you try doing it monthly, you're in for some strange looks, not to mention rashes.

Once you get the hang of this, you'll see you don't need more than one set of clothes. If you wash the clothes before you go to bed, hanging them on a clothes line outside, they'll be dry by morning. If you wash the clothes before taking a siesta in the afternoon and hang them in the sun, they'll be dry in about forty minutes.

bring as much as you feel like. Two suitcases the size of Japanese import cars aren't an issue. They only have to be dragged into and out of the airport. The problem, you're thinking, is that it was difficult enough to figure out how to get a week's worth of stuff into just two enormous suitcases. How on earth are you going to get several weeks' or months' worth into a single tiny backpack?

To customize your packing list, there's one important question you need to ask. What clothes do I need to survive a day (not just any day, though: a day in which you go from swimming in the ocean to tanning on the beach to a cool evening walk in the rain to a moderately nice dinner at a place where there's casual dancing), and be able to wash it all in the sink afterward?

Let's start with the swimsuit. For guys (and possibly women), make sure it's quick-drying and has pockets you trust enough to put car keys in while you swim – probably some kind of zipper–Velcro combination that'll foil pickpockets as well. The shorts should cover your legs modestly so they can be also used for city exploring – they're the only shorts you have along. For women, it doesn't matter if it's a bikini or a one-piece, as long as you can use the top as a top in a casual setting (in most European settings away from the beach, however, it won't be appropriate). You'll also want a beach towel. It should be fairly thin, but long enough to stretch out on comfortably and wrap yourself in modestly (there are special travel towels that work a treat). Later in the day, you'll want a hat and T-shirt to help ward off additional sunburn after your stint on the beach, and to cover yourself when you run over to a café for a snack.

For a cool evening walk, you can get by with sandals or sandals with socks in a fashion-free setting. You've got long, comfortable walking trousers. They should have deep front pockets that will deter thieves and not spill your valuables if you need to make a pit stop in the woods (front pockets, like the type found on jeans, tend to work the best). On top you've got a long-sleeved polypropylene shirt that wicks away sweat, a micro-fleece pullover (not cotton), a nylon rain jacket and a bandanna on your head to absorb any sweat and prevent a chill. You're carrying your plastic poncho in your small daypack in case it really starts to pour.

Clothes pack list

- ❏ 1 T-shirt – women, if the T-shirt is a little longer, it can double as a night-shirt.
- ❏ 1 long-sleeve polypro shirt.
- ❏ 1 micro-fleece – keep it stylish and it can be worn as a pullover in a nice restaurant.
- ❏ 1 rain jacket – even expensive Gore-Tex and similar high-tech rainwear won't help much when it pours for hours, and cheaper versions are less likely to get stolen.
- ❏ 1 plastic poncho – this covers your pack as well.
- ❏ 1 thin beach towel or sarong – an XL special travel towel is ideal.
- ❏ 1 swimsuit – doubles as walking shorts for men and a casual top for women.
- ❏ 1 pair of trousers – not black, but a good, dark dirt-hiding colour is ideal. Also, make sure they're lightweight, wrinkle-free, comfortable, fairly stylish and easily washable, with good deep pockets.
- ❏ 1 wrinkle-free travel shirt – short- or long-sleeve is fine.
- ❏ 1 pair of socks – for cool overnight bus rides and cold hostel floors.
- ❏ 2–4 sets of underwear – special travel underwear dries quicker and lasts longer.
- ❏ 1 pair of sports sandals. You don't want to skimp on these. They should be reasonably stylish (smart enough for a decent restaurant), have good support, stay on during a swim, not rot when they get out of the water and allow you to run for a train.
- ❏ 1 collapsible hat.
- ❏ 1 bandanna – soak it with water to keep you cool on warm nights. Cover your mouth with it to protect your lungs from dust. Use it to dry off in the shower when you don't have time to let your towel dry.
- ❏ 1 wrinkle-free travel skirt (women).
- ❏ 1 pair of shorts (women).

For dinner, you can still get by in sandals, especially if they're black or solid earthy colours. You've got a smart, short-sleeved or long-sleeved lightweight, wrinkle-free shirt/blouse. If it's still a little chilly inside, the micro-fleece should be stylish enough to wear. Men, your walking trousers will suffice, provided you didn't get those "adventure travel" ones with more zippered pockets and removable bits than a 1980s breakdancer. They should be dark enough to hide any dirt you might have picked up on your walk. Women, you might also elect to go with a long wrinkle-free skirt.

For day two, wash and repeat.

If you're heading to Europe in the winter, you'll want, of course, warm shoes, wool socks (or "smart wool"), a good jacket, hat and gloves. If you find you need long underwear, you can pick that up once you arrive.

Sleeping items

Brace yourself: for summer travel in Europe, you don't need to take a sleeping bag. Yes, many people take them and find occasion to use them, but not necessarily because they need to. Nearly every hostel can produce a blanket for you as long as you have a sleepsheet (which you do need). And in budget digs where air conditioning is typically not included, you'll rarely need more than a sheet. Beyond that, if you layer on all your clothes for a rare chilly night on a train or bus, you should be fine. In a worst-case scenario, if the weather does get a bit cold and there is no blanket available, you can pick up a cheap secondhand one for less than €3 or move on to a hostel that does offer blankets.

The previously mentioned sleepsheet is – well, just that – a sheet in the form of a sleeping bag. You can sew one yourself from a queen-size flat sheet or buy a pre-made model. The nicest are silk, which cost a fortune, but can be worth it, as they keep the occasional bed bug out better then the others.

Leave your pillow at home. Instead, use the ones provided at the hostels, hotels and pensions. You can bring a pillowcase, but it's a better use of space to simply use your T-shirt or micro-fleece as a pillowcase. If no pillow is available, stuff your towel and micro-fleece and a few other items into your T-shirt and use that. On train rides, if you put your towel in your micro-fleece and gently tie it around your neck, you'll get the same effect as one of those inflat-able neck pillows, which can also be left at home.

Toiletries

Start out by buying a toiletry kit with a built-in mirror and hanger, since you can't count on much counter space in the bathroom. Then transfer your perfume/cologne from the heavy, breakable, chic bottle to a small sturdy glass one with a tight, screw-on lid (plastic ones can taint the odour). Extended sandal- wearing takes its toll on your feet, so bring a foot file to help shed unwanted calluses and keep people from smelling you before they see you.

Major-brand contact lens fluid can be found at supermarkets, opticians and pharmacists, so there's no need to bring enough to last an entire journey. Bring a pair of glasses along just in case, plus your prescription in case something happens to your glasses. Pity to travel the world, then have to check your photos back home to see what it looked like in focus.

Again, only buy the miniature travel containers and restock as you go. Local toothpaste is especially interesting to sample and – there's at least one traveller doing this – collect.

For women, tampons and pads are no harder to find in Western Europe than they are at home. On remote Greek islands and in countries like Romania, Hungary and the ones that comprise for-mer Yugoslavia, they may be slightly more difficult to come by, so make sure you have what you need, especially if you'll be out in the countryside.

Toiletry packing list

(Mini-sizes only)

☐ Toothpaste	☐ Comb/brush
☐ Toothbrush	☐ Lotion
☐ Dental floss	☐ Razor
☐ Cologne/perfume	☐ Sunscreen
(in plastic bottle)	☐ Mosquito repellent
☐ Foot file	☐ Mirror
☐ Contact lens fluid	☐ All-purpose soap
(if needed)	☐ Conditioner (if needed)
☐ Lip balm	☐ Deodorant

Miscellaneous gear

There are a few tiny items that, when you need them, you need them immediately. And they're not always easy to find. Keep the following items in a separate bag:

- Earplugs – don't leave home without them. Hostels have a nasty habit of occupying the space above nightclubs and next to busy streets. Plus, every dormitory seems to come with at least one snoring champion.
- Permanent marker – for making hitchhiking signs and other notices.
- Superglue – this fixes just about everything (keep it in its own plastic bag).
- Duct tape – this fixes nearly everything the superglue doesn't (wrap it around the marker to save space).
- Guitar string/wire – fixes whatever's left.
- Sewing kit – OK, that's a lie. *This* fixes whatever's left.
- Lighter – you don't need a €50 lighter that works on top of Mount Everest.
- Power adaptors (if needed) – the Brits have one bulky kind, the rest of Europe uses another. You can pick them up at major airports when you land, or before leaving (see ⓦwww.kropla.com for country requirements).
- Pocket knife – you can leave the Rambo survival blade at home. (If you plan to carry your small pack onboard, your knife will likely get confiscated by security. You might just wait until you get to Europe to pick up your knife. On the way back, you'll likely be checking in a bag with souvenirs, anyway.)
- Spoon – just grab one for free on your first flight. It comes in handy for supermarket-food dining.
- Clothes line – you'll need about ten metres of nylon cord. The slightly more expensive version found beside the climbing rope at outdoor shops tangles less.
- Water bottle – tap water is fine for drinking even if it doesn't always taste great.
- Sink plug – chop the top third off a tennis ball or split a racquetball in two and you've got one.
- Plastic bag – for wet clothes.

Optional extras

Here are a few extras that you might want to bring along.

- Small travel games: backgammon, chess and cards are the most popular. They can keep you sane on an overnight train ride, and can be a nice way to meet locals.
- Instrument: a guitar can be worth the effort, especially if you're good and plan to earn money playing it, but a harmonica is better suited for transport.
- Frisbee: doubles as a plate and soup bowl.

First aid

Most prepackaged first-aid kits sold in outdoor stores are borderline worthless. And those nylon sacks don't keep your bandages and pills from getting wet or crushed. Make your own. Start out with a tupperware container large enough to hold about four muffins. You should be able to resupply all you need – see the box on p.134 – on the road.

A lot of travellers like to take antibiotics along. And if you're whacking your way through a rainforest for weeks, it's probably not a bad idea. But in Europe you're never that far from a local doctor or hospital. If you get sick enough to require antibiotics, you should be visiting a doctor, who can prescribe the best ones for your condition. Plus, many antibiotics don't travel well. If you do take antibiotics, take the full course, even if your symptoms abate after just one or two days. Otherwise, the few microbes that don't get killed off tend to mutate and come back stronger.

Daypack

Even a relatively small, internal-frame pack is not a joy to lug around the entire day while you explore ruins, museums and cities. A daypack is a more sensible way to carry the few necessities you'll need.

Most travellers opt for small backpacks, such as the detachable ones that come with packs. To avoid quick-handed thieves and (for women) groping hands in crowds, wearing the daypack on your front is an excellent idea. While it's on your back, though, it can be hard to protect. Some prefer the comfort of a waist pack, but this, too, is something of a thief magnet and looks awfully odd when worn in front. A better idea is a shoulder bag. It's easy to tuck under your arm to protect from pickpockets, can be accessed

Medical pack-list

European pharmacists have the authority to prescribe many medications that require a doctor's note in North America, and you'll find any medication you might need in Western Europe. Since you usually won't be more than a short 9-iron shot from a pharmacy, few items are really that essential. It's nice to have a small kit, though, just in case. You don't need much medicine for a few weeks or months of travel. A few pills of each will usually do the trick. Make sure you bring the directions for consumption, and label the pills if you don't bring the entire packet.

❏ Elastic wrap bandage – if you or a fellow traveller has a major accident, this is the most important thing to have within arm's reach. Vital for twists and big cuts

❏ Anti-diarrhoea medicine – few forget to bring these.

❏ Laxatives – few remember to bring these; specially useful for those who don't like unclean bathrooms.

❏ Antihistamines – you never know what will spark an allergic reaction.

❏ Hydrocortisone cream – cures most rashes and skin irritations.

❏ Aspirin/paracetamol – for minor aches and major hangovers.

❏ Compeed – modern science has created the wonder blister cure.

❏ Band-aids – put them into a clear plastic sleeve that holds photos or credit cards.

❏ Iodine – for sterilizing cuts and purifying particularly spooky-looking water (a few drops). If you can't deal with the taste, then water purification tablets are a good idea.

❏ Rehydration packet – one is enough to get you started (in a crisis, make your own mix: 1 litre water, 1 teaspoon of salt, 8 tablespoons sugar, dash of juice if available).

❏ Condoms – more readily available in Northern Europe.

❏ Motion sickness pills – curvy roads and stale air on bus rides make a lethal combo, not to mention stormy ferry rides.

Medical extras

If these don't fit in your first-aid container, toss them in the gear bag:

❏ Tweezers – find a good pair with a sharp point for removing splinters.

❏ Vaseline – prevents chafing and blisters during long hikes.

❏ Sports tape – it's mostly for blister prevention, but helps hold band-aids on.

❏ Antiseptic wet wipes – a great refresher for when you're stuck in a hot bus seat for hours, trying to clean up before a meal, or helping dab a wound.

❏ Tiger balm – the all-purpose sports cream that also clears up clogged sinuses and soothes headaches.

more quickly while you're on the move and doesn't peg you as a tourist, especially in bars and nightclubs. If the top compartment of your backpack detaches, a camera or guitar strap can turn it into a decent shoulder bag. If not, a collapsible one with zipper/Velcro closure is fine.

What to keep in your daypack

- Guidebook – you can lighten the load by ripping out unneeded sections.
- Sunglasses – shades without UV protection allow your pupils to widen and expose your eyes to more damaging rays. You'll want a hard case to keep them in one piece.
- Journal/address book and pen – a necessity. Some photos of home and friends are also nice to include for letter-writing inspiration.
- Something to read – for more info on how many books to bring and how swapping books works, see p.149.
- Pocket knife (but not on flights) – you don't need the Swiss Army knife with all sixty functions.
- Flashlight – the little LCD key-chain ones work well, the LCD headlamp with retractable band even better.
- Pocket camera – you can get a good one for under €75. See "Documenting your trip" (p.218) for advice on which type of camera to bring.
- Cellphone and charger (optional) – a tri-band phone works almost everywhere these days and, even if you keep it off, it can be worth it in the one emergency you need it. See p.176 for more.

Camping gear

If you already have camping equipment, using it can save you money, but will more than double the size and weight of your rucksack, so think twice before carting it along. It's really only sensible for those planning to camp the entire time. If you're not sure, leave the gear at home. Even if you only thought about camping a little, you'll be happier with less stuff and a few extra nights in a hostel. Yes, it is legal to "free-camp" in Sweden, and it is possible to pitch a tent after dark on the edge of small towns elsewhere – if you're sneaky about it – but in most decent campgrounds near popular cities, it's not all that cheap and you'll be spending more time and money on local transport getting in and out of town. And you may worry about your belongings when your tent is unattended. If you're not swayed, make sure you have the right gear:

- Light, rainproof tent
- Cooking stove
- Pot with lid
- Cooking utensils
- Sleeping bag
- Sleeping pad
- Tarp to lay under tent

What you don't need and why

- Shoes – this may come as a shocker, but if you're travelling in May to September in Europe with a decent pair of sandals, you can get by without shoes. If you find you're going out clubbing regularly or need shoes for work or if it's just getting too cold, buy a cheap pair for €10–25 and ditch them when you're done.
- Walkman/Discman – this is a great way to tune out and relax. However, you're also cutting yourself off from the sounds of the country, which, though often aggravating, are part of the experience. More importantly, it discourages locals from making contact with you. Besides, it's something else that can break, get stolen, take up space in your pack and chew expensive batteries. Read a book instead.
- Electronic language translator – just try to have a conversation with one of these! I have yet to see someone pull it off. The most common words and phrases can be looked up in nearly all guidebooks. Better yet, take twenty minutes and learn a few words and phrases before you arrive.
- Currency converter – your primary-school maths skills should get you by nicely.
- Pro-camera setup – if you're a serious amateur or professional photographer, bring what you need. If not, this is probably not the time to start. Forget the SLR, lenses and tripod. Stick with a pocket camera and you'll get more use out of it.
- GSM – if you're charting new territory, fine. If not, leave it at home.
- Jeans – resist the temptation to pack your favourite pair, no matter how good you may look in them. They're too warm in hot weather, too difficult to wash by hand and take too long to dry.

- Sweatshirt – the comfort is alluring, but it will take up far too much room, offer no warmth when wet, and require about two days to dry on its own. A micro-fleece (or some petrochemical equivalent) is the way to go. Besides, they're more culturally sensitive than sweatshirts sporting giant university or fraternity logos.
- Water filter – the water in Europe isn't going to kill you. It's easier and more affordable to drink from the tap; just buy bottle water in extreme situations.
- Compass – the sun rises in the east and sets in the west. That sentence should get you by. At least, if you're not in Scandinavia, where the summer sun never seems to set. If you feel better having a compass along, take a tiny key-chain model. If you set off without a compass, and regret it, you can always buy it along the way.
- Mosquito net – there are mosquitoes in Europe, but such measures aren't necessary.
- Mini "travel towel" – the beach-towel-size ones are great. The mini ones preferred by Olympic divers and car washers aren't as practical for the traveller as a bandanna, even if you have to wring it out a few extra times to get the same effect.

Resupply on the road

There may not be toilet paper in every stall or ice in the drinks, but you can get sweaters, T-shirts, socks, toothpaste, soap, band-aids, contact lens fluid, superglue, all kinds of film, sport sandals, trendy clothes, hats – nearly everything – almost everywhere you go. If 700 million Europeans can survive with the supplies they have, there's a good chance you'll find what you need to get by for a couple months. Just take the smallest tubes and bottles, plan on buying supplements, and stop at an Internet café and special-order something to your next destination if you simply can't find it. If you're taking medication, bring what you need or bring along your prescription for a refill.

Sending gear ahead

If you're going to be trekking in the Alps or Pyrenees, or hiking national parks every other week of your trip, bring your favourite hiking boots. If not, they're going to take up thirty percent of your pack and make the other seventy percent smell. Tying them to the outside of your pack may be even worse: the dangling-ornament look makes it tricky to run for departing transport, knocks people in the head as you enter and leave trains, and creates a stench that circles you like the moons of Saturn. Better to use the postal service to get your boots to the place you'll need them (and send them back when finished). Or simply rent boots when you get there. All major trekking centres have boot rental and cheap secondhand ones for sale but make sure you give yourself a day or two to wear them in before taking off on a serious hike.

Sending souvenirs home

Many souvenirs get bought, but far fewer make it home in one piece. The best way to make sure your purchases survive the journey home is to send them back as you buy them. With almost daily packing and unpacking, plus the normal wear and tear of the road, your souvenirs have a far better chance of getting lost, broken or stolen in your backpack. Check the local postal regulations before you start boxing up your items. Sometimes there's a certain weight or container size that's extremely cheap, and you can divide your purchases into separate parcels accordingly and save a mint. Overland shipping takes a few months but it usually gets there. If you'd rather not take the chance, try registered mail. (Simply request it at the post office and pay the supplemental fee). Or, if it's of considerable value, look into FedEx, DHL or another reputable courier. If you can wait until your last stop before stocking up on trinkets, simply buy a cheap duffle bag for €5–10 and courier home the items yourself.

Carrying valuables

The euro may have simplified pricing in Europe, but it hasn't made your money any safer from theft. With a steady stream of Europeans walking the streets in designer suits and custom-made leather shoes, you may not feel like much of a target. However, with half a glance thieves can see that you're a foreigner and, as such, are probably carrying a bundle of cash, credit cards and a camera. And, with a backpack on, you may not notice their quick hands or be able to give chase if you do. Therefore, you need to handle your valuables with care.

There are several options these days. Passport pouches, also known as money belts, come in a variety of styles. Some go around the waist (just under the pants), some hang around the neck and still others fasten to your leg. Choosing which one to wear is a combination of personal preference, how it works with your clothing and how easy it is for thieves to spot (see p.186 for more info on this). Try a few on before you make a purchase, since this is something you'll be wearing round the clock.

Before you leave home, remember to photocopy the contents of your money belt (except the cash!), leave a copy with your parents or trusted friends, and take a copy with you and store it separately from your money belt or with your travel partner. If you're using a service like ekit (see p.171), upload the data into their digital vault.

Credit cards

Don't leave home without one of these. Two is even better. Visa and MasterCard, respectively, are the most widely accepted. You should have PIN codes for both to access cash machines and make sure they're compatible with one of the following automated telling machine (ATM) services: Plus, Cirrus, Visa, MasterCard or EuroCard. In the event a cash machine can't be found, most banks will still allow you to use them for cash advances. That is, you can go into a bank, let them swipe your credit card and buy cash (for a fee, of course). Also, you may have to call and activate your credit card for international use when travelling overseas.

The benefits

- You can access emergency funds and cover many daily expenses without carrying a thick bundle of cash.
- You can track your finances easily, even from the road, if you set up an Internet account.
- Parents, relatives and friends can send funds to your account, which you can quickly and easily withdraw.
- Cards can be quite easily replaced if stolen or lost.
- You're entitled to additional insurance when you use the card to make purchases (see p.113).

The drawbacks

- Most credit card companies charge a flat fee (usually about €2) for foreign ATM use, as well as a clearing-house surcharge. More recently, they've tacked on "conversion fees" (up to five percent) for cash withdrawals and regular credit card purchases.
- As if that wasn't bad enough, you'll have to pay interest (around seventeen percent) on the withdrawn cash until your next bill is paid.
- Hold on; it gets worse. If you buy something with your credit card, find it doesn't work, give it back and get the purchase removed from your credit card bill, it gets reconverted back through the whole process, with the credit card company getting a commission and conversion fee again.

- Merchants who accept credit cards pay a small percentage fee to the credit card company for the right to accept their card. Although they're not supposed to do this, many smaller companies make no secret about passing that percentage on to you (though paying it is still often cheaper than withdrawing money from a cash machine, especially for one purchase).

Choosing a credit card

- Some credit cards are better than others. It depends on the bank or financial institution behind them and what deals they're offering. When deciding on a credit card, make sure you ask about the surcharges for foreign purchases and cash machine withdrawals. More and more cards are adding a three percent conversion fee. Try to find one that doesn't. If you do, cancel your current card and tell them why.
- Try to boost your spending limit before leaving. Simply call the credit card company and ask if you can get your limit raised. You may have to put more expenses on the card (or cards) than you're used to, and with an emergency purchase, such as a plane ticket or hospital bill, you might be quickly out of funds.
- Many credit cards or bank accounts can be set up for "Auto-pay". Each month, your credit card bill will be automatically paid from your checking or savings account. That way you don't have to worry about missing any payments and getting hit with the high interest rates credit card companies thrive on. Of course, what you may have to worry about is having enough money in your bank account. To be safe, meet with your bank manager before you leave and set up a line of credit (€1000–5000) to cover you in a pinch. If you get Internet banking, all this can be easily monitored from any Internet café.

Bank cards and debit cards

Try to take along a card that taps directly into your cheque or savings account. Some of these bank-issued cards can be used for purchases ("debit cards"), some can't ("cash cards"). Both types can be used to withdraw cash, though. You'll still be slapped with a withdrawal fee and perhaps a conversion fee, but you won't have to pay interest on the money withdrawn, which makes them better than credit cards for this purpose. For those who don't trust themselves with the spending limit granted on a credit card, this can be a good alternative, but the drawbacks are clear cut: there's no credit, which is no good when you're faced with unexpected, urgent expenses. "Offline" debit cards are generally less secure (they don't require a PIN and it's a few days before the money is taken from your account). "Online" debit cards ("Chip and PIN" cards in the UK) require a PIN but have instantaneous processing; if they land in the wrong hands, your money could be as good as gone, especially if the loss is not reported immediately. Check the written policy of the card: some limit the stolen amount to €50, others €500, depending on how long it takes you to report the theft. If you can't arrange a credit card, or want to use this as a second credit card, you'll need to ring or meet with your bank.

Cash machines

Holes in the wall, or ATMs, are everywhere, but they're not infallible: they sometimes run out of cash, break down and even occasionally swallow your card for no good reason. When that happens at home, it's a hassle. Abroad, it can make for a very unpleasant day. With all the fees involved, it can cost as much as €4 to take out as little as €20, so the fewer the withdrawals, the better. To find Visa/Plus cash machines, see ⓦwww.visa.com/pd/atm/main.html; to find MasterCard/Cirrus cash machines, see ⓦwww.mastercard .com/atmlocator/index.jsp.

Travellers' cheques

For the last decade, the conventional wisdom has been that travellers' cheques are defunct, replaced by convenient ATMs. You can certainly get by without them. However, with all the new ATM fees, travellers' cheques may start making a comeback.

Here's how travellers cheques work: you buy the cheques (for a small fee) and keep a list of their serial numbers, so if they get stolen or lost you can report exactly which cheques are missing and get the amount refunded. In order to do this, you need to keep the list updated and separate from your unused cheques and hope the bag with the list in it doesn't get stolen or lost as well. Some places accept travellers' cheques as cash, but not the smaller places where budget travellers often hang out. You can easily encash them, and sometimes for free (you can cash American Express cheques at AmEx offices for free, for example – for a list of locations, see

ⓦwww.americanexpress.co.uk), but you may not be anywhere near the relevant office. So, you're more likely to be paying a fee to convert your cheques into cash in addition to the cost of exchanging the currency. Understandably, some people find this to be a hassle – one that outweighs the security factor.

In general, places that take travellers' cheques also take credit cards (or are not far from a cash machine or bank that allows cash advances). However, if you plan to spend an extended period in a rural area, and have read in your guidebook that cash cards and credit cards are of limited use but that travellers' cheques can be encashed, you can always pick some up in a major city if you're uncomfortable carrying the amount of cash you'll need to get by.

Visa, Thomas Cook and American Express issue the most commonly used travellers' cheques. There are no real advantages in terms of acceptance (though AmEx does allow clients to collect mail at some of their offices, and AmEx and Thomas Cook allow two people to sign the cheques). Remember to make sure the assistant watches you countersign the cheques. Don't let them walk off while you're busy scribbling your name, or the whole thing may be void.

AmEx also has a "travellers' cheque card", which you can load up with money, then use to withdraw funds from bank machines. When it's empty, simply toss away the card. However, if you've got a cash card from your bank or a debit card, this seems unnecessary: you don't need both.

Cash

Of course, you'll want to carry cash as well. The question is how much. For starters, you should try to keep a €250–450 emergency stash on you at all times because… well, you never know – a bank's computer system is down, you get fined by a conductor for failing to make a reservation on an overnight train, the guy selling the last ticket to a Sting concert in a stone amphitheatre in Greece will only take cash, and so on. I've had to dip into my emergency fund more times than I care to count. Consider keeping €50–100 separate from your passport pouch. Perhaps in a pocket in your address book or taped to the inside of your backpack – just enough to spend a night in the hostel, get some food or take transport to the nearest embassy.

△ Always keep some cash on you... just in case

If you're using credit cards and bank cards instead of travellers' cheques, it's a better idea to use them for as many purchases as possible. That way, you've got records of your expenses and you can limit the amount of cash you need to carry. Minimizing cash withdrawals (ie the cash withdrawal fees) is a huge saving. You'll still need some pocket change, though, as it's not possible to put every beer, postcard or subway ticket on a credit card. Finding the balance between minimizing your withdrawals and not carrying too much money is largely dependent on your comfort level and how much you're spending. Some find €50 is fine for pocket change. Others prefer €250. It may take a week or two to find an amount that works best for you.

Others items for your money belt

Passport

The money belt is, in fact, where you want to keep your passport. To find out how to get a passport, see p.108.

Flight tickets

E-tickets mean, if nothing else, more comfort for the traveller. If you have paper tickets, remove the bulky folder and cover them in plastic wrap or a small zip-lock bag. A little water or sweat is all it takes to render the tickets virtually unreadable.

Train/bus pass

For a long trip, you may want to protect these with a bit of plastic wrap or a zip-lock bag as well.

Driver's licence

It's helpful to have an official photo ID besides your passport, especially since there's a chance you'll end up driving a car at some point. There's little need to get an International Drivers' Licence (which essentially makes it easier for the police to write you a ticket), but it is "recommended" in Austria, Germany, Greece, Italy, Portugal, Spain and Eastern Europe – to find out exactly where it's required, see the updated list at ⊛www.theaa.co.uk. They are easy to get (Australia ⊛www.aaa.asn.au; Canada ⊛www.caa.ca; New Zealand ⊛www.nzaa.co.nz; UK ⊛www.rac.co.uk; US ⊛www.aaa .com) and cost about €13–18. Should you decide to pick one up, be warned this maplike document won't easily fit in your money belt.

Student ID card/under-26 youth card/teacher card

If you qualify for one of these, probably best to keep it close by. It's not as valuable as the other items in your money belt, but its size makes it easy to lose. For more information on these cards, see p.70.

Hostel cards

If you plan to get a Hostelling International card or VIP Backpackers card, remember they need to be purchased before you leave home. For more info on both cards, see p.70.

Six extra passport photos

This seems like a lot, but when you apply for visas and such you often need three photos just for one application. Local transport cards sometimes require them as well. Better to take a few extra than have to wander off looking for a place to get a snapshot in a hurry.

Insurance card

If you've got insurance, carry the card. If you're just issued a large piece of paper, make your own card with your account number and emergency telephone number and laminate it. See p.113 for more on insurance.

Phone card

These cards list the local access numbers you'll need (available online if you misplace the card), so you have them handy in case of an emergency. You can get them free from the phone service you plan to use.

Other licences

If you're a trained scuba diver or pilot, or hold other such licences that easily fit into a money belt, bring them along. You never know when you might need them.

One anti-diarrhoea pill

It's hard to predict when dysentery is going to strike. Inevitably, it'll happen while you're out wandering around town or on a long bus ride with your medical kit stored in the luggage hold below. Best to keep one pill handy for such emergencies.

10

Guidebooks and
other reading

This is precisely where you might expect to find a few
sentences of Rough Guide propaganda. Happily, you
won't. Not much, anyway. Naturally, the editors and
writers at Rough Guides are proud of the guidebooks they produce, but they also understand it
comes down to individual taste, trust, and how you like your information gathered and presented.

Besides Rough Guides, guidebook publishers aimed at the independent traveller include Fielding's, Footprint's Handbook series,
Let's Go, Lonely Planet, Time Out city guides and (for French
speakers) Le Guide du Routard. For more mainstream travel,
there's also Frommer's, Fodor's, the design-intense Eyewitness
guides by DK and Rick Steves's self-guided tours.

You'll want to bring some pure pleasure reading as well. This
chapter will explain how many books you'll need to cart along on
your trip, no matter how many weeks or months you'll be spending on the road.

How to pick a guidebook

The best thing is to "test-drive" a few different guides in your home
town or on your next short trip and see which suits you best. At the

very least, you should go to a bookstore, so you can pick up a few guides on the same country and compare a few paragraphs on the same topic. Start with a city or town you're particularly interested in. Is the layout and writing easy to follow? Are the maps clear? Also take a look at the author bios – you'll want someone (or several people) who have spent considerable time in the country they're writing about. It's always helpful if they speak the language and have been able to get information by conversing with the locals.

How to use your guidebook

If this trip to Europe will be your first time using a guidebook, you'll be amazed. Guidebooks have everything you need to know to get around: where to stay, where to eat and what to do while you're there. However, this does more than just provide incredible help; it removes some of the adventure. Moreover, it sends everyone to the same places; not just the same towns, but the same cafés, hostels, bars and scenic overlooks. Ask nearly any guidebook author and they'll tell you their book is best used as a reference, not a bible or substitute tour guide. The little maps are great for helping you navigate your way from the train station to a hostel at 3am or finding a vegetarian restaurant in Scandinavia, but, as any guidebook author will also tell you, your best guide is still your own nose. Find your own undiscovered restaurants and lodgings, and you'll likely have a much more memorable experience.

Here's another common misuse. The temptation is to sit on the bus or train approaching the city and scrutinize the hostel descriptions. Then, you compare your favourites over and over until you get them into your head, and before you know it you've got the experience largely mapped out before you've even done it. Save yourself the effort; it's not worth it. There's not that much difference between four recommended hostels. And if you don't like it you can either move out the next day after you've had a chance to look around, or just crash there at night and spend your waking hours elsewhere in town (or lounging in the lobby of a four-star hotel, if you prefer).

You'll eventually find a system that works for you, but mine is something like this: if I'm tired out or staying somewhere a bit longer, I'll pick a place further from the centre. If I'm just staying a day or two and feeling fresh, I'll go for the best-rated of the fleapits in the centre. If I'm not feeling well, I'll go for the cheapest room with an attached bathroom. If there are a few decent choices in any of these categories, I'll typically go for the ones that are the easiest to get to and within walking distance from the centre. But, whatever the case, I won't spend more than five or ten minutes deciding. However, if I want to splurge on someplace special for a night, I'll spend a day in town first and ask around at the tourist office, looking at a few brochures before I decide.

How many guidebooks to bring

Here's some good news. Just because you're planning to hit twelve European countries doesn't mean you need to pack twelve guide-books. You'll get by just fine with a single, double-Bible-thick Europe book.

However, if you're going to be spending considerably more time in one city or country, a country- or city-specific book is well worth the money. If you're not sure in advance how much time you'll be spending in each spot (or if you simply prefer more background information), then you can easily pick these up once you arrive, from hostels, hotels, bookstores and airports – virtually everywhere. Ideally, you'll be able to find someone who's heading in the direction you just came from and make a straight swap. If you're trading with a hostel or secondhand bookstore, you may have to throw in some money or a novel to complete the deal.

Another type of guide worth considering, either locally or before you leave, is a special-interest guide: hiking routes, architecture, great restaurants, bicycle trails and so on. Books bought locally are often more comprehensive, but may not be as professional as those found in your own bookstore back home.

What to read along the way

One of the very best ways to add richness to your trip and bring the locales to life is to read up on them. This entails putting aside the iPod, getting beyond the brief guidebook descriptions and finding stories that explore cultural nuances and history easily missed while searching for your hostel or a better exchange rate. The Travellers Tales series published in San Francisco offers diverse and well-crafted anthologies on popular destinations that do just this, and has most European countries (and many of the cities) covered. If you can find room for (or manage to lift) any of the country-themed James Michener tomes, you're in for a treat, with folklore and fiction woven into the locales named in the title. But it would be a pity to miss out on some of the classics, especially in the regions where they are set. Reading books like *Ulysses* in Ireland, *Crime and Punishment* in Russia or *Death in the Afternoon* in Spain is not just one of the great joys of travel, it's a snap. The classics are among the most popular titles along the appropriate routes and can be bought or traded quite easily. Even the popular modern travel books, such as Bill Bryson's *Neither Here Nor There: Travels in Europe* or Adam Gopnik's charming bestseller *Paris to the Moon*, are easy to find. So, when you're starting out, one paperback will do. Pop fiction authors like Clancy and Grisham tend to serve as the strongest currency, but start with something you like and let your continuous swaps serve as a literary adventure that runs parallel to your trip.

How to pick a map

You can pick up maps for free or for a small charge in every city you visit, and you'll find several maps in your guidebook. The problem: most of them stink. They're either too small, too big, too cluttered with ads, or simply impossible to fold without a PhD in origami.

For larger cities where you plan to spend more than a day or two, it's often worth buying a decent map from local bookstores, tourist shops, or at the tourist information offices when you arrive. You can also try to trade them as you go, but it's not that easy, since most get damaged during the folding process. Maps are also a matter of preference: some prefer the more discreet book-style ones that contain blown-up sections of each part of the city on a different page; others like something they can spread out on the table back at the hostel when looking over the ground covered or the following day's route.

Whichever you choose, you'll probably want to avoid anything that folds out like a picnic blanket and has enough detail to conduct a geographical survey. Look instead for easy folding (if any) and for paper that will survive some rough treatment. Rough Guides has − brace yourself for a dose of propaganda − a line of weatherproof, tearproof maps that combine the book and fold-out formats for those who aren't on the very tightest of budgets. Others worth considering are Insight fleximaps, Hallwag City Flash maps and Artwise/Streetwise maps.

11

When you arrive

Take one step off the plane into the cultural mystery of Europe and - bam! – everything is still in English. Most of the major European gateways provide soft landings in this respect. There are free luggage carts and easy-to-use automated ticket machines (with English directions) that accept credit cards. High-speed rail links whisk you to the city centre. Tourist information booths provide enough brochures to fill a small library, and the person behind the desk will answer any question you can think of, probably in no fewer than three languages.

Some people like to book a room for a few nights in advance. That's fine. You can let your travel agent do it or you can find a hotel/hostel on the Web. Others prefer to begin honing their room-finding skills right off the bat. That's not a bad idea, either. After consulting your guidebook, you might book a room from the airport through a tourist office. Or take a train or bus into the centre of the city and book via a tourist office there. Or you might buy a local phone card in the airport and make a few calls to see who has space. Or simply use public transport to get to an area with several hostels and walk from one to the next to check them out on your own.

OK, you've found a place to stay and put your pack down. Now it's time to see some of Europe's sites, right? Sure, but don't forget that you're already travelling. The subway ride to the hostel, asking

Points of confusion

- ❏ Cities aren't always spelled the same way in their native tongue
- ❏ For example, Cologne is Köln, Copenhagen is København, Florence is Firenze, Geneva is Genève, Munich is München, Prague is Praha, Venice is Venezia and Vienna is Wien.
- ❏ Nor are countries For example, Austria is Österreich, Finland is Suomi, Germany is Deutschland, Italy is Italia, Norway is Norge, Spain is España, Sweden is Sverige, Switzerland is Schweiz or Suisse, and Turkey is Türkiye.
- ❏ Often the countries have abbreviations, commonly seen on vehicle licence plates or as a sticker. Some are less than obvious. For example, BIH is Bosnia and Herzegovina, CH is Switzerland, D is Germany, E is Spain, FL is Liechtenstein and GB is the United Kingdom.
- ❏ A comma is used instead of a period or full stop in prices. €3.50 is often written €3,50.
- ❏ The date is typically written day/month/year.
- ❏ Time is posted military style when written – 0900 is 9am, 1400 is 2pm, 2300 is 11pm. Orally, the am/pm system (ie "meet you for dinner at seven") is used.
- ❏ A road sign of a town's silhouette with a slash through it means you're leaving the city and can go back to the speed limit you were driving at before you had to slow down to pass through the town.
- ❏ European banks often close at three o'clock, and at midday on a Saturday, if they're open during the weekend at all.
- ❏ Many stores in rural areas close for lunch.

directions, finding a bite to eat en route… that's all part of the experience. Travelling is just as much about getting there as arriving, or maybe even more.

One of the best ways to take advantage of your time on the road is to vary the way you travel down it. How you get around, whether it be in the air, through the water, on wheels or on the back of an animal, will shape the memories you bring home. And that doesn't just apply to transport. You can be adventurous or timid in your choice of accommodation, what you eat, even the bathrooms you decide to use. It's always going to be easier to travel in the style you are accustomed to at home, but making the choice (often several times a day) to try the local alternatives will ultimately enrich your trip. This chapter will provide you with a little taste of what's lies ahead.

Transport

Take as diverse a range of transport as you can. Try a black cab in London, a tram in Vienna, a bike in Amsterdam, and hop on every subway you come across. If you have the chance, skip the air-conditioned bus and try… well, anything. Here's a guide to getting yourself around. To find the transport that best fits your schedule and budget, see the "Getting there and around" chapter (p.26).

Aeroplanes

Confirm your flights by phone or email 72 hours in advance. You won't be automatically bumped if you neglect to do this, but it's nice insurance and more important in some places than others. Most carriers will have English speakers manning the phones, but have the hostel receptionist or tourist office help out if you experience a language barrier. And remember to confirm your in-flight meals if you have any special dietary considerations.

With the budget carriers, you may not experience the sort of service you get on flights at home (if, indeed, you get such service at home). If you're nervous about flying with budget companies, that's normal, but remind yourself that they have a strong safety record and it's statistically safer than other modes of transport, including walking. Flying during daylight may help with some of your worries.

Bicycle rickshaws

Some cities offer a sporadic bicycle rickshaw service. It's essentially for tourists and, as such, overpriced, especially compared to the place where the bicycle rickshaw probably came from. There's no meter, so always fix the price before you depart.

Bicycle

Bikes can be rented nearly everywhere. And where they can't be rented you can pick up a low-tech, used model for €32–65. Take advantage of this. It's an ideal way to get to know an area, particularly the ones set up to accommodate bicycles: you can stop whenever you get the urge, yet you're more inclined to venture further off the main tourist routes, which will afford you some of the most interesting views.

Buses

Long-distance buses are convenient, and well air-conditioned. Try to get a window seat near the front to help avoid nausea on curvy roads. Sit on the side that's not getting direct sunlight (take a moment to figure this out before you step onto the bus – heading south in the afternoon, you'll want to be on the east side, the side to the right when entering; that way, you can keep the window shade open and get a nice view.) For safety, keep a few rows between you and the front to cushion any collision. (For Busabout and Eurolines info, see p.40.)

Canoe

Paddle your way around parts of Iceland, Scotland or France. You can find places to canoe just about everywhere, as well as places that will rent you canoes. Pick up a good map, some local tips and a few trash bags to waterproof your backpack, and you're ready to go.

Car

See p.41 for general information on transport, and buying, selling and renting cars as you travel.

Cruise ship

This doesn't fit the traditional traveller image. The cabins aren't conducive to drying hand-washed laundry, the staff don't appreciate people walking down the corridors in just a towel, and body art and piercing may frighten some of the other passengers. But this can be a way to connect certain legs of your trip at a decent price.

Ferry

Many of these are nearly as luxurious as their cruise-ship cousins, with hot tubs, saunas, movie theatres and discos, and all are more expensive if you try to bring along a car. See map on p.52 for the ferries around Europe.

Horse

Equestrian travel can be incredibly romantic and exciting. You can take a horseback tour on the coasts of Ireland or Spain or in the forests of Germany. But in the words of Ian Fleming, "A horse is dangerous at both ends and uncomfortable in the middle." Make certain, therefore, that you get a little practice before you head out on a longer journey, and spend some time getting to know your steed's signals before you need to interpret them in an emergency.

Motorcycles

There are probably two hundred safer ways to navigate your way around Europe, but few that offer the opportunity to do so in leather. Helmets and protective clothing are a must, as road conditions change around every mountain curve, and European drivers can be… well, capricious.

River kayak

These are short and rugged, and they tip over easier than a toddler on Rollerblades, so it's best to take a course when getting started. Because handling is so sensitive, most kayakers prefer their own boats. However, on a long trip, you'll probably just have to make do with what's available. If you stick to the rafting epicentres (Austria, Germany, Slovenia, Czech Republic, Switzerland), you'll find there's good equipment on hand and, depending on your skill level, you may be able to catch free rides with rafting trips, working as a safety kayaker.

Sea kayak

Both the hard-shell and the collapsible variety have their merits, depending largely on how you're able to transport them. They're increasingly available for rent, so enquire before you drag yours halfway around the globe. You'll also need to check with airlines to see what additional fees are involved for taking them on board.

Subway

No matter how little there is to see out the window, a subway is an integral part of any big city's character. Some offer incredibly high-speed and efficient transport, some are overdue for repair and some are simply underground marvels. The lines in Moscow, St Petersburg and London, and some of the stations in Stockholm, are particularly worth a look.

Taxis

At home, you might order a taxi or flag one down for a short ride. You can do that on the road as well. From a financial viewpoint, make sure you know what you're getting into. A ten-minute ride in a Swiss taxi might cost you as much as €41. Also know that, possibly as a result of petrol being priced like twelve-year-old Scotch, many taxis wait at designated spots around the city instead of driving around. So it may be far quicker to ask directions to the nearest taxi stand than wait for one to pass by.

Trains

Important: remember to check that the train carriage you are boarding has the name of the city you are going to posted on the side, or at least a city beyond the one you're heading to. If the individual carriage says "Hamburg" on it, that's where it's going. But that doesn't mean the entire train is going to Hamburg. In fact, there's a good chance it isn't. Trains drop off some carriages and pick up others along the route, so you can easily end up someplace you hadn't counted on – and many people do.

It's tempting, especially with rail passes, to save money by spending a few nights on the train. Overnight trains aren't the safest form of accommodation or quite the bargain they might seen, so see p.71 to learn about supplementing your pass with other cost-effective travel.

France's TGV is the world's fastest train. There are several other high-speed services in Europe: Germany's Inter-City Express (ICE), the Netherlands' and Belgium's Thalys, Eurostar, Spain's Alta Velocidad España (AVE) and Italy's Pendolino. It hardly feels like you're moving, never mind travelling. Until, that is, you catch the 250 kilometre-an-hour blur out the window. When high-speed trains are involved, it's almost always cheaper to get some type of rail pass. (It may even be cheaper to fly.) There's a monopoly on the food, so plastic-wrapped sandwiches are priced like Michelin-star entrées; fortunately, though, the rides don't last that long, so a few pack-along snacks should see you through.

Water taxi

These are found in several cities, from Venice to Stockholm, and are usually priced for vacationing millionaires, so make sure it's a special occasion before you flag one down.

Accommodation

İstanbul is a little too far to travel to stay at the *Hilton*. And your budget is likely to suffer from even one night's plush rest. It may take some time to get used to staying in budget digs, but it's more rewarding than it might initially seem. There's a sense of camaraderie that you simply won't find at the *Ritz*. You can swap tales at breakfast, make dinner together, play backgammon – it's a nomadic commune of sorts. The atmosphere changes from place to place, even from day to day if enough new travellers pull in. You can also seek more interesting places from time to time: a hostel in a cave, a bed in a backyard tree house, an ice hotel. Even if these unconventional digs cost a little more, it's usually worth the experience.

Camping

Traveller camping falls into two categories: free camping, which is usually illegal but pretty easy to do outside of big cities; and paid camping, at designated campgrounds with bathrooms and other amenities. If you plan to do go down the free-camp route, you'll probably need to give big cities a miss. Many of the city parks are too dangerous to sleep in, or too likely to be patrolled by police. Either way, you're in trouble. In smaller towns, you can usually find a field, perhaps even a remote part of a park, if you're discreet. Some designated campgrounds are quite extravagant, with a restaurant, supermarket and pool, but even the smaller ones can be surprisingly expensive. For just a little more, you can often rent a walk-in tent with a "real" bed. Sweden and Norway allow you to put up tents legally, even on private property (if

100–150m from the nearest residence and you don't stay more than two nights; as a matter of etiquette, ask the permission of the owner if possible), which makes these ordinarily expensive destinations a good deal cheaper.

Farmstays

The name conveys the gist. You stay on a working farm where the family has made a few rooms available to those who are willing to pay for the experience. It's a bit like a B&B with animals. There's a significant range in comfort and price, but many of them dip well into the budget range (€24, including breakfast). Some offer courses in riding or gardening, many provide family-style meals, and you can sample everything from grape-growing to feeding pigs to making cheese to horseback riding. For lists of farmstays all over Europe, visit ⓦwww.agrisport.com/europa.htm.

Guesthouses/pensions/B&Bs

These are typically private homes or apartments with a few spare rooms or bungalows in the backyard. They're often run by older people whose children have moved out, and who are looking to earn a little extra money by letting travellers into their private living space. This means showing a little more respect and courtesy than you might at a hostel. Even if these places are rather lacking in services, keep in mind you're living in someone's home.

Homestays

Like farmstays (and some pensions and guesthouses), these are run by people who have opened their homes to paying visitors. They're often very reasonably priced – sometimes better than hostels – and give you a little insight into the way people live. You typically receive a private room and breakfast. You'll get your host's personal take on the country or city, which (for better or worse) is at least genuine and often interesting. It can otherwise be challenging to make contact with people who live in the country you're visiting. Some stipulate that they only accept women, couples or enrolled students.

Go to a search engine, type in the name of the city you're heading to plus the word "homestay", and you'll probably get a selection to choose from. For starters, try:

- **Global Freeloaders** A network of travellers (12,000 worldwide) who share their home for free. Ⓦwww.globalfreeloaders.com.
- **Servas** A reputable non-profit homestay community. Ⓦwww.servas.org.

Independent hostels

Independent hostels come in as many different shapes and sizes as rocks, which, coincidentally, is what some of them seem to stuff their mattresses with. You'll find some setups extremely professional and others, well, lacking. Some have great bar scenes with cheap food and people dancing on the tables in the evenings, others feel like giant, anesthetized, dormitory-type buildings with concierges that could easily double for nurses in *One Flew over the Cuckoo's Nest*. Others are blissfully charming and serene with hammocks and sofas. They can be both centrally located and fiendishly remote, with little commonality other than being the cheapest digs in town.

For general hostel bookings around Europe, try Ⓦwww.hostels.com, Ⓦwww.hostelworld.com or Ⓦwww.eurotrip.com. Also, Ⓦwww.hostelz.com offers reviews.

International youth hostels

No, you don't have to be a certain age to stay at a youth hostel. Being young at heart is enough. With all the senior travellers around, some hostels even seem more like retirement communities. Official Hostelling International (HI) hostels are part of an organization, which means there are certain standards, although it doesn't mean the standards are terribly high. Nearly all of these are well cleaned, some practically sterile, with dormitory-style rooms and separate quarters for men and women, self-service kitchens, common rooms, lockers and a cost of €8–24 per night if you're avoiding any of their "luxury" rooms. Some are equipped with pools, hot tubs and barbecues, while others are about as basic as their tree-and-hut logo. There are some notable exceptions, but HIs don't usually earn many points in the architecture, cosiness or roaring-social-life departments. Most are located a little way out of the centre of town and come with a curfew (during the day and/or night). There are almost always budget alternatives, but if this sounds like your cup of discounted tea, pick up the membership card. Without the card, you're still welcome, but will pay slightly more. Try to book in advance if you know when you're arriving, especially in high season. (See p.70 for more info on discount cards.)

- **Hostelling International** A not-for-profit association (and brand name) of hostels (over 4000) around the world, with discounts for members. ⓦwww.hihostels.com.
- **European Alliance of YMCAs** Similar in atmosphere to the HI hostels, the YMCA also offers health club facilities and fairly inexpensive accommodation for members. ⓦwww.eay.com.

Sleeping rough

Ah, the last resort of the traveller, the safety net that leaves your back out of alignment, the experience that will help you overcome whatever was annoying you about hostels. At some point, it's possible you'll be spending the night on a park bench or in a train station or airport lounge. There are obviously risks associated with sleeping rough. In particular, it's not a good idea for single women travellers, especially in (or just outside) a train station – in fact, train stations are best avoided by all, really. And a secluded park beach at night is even riskier.

But it you do find yourself having to sleep rough, bear in mind the following tips. Firstly, you probably won't be the only one doing it, so when it looks inevitable start trying to secure a good spot. What's a good spot? You'll know it when you see it (if there is one). Not too hidden, not where people have to step over you, not right under bright lights. Corners are usually quite nice, and frequently coveted. You may be inadvertently borrowing the resting place of a "regular" – so be forewarned that many of them don't take too kindly to this. Look for newspaper or cardboard to place under you; a cold marble floor will drain your body heat and make it difficult to rest. If you've got a travel partner, take turns staying awake. If not, make sure you're bear-hugging your backpack while you sleep. Alternatively, look for an all-night snack shop or bar and sip tea or coffee until the sun creeps up, then find a more comfortable place to sleep at a park or beach.

Eating

No matter what level of comfort you choose to travel in, you don't want to circle the globe without sampling the local cuisine. Check out the produce, meat and fish markets, or follow your nose into a tiny restaurant and discover hand-rolled pastas in Sicily or fresh tapas in Seville. There's no need to be paranoid about what passes your lips. If it looks truly vile (like greenish drinking water, for example), you might want to give it a miss. Otherwise, eat, drink, be merry, and see p.203 for lightning-fast cures for diarrhoea.

Hostels

They know the budget of their customers better than anyone. They also take advantage of traveller physics: a traveller not yet packed tends to stay that way for a while. Once in "hang-out" mode, it's tempting to stick around the hostel. Many hostels offer extremely cheap stews, sandwiches and plates of pasta. The ones that don't may offer cooking facilities. Team up with another traveller, or an entire group, head to the supermarket and make a meal together.

Restaurants

Eating at restaurants can run up your expenses quicker than Imelda Marcos with an hour to kill in Milan, so choose where you eat with care. As comforting as it may be to dine with other travellers, you'll often get a better deal ditching the guidebook, heading to the poorer parts of town and checking out the places (normally packed with locals) that don't take credit cards.

McDonald's

On one hand, there's simply too much wonderful food out there to justify a trip to the Golden Arches. On the other, *McDonald's* has some rather interesting (albeit processed and chemically enhanced) dishes in addition to the old classics. Italy (some argue you should be shot for entering a *McDonald's* while in Italy) has a Caprese salad with mozzarella and tomatoes; Austria has a Gemüse-Mac, whatever that is; in Slovenia, you can find a Dvojni Hamburger, with broccoli and maybe corn mixed into the meat; Turkey has the Köfte Burger, a spiced patty inside a bun enriched with yoghurt mix. The point is, if you absolutely must get your McFix while you're on the road (and these places are packed with travellers), you can at least give yourself a push by trying something you haven't seen or can't pronounce.

Street vendors

Don't believe the intestine-quivering rumours. Not every street snack leads to a week in squatter solitaire. In fact, buying food from street vendors is a wonderful way to supplement your diet: some travellers manage to exist entirely on these budget snacks.

Personal hygiene

Staying clean on the road is a challenge at times. It becomes particularly rough during the back-to-back long-transit stretches (an overnight train ride followed by a day walking around a hot city followed by another overnight train ride). If you encounter some intimidating toilets, that can be a problem as well. Either way, relief can be found.

Airports and buses

Many airports now have showers available for a small fee. Some have a sauna and gym as well. You may have to hunt around a little, as they're not as well situated as the duty-free items and postcards. Even if you have to put your yet-unwashed clothes back on, a refreshing shower (€1–3) can be an enormous boost. And you'll probably have some spare coins to get rid of anyway. If you don't take the opportunity during a long haul, the smell is only going to get worse. The budget route, of course, is simply to wash up in the restroom, perhaps with a damp paper-towel "shower", and swing by the duty-free and take a squirt of perfume before the next leg of your journey.

On nicer bus rides, particularly around Eastern Europe and Turkey, don't be surprised if an attendant comes by and offers you a splash of unisex perfume or some fragranced towellettes. They're not as pleasant as the warm washcloths distributed by many airlines, particularly considering they have the olfactory properties of toilet-bowl cleaner, but it's still better than being trapped beside someone with nuclear BO. The individually wrapped moist tissues function better, since they also remove the dirt and odour rather than simply masking it. Bring some of your own just in case.

Turkish baths

You'll find some classics in Turkey but also in other cities around Europe, like Paris, Stockholm and London. Look for the word "*hamam*". They're a perfect remedy for travel grime – the accumulated film that covers your body after weeks of low-pressure showers. These medieval bathhouses are mild steamrooms with washbasins, and most offer, for an additional fee, a joint-cracking, back-popping, skin-blasting "massage" that will leave you feeling like a boneless chicken. Upon exiting, you can cool down wrapped in towels with a refreshing yoghurt drink.

Hot hamams

Galatasaray Hamam
Built by Sultan Beyazit in 1481, now an upscale classic more popular with visitors than locals.
€19 with full treatment
24 Turnacibasi Sk İstanbul, Turkey
☎0212 252 4242

Les Bains du Marais
Elegant upscale *hamam* and sauna, with a restaurant and hair salon there as well.
€30 entry fee
31–33 rue des blancs Manteaux, Paris, France
☎1 44 61 02 02
ⓦwww.lesbainsdumarais.com

Paris Mosque baths
Marble baths built in 1922. Moorish courtyards with gardens for relaxing afterward with a cup of mint tea.
€15 entry fee
39 rue Geoffroy St Hilaire, Paris, France
☎1 43 31 38 20
ⓔnour-l@wanadoo.fr

Portobello Centre
An old restored bathhouse at a good price.
€6 entry fee
57 The Promenade, Edinburgh, Scotland
☎0131 669 6888
ⓦwww.edinburghleisure.co.uk

The Royal Baths
England's most famous Turkish baths.
€18, off-peak (Tues) €12
Royal Baths Assembly Rooms, Crescent Road, Harrogate, England
☎01423 556746
ⓦwww.harrogate.gov.uk /turkishbaths

Sturebadet
Upscale, luxury bathhouse in the city centre.
€65 for two hours (with a group of 4–9 people).
Sturegallarian 36, Stockholm, Sweden
☎08 545 01500
ⓦwww.sturebadet.se

Toilets

To find out how to sidestep pay toilets see p.77, and to keep from having to visit too often, see p.203. Meanwhile, here's a look at what you may end up facing.

There aren't too many squatters left in Europe, but you may stumble across one. The trick is not to stumble while you use it. Place your feet on the small foot-size platforms provided and align your hole with the one in the floor, which usually means facing the way you came in as you would on a Western toilet. There's rarely anything to hold on to, or anything you'd *want* to hold on to, so beyond the obvious danger of tipping over, the position causes your pants pockets to become somewhat inverted, so your valuables may go sliding irretrievably down the hole. And if this doesn't sound challenging enough, remember you may have to hold a flashlight in your mouth, since these lavatories often don't have any lighting. How to flush the hole is not entirely apparent. There's no little handle to push. No knob to turn. You have to fill up the plastic bowl a few times and dump the water into the hole and let water displacement take care of the rest.

More commonly, you'll happen upon loos that look like Western models, but which were installed by someone who may not have fully understood the directions that came with the assembly kit. Or who lacked the necessary tools. If so, notice the seat has usually been secured by something with the equivalent strength of chewing gum, so if you don't sit down exactly straight, the seat detaches and you slide right off the porcelain rim, which – take it from me – can be pretty painful. More commonly, however, the plastic seat is missing altogether. This means that you're squatting again; only now it's more difficult than a standard squatter, because you have to do a "standing squat" to clear the rim of the toilet. This usually entails bracing yourself with one hand on the wall behind you, which is highly exhausting for your arm and leg muscles and often makes them cramp painfully.

A few of these bathrooms do come equipped with paper, but it's often the sort that Rambo would be afraid to use. So, while you're sitting there (or semi-squatting), use your time wisely by crumpling and uncrumpling a piece of paper (from an unused section of your guidebook if necessary) until it's almost tolerable. This takes about five minutes (twenty with the glossy stuff), so you may want to start working on it before you actually get to the toilet. Whatever you use, if there's a little waste bin beside the toilet, put your used paper there. Don't even think of throwing it into the toilet. Though they may look vaguely like the loos you have at home, they can have a violent reaction to toilet paper: just one square of proper loo paper can clog it beyond repair.

12

Culture shock

I t may sound like what happens when Britney Spears visits the opera, but culture shock is simply a dramatic way of saying that things aren't quite the way they are at home. When you change everything you eat, say, do, smell and hear at the same time, the effect can be jolting, especially if amplified by sadness or apprehension about leaving home, fatigue from the journey or illness. The natural tendency is to return home immediately. But if you give yourself time the bout of anxiety or despair will almost certainly pass.

Combating culture shock

On the face of it, Europe, especially its larger cities, may not be all that different from the way of life you're accustomed to. There are a few more cobblestones, the architecture's more impressive, the clothing more stylish and there are more tiny cars with drivers who seem to be trying out for the Formula One circuit. But the closer you get, the more differences you'll see. To help people cope, researchers Furnham and Bochner developed an idea in the 1970s and 1980s that the individual traveller didn't need to embrace all or even most aspects of the society, just some key features to be able to operate within the culture. By reading this and simply being aware of the phenomenon, you're already a step ahead.

Here are several practical things you can do to minimize culture shock:

Four stages of culture shock

Anthropologist Kalfery Oberg first introduced the term in 1960 and defined it as a state precipitated by the anxiety that results from losing all our familiar signs and symbols of social intercourse. Everyone has slightly different reactions, the speed of the process varies and many people go through different phases more than once, so this may not provide a complete blueprint for your adaptation.

1 Honeymoon
Cultural differences are intriguing and new sites fascinating. You are still comforted by the close memory of your home culture.

2 Crisis
After some time abroad, differences begin to affect you. Differences in language, concepts and values begin to create feelings of confusion and anxiety. This is normal – it's a sign you're reconnecting with your own cultural values.

3 Recovery
You begin to accept the differences and feel comfortable in new situations. Often the crisis dissipates as lingual skills improve.

4 Adjustment
Despite occasional bouts of strain, you're enjoying the new culture and able to make choices based on preferences and values.

- Recognize it for what it is: a reaction to sensory overload and unfamiliar surroundings ("Oh, that's just a bout of culture shock – I'll be fine soon"). Look at the upside of what it represents: you're getting new experiences, new insights, and a new perspective. How bad is that?

- Start your journey in countries similar to your own. The UK is ideal in this respect.

- Read up on the place before you arrive. You're going there to experience what that country has to offer, but a little knowledge can decrease the number of cultural surprises. It can be enough for some just to buy the guidebook a day before departure and start reading background information, but reading a novel set in that country will do far more to get you in the mood.

- Jet lag gets your trip off to a poor start (see p.206), so get some sleep on the plane.

- If you're making a large cultural jump early in your trip, you can do a number of things to ease into your new location. Start by staying in a Western-style hotel for a day or two, and looking for cheaper, local digs after you've had a chance to acclimatize. Or simply spend some time just relaxing in a nice hotel lobby free of charge and don't return to your hostel until you're ready to examine the back of your eyelids.

- Speak to other travellers and compare observations.
- Keep a journal.
- Allow yourself to get excited about your trip. It's natural to be a little nervous about what's ahead, but focus on converting that into positive energy.

Your travel philosophy

What you take with you on your trip will, to a large extent, determine the experience you take away from it. And in this

Finding the real Europe

Everything seems so new and exciting when you first arrive, it's possible to overlook the tourist infrastructure that surrounds you. But after you notice it, you'll wonder how it ever eluded you. A well-decorated Greek restaurant in Paris with an overpriced menu (in six languages) on a touristy street may seem exotic, but it couldn't be less authentic, even with Greek waiters and a Greek owner and food imported from Greece. You may be used to these things in your own country (a *Texas Steakhouse* in Vancouver with waiters wearing cowboy hats, for example), but in Europe, where you've come to see the culture of the places you're visiting, it seems somehow painfully phoney. There may be an excellent Greek restaurant tucked away in an immigrant area, but that's a different story. As a rule of thumb, if you're the only traveller in the tavern, you've stumbled into an authentic place.

Naturally, in your hostel, you'll be surrounded by other travellers, as you will be at all the major attractions, on popular beaches and along the most famous shopping streets. You're not likely to escape this bubble by travelling longer or further or faster. Instead, go deeper. Hang out in places where the tourists don't go. Learn a language, communicate with the locals, spend time with them (a lot of time), and form your own firsthand perspective.

One of the best ways to do this is to work for them or alongside them. Volunteering is another excellent path (see p.99). Joining a local sports club or choir will also create inroads. Since there's no membrane on this bubble, it's impossible to say when you've burst it. But there are a few signs. Can you describe the character of the local people to someone back home? Do you have the phone numbers and addresses of local friends you've made? Have you been invited over for dinner? These are certainly more worthy things to strive for on your trip than passport stamps.

case, I'm not referring to the duel-current hairdrier that you should probably leave at home. I'm talking about your travel philosophy; your approach to dealing with the cultures you encounter.

You'll face this the moment you begin your journey. The locals you meet in more out-of-the-way places will tend to be more genuine, as they haven't been hardened by years of loud tour groups and tough-bargaining backpackers. Likewise, the travellers you run into off the main routes are likely to be a bit more interesting and into their trips. If you're passing through small towns not plagued with tourists, you're in a more cultural- ly fragile environment and should thus move about and interact with care.

Here are a few concepts to keep in mind:

- You are a (uninvited) guest in a foreign country. Be gracious. Travel with an open mind and a desire to learn.
- Familiarize yourself with local customs and make an effort to learn at least a few words of the local language. Your efforts will make an impression on those you meet. (How would you react to some- one who came to your country and asked you for directions in another language, then spoke louder and slower when you didn't understand?)
- Be a sensitive photographer. Be discreet or ask permission before you take someone's picture. And consider the long-term

Tourism impact

With good reason, travel publications have long asserted that mass tourism destroys the very things – quaintness, genuine hospitality, serenity, unique culture – that attracted visitors in the first place. There are still thousands of small, picturesque towns and villages around Europe that haven't found their way into guidebooks and are yours to discover. But it doesn't take long before they've got parking lots to handle dozens of tour buses; view- blocking, shadow-casting luxury hotels right on the beach; colourful costumes for evening cultural dance programmes; light shows with multi- lingual recorded voiceovers; and air-conditioned restaurants serving food the locals would never touch. Truth be known, we independent budget travellers contribute to this as well, probably more than we'd care to admit. Simply by being aware of your impact, though, you'll probably make more thoughtful decisions about where you spend your money and how you interact with people.

implications before paying someone in cash or candy to take their photograph.

- Resolve conflicts with a smile.
- Look beyond the tourist streets and resorts. Here's a worthy goal: meet and spend time with at least one local who is not trying to sell you any goods or services.
- Pay attention to what the locals are wearing. Shorts, vest tops and other revealing items often aren't appropriate. Better to choose styles and colours that help you blend in rather than display the latest fashions from your own country.
- Don't litter or waste electricity and water.

13

Staying in touch

Just twenty years ago, staying in touch from Europe meant dealing with fickle overseas operators while you pumped a pocket full of coins into a payphone that would, like an Italian Vespa driver, cut you off at will.

Today, perhaps the most vexing aspect of staying in touch is choosing how you want to do it. On a nut-and-bolts budget, you can get by with a free email account and the occasional collect call. And if you're armed with the right phone numbers and know where to look for cheap Internet access, it's a breeze.

Communications kit

Finally, there's proof that the Internet has more purpose than circulating porn and driving Viagra sales. ekit (www.ekit.com) is the long-awaited all-in-one communication package designed for travellers that *is* actually useful. It slices! It dices! It uploads! It faxes! ekit provides a discount calling-card account that works in eighty countries; a voice-mail account that enables you to listen to messages by phone or for free over the Internet; an email account with 50MB storage; access to a Web service, which you can use to send and receive faxes as easily as email; and an electronic vault where you can securely store backups of your passport, travellers' cheque numbers, credit cards and other essential documents. The vault is free (and worth using even if you don't bother with their other services) and you're essentially just paying for your calls and faxes – an account you preload by credit card. For example, typical calls from Europe to cities overseas cost €1.25–2.50 for four minutes' of international chatting. They also provide a 24-hour customer service operator in English, German, French, Spanish and Portuguese. It's not ideal for local calls, but that's fine – you have cheaper options for those. However, not every country has access numbers (Bulgaria, Croatia, Romania, Slovakia, Slovenia), in which case you'll have to use one of the other methods listed below. The other downside is that there are probably a few pure international phoning services that are slightly cheaper.

Phoning

There's nothing quite as comforting as hearing a loved one's voice. And from most phones in Europe, the connection is clear enough that your mom won't sound like your husky grandfather. If the signal does sound like it's being bounced off Mars, hang up and call back after a few seconds, try a different phone or have your family call you.

△ Sometimes, you may have to go the extra mile to phone a friend

Example: Sweden to the US, four-minute call
Private phone: €0.40
International prepaid card: €1
ekit phone service: €1.90
Monthly billed card: €2.65
Mobile phone (not including minimum €16 monthly fee): €3.30
Satellite phone (not including minimum €20 monthly access fee or €40 activation fee): €6
Hotel room phone (with hotel charges): €12
Callback call: €0.50
AT&T calling card: €15
AT&T collect call: €16

There are several ways to place a call: direct, collect, credit card, calling card, mobile phone, and more. The rates differ dramatically; making the right choice (much of which depends on if you're on the move or staying still) could save you over €10 on a single five-minute overseas conversation. Plus, bringing a mobile phone is becoming an increasingly viable option, and with the right approach you won't even feel shackled to it.

Direct calls

Making a direct dial call from Europe (that is, one you are making from a private phone, hotel phone, or phone booth with coins or a locally purchased calling card), dial 00 plus the

Calling Europe

In case you want to make some pre-trip plans, here's a list of country codes at a glance:

Austria 43	Estonia 372	Latvia 371	Russia 7
Belgium 32	Finland 358	Lithuania 370	Slovakia 421
Britain 44	France 33	Luxembourg 352	Slovenia 386
Bulgaria 359	Germany 49	Netherlands 31	Spain 34
Croatia 385	Greece 30	Norway 47	Sweden 46
Czech	Hungary 36	Poland 48	Switzerland 41
Republic 420	Ireland 353	Portugal 352	Turkey 90
Denmark 45	Italy 39	Romania 40	

Time zones

Britain, Ireland and Portugal
Five hours ahead of New York, eight hours ahead of Vancouver, eleven hours behind Sydney.

Austria, Belgium, Croatia, Czech Republic, Denmark, France, Germany, Hungary, Italy, Luxembourg, the Netherlands, Norway, Poland, Slovakia, Slovenia, Spain, Sweden, Switzerland and Turkey
Six hours ahead of New York, nine hours ahead of Vancouver, ten hours behind Sydney.

Bulgaria, Estonia, Finland, Greece, Latvia, Lithuania and Romania
Seven hours ahead of New York, ten hours ahead of Vancouver, nine hours behind Sydney.

country code and number. So, to dial Australia, ring 0061 plus the number; for Canada and the US, it's 001 plus the number; and for New Zealand, it's 0064 plus the number. See the box on p.173 for how to dial the UK.

Calling Europe is just as easy. To call from Australia, Canada or the US, dial 011, then the country code and number. To call from New Zealand, dial 00 then the country code and number. If the European number you're calling starts with a zero or has it wrapped in parenthesis like this "(0)" after the country number, you typically don't dial it when calling from overseas. So, if calling England from the US, and the number is written like this "+44 (0)70 222 2222", you would dial 011 44 70 222 2222.

Callback

Callback is aimed at people staying in one place for a while (eg with work or study) and who have access to a private phone. It may sound a little complex, but really it's quite simple. Once you set up an account by contacting a callback service and providing a billing address and credit card number (or preloading it with funds), it works like this: you dial a special number, let it ring once, then hang up. This part doesn't cost a thing. In a few seconds, you get a call back. When you pick up the receiver, you get a dial tone. Then you just dial as if you're in your home country. You can make several calls without hanging up by pressing a few designated keys after each call (such as "#" three times). You don't even have to initiate the callback with the phone; you can, on some accounts, trigger it with an email or SMS. For the non-prepaid sort, the phone bill is automatically paid by credit card and sent wherever you'd like it. For a list of callback companies, see ⓦwww.gphone.com, ⓦwww.telestial.com and ⓦwww.kallback.com. Make sure there's no monthly service fee (or not much of one) and you're not committing to a long contract.

Collect calls

Many of the major national phone companies in your country have set up special numbers abroad so you can be connected directly with an operator back home (and so they can keep your money!). This enables you to reverse the charges (or use a calling card account number you have with that phone company), all while speaking with an operator who shares your language. For example, to call the US from Belgium using a public phone, you'd dial 001 800 100 10 to reach an AT&T operator. After entering or saying the area code and local number you're calling, you get a voice prompt, at which point you can either enter your calling card account number or wait for an operator and request a collect call. The other option is to use a local operator to reverse the charges. The directions for that are often on the payphone itself or in your guidebook. Collect calls are convenient but they're not cheap, working best in emergencies or if people back home are so happy to hear from you that they won't mind the obscene charges.

Fax

Email hasn't rendered these machines obsolete just yet. In remote locations where you need a document quickly, can't access email or can't afford the local calls, faxes are an ideal alternative. Keep those fax numbers handy just in case.

Phone cards

Phone cards are the best option for local calls and sometimes prove a great deal for international calls. They look like flimsy credit cards and are typically sold in different denominations (and different types – some are specially designed for international calls) at newspaper stands and grocery stores across Europe. They are either inserted directly into the public phone, with the units ticking by as you talk or (as with some international cards) the card's number and special code are dialled first to access a special account that lets you call overseas. Before you buy any card, ask if it works internationally, how many minutes you get and if it has an expiration date (some become invalid after one to three months). If you want to keep things simple, pick up local cards as and when you need them. If you prefer to arrive with one in your pocket – and you don't mind spending a bit more – you can buy similar cards at special websites (such as ⓦwww.besttelephonerates.com) before leaving home. Either way, it's much cheaper than using a national phone company's service. In fact, chances are you'll be able to find a card that has better rates than ekit.

Local phones

You're still going to encounter the coin-eating dinosaur phone, but they're heading toward extinction and it's much more likely you'll be using a phone card (see above) that can be inserted into the phone. Sometimes there are special overseas phones that offer better rates; your guidebook should advise you on that.

Mobile phones

Carrying a mobile phone is a decision worth thinking about, but if you're coming from the US, chances are the phone you bring with you will be about as effective as a refrigerator magnet, so it's important to get the right phone and service plan (see opposite). In that one emergency situation, a mobile phone could save you, or at least make your life much easier. But it may feel like an expensive and obtrusive umbilical cord. One simple solution is to leave it turned off and have the calls diverted to your voice-mail service or a family member, or simply leave a message instructing people to email or text you. Europe has extensive mobile phone coverage, but be careful not to use your phone as a crutch when venturing, say, up into the mountains. You can get yourself into serious trouble thinking that a rescue team is just a call away. Coverage is especially patchy in rough and remote terrain, so that helicopter ride out may take longer to arrange than you think. Better to go in prepared with the right equipment and solid backup plans, as if you had no phone with you at all.

Choosing the right phone and service plan

Most of the world uses 900/1800 GSM, but the US and Canada use 1900 GSM and there's no way a 1900 GMS phone is going to work with an 1800 network. Sucks, doesn't it? So, if you want something that will work well in both places, you'll need a tri-band phone. These start at around €100, not including monthly fees, rising to €450 for the top-end models with a colour screen and camera – more important, though, is that it operates on 110–240V and has a lithium-ion battery.

If you opt for a tri-band phone and stick with your subscription back home, remember that each local call you make in Europe will be "international" – calling one end of Paris from the other, for example, will use a US network, so you'll end up getting fleeced on both ends. Furthermore, you'll have to pay surcharges for accepting incoming calls as well. To put it another way, if you use your phone for anything but emergencies, the bill will be frightening.

There is a (sort of) solution for people who want to make more practical use of their phone. If you plan to stay somewhere for a while and want to use your mobile phone locally, buying a local SIM card makes the most sense. These cost €8–25, can be topped up easily and, best of all, incoming calls are free and local calls cost around 20–80 cents a minute, instead of a few euros. And, for international calls, you can simply use that local card to ring ekit or another callback service and make a cheap call (double-check to see that the service will call back to a mobile phone first, though). Only one small problem: many US service providers "lock" in your subscription SIM card, stopping you from switching networks. At the moment, only T-Mobile (in the US) lets you switch (you have to wait fourteen days after purchasing before putting in a request).

You could, of course, buy a used 900/1800 GSM phone once you arrive in Europe (for about €35), and buy a SIM card in every country (which you could keep loaded up as needed), but after about three countries those cards are going to really add up. So, if you're travelling through many countries, consider a HopAbroad roaming SIM (see ⊛www.telestial.com). For €82, you get one phone number and €12 of talk time; it costs about €1 per minute for outgoing calls and thirty cents per minute for incoming calls. As long as you keep funds in your prepaid account, you can make and receive calls. Yes, it's pricey, but if you want to use it in ten or more countries over the summer, it's probably the cheapest option for semi-regular use. And if you decide to stay in one country for a month or so, you can just slap in a local SIM card. You can use it with both a US/Canadian tri-band phone or a European dual-band.

Of course, there are mobile phone rentals, as you'll no doubt see in the airport, but after more than a week or two of travel they make these other options seem like bargains.

Satellite phone

Maybe you've heard about this and conjured up some notion that it's exactly what the doctor ordered for overseas travel. Well, for field researchers on a corporate account it might be (Globalstar makes a 12oz model that uses 46 orbiting satellites), but for budget-minded travellers, price (€650+), weight (heavier than normal phones) and rates (relatively high per minute) make it impractical at best. Besides, it doesn't work indoors.

Telephone centres

These old phone centres can be charming; there's no reason to be intimidated by them. The hardest part is actually finding one. Once there, you simply fill out a form stating who you want to call and the number where they can be reached. When the operator gets them on the line, she points you to a phone cabin and connects the call. You pay after the call is completed, so make sure you check the rates first. It's often possible to make collect calls this way as well.

Webphone

A webphone, or VoIP – Voice over Internet Protocol, allows you to dial from a PC to a phone and pay a fraction of the best rates (2–4 cents a minute to the US, 4–6 cents a minute to Australia and 4–10 cents a minute to Britain on one plan).

With special software and a headset (€8), you can connect with others using the same software for free. Currently, few Internet cafés offer VoIP, but it's a smart idea and will probably soon be turning up at more. The downside is that audio (and especially video, if you want PC to PC) quality may not be up to par, but a little echo isn't such a bad trade-off for the big savings. If you're bringing a laptop and want to do it yourself, you'll need a headset, special software installed (see ⓦwww.skype.com), and access to high-speed WiFi "hot spots" (a bulky and expensive set-up that can get stolen and break easily when dropped or rainsoaked). To find WiFi hotspots around Europe, see ⓦwww.wifinder.com.

Email

With time zones and long-distance charges, email is going to be your best ally for almost-immediate contact. You can knock off one letter and send it in bulk, or alter it for specific people with a little cutting and pasting and save yourself (not to mention your metacarpal ligaments) the hassle. Unless you're writing a novel along the way, there's no reason to bring a laptop. You can get Internet access virtually anywhere. And by anywhere, I really mean anywhere. Nearly all hostels are now equipped with a connection, and if they're not you shouldn't have to walk more than five or ten minutes to find an Internet café. Expect to pay anything from €0.40 to €2 for fifteen minutes, although libraries, universities and many hotels offer free access. Just make sure you're set up with an account you can check from the Web. If the email account you currently use can only be accessed from your work or school workstation, consider getting a free account. There are many to choose from, but Hotmail (ⓦwww.hotmail.com) and Yahoo! (ⓦwww.yahoo.com) are among the largest. Gmail (ⓦwww

Overconnected

For as little as a couple of euros an hour, you can walk two blocks from your hostel to check email. It's cheaper than entry to a museum, lasts longer than a meal and it's easy to justify wasting time by calling it a cultural experience ("Well, the keyboard layout is different, at least"). But when you realize you've spent a small fortune on the Internet, the only language you've mastered is typing with the ñ, and you're starving, it's time to move on to another country. Try for a hostel where the Internet café is at least three blocks away and the keyboard is in Cyrillic.

Chris Heidrich,
Chief editor, ⓦwww.bootsnall.com

Secure Web surfing

Surfing on the road is not like surfing at home. The connection may be fine, but you need to be aware of a new breed of pickpocket – the kind that watches you type in your various passwords or logs on to your machine after you're gone and accesses your private accounts with the info that you've unknowingly left in the far reaches of the computer's memory. There are a few things you need to do to adjust the browser settings every time you sit down at a terminal. You'll want to do it for any online shopping and banking especially, but to keep them from getting your email access info you'll probably want to do it every time you go online. Practise getting the settings switched quickly so it doesn't tie up your paid minutes.

With Internet Explorer (it's similar with Netscape), click on "Tools", then scroll to "Internet Options". Start by setting "Days to keep pages in history" to zero. Then, also under "Tools/Internet Options", click on "Security" and then "Custom Level" and *disable* both "Download unsigned ActiveX controls" and "Initialize and script ActiveX controls not marked safe for scripting". There are a few more changes needed in that same box: set "Java Permissions" to "High Safety"; set "Software Channel Permissions" to "High Safety", and disable the following: "Meta Refresh", "Launching programs and files in an IFRAME", "Userdata Persistence", "Active Scripting", "Allow paste operations via script" and "Scripting of Java applets".

Back under the "Tool/Internet Options" menu, click "Advanced" and look under the "security" heading. Untick "Enable Profile Assistant". Then tick "do not save encrypted pages to disk" and tick "Empty Temporary Internet files folder when browser is closed". Almost done. Click "Control Panel", then "Network", and check that file and printer sharing are disabled. (An Internet café controller can access what you're doing from another terminal.) Accept session cookies but not stored cookies. Never, never allow Windows to save any of your passwords. And, finally, make sure there's no one peeking over your shoulder.

.google.com) is a new free service that gives you 1000MB of storage and you don't have to delete your old mails; they're saved and searchable. If you have a digital camera, you can easily include photos as you go. Some Internet cafés are equipped with a scanner, so developed film can be sent for a slight additional cost. (For other photo options, see p.219.)

Need a safe way to keep track of all your online passwords? Try ⓦwww.passwordsafe.com or ⓦhttp://briefcase.yahoo.com.

Snail mail

Sadly, letter writing is becoming a lost art. There's still nothing quite as nice as receiving an actual letter from abroad: the stamps, the smell and knowing it had to travel across oceans and continents to get to you. The proliferation of email simply makes the occasional postcard or letter all that much more special. It's easy to forget this while you're on the road hopping from one Internet café to the next, but it's worth the effort and is likely to strengthen friendships and ensure you'll be getting mail from your travelling friends in years ahead. Bear in mind that most letters take five to ten days to arrive.

Sending packages

There are a few tricks you can use to simplify the process, but they all revolve around the same concept: scout out the requirements before you try to mail something. In many European countries, there are special postal boxes you can buy that will speed up the shipping process and bring down the costs. More often, there are package weight limits in various price categories (it's a drag to show up with your carefully wrapped package, only to learn you're 20g over a price cutoff, which will cost you an additional €10.) Sometimes, you can get good bargains within a lower weight range, so if you divide up a larger package you can actually save money. Consult your guidebook for local tips.

Surface mail

Surface mail from almost everywhere in Europe is cheap and slower than a worm with a hangover. It's perfect for sending home items you realize you no longer need (or never did), inexpensive souvenirs, worn-out clothing you simply couldn't part with, and so on. Just about the time you've forgotten you sent it, it'll arrive, prodded and shaken by countless customs officers, like a gift from the heavens.

Registered mail and major couriers

If you're sending anything of value, such as jewellery you purchased, a filled diary or film, it's better to be safe than sorry. Spend the extra money for registered mail to make sure it arrives. Or go straight for a private delivery company, such as DHL or FedEx.

Sending film

To protect your film from the strong postal X-ray machines, make sure you wrap it in aluminium foil or purchase a special film-safe bag found online or at a well-stocked camera shop for around €15. Obviously, foil has a slight price and transport advantage. Tear off a long sheet before leaving home and fold it neatly into a flat rectangle that can easily fit between the pages of your journal or address book. Then rip off palm-sized pieces in which to wrap each used film roll before putting it into its little black plastic canister. The question is where to send it: to your family for (hopefully free) development, or an online photo developing service that will put your pics on the Web before sending the negatives and prints home to your family (see p.222). Once online, you can access and caption your pics from the road. Carrying your film around puts it at risk – either through getting stolen, damaged or dragged through the airport X-ray machine a few too many times (see p.224 for more on film at airport).

Receiving mail and packages

If you're organized enough to make an itinerary, you could send it off to your friends and relatives with a note trying to encourage some letter writing. Mail and packages can be sent to you marked with the city, country, and the words "Poste Restante, Central Post Office". If you have an American Express Card or at least one AmEx travellers' cheque, you can pick up your mail at their global offices found in nearly every major city, though it's better to shoot the individual office an email before you get sent anything of real value, as some don't have space for packages or have specific guidelines for handling them. Addresses can be found on the Web at ⓦwww.americanexpress.com. Note that most AmEx offices do not accept parcels, just letters. If you don't have an AmEx card or travellers' cheques, and don't trust the main post office with a valuable delivery, you could, for a small fee (or perhaps nothing, if you find a kind clerk) make a delivery arrangement at a top-end hotel.

Forwarded mail

Check with your national mail carrier to see if your post can be forwarded for free or an additional charge. In Australia, a year of forwarded mail costs AUS$66 (not sent internationally) and mail holding rates are AUS$9 for the first week and AUS$4 for each additional week (www.auspost.com.au). Canada Post offers international redirection for CAN$54 for three months and CAN$18 per month thereafter. Holding mail services cost CAN$6 for the first ten business days and CAN$3 per additional week (www.canadapost.ca). New Zealand Post (www.nzpost.co.nz) will hold mail for an unspecified period of time at no cost. The Royal Mail (www.royalmail.com) charges £13.15 for one month, £28.60 for three months, and £44.05 for six months if you know where you'll be. The catch is that you have to stay in one place for at least a month. For up to two months, they'll hold your mail for £15.75. In the US, they'll only hold your mail for up to thirty days, but won't charge for it (www.usps.com). Best, of course, is if you can have a friend or relative filter out the junk mail and send it along.

Keeping up with current events

When you're in travel mode, current events can feel as distant as some of the relatives you've been meeting. Shelling out for a newspaper at newsstand prices seems like beer and museum money put to bad use. Some distance can be wonderful, but keeping an eye on things can also keep you safe. You don't want to unwittingly walk into a strike (which, in France or Italy, is a monthly occurrence). Don't neglect the local press, provided you can read the language; besides, there's often an English edition. These are usually the cheapest newspapers and magazines and the ones most likely to tell you about local security issues as well as events, shopping sales and performances you may not want to miss. For a taste of home, you'll be able to find most major international newspapers in big cities. They're expensive, but sometimes provided for free in nice hotel lobbies. And there's always the Internet. Check out your home-town paper on the Web from time to time; there are usually things going on that your family and friends forget to tell you about.

14

Security

E urope is, for the most part, no more dangerous than your local health food store. However, though violent crime is rare, Europe is hardly devoid of thieves. Your rental car and pockets are at risk virtually everywhere if you're not on your toes. To find out how to avoid becoming a victim, read on.

Is my destination safe?

If there's no G8 or World Bank summit in town, your first guess can be "yes". Europe is wonderfully low on homicidal maniacs and civil wars. Nearly all the major guides have good security information, but even recently updated ones can't stay up to the minute with security issues. So get the official position of state departments; just keep in mind that a country can be very safe but for a single border dispute or town. Consider London, for example. There are places you wouldn't want to wander in at night, but that doesn't mean the entire city or country should be put on a warning list. The UK Foreign Office website (✪www.fco.gov.uk) is more likely than others to specify the volatile area when they place an entire country on warning; cross-check with Canada's Consular Affairs Department (✪www.voyage.gc.ca), Australia's Department of Foreign Affairs (✪www.dfat.gov.au) or the US State Department (✪http://travel.state.gov).

If you're still uncertain, surf the Web for tourist bureaus (ⓦwww .towd.com). You can almost always find an email address of a specific office within that country. The people who staff the counters meet travellers all day and generally have a good feel for travel conditions. Tell them your nationality, when you're planning to travel and rough-ly where you hope to go. Ask if there are any security issues you should be concerned about. Lastly, check with other travellers. Visit Internet chat sites so you can hear directly from travellers who've been there in recent weeks, or are still in the country: try the Rough Guides message board, Travel Talk (ⓦhttp://roughguides .atinfopop .com); Let's Go's Forum (ⓦwww .letsgo.com/forums); or Lonely Planet's Thorn Tree (ⓦhttp: //thorntree.lonelyplanet.com).

If the political conditions take a turn for the worse, you probably

Stay alert

I've never had anything stolen in a war zone, but my track record isn't nearly as impressive in developed countries. You're on vacation, your guard is down, and you're thinking, "Hey, I'm a tourist, there's a cop, nothing to worry about." That's when I always get nailed. Heading for a tour of the Vatican, I parked and locked all my possessions in the trunk of my rental car. When I returned, everything was gone except a few rolls of film on the trunk floor.

You have to remember that just like everyone else in civilized countries, Europe's criminals go to work everyday. They feast off the herds of roaming tourists, showing up in droves at the same place and same time every year. The crooks get away with it because they use kids for the theft, and keep it mostly nonviolent – so as far as the police are concerned, it's a catch and release sport.

Robert Young Pelton,
Author, *The World's Most Dangerous Places*
ⓦwww.comebackalive.com

don't want to stick around, no matter how exciting it may seem. And if you're American you probably don't want to go to the US embassy either (often a prime target, so they shut their doors when the going gets rough). The Australian embassy, Canadian embassy, New Zealand embassy, UK embassy and others should be fine – even for American citizens. The other option is to get out of town immediately (it's rarely a country-wide riot). If you hadn't picked up some discreet local clothes yet, now would be the time. Keep an eye on the local news, and head to an Internet café, if necessary, to find English updates.

How to avoid being robbed

The trick here is to blend in, keep out of areas where you're likely to become a target, stay alert, carry your valuables securely and provide yourself with a quick exit when you need one.

- Start by removing all jewellery (if necessary, covering a fancy engagement ring with a band-aid or tape). Wear a cheap digital watch or no watch at all. Keep your camera well hidden and pick clothing that won't make you stand out. Earth tones and reserved patterns generally do the trick.
- Show that you don't have much to steal – or that you have less than other potential targets. With just a backpack and no carry-on bag, you have both your hands free and can remain mobile for a quick getaway or to give pursuit, so robbing you looks like more of a challenge. The small padlocks and wire-mesh pack-covers will do little to protect your pack, but they will draw attention to the value of its contents.
- Be on high alert on subways and city buses, as well as in flea markets and train stations.
- On overnight trains, use your pack as a pillow or bear-hug it while you sleep. It's not enough to put your pack up on the luggage rack overhead or beneath your seat, where any thief could get to it without waking you.
- In restaurants, get in the habit of avoiding the tables near doors or bordering sidewalks in cafés. A quick thief can grab your gear and run. Keep your bag under your table while you eat, with the strap around your leg. If you need to use the restroom, take your bag along. You can't expect another diner to guard your bag as closely as you do.

Packing for safety

Don't keep your money and passport in a handbag or daypack. Use a secure travel pouch. A money belt (see p.139) kept under the waistline of your trousers is quite effective, and similar pouches that hang around your neck (under the shirt) or fasten to your ankle are also available. Just make sure you don't access it in busy areas like train stations and markets. Walk over to a quieter spot (if you have a travel companion, you can make a privacy shield if you stand between them and a wall so that your actions are hidden).

Even with your funds in a travel pouch, you might consider using a fake wallet; that is, a cheap wallet with some old cards and some pocket change in it. This can prevent a pickpocket from getting at your real valuables and provide you with something to hand over should you ever come face to face with a mugger.

To protect your slightly-less-valuables, wear your backpack on your front in crowded places and don't use a backpack for a day bag. Because it's inconvenient to wear a day backpack on your front all day for city exploration, use a shoulder bag and keep it tucked tighter under your arm in crowded places. Try to find a model with Velcro flaps, which are difficult to open without you noticing, or a double-entry system (eg a zipper plus a clasp). "Bum bags" (waist packs) are thief magnets and as such are best avoided – at least refrain from keeping your valuables there.

And finally, don't keep all your money in one place. Stash some emergency funds (€50–100) in the secret compartment of a belt, or tape some (in a small plastic bag) to the inside of your backpack.

Avoiding dangerous areas

Just because Europe is a safe continent doesn't mean every street is safe 24 hours a day. Often, 100m can be the difference between a completely safe street and a dangerous one. And these boundaries may change after dark. Ask your hotel clerk or tourist office staff to mark any dangerous areas on your map (both day and night). Be particularly aware after dark. Muggers can easily hide in doorways, so the closer you are to the street, the less chance they have to surprise you. If you spot one or more suspicious characters in a doorway up ahead, cross the street. Or hop in a taxi, if you've got a bad feeling about the area. Trust your instincts and always keep enough change ready to pay for a short cab ride. For less than €4, you can quickly get yourself back to a safer area. Otherwise, walk with confidence. When you're in an area you're not sure of, resist the temptation to pull out your map on a street corner. Keep up a brisk pace and duck inside a coffee shop or store to study the map or ask directions.

Accommodation safety

It's not just local thieves – travellers steal as well. Sad, but true. There's little threat to your dirty laundry, but your valuables still need to be guarded. And travellers know the value of a brand-name Gore-Tex jacket no matter how crumpled it may look. At night, cameras and such are better left at the reception desk in a safe, in a hostel locker, or behind the counter if there's someone keeping an eye on it. If you can tuck it away deep under your bunk bed without anyone noticing, that's often good enough. Some places also offer the reception safe to travellers who need a place to keep their money belt while at the beach – which is better than taking it along. Otherwise, treat your money belt like your spleen: wear it to bed (or put it in your pillowcase) and take it along when you shower – you can hang the pouch on the hook, just under your towel *inside* the shower stall.

Some hotels require your passport for a few hours to gather information. They should not require it any longer than that. Ask for it back as soon as they're done.

If you're particularly concerned about safety while you sleep, request a room that's not on the ground floor or on the roof, where burglars have easiest access. And don't book a room higher than the seventh floor – the highest ladders on fire trucks stop about there.

Rental car safety

Rental cars are popular targets for thieves, especially at night. There are a few things you can do to make yours less appealing to them. Start by taking the rental sticker off. That's like putting up a neon welcome sign, and thieves may cross the parking lot just to check it out. Take off the face of the radio (most have this feature) and store it out of sight. Empty the car of virtually everything. Leave the glove compartment open so they can see there's nothing in it and, if there's some sort of screen in the back of a hatchback/wagon, leave that open so they can see the car is empty. If you must leave items in it during the daytime, put them in the boot (trunk). And always ask your hotel receptionist for a safe place to park.

If you have everything stolen

Even if you do lose the lot, it's not the end of the world and you shouldn't let it ruin your trip. It's happened to enough people that a system is largely in place, so it's not the hassle it used to be. You could very well have everything you need – credit cards, passport and cash – in one to ten days. But act immediately to get the process started. Your first job is to file a police report. Go to the nearest police station, report the robbery and ask for a numbered copy of the police report. Presenting this at your embassy will expedite the issuance of a new passport. Your insurance company will also want a copy.

You may be waiting a while at the police station for the forms to be processed, so use this time to make phone calls. Try a guide-book, local operator or take a peek at the back page of the *International Herald Tribune* for collect-call numbers. Start with a collect call to your travel insurance company (assuming you have one). A good insurer takes collect calls and keeps you on the line while they cancel your credit cards and have new ones issued. Otherwise, you'll have to cancel them yourself by phone or email. If your insurance or credit card provider doesn't supply emergency cash, Western Union (www.westernunion.com) or Money Gram (www.moneygram.com) can assist, as long as you have someone at the other end put money in. Expect to pay a fee of four to seven percent, depending on location, so sending €1000 will cost around €50.

If you're not going to have copies of your documents stored in an ekit online vault (see p.171), you should scan and leave copies of your credit cards, passport, tickets, ID cards, a list of the contents of your backpack with photos of any expensive items (camera, laptop, tent) and insurance papers with your parents and/or trusted friends. Give it to them in a FedEx envelope that can be dropped in the mail in an instant or on a disk that can be emailed. Sending docu-ments by email is not secure, but if you decide to do it give the attached file a vague name (eg "travel stuff"). Do not label it "Visa card" or "Passport number" or include any of that info within the email. At the very least work out a private code on the phone for a special "dingbat" font or number system.

Then call your embassy, tell them what happened and that you'll be on your way over as soon as you get the report. Ask for an appointment or a specific name you can request at the gate to help bypass any queue. If you can, try to get a few passport pho-tos before you show up at the embassy.

If you have no copies of your documents or any cash, throw yourself at the mercy of your embassy. If you're travelling with another citizen from your country with a valid passport, have them come along and vouch for you. And have your friends or parents fax any documents they have (old photo ID, pictures, birth certificate, etc) directly to the embassy.

How to avoid sexual harassment

Most harassers are trigged by appearance, so let's start there. Women travelling alone, especially in southern Europe, should dress conservatively. Even if your clothes aren't racy by your own standards, they might send out the wrong signals. Shorts, short skirts, tank tops and tight-fitting clothes are popular in Europe, as elsewhere. But to avoid getting the attention of the wrong sort of admirer, try to find a modest alternative.

To help fend off would-be suitors, you can always pick up a cheap, simple ring when you arrive. You'll need a story to go with it – something about your husband coming to meet you in a day or two. Talk of children can also be off-putting.

That should take care of much of the harassment, but don't be too surprised by the occasional rude remark, catcall or quick pinch in a crowded public place. Do your best to ignore them and keep walking. Or, alternatively, react with clarity and confidence and tell them you don't like it. If you get followed, head into a nearby busy shop and tell the owner.

If you're alone and see a crowded or well-lit area in sight, consider running (but make sure you have shoes that allow you to run). If the harasser chases or grabs you, scream for help. This is, in fact, how most women escape rape. Pleading and stalling are not very effective. Kick in the knees or privates and don't think twice about jabbing him in the eyes. Feel free to use any objects nearby to aid your fight: pen, car antenna, rock or camera.

How to avoid scams

The best trick, really, is just to learn some of the most common scams. Con artists are hatching new plans all the time, but they tend to be slightly mutated versions of the ones you'll read about here.

For information on hitchhiking safety, see box on p.48.

Keep your guard up, but not too high. Not all foreigners are out to scam you. Many of their gestures, although odd, are genuine acts of hospitality that you wouldn't likely experience at home. You'll have to learn to trust your instincts.

Cardboard scam

You're walking from one ancient architectural treasure to the next in Rome when a group of kids approach you, one carrying a big piece of cardboard. The seemingly innocent kids in rag torn clothes swarm around you while one holds the piece of card-board to your chest much like you might hold a map. While you're trying to give them a few coins, explain you don't under-stand, or even back away, the other kids have picked your pock-ets. Some aren't even subtle about it, but what are you going to do: push or kick a small child?

How to beat it: when you see them coming, keep a firm hand on your belongings and head quickly in another direction. Throw in a firm "Go away!" if they start to follow.

Local "assistance"

Having trouble with a subway ticket machine, train station locker or ATM? If someone starts offering help before you've had any problems, beware. They get a free look into your wallet or chance to guide you to a locker that they have rigged.

How to beat it: thank them, but refuse help. Look around for someone to ask; chances are you'll find a good Samaritan happy to help within a few seconds.

Credit card scam

A store owner takes your credit card to a back room to swipe it, then swipes it again for another price. You sign one, then he forges your signature on the other.

How to beat it: keep a close eye on your credit card and ask the person to run it through the machine in front of you. Take a busi-ness card from the shop when you make any purchases so you can better alert the credit card company in case you later learn you were robbed.

"Drug-buy" scam

Especially common for those heading over to Morocco for a quick visit: you buy a small amount of hashish from a local dealer, then he tips off his buddy, the police officer, who comes knocking at your door to demand a fee for not taking you to prison.

How to beat it: it's a dangerous game of chicken. You can pay the fine, try to bargain a little, or call their bluff and tell them you have no money, you were set up and that you're happy to go to police headquarters and explain it. Best just to avoid buying the drugs in the first place.

Taxi dash scam

You've paid your taxi and the driver leaves before you can get your bag out of the trunk.

How to beat it: leave your door open or don't pay up until you've got your bag.

"Fake travel agent" scam

You buy a ticket from a travel agency you found on the Web in your own country or even in Europe (most likely in London). The ticket never arrives, and when you try to call you find out the place has gone out of business.

How to beat it: make sure you're signing up with an accredited agency. In Australia, check with the Australian Federation of Travel Agents (⊛www.afta.com.au); in Canada, the Association of Canadian Travel Agencies (⊛www.acta.net); in the UK, the Association of British Travel Agents (⊛www.abta.com); and in the US, the American Society of Travel Agents (⊛www.astanet.com). And pay with a credit card so you can stop payment, if necessary.

Help from your embassy or consulate

If you think of your government's embassies, consulates and high commissions as a safety net, you're liable to slip through one of the holes. They can't do much if you've been arrested for violating local laws, and they won't help send you home or give you a place to sleep if you run out of money. They can, however, help you in the event of a lost or stolen passport. They can also provide contact information during emergencies; give you the latest travel advice; allow you to register your travel plans if you're heading into areas for risky adventures (don't forget to check back in); and assist with overseas marriage and birth documents. And most of them make excellent cocktails, should you manage to attend one of their functions – consider swinging by if you're in the neighbourhood during a national holiday.

15

Health

urope is hardly a Petri dish of virulent microkillers waiting to pounce on unsuspecting travellers. In fact, many of the vaccinations and precautions recommended below are also recommended to European travellers heading to your country. The things you should concern yourself with are actually quite basic: get your pre-trip health details in order before you leave (including any necessary immunizations); take some fundamental precautions; keep an eye out for some specific symptoms, and get yourself to a doctor if you encounter any of them. Despite the tales you may have heard, many of the common illnesses are avoidable or easily curable with some of the basic information you'll find in this chapter. If you want more details, there's always *The Rough Guide to Travel Health*.

Health warnings for Europe

According to the Centers for Disease Control and Prevention (CDC), diarrhoea is the top illness among travellers in Europe and motor vehicle crashes the leading cause of injury. There's risk of salmonella, cholera (in Eastern Europe only, and only where there are public warnings), hepatitis, *E. Coli*-associated diarrhoea, tick-borne encephalitis (certain areas) and Lyme disease (certain areas). Read on to see which vaccinations you need.

Pre-departure checkup

Far too many travellers neglect basic pre-trip medical arrangements and suffer needlessly as a consequence. Your first order of business is a checkup. Don't make the common mistake of putting this off till the last minute. A month or two before departure is a more sensible time to schedule an appointment (though some vaccinations require more time before they start working). If the doctor finds something during the checkup and wants you to come back for a second consultation, your next-day flight is buggered. Besides, you'll want to get your checkup before you start getting your vaccinations. Some vaccinations should not be given if you have so much as a cold, or if you're taking other medications. Make sure to ask for a copy of your clean bill of health to take along so you don't have to pay for one again if you end up working or volunteering for an organization that requires one.

Schedule a visit to the dentist as well. It would be a serious setback to get a gnawing tooth problem while you're in a country like Romania or Turkey, which are not exactly world-renowned epicentres of dentistry. Needless to say, getting this taken care of beforehand is a lot cheaper than flying home to do it.

If you wear glasses or contacts, you'll want to swing by the optician. Make sure you have enough contacts and fluid to keep you going (you can always send some lenses ahead as well). Glasses are important backups, even if you never wear them at home – you may find yourself in dusty environments where contacts don't function well. If you're trying to decide between two frames for your glasses, take the most durable, even if they're not the most flattering. Make sure you bring along a copy of your prescription and your optician's telephone number in case you need emergency replacements on the road or ordered from home.

Vaccinations

Once you decide the jabs you want (visit the CDC's website, ⓦwww.cdc.gov, for updated info), call around to make sure you get a good price. A full course of shots might set you back €165 in the US. If your country has a national health plan, a number of the shots (eg hepatitis A and polio) may fall under that policy and can be received free from your GP.

Confirm the information you get from the CDC with the doctor or clinic administering the shots, and be sure to inform them of any medical conditions (even allergies) and medications (including the contraceptive pill) you're taking. Also, explain where you'll be staying and how long you'll be there.

Some vaccinations require a course of shots over six months to take effect, so don't leave it until the last minute, or even the last month. If you're getting several jabs, bear in mind that you may not be able to get them all on the same day. They may conflict with one another, require more than one injection or take time to become effective. However, if you're not entirely sure where you're headed, you don't need to get every needle in the cabinet. Vaccinations are all available on the road. Just make sure the clinic looks clean and professionally run, and that it uses sterile needles. If you have the option, try to get this taken care of in more developed countries.

Get a vaccination record card and keep it with your passport while travelling. It's nice to have it to hand. With all these mega-syllabic names, it's hard to remember what you got, what you didn't want to get but got anyway, and what you were going to get but decided not to get at the last moment.

Update your basic vaccinations

Start by dusting off your medical records to see which boosters you're going to need.

Diphtheria

You'll definitely want to make sure you're vaccinated against this bacterial illness. It's passed person to person quicker than an email chain letter, and typical unpleasantness includes fever, chills and a sore throat. Eventually, it can cause heart failure and paralysis. Be aware that if someone you know has it, they're highly infectious for ten days. Seek medical help if you suspect it; a quick throat swab can determine if you've got it or not.

Tetanus

You've probably been vaccinated against this already. However, you may be due for your ten-year update. Check your records to be sure the booster is taken care of. With tetanus, spores enter the body through open wounds as small as a pinprick, and can be picked up through contact with dirt, manure and – the classic – rusty nails. You won't get the symptoms for five to twenty days, but the one that should get your attention (and any doctor's) are spasms of the jaw muscle. Those will spread across your face and into your torso, and that's when things get really nasty. It is potentially fatal, so if you recognize these symptoms yourself, get thee to a hospital immediately.

Other possible vaccinations

Cholera

Only found in parts of eastern Europe during outbreaks, this particularly unpleasant diarrhoeal disease is caused by consumption of contaminated water or shellfish. When you hear warnings about it (it seems to follow natural disasters and wars), avoid the area if possible and be very careful what you eat (no ice, only bottled water; no raw food unless peeled). There's no vaccination recommended by the CDC for this, but two relatively new oral vaccines (Dukoral and Mutacol) have proven effective (85–90 percent immunity within six months of taking the vaccination, decreasing to 62 percent immunity after three years) and should be considered if you're heading to areas where outbreaks are occurring. Because the vaccine is new, it may not be available everywhere.

Hepatitis A

This is one I'd get. It'll come in handy if you're plannning on eating seafood (particularly shellfish) in southern Europe, where high

What if I don't get any shots?

No one says you have to. You'll still get into Europe just as immuno-under-equipped as you are now. And you'll most likely do just fine. European travellers don't always follow the advice of getting a Hep A shot when going to the US (or bringing a bulletproof vest) and still make it home alive. The idea is that a little inconvenience now will help prevent a major hassle later. It's like giving your car a tune-up, oil change and new air filter before a big road trip. Only, when it's your motor that's at risk, and not the car's, the stakes are substantially higher.

temperatures and dodgy refrigeration can provide ideal breeding grounds for the disease. Contaminated water and people (who don't wash their hands well) also pass this bowel blaster along. Good news: there's a vaccination. One poke with a Havrix vaccine will last a year. Follow it up with a second injection six to twelve months later and you're good to go for a decade. The downside is it takes nearly a month after the first dose to take effect. The more traditional gamma globulin shot works right away, and provides protection for three to six months. In the UK, a Hep A and Hep B combination, which will also give you ten years of immunity, is available free from GPs, but you'll need half a year to get all three shots taken care of. Or ask your doctor about Hepatyrix, fifteen-year protection against Hep A and typhoid in one stab.

Vaccination roundup

Cholera

Full course Two oral doses

Booster One week apart ("killed vaccine") or one single oral dose ("live vaccine")

Comments Eighty-five to ninety percent protection for six months after two doses of killed vaccine; 62 percent after three years. Considered for people going to endemic areas. Should be taken at least three weeks (one week for live vaccine) before departure. Avoid antibiotics and malaria prophylaxis with proguanil one week before and one week after cholera vaccine

Time before effective immunity One week after final dose

Hepatitis A

Full course Single dose

Booster After 6–12 months

Comments Gives good protection for at least twelve months; booster protection lasts more than ten years

Time before effective immunity One month

Hepatitis A (immunoglobin type)

Full course Single dose

Booster Only gives protection for 2–6 months, depending on dose

Comments Needs to be given close to departure

Time before effective immunity Immediately

Hepatitis B (optional)

Full course Two doses one month apart, plus a third dose six months later

Booster Provides protection for at least ten years; booster dose is not recommended for adults with intact immune system

Hepatitis B

This vaccine is recommended for heath care professionals, but it's transmitted through sexual contact and needles, so if you're planning on some heavy romance or heavy knitting (in the vicinity of drug users), it's probably worth the extra jab. Even if you're just considering a tattoo, it's not a bad idea. The vaccination is a bit of a drag – three jabs over seven months – but well worth it for a long trip. For those who put it off to the last second, it's possible to get three jabs in three weeks with an additional booster, but this is slightly less effective. As previously noted, in the UK there's a Hep A and Hep B combination jab, which will also give you ten years of immunity, available free from GPs.

Comments More rapid three-week courses are available if you're close to departure, but this gives lower immunity and requires a booster after twelve months

Time before effective immunity One month after final dose

Rabies (optional)

Full course Three doses over one month

Booster After 2–3 years

Comments Pre-exposure immunization gives greater protection but does not eliminate the need for prompt treatment if bitten by a rabid animal

Time before effective immunity Two weeks after completed course

Tetanus

Full course Three doses: four to eight weeks between first and second doses; third dose six to twelve months after second. Usually given with diphtheria

Booster Every ten years

Comments Full course usually given in childhood. If pressed for time before departure, only first and second dose can be given

Time before effective immunity A few days after third – or second, if only two can be given – dose

Tick-borne encephalitis

Full course Two doses over a month

Booster After 1–3 years

Comments Fever a common side effect after first dose. Not needed for children under 7. Get in Europe once you arrive, if necessary.

Time before effective immunity Ten days after final dose

Rabies

The CDC recommends this one, but a lot of people survive in Europe without it. If you steer clear of packs of wild dogs in İstanbul and strays in rural areas, you'll probably be fine. Always enquire about a dog's biting habits before petting – it's cheaper than getting the vaccine (three shots over a month, plus another two if bitten, scratched or even licked by a rabid animal), but possibly not as effective. Without the vaccine, you're looking at nearly twice as many shots – although no longer the nasty ones in the stomach. If you have an encounter with an animal that puts you at risk, get tested immediately.

Tick-borne encephalitis

This viral infection of the central nervous system comes from tick bites and is untreatable. The CDC says it exists in Central and Western Europe, but that doesn't mean it's everywhere. For example, if you're going to Stockholm, you're not at risk. But if you're planning a kayaking trip down the east coast of Sweden, where you'll be camping in the forest, you are. Some Stockholmers who live in these tick-infested areas in the woods get the vaccination. Others chance it. Taking away the tick doesn't work – if you find one, you may be too late. But just one tick bite is very unlikely to bring on the virus, and only one in 250 who get infected develop the symptoms. For those who do, it starts out like a flu, and then causes dizziness, tremors and paralysis. The risk is seasonal, occurring when ticks are out and about: May to September. At the time of writing, the vaccine can easily be obtained in Europe if you have trouble locating it in your country.

What you can't get vaccinated against

These are the ones you'll have to watch out for, and may just get anyway. Some maladies are more common than others and some

---

Where **medications** are listed, you'll only find the generic medical name. These are known by various commercial names in different countries. Simply check the label or consult your pharmacist or doctor.

more severe, so read through the descriptions to get acquainted with the symptoms and dangers you may face.

AIDS/HIV

You've probably heard an earful about this already, but it can be caught in Europe as well – something to consider before you have unprotected sex or share a needle.

Travelling with AIDS/HIV

If you have special health considerations that render you immuno-compromised, keep in mind that the bacteria and bugs that affect all travellers may have a more profound effect on you. Less developed countries in particular pose significant risks for exposure to opportunistic pathogens. Your consulate or the International Association of Medical Assistance to Travellers (🌐 www.iamat.org) can provide trained English-speaking physicians in Europe.

Vaccinations

The CDC currently recommends that "killed vaccines" such as diphtheria, tetanus and hepatitis A are OK for "healthy" HIV-infected travellers. However, the degree of immunity after a vaccination may vary with the degree of immunodeficiency caused by the HIV. For more information, visit 🌐 www.cdc.gov.

Medications

Discussing an emergency plan with your doctor prior to departure is an excellent idea. The CDC advises all HIV-infected travellers heading to Bulgaria, Romania and Turkey to bring an antimicrobial such as ciprofloxacin (500mg twice a day for three to seven days) for empirical therapy for diarrhoea, although alternatives (such as TMP-SMX) should be discussed with a doctor. If the diarrhoea does not respond to this treatment, there is blood in the stools, fever and shaking chills, or dehydration, get to a doctor.

Going through customs

If you are carrying a full array of HIV drugs, or just the virus, be aware that some European countries have vague restrictions preventing those with "communicable diseases" from entering. So, faced with an inquisitive customs officer holding your medications, you might offer other half-truths about the things you're suffering from first (such as liver/heart/kidney problems), and delay mentioning HIV. If you're staying for an extended period to work or study, you may face a serological screen in many countries. Check out the unofficial list compiled by the US State Department at 🌐 www.travel.state.gov/travel/HIVtestingreqs.html.

Allergies

If you experience allergies at home, you'll probably encounter them on the road. Watery eyes, a runny nose, sneezing... you know how it goes. Pack an antihistamine (chlorpheniramine or loratadine) to relieve the symptoms. If these don't help, visit a doctor.

Altitude sickness

This is more dangerous than most people believe, especially when those who don't have it are egging you on to keep going up. "High altitude" is considered 2438–3658m; "very high altitude" is 3658–5487m. If your head feels like it's about to implode or you're dizzier than a wino trapped on a Ferris wheel, then head down the mountain. It doesn't mean making a beeline for the bottom (unless it has reached a critical stage). Usually, the symptoms will abate after just a little descent, and you may even be able to continue once your body has adjusted at its own pace.

Fitness is only one factor: you could be a champion triathlete or an Olympian on performance-enhancing drugs and still get a case of altitude sickness worse than the couch potato with a liver condition hiking beside you. Follow a careful acclimatization plan and, most importantly, listen to your body. If you want to try a short cut, the drugs acetazolamide and nifedipine have been known to help combat the sickness.

Bed bugs

These aren't merely bedtime-story myths. They're out there, typically in the cheapest hotels, and they do bite. The bites aren't serious, but they seriously itch. And you'd have a better chance spotting Elvis than some of these critters. Your best defence is a good sleepsheet: make sure it's big enough to cover the pillow as well. A tight weave should keep most of them out. The bites look like two or three little red dots in a row. Treat with hydrocortisone or antihistamine cream and – easier said than done – refrain from scratching.

For a list of basic medical supplies you should take with you, see p.134.

Cold sores

Don't kiss people with lip sores or blisters. Don't share water bottles with them either. There's really nothing cold about these sores, which are actually herpes picked up by oral contact (fellatio and cunnilingus included). If you get one, you've got a recurring menace for life, often triggered by too much direct sunlight. To keep the sores at bay, keep your lips well glossed while exposed to the sun and apply aciclovir cream (may require prescription) as soon as you feel the tingling sensation coming on (apply five times a day for five days). Once the sore breaks open, the medicine won't help.

Constipation

Travellers get all worked up over diarrhoea, but forget about an opposite ailment that is nearly as uncomfortable and troublesome. Travellers who are new to the trail and spending time in Eastern and southeastern Europe are especially susceptible. They take one look at a squat toilet (or even an unsanitary Western version) and suddenly they don't need to go any more. A few days later, the mental block has become an intestinal one. This can be solved by simply carrying some laxatives (such as senna) and not waiting too long to use them. Better yet, force yourself to go when you have the urge, no matter what the loo looks like. And a little diet altering won't hurt: more fruit, bran and fluids.

Dehydration

The trick here is to drink before you get thirsty. For a full day of walking in, say, Rome, you should be drinking about four litres of water. In the Alps, you'll need even more, and wind masks the amount you're sweating away. Once you're dehydrated, you'll experience a dry mouth, dark urine, headache and, in extreme cases, fainting. Find some shade, take it easy and mix your water with a rehydration solution so you get your salt balance back, and if fluid can't be taken orally get to a hospital for an IV.

Diarrhoea

The good news is that it's most often extremely treatable and the troublesome symptoms can be cured in less than a day. The following advice may save you a week of traumatic toilet dashes and, as such, this book will have paid for itself a few times over. You'll meet numerous travellers suffering from diarrhoea for days or weeks. The typical reason is that they're trying to ride it out. You want to do exactly the opposite.

The moment you start to "go liquid", drink a bottle of water mixed with a packet of rehydration mix that you should be carrying in your first-aid kit. And keep drinking. The biggest danger with diarrhoea is dehydration. The next biggest risk is that you sit by the toilet for days waiting for the diarrhoea to abate. As soon as possible, bring a little plastic film canister (or something similar) and put a stool sample in it. Either take the sample to a nearby clinic yourself or have a trusted fellow traveller do it for you if you can't risk leaving a toilet for that long. With a quick look under the microscope, a doctor will most often be able to identify the cause. If so, they'll write a prescription on the spot, which will likely include the pharmaceutical equivalent of a cork. Less than a day after you start taking the medicine, you may feel back to normal, or at least better. While recovering, stick to simple, unspiced foods like rice for a day or two just in case. Little tip: carry an antidiarrhoea pill (such as Loperamide) in your money belt. If you're

△ Most health concerns will be sorted with a trip to the local chemists

on a long bus ride with your pack in the baggage bin underneath or you're walking around town, it will come in handy more than you can imagine. Women travellers should be aware that diarrhoea can reduce the effectiveness of the contraceptive pill.

E. Coli diarrhoea

You may hear this name tossed about. It also goes by its given name of *Escherichia coli*, and it is about the most common type of diarrhoea, though it comes in several different strains. It's about as nice to contract as it is to spell. Often picked up from eating undercooked, contaminated ground beef, it can also be passed from person to person. Drinking raw milk and swimming in or drinking sewage-contaminated water may also do the trick. The infection makes itself know with bloody diarrhoea. Hang out with people who wash their hands carefully.

Hepatitis C

Less common than Hep A and Hep B (but with no vaccination), to catch this one requires contact with contaminated blood, which means stay alert where any needles are concerned. It can be spread by sexual activity, but this is rare. Symptoms include dark urine, nausea, jaundice, abdominal pain and loss of appetite.

Hiking blisters

The face of Mont Blanc is not the ideal place to try out a new pair of hiking boots. If you buy or rent some, give yourself at least a day or two for your feet to adjust (especially with new boots). For serious treks, make sure you bring Compeed (a skin-like blister cover), sport tape, Vaseline, or a silicon spray and a needle (with antiseptic to sterilize) to drain blisters. Always make sure to puncture the blister in the centre, not on the sides where the skin is more sensitive. Also, give them as much time to dry out as possible before taping them up again. Some people have success with a needle and thread, leaving the thread in the opening for better drainage. Tape can be applied in advance to trouble spots, then sprayed with silicon. Two pairs of socks are advisable, neither of them cotton. Polypropylene or silk (next to the skin) and wool (or Smartwool) make an excellent combination.

Infected cuts and scrapes

In humid coastal environments, cuts don't tend to heal that fast. They're easily infected and can actually grow in size. So if you pick up some scooter road rash around the Med, head up to the Alps where it can more easily dry and heal. Visit a doctor if you're unable to stop the growth of the wound on your own.

Jet lag

It's a fancy way of saying you spent your flight over watching a B-movie or glued to a John Grisham book instead of getting much-needed sleep. An alarming number of travellers don't take simple steps to combat jet lag, and are then plagued by fatigue for days (typically, one day per time zone), starting off their trip on the wrong foot. If you can sleep on the plane and get a good night's sleep the first night in the new time zone, you're not going to experience much, if any, jet lag. Sleeping on the plane, if you're not naturally gifted at the art, can be achieved with an over-the-counter or prescribed sleeping pill.

According to studies, drinking alcohol is exactly the wrong approach. The next worst thing you can do is stay up late. There's no reason to eat dinner at 11pm, then watch a movie at midnight simply because you're at 30,000ft. Eat a meal in the airport, pop the sleeping pill when the plane leaves the ground and drink plenty of water when you wake up. Then refrain from naps until bedtime (here's a great chance to try some of that strong European coffee) and take another sleeping pill if you wake up during that first night, or pop a Melatonin tablet before bed to ensure you sleep a little longer.

Lyme disease

Ticks carrying the disease are found in the forest, long grass and trees, waiting for a host animal (typically deer, but humans will suffice) to pass by. The ticks need around 24 hours attached to your body to transfer the disease, so, if you give yourself a good check a few times daily, you'll spot them in time. You'll have to check in hard-to-view places, though, including your hair. And the hair on your head as well. If you miss it at the time, then you'll notice a few days or weeks later, when the classic "bull's eye" appears at the bite site. It can affect the nervous system, joints and heart, and can become very serious if not treated (with amoxycillin or doxycycline).

Motion sickness

It's not serious, but it's bad enough to ruin a day or two of your trip. On a winding bus ride, try to sit near the front (although not in the front, where you'd be the first one through the windshield in the event of a crash) and next to a window or air vent. Make sure you get out to stretch your legs whenever the bus stops. On a boat, stay above deck and try looking at the horizon. Take deep, relaxing breaths or simply try to stay busy. And, in any event, have a motion sickness pill or a skin patch (such as Hyoscine or Scopolamin) ready just in case. It takes at least an hour before the effects of these pills are noticeable, so you may need to take them in advance of boarding.

Rashes

You'll be encountering plants, fruits and bugs that your skin has never been exposed to before. It's common for travellers to experience a host of new body art. Try applying topical antihistamine, calamine lotion or steroid creams (hydrocortisone) to the area. If it persists, visit a local doctor.

Salmonella

This is the one most commonly associated with eating undercooked chicken. Or when the cooks forget to wash their hands after a trip to the restroom. The foods get contaminated from animal (or human) faeces. And here's the scary part: you won't be able to smell or taste infected food. Most of those who get salmonella develop diarrhoea, fever and abdominal cramps 12 to 72 hours after infection. That's the bad news. The upside is that most people recover without treatment (four to seven days). However, if the person becomes severely dehydrated (see p.204) or the infection spreads from the intestine, it should be treated promptly with antibiotics (such as ampicillin or gentamicin).

STDs

Just because you're choosy about whom you have sex with, doesn't mean *they* were. And once is all it takes to wake up with syphilis, gonorrhoea, chlamydia, chancroid, trichomoniasis or herpes. Symptoms include: unusual vaginal or penile discharge, pain when passing urine, itching, abnormal vaginal bleeding and genital ulceration. There's only one thing to do if you get any of these: go to a doctor. With chlamydia, it's a little trickier. Most women don't know they have it. Some never find out. Some only learn of it at an infertility clinic while trying to find out why they can't get pregnant. A condom is your best defence.

Sunburn

Sunscreen keeps you from burning, but it also keeps people out in the sun longer with more UV exposure, and the long-term effects of this are yet to be determined. Still, burning is bad. So get in the habit of using SPF 25 sun block and reapplying it frequently. For those on medications, note that some reduce your skin's ability to fend off the sun's powerful rays: ciproloxacin, tetracycline group antibiotics, sulphonylurea (taken for diabetes) and thiazide (taken for high blood pressure).

Vaginal thrush

Warm climates, tight nylon underwear and increased sexual activity are among the factors that lead to a higher incidence of yeast infections on the travel circuit. Men who carry the fungus rarely show any signs of it. For women, soreness, discomfort during sex, pain while urinating, and passing a white or yellowish discharge are among the symptoms. It's easily treated by an antifungal preparation that should be straightforward to find in most countries, but you may want to carry one just in case. In a jam, try applying regular plain yoghurt and altering your diet briefly: no sugars, breads, beer, wine, mushrooms, Vegemite or other yeast-containing or yeast-encouraging foods.

If you do get sick

Here's the basic approach: with a high fever, loose stools or vomiting – anything very painful or unusual – get to a doctor and have blood and/or stool tests conducted. It's generally quick and cheap and far better than trying to ride it out. With a quick diagnosis and the right medicine, you could be feeling fine within a day or so.

This is also a great time to check into a decent hotel with a private toilet and phone. You owe it to yourself and your fellow travellers. Hostel dormitories are not meant as recovering wards (beyond temporary alcohol-related afflictions). When you check in, tell the desk clerk that you're not feeling well and see if they have a doctor who can pay you a visit. You can always ring for an ambulance or taxi if things take a turn for the worse.

If things seem serious, don't take chances. Get yourself to a hospital and contact your family and travel insurance company. If you're in a remote area, get to a major city immediately.

16

Travellers with special considerations

For many, just navigating your way around Europe – or even just one large city – with transport strikes, spaceship-like pay toilets and incomprehensible menus is challenge enough. But there are some groups who must also cope with a number of issues, from a medical condition to sexual-preference discrimination. This chapter focuses on the concerns these travellers face and offers a few tips that will hopefully smooth out their journey.

Senior travellers

Retirement can be a perfect time in your life to travel, and you don't need to be in outstanding physical condition, as long as you plan you trip well and stay prepared. There are a number of speciality items available these days from lightweight canes that can be collapsed and stored in a handbag to inflatable back-support rests – that can make a mild trip comfortable and a rough ride tolerable.

Health

When planning your itinerary, consider the medical facilities of the country you're visiting. The Netherlands or Denmark, for example, will have a more modern health care system than Romania or Estonia.

Consider the temperature of the places you're headed. Even if you've experienced such sweltering heat before, it can be another thing entirely if you're out walking in it most of the day or staying in places without air conditioning. And air conditioning in Europe is less common than it is in the US or Australia.

If you're concerned about pre-existing ailments, discuss them with your doctor before leaving and come up with a game plan if you spot symptoms en route. Depending on your case, it may not be a bad idea to bring a copy of your medical file along, or at least the relevant pages. Check your medical insurance for travel coverage and supplement it with any special travel insurance you may need (see p.113).

Medications

Bring your prescriptions if you want to get refills, but ask your doctor to include the generic name, since some brand-name prescriptions are not available abroad. Keep medicines in their original labelled container to avoid problems at customs and have the prescriptions handy; the label on the plastic bottle is not always enough, especially if you're transporting stronger pain medications, which may require a special permit obtained at the pharmacy. If you need medication refilled in an emergency, a good travel insurance plan will assist. And keep the phone number of your doctor and pharmacist with you for backup.

Security

Europe is a very safe place to travel. Perhaps as safe as or even safer than where you live. However, seniors are especially venerable to theft while travelling. It is perceived that your guard is down more often, you're more likely to be carrying valuables and are less likely to give chase or fight back. To combat this, take special notice of the tips in the "Security" chapter, (see p.184). As always, you can best avoid putting yourself at risk by carrying very little and disguising what you do have. Then take special care when and where you wander. Get good information from the reception clerk on which areas are dangerous and which to avoid after dark.

Discounts

There's enough material to write an entire book on senior discounts. In fact, someone has. Actually, several have. One of the things that seems to get better with age is the number of rebates available. Seniors might get anything up to fifty percent off museums and other sites, and local transport. Look for notices at ticket windows, check your guidebook, and get into the habit of asking.

Flights

On airlines, the magic discount age is usually 60 or 62. Rates vary, but you can typically get ten percent off "the lowest published fare" (and that's exactly how you should phrase it when you ring a travel agent). Not only that, but you're often allowed to bring someone of any age along at the same rate.

Accommodation

There's nothing that says you have to be a youth to stay in a youth hostel. In fact, in many of the calmer hostels, senior travellers far outnumber the youths. International Youth Hostel cards for seniors cost just €12. There are also special organizations, such as the non-profit-making Elderhostel (❿www.elderhostel.org), which run trips around the world for those aged 55 and older. For roughly €40 a day, you get a room, food, educational classes on a variety of subjects and the chance to meet plenty of like-minded, interesting people. Seniors may also be offered ten to fifty percent off normal rates at major hotels (and some minor ones) across Europe. Always enquire when you book.

Travel agents

- **50+ Expeditions** Adventure trips for the over-50 set ready to hit the road. ❿www.50plusexpeditions.com

- **CARP** Not the most inviting acronym, CARP is a travel agency for Canadians over 50. Ⓦwww.50plus.com/travel
- **Saga** Guided tours, cruises and adventure holidays for "today's over 50s". Ⓦwww.saga.co.uk/travel
- **Senior Women's Travel**. They bury the "old lady" image for the 50+ set with a thirst for active travel. Ⓦww.poshnosh.com
- **Wired Seniors**. Under "Travel", they have lists of "senior-friendly" travel agents and hotels. Ⓦww.wiredseniors.com

Travellers with disabilities

If you can get to the store to pick up this book, don't let anybody tell you that you're not physically able to get to Europe. There's going to be more planning than an able-bodied person may face, more hassles, and you may have to give up more independence than you'd prefer at times, but if you're prepared to accept this the rewards are immeasurable.

Some parts of Europe will be better suited to deal with your disability than others. But no matter how much planning you manage, you'll still need to prepare yourself for the unexpected: unstable or missing handrails, faulty ramps, narrow passages, and assigned assistants with little training and even less enthusiasm. Greet them with good humour and look for ways to solve the problems on the spot.

What you can do to prepare

Much depends on your degree of disability, and no one has a better grasp of that than you. Stay in control of your options. An activity that may not be a possibility for someone else could be fine for you. But if a travel agent or tour operator hears that you're disabled first, they may decide which things are appropriate for you and present you with an inappropriately limited selection. In other words, look into things you'd like to do, then ask questions to find out if you can be accommodated. Don't simply look for "disabled activities".

Before you begin your trip, whether you're joining a tour or doing it alone, think about ways to enhance the experience of travel and remove potential obstacles. For example, a deaf person may wish to purchase a rail pass in advance to avoid the hassle of buying individual tickets at a station counter, and a sight-impaired traveller might pick up souvenir replicas of the famous monuments once they arrive to help get a better feel of the structures they're standing in front of. Consider activities that can be done on an equal level. For those in a wheelchair, a cultural show, botanical gardens and recommended restaurant should take minimal preparation beyond confirming that they can accommodate you where stairs and doorways are concerned.

What you'll face

In most European countries, you'll find a mix of excellent accessibility and complete lack of it. However, there should be a fundamental infrastructure in place and your requests for assistance will often find an experienced ear. In less developed countries, expect to find little infrastructure, if any at all. What you may experience, however, is a refreshing abundance of helpers with an enlightened indifference toward disability. On the other hand, you may feel like a novelty act at times. If so, keep in mind that you may be one of the first independent disabled people that locals have seen. And even if it doesn't seem appreciated at the time, the inspiring tale of seeing you will likely find its way to those locals with disabilities who need to hear it most.

Most of Europe's great attractions are accessible to all. A few aren't or are at least extremely difficult for manoeuvring, like the tower of Notre-Dame. At such times, you'll either have to content yourself with a view from afar, have a travelling companion videotape it and replay it on the spot, or find alternative activities.

It's not impossible to find accessible toilets, but it may not be easy everywhere you go. Make sure there's one at your hotel. These websites should prove useful:

- **Mobility International USA** Sponsors international exchange programmes for people with disabilities, and sells books and even a video (All Abroad) to help those with disabilities cope on the road. Ⓦwww.miusa.org.
- **The Society for Accessible Travel and Hospitality** A nonprofit organization with membership and a magazine and special deals for seniors and students. Ⓦwww.sath.org
- **Britain's Royal Association for Disability and Rehabilitation** Publishes a guide for disabled people in Britain and Ireland, with over 1400 places to stay in the UK and Ireland. Ⓦwww.radar.org.uk

Getting around

Around Europe, trains may just be the best of your options. You can see on the Thomas Cook Timetable or on the individual country's rail website (see the country profiles for these) which trains are specially equipped to handle wheelchairs.

Next in this somewhat sorry selection is air travel. The toilets may be impossibly narrow and the seats painfully uncomfortable, but at least it's generally the quickest option. Always call the airline well in advance if you need any special assistance. If you have a wheelchair, let them know which kind and be prepared for a transfer to a special aisle-sized chair. At All Go Here (🅦www.allgohere.com), there's a list of airlines that cater to those with disabilities, with detailed information on what they do.

Taxis are usually the most convenient, most comfortable option for getting around a city, but also the most expensive. In some enlightened cities (Stockholm, for example), there are elevators that take wheelchairs down to the subway at every station and buses that dip down and provide space to roll on.

With assistance, the transport possibilities are as limitless as your imagination. If you need some inspiration, pick up Patrick Simpson's book *Wheelchair Around the World*.

If you're not ready to go it alone, there are tour agencies for the disabled:

- **Accessible Europe** Has a collection of European travel agents and tour operators who specialize in disabled travel. 🅦www.accessibleurope.com.
- **Flying Wheels Travel** Specialize in escorted and disabled tours. 🅦www.flyingwheelstravel.com

Where to stay

Not all hotels and hotels have special facilities, but many do. Often, the local tourist bureau is well versed with this information. Find them at 🅦www.towd.com.

Access-Able (🅦www.access-able.com) has a database of hotels that accommodate those with disabilities, plus listings of places where you can rent special medical equipment and get it repaired.

- **Hostelling International** Has a listing on their website of the hostels that can accommodate disabled guests. Ⓦwww.hiayh.org
- **Independent Living's Accessible Vacation Home Exchange** Website helps those with disabilities swap homes with similarly disabled Europeans. Ⓦwww.independentliving.org/vacaswap.html

Gay travellers

It's certainly much easier now for gay people to travel openly than it was twenty years ago, with scores of guidebooks, travel publications and websites devoted to gay travel. And Europe offers numerous social scenes, if that's what you're looking for.

Europe is about as enlightened as a continent gets, but that doesn't mean that public affection is welcomed in all settings. Holding hands won't land you in jail, but it can do more than turn a few heads. Just make sure you look around and enquire about any potential risks before you make an active protest against an intolerant rural community. If you're not sure, simply avoid public affection, which is often frowned upon no matter who's doing it.

Vegetarian travellers

It's one thing to organize your diet at home, and quite another to maintain your eating habits in a new setting every day. But it can be done. And it doesn't even have to be stressful. Naturally, your chosen destinations are a major factor. Knowing where to look is another. A number of supermarkets, restaurants, resorts and B&Bs around Europe cater specifically to vegetarians.

Scandinavia doesn't offer much of a vegetarian selection outside of major metropolitan areas, but delicious non-meat Italian pastas and pizzas can be easily found, not just in Italy but all across Europe. Salad bars are becoming more and more common; large supermarkets are increasingly well stocked with vegetarian food; and the produce in southern Europe is outstanding (Italian tomatoes alone might convert thousands of meat-eaters).

To pinpoint vegetarian restaurants everywhere you go, check your guidebook. For a more complete listing, you might pick up a book such as *Vegetarian Europe*, which lists three hundred vegetarian and vegan restaurants. Or search the Web for each specific city at ⓦwww.happycow.net, where you can also find some short reviews and helpful translations on how to explain your dietary requirements.

Eating veggie as you travel

Start by booking a vegetarian meal when you arrange your flight, then confirm it when you check your luggage. It's that easy. If you forgot, you can usually request the meal up to 48 hours before departure. Some veggie meals receive better reviews than their carnivore counterparts, while others are dire. See ⓦwww .vegparadise.com/airline.html for airline contact information, and to view the different vegetarian menus.

Trains, ferries and buses have captive audiences, and that doesn't just apply to the music some are fond of pumping at you. Your best shot at feeding yourself a decent vegetarian meal during the trip is if you buy one at a supermarket before boarding. Doing this is also a great money-saver, so you're helping your wallet as much as your digestive tract.

17

Documenting your trip

For many, the time spent travelling will provide some of the most vivid memories of their lives. However, memories fade. Even travelling with your best friend, or an entire overland group, doesn't mean you're going to collectively remember everything. When you're going solo, it's even harder. A journal, camera, tape recorder, video camera, colour pencils, paints and watercolour set are the most common tools for recording your journey and its impact on you. Taking along all these is overkill, but keeping some record of your trip is an excellent idea and will help keep the experience fresh in your mind long after your return.

Keeping a journal

Many travellers say this is the single best thing they brought on their trip (or bought when they arrived – you certainly don't need leather-bound hand-pressed paper from France to record your thoughts, but it makes for a nice souvenir). If you've kept a journal before, you'll be bringing one anyway. If not, this is the perfect time to start. It's not easy to process, or even remember all the places and people and stories, but simply putting your thoughts

down on paper can have a sooth-
ing, therapeutic effect. It can be a
friend when you're alone or provide structure for your day. If you
have some artistic skill, spend a little more and get paper that will
soak up your watercolours or hold
ink better.

Taking photographs

Deciding whether or not you're
going to bring a camera doesn't
usually invoke much of an internal
debate. Which kind, how to use it,

and what to do with your film should. The temptation for many is
to get a "good camera" – that is, one above their level of expertise.
If you're a professional or exceptional amateur, bring what you need.
Just be aware of the security risk of carrying valuable gear. Remove
the brand names from the bags, try to select a case that doesn't look
like a camera case, and minimize your lenses and accessories. If you're
not a pro, go for an inexpensive pocket camera with APS (Advanced
Photo System) or regular film – both types are readily available
around Europe. Because you can keep a pocket camera handy in a
day bag (and if it's really small, even a pocket) and pull it out quickly without attracting much attention, you're much more likely to use
it. And – here's one of the oldest photography tricks in the book –
the more photos you take, the more likely you'll get a great photo. If
you find a good camera deal, fine. If you're not sure, take a look at
the Yashica T4, the tried and trusted pro favourite that has been dis-
continued but can still be found on eBay and at used camera shops
for under €125. A digital camera is also a solid option, but we'll get
to that in a minute. A full-size SLR (single-lens reflex – the traditional large-body type) will have more features than you need and
won't make up for poor photo composition. Plus, they're bulky,
expensive and more likely to get stolen.

The real decision here is between digital and film. And it's a toss-
up. For the budget-conscious, a regular pocket camera may be your

best bet, especially in terms of an upfront investment. These days the quality of a basic €60–175 point-and-shoot is remarkable. Skip the zoom, though. It jacks up the price, runs down the battery, brings down the quality, and is not very powerful on these small cameras. If you take one to three steps forward, you'll get the same effect for free. Plus, if the moving zoom parts get so much as a grain of sand in them, kiss the camera goodbye for a month or two while it gets sent back to the manufacturer.

Digital cameras have the obvious benefits of being able to see the result immediately, skipping the whole developing process. They lack the bulk of SLRs, but the decent ones are nearly as expensive and therefore nearly as likely to get stolen. The older ones eat up AA batteries like a starving sumo wrestler; the newer ones have longer-lasting rechargeables, but require schlepping along a load of extra wires and hardware (some of which are bulkier than others, so ask to see it before buying the camera).

Perhaps the biggest issue, however, is film versus memory cards. Quality is close, but still goes to film, at least for pocket cameras. But dealing with film can be a real pain on trips that run more than a few weeks. If you carry it on too many flights, it's likely to get damaged from all the airport X-rays. Even if you're not taking planes, there's a decent chance those small canisters can get lost or go bad collecting mildew in the bottom of your pack. If you develop film on the road, the prints become heavy to carry and can get ruined. Plus, in remote areas, you may be taking your chances with a local developer who may not have the finest equipment. The best way to handle film is either to avoid it altogether (with a digital camera and memory card) or to mail it to an online developer. They'll place all the photos online, which allows you to access them from the road and create a digital photo album for others to view, send photos as email attachments, or have glossy prints made and sent (along with the developed film) home. If this is what you plan to do, bring along some aluminium foil in which to wrap your film (inside the plastic canister) to protect it from postal X-ray machines. A large sheet of foil can be neatly folded and kept flat between the pages of your journal.

Naturally, memory cards take less space, but the big question is typically cost. Online, you can buy eight rolls of film (192 exposures) for about €12. Online developing costs about €3 per roll. Price for prints (assuming you opt to get 150 of your 192 shots printed) will set you back a further €36. And let's say you send the rolls registered mail in three separate batches to an online developer back home: that's €12 for postage. Total cost: €84. So, if you're starting from scratch, the film option will cost about €170 (including a €83 camera). Those who are worried about sending film home could take the extra precaution of having it developed at a professional outfit in Europe, then scanning the best ones and emailing them before sending the prints and negatives home. Or you could use a private courier company (DHL, FedEx, etc). Both of these measures will jack up the expense, but even with pricey developing and shipping costs, you won't be entering the digital price range.

With a digital camera, you'll want to use high resolution for all your photos in case you snap a winner you want to print and enlarge. If you have, say, a 4-megapixel camera on the highest-quality setting, you should be able to get about 200 images on a 1GB card (€165) and 100 on a 512MB card (€83); you can get smaller cards, but that's a lot of swapping in and out, and they're easy to misplace. Of course, you'll be able to use these cards for ages, so if you already have them or plan to use them extensively after returning, it's a good investment.

You might consider uploading them to an online developer such as ⓦwww.ofoto.com, ⓦwww.snapfish.com or ⓦwww.shutterfly .com (UK ⓦwww.kodak.co.uk; NZ ⓦwww.extrafilm.co.nz; Australia ⓦwww.extrafilm.com.au, ⓦwww.fujicolor.com.au and ⓦwww.metrophoto.com.au), so your friends and family can easily view them and even have prints made if they want to, but that will take a while, even with a high-speed connection, so you have extra Internet café costs to consider (many cafés will copy images to a CD-ROM for you, though). Then you're just paying for the prints, which would be the same as with film (€36 for 150 prints). Starting from scratch, the digital option is about €540 (including a €300 camera).

Turning your film and digital images into prints

The cheapest and most practical way to get your film and digitized images turned into prints is to send (or upload) them to an online developing/printing company. They'll develop your film, send the negatives home and post all the photos on the Web so you can caption them, share them with friends and – best of all – let them pay for the prints they want. Also, when sending film, remember to wrap it in aluminium foil (you can fold up a few sheets of foil and keep them tucked away between your journal pages), to protect it against postal X-ray machines (see p.182). The US and Canada offer the most competition (see comparison below to help navigate the field), and no two companies seem to offer the exact same deal or features… at the moment. But the sites often upgrade tools and juggle pricing, so take a good look before deciding. It's not a bad idea to test the service with a roll or a few digital prints before leaving home.

- **Club Photo** ⓦwww.clubphoto.com
- **Developing:** No developing, just digital uploads
- **4″ x 6″ print:** 14 cents
- **Comments:** Least expensive for digital photographers. Joining is free, but you can pay €8.70 for a five percent discount or €14.50 for a ten percent discount. Photos can be ordered at 4″ x 5.3″, the size used by most digital cameras, if you'd rather not risk distortion by stretching the shot to fit the traditional 4″ x 6″ parameters.

- **Ofoto** ⓦwww.ofoto.com
- **Developing:** €3.27 per roll
- **4″ x 6″ print:** 24 cents
- **Comments:** Good online editing tools (photos can be cropped and red eye removed), but it's not as cheap as its competitors. Registration is free and you can store and share your pics for up to a year without buying anything. Ships internationally.

- **Shutterfly** ⓦwww.shutterfly.com
- **Developing:** €3.30 per roll
- **4″ x 6″ print:** 24 cents
- **Comments:** Visitors don't need to register to view your online album, so sharing your pics is more convenient. Membership is free and you get unlimited storage and discounts on large orders.

- **Snapfish** ⓦwww.snapfish.com
- **Developing:** €2.47 per roll, includes set of prints (plus €1.65 for shipping and handling per roll)

- **4″ x 6″ print:** 12 cents
- **Comments:** Easy to use. The only site that enables digital photographers (and Photoshop users) to upload their non-JPEG images. You can also email your pics in if you're not comfortable with uploading. Also allows 4″ x 5.3″ printing.

Other sites

Australia: ⓦwww.extrafilm.com.au, ⓦwww.fujicolor.com.au and ⓦwww.metrophoto.com.au

New Zealand: ⓦwww.extrafilm.co.nz and ⓦwww.frogprints.co.nz

UK: ⓦwww.ofoto.co.uk and ⓦwww.photos-by-post.com

US and Canada: ⓦwww.dotphoto.com, ⓦwww.ritzcamera.com, ⓦwww.walmart.com and ⓦwww.winkflash.com

Essential tips for pocket-camera users

Postcard photographers use the best equipment, know the best vantage points and wait until the lighting is perfect. For monuments and panorama shots, chances are slim you're going to do better yourself. If you want a great shot of the city or a favourite attraction for your album back home, just buy the postcard. Besides,

△ Getting to know your subject will add a new dimension to your photography

nothing will put your friends and family back home asleep quicker than endless landscape shots.

Instead, photograph things that show your life on the road. It takes some effort to remember to photograph them (doorways, weird meals, freaky buses, scary toilets, charismatic taxi drivers and so on), and it may feel odd taking out your camera in the middle of the restaurant and snapping a picture of the meal, but those are the shots that'll spark your memory the most back home. Also, resist the urge to photograph your travel companions posing. Catch them off guard and you'll get a more honest, interesting photo.

With scenery, and often even with people, try to compose the photo so there's something very close, something mid-range and something in the distance. If you want to photograph someone standing in front of a waterfall, for example, try positioning yourself just behind a texture-rich tree branch and allow it to appear in a third of the picture.

Despite the fact that things seem brighter, midday sunlight actually flattens images and makes for unappealing photos. For people, animals and objects, you want overcast skies or indirect light. A cloudy day is the perfect time to get great pictures. If you must shoot people in the middle of a sunny day, use your flash to eliminate unattractive shadows or have your subjects step into a shaded area.

For pocket cameras, 100–400 ISO film is pretty versatile for action, both indoor and outdoor, and it's available everywhere. Special professional films, conversely, are not always easy to come by in smaller towns, so make sure you pack enough.

Airport X-ray machine

Never pack your film in a check-in bag. The strong X-ray machines used for checked luggage can fog your film with a single pass. With carry-on luggage X-rays, even if the machine is covered with signs stating that it will not harm film, that's not entirely true. One or two passes through may do nothing, but repeated exposure can fog unprocessed film, especially high-speed film. Ask nicely to have your camera and film hand-checked. After 9/11, airport security is more reluctant to do this, but it's worth asking. Even if this isn't allowed everywhere, it may save your film a few extra zaps from the machine. Keeping all your film handy in a clear zip-lock

When not to take photos

There's a reason it's called taking a picture: rarely is permission requested. It may be your camera, but it's their image and privacy and that trumps whatever you've got in your hand, even if you're holding a Nikon with a Zeiss lens. The path to pictorial enlightenment involves respecting local bans on photography and asking all subjects for the right to snap their photo. Everything else – including the temptingly easy zoom-lens sniper approach – is nicking pictures. That sounds a bit dramatic, but for many travellers photography is their only interaction with locals, and it's a relationship largely based on selfishness and insensitivity (the author has been guilty of this as well at times). For some, our swinging lenses can feel as intrusive as if someone walked up and took your picture while you were lying on the beach half-naked or stuffing your face at a restaurant. To get those great portraits you see on guidebook covers and in magazines, simply ask permission. Or go one better and try to initiate conversation. Make a few friends or even a small connection and it will add another dimension to the picture. Then, if you can, get an address and send them a copy. Or bring along one of those little disposable cameras that creates instant photos and take one with that. Giving photos has a much nicer ring than taking them.

bag should speed up inspection. Otherwise, you may wish to try a portable lead-lined pouch for protection.

Recording sound

If you think the sounds of Europe – French chatter in a trendy café, Italian Vespas zipping by, an animated story told by a drunk German in an old beer hall – will conjure stronger memories than photos, or if you'd prefer to dictate your journal, mini-cassettes and mini-discs are both good options. If it's a digitised format, you may be able to upload sound clips and attach them to emails at Internet cafés. Consider what you'll be using it for when you select a microphone. For voices, go for a unidirectional mic. For ambient sounds, you'll want a wider spread. Some of the better microphones are equipped with both, and you can toggle between them with a simple switch.

Making videos

Many of today's smallest digital video cameras can slip into a jacket as easily as a pocket camera. Plus, they record sounds and make still video images. The downside is that they cost €800–2000, take fairly low-resolution digital stills (this bit seems to be improving in recent models, though), and don't record sound that well without an additional microphone.

Like photography, video has spawned stacks of books on method and technique. If you're going to shoot, here are two simple tips: first, hold the camera very steady, even if it's equipped with an electronic stabilizer. That may mean leaning against a tree or lamppost. Better, however, is to bring a simple tripod – nothing induces headaches and screams "amateur" like shaky footage. The second tip is to resist letting the camera follow your natural head or eye movement all the time. For example, allow someone to walk across the field of vision – entering on one side and disappearing on the other. This will make editing much easier once you return home.

Drawing and painting

No one will see Europe quite the way you do. To personalize the visual impact, you might consider toting along watercolours, colour pencils or sketching charcoal – all relatively cheap and extremely easy to transport. Even if you don't have much artistic skill, or much that you're aware of, this is an ideal time to give it a shot. It's a nice alternative to reading or writing when you're stuck somewhere for a long time, which, invariably, you will be at some point.

What to do with souvenirs

Send them home. That Venetian lace tablecloth, stolen gelato spoon and Mona Lisa bottle opener will make nice mementos, provided you get them back. Dragging your souvenirs around Europe in your backpack is a great way to get them ruined, lost or stolen, but is not as effective as the postal service for actual delivery to the final destination.

No matter how small, lightweight and space-saving the items may seem individually, they can take over your pack like Dutch elm disease. The obvious exception is waiting until the tail end of your trip for a big shopping splurge.

Naturally, there are several levels of security available (as well as private couriers) at a range of prices. Consider the reliability of the

Mementos of your trip

Memories fade, surprisingly quickly. After a few days back home on the sofa in your old pair of jeans, the entire experience can feel like it never actually occurred. Best to jot things down while they're still fresh in your mind.

One way is to create an online scrapbook with a service such as My Yahoo! (it will basically happen on its own if you use one of the online photo developers). Just make sure you don't forget to label the photos with names and places as you go. It may seem obvious at the time, but several months down the road, when you finally return and get around to assembling the photos, it's not going to be quite as clear. (If you're getting film processed along the way, remember to write names and places on the back of the prints.)

Until we know that digital memory lasts (and lasts well), you'll eventually want to convert your photos to prints. And make sure you've got a friend or parent saving and printing out the e-dispatches you're sending back. Those can provide the backbone of the memorabilia you may wish to piece together later. Toward this end, one of the best things you can do aside from taking photos or painting is to collect small, flat items that catch your eye and evoke a memory: concert and train tickets, a beer label, a fortune-cookie prediction, even a sample of the abrasive toilet paper that once gave you some trouble. Send it home with your film or wedge it into your journal for safe transport.

postal service (are you in Denmark or Russia?), the weight of the package and the value of what you're sending, before you ship. There's no magic formula, but it's not uncommon to pay more for postage than the actual item enclosed. Keep that in mind when you're about to buy that set of terracotta roof tiles in Spain.

Another thing to remember is that not everything you buy may be allowed back into your country, and that's not just a veiled reference to the popular agricultural products in Amsterdam. All plants, seeds and items made from wild animals may be removed by customs officials. You won't be reimbursed, but you may get fined.

18

Returning home

Except perhaps for getting your gums scraped, nothing seems less appealing during your trip planning process or the trip itself than taking a moment to work out your return details. But this information may affect your planning, so best that it's addressed, at least briefly, now. Let's assume you've conquered Europe. You've picked up six languages, run with the bulls, bungy-jumped off the Eiffel Tower, foiled pickpockets, fallen in love, fended off dysentery and learned the difference between a Châteauneuf du Pape and a Châteaupape du Neuf. All you have left is to return home.

But here's where things can get problematic. With a comfortable bed and a fresh set of clothes in sight, it's tempting to lower your guard. Instead, you're going to need to brace yourself for a potentially rough re-entry.

Re-entry shock

Even if Europe is similar in many ways to your own culture, many people coming home from a long trip still experience a shock – it's often bigger on their return than when they first went abroad, and at a time when they're least prepared for it. On the bright side, there are a few simple things you can do to turn the experience into a smooth landing, and the most important of these is learning what to expect.

The stages of re-entry mirror those of culture shock: honeymoon, crisis, recovery and adjustment. The honeymoon is the initial exhilaration of returning home, and is precisely what most are expecting. The surprise left hook is the "reverse culture shock", which lasts until you acclimatize to your home surroundings and eventually return to your old self (with a bit more wisdom and experience).

The degree of the reverse culture shock you experience largely depends upon how integrated you became into foreign cultures during your journey, and how different they are from your own. Upon returning, you may miss the regular and close social interaction you had with your foreign community and other travellers. You may find yourself revolted by the TV commercials and telemarketers you had previously learned to ignore. More likely, you may feel a distance has come between you and your friends and family because they can no longer relate to your "new" well-travelled persona – one that has grown and been shaped by your range of different experiences. Instead, they're treating you the same way and don't have the patience to hear the thirty hours of stories required to bring them up to speed. And if you're returning to a job, you may notice reduced responsibilities and little acknowledgement for your overseas accomplishments.

This is compounded by The Questions. If you've ever broken your leg and had to explain what happened to everyone you met for a month, you already have a good understanding of what it's like to be a human recording. But when you're trying to sum up a few incredible weeks or months of life-changing experiences in one or two cute lines, it's even more frustrating. The Questions tend to be the same worldwide. They'll start with "How was the trip?", move on to "What was your favourite?" and quickly get to "So what are you going to do now?"

Coping strategies

Scuba diving and cultural immersion are similar in at least this one respect: a little decompression is a good idea. Before you return home, try to build in a little stop for mental refuelling. It needn't be a month of silence at a monastery; a beach will do fine. You just need a place with minimal stimulus. It can take a while to process the lifetime of experiences that you've just crammed into a ridiculously short period. And, more important still, you need to begin to engage the concept of returning home. You're going to have enough to worry about when you get back, so try to work out a game plan in advance – where you're going to stay when your plane touches down, who you plan to visit, and so on.

Bracing others for your arrival

The best single thing you can do in this respect is keep your friends and family up to speed during your trip with short, regular dispatches from the road. The easiest way to do this is with a group email. Let them know where you are and what you're up to. In general, people will have more patience to read about your experiences in bite-size chunks than to listen to them all in one go.

Writing that last dispatch from the road

When you're just about to head home, take some time to sum up your trip in your last email or letter. Answer the questions they're likely to ask. Tell them what your favourites places are, if in fact you have any. Tell them what your plans are. Those around you will want to get that extra dose of info when they see you in person. Help them out. Give them something they can ask about. You might say, "For a beer, I'll be happy to fill in the details on the time I was gored in the backside by a bull. But the time I had a few shots of vodka and woke up in a

Siberian prison camp is worth at least two." Some people will be more interested to see your photos than others. Prepare them for it with a bit of humour and the option to back out of the full seventeen-roll photo presentation. You might try something like "I'll be carrying around a very small selection of photos in case you're curious to see some of the things I've been writing about. If there aren't clean sheets on the bed when I visit, I'll be forced to show you all 824 photos."

Staying in touch with people you met

Stay in touch with the friends you made on your trip. It improves the chance you'll see them again, have a free place to stay (and a cultural guide) when you head back to Europe next time, and gives you a free support network.

Keeping involved with the places

Study that language you were dying to speak at the time but couldn't. Read fiction or non-fiction books on the subject. If you do eventually head back to any of these places, you'll be able to appreciate them on another level.

Seeking out travellers in your area

There's probably a hostel in your area filled with Europeans (and Aussies and Kiwis and Americans and Canadians, if that's who you miss). Spending time with travellers, visiting students or an immigrant crowd can be just enough of a dose to remind you that you're sane after all.

Finding patience

It's common to feel superior to those around you who haven't had such international experiences. Suddenly, their views may seem pedestrian and insular and you feel the continued need to "set them straight". Just remember: your own views may not be that popular, either. Time outside your own country tends to highlight its faults, and you may come off sounding like a born-again critic. Take heart. You will have enlightened perspectives, but don't expect others to come around easily.

Reviving the memories

If you need a quick fix, you might try escaping back into your travels for a brief tour. This is where a good scrapbook and well-kept journal come in handy (see p.218). Using your notes and images, it can often be helpful to write about your experiences more fully. Who knows? This may be the chance to release that budding travel writer within.

Getting busy

If you have the possibility to arrange your work/study schedule before returning, keep this in mind: a little down time at home is wonderful, but too much can be self-defeating. Finding that right balance is up to you, but in general the less, the better. One or two weeks is usually sufficient.

Start travelling again

If all else fails (except your finances), hit the road again. It doesn't have to be a long trip, or even a European one. Just taking some trains and buses, packing up your rucksack, sleeping in a few ratty hostels and meeting some other travellers can be enough.

First-Time Europe

Country profiles

Austria

Capital: Vienna
Population: 8,175,000
Language: German
Currency: Euro (€)
GDP per capita: €24,500
When to go: Mid-December to March for skiing, July and August for hiking, or June, when the Alps are in full bloom, crowds are manageable and prices have yet to hit their peak
When not to go: Many theatres and performance centres close during July and August
Minimum daily budget: €32

As the homeland of personalities as diverse as Mozart, Hitler, Freud and Aaahhhnold, you could say Austria brings out the best and worst in people. It is one of the world's richest and most stable democracies, but it has plenty of the Alps thrown in for those who enjoy risking life and limb. Fantastic skiing and hiking in western Austria draw the outdoor adrenaline nuts, while there is enough grand imperial art and architecture in Vienna to leave the culture crowd gasping for air. What the kleptomaniac Habsburgs couldn't steal from their vassal states, they commissioned themselves, leaving the Kunsthistorisches Museum with one of the four largest art collections in the world. There's a lot of Klimt and Schiele, but also enough of Ye Olde Masters to fill entire rooms.

If your taste leans to the less dusty side of culture, Austria has a bubbling electronic music scene, too. It might not be the zaniest of countries, but it's making strides in that direction. Traditionally pork-loving Austrians are even warming to such unheard-of concepts as vegetarian dining. What will they embrace next?

Main attractions

● **The Austrian Alps** Hundreds of 3000-metre-plus peaks will take care of most of your climbing needs. If you prefer the assistance of a ski lift to get you up the mountain, every self-respecting village has at least a dozen.

● **Schönbrunn, Vienna** If you find the Habsburg Palace in downtown Vienna confusing and gridlocked, this 1685 "summer cottage" commissioned by Emperor Leopold I gives you a much better idea of how Viennese royalty spent the taxpayers' money. When crowds arrive, head outside – the park out the back is bigger than Monaco.

● **Eisriesenwelt caves** A walk-in refrigerator of gigantic proportions, these caves have over 40km of frozen waterfalls and weird-looking ice sculptures. They're easily accessible from the town of Werfen, south of Salzburg, and are open between May and October. Even in the summertime, the temperature hovers around freezing point, so bring a fleece.

● **Mozart's Salzburg** This famous border town is not only worth a visit to pay homage to the man, but also has churches so cute you want to pinch them, plus plenty of art, city squares and chocolate galore.

● **MuseumsQuartier Wien, Vienna**
The shape of things to come, within the world of a museum building. The Viennese complex houses, among other things, the Leopold Museum (Austrian Art), the Kunsthalle Wien, the ZOOM Children's Museum and the Tanzquartier Wien (the New Centre for Contemporary Dance). A total floor area of 60,000 square metres makes this one of the most impressive mega-museums in the world.

Alternative activities

● **Cruise the Austrian Alps on a motorbike** Long and winding Alpine roads offer unparalleled two-wheel riding. Classic tours include the Grossglockner mountain, the Silvretta high-Alpine road, the Tauern mountains and the tour around the Hochschwab.

● **Ski the Hahnenkammrennen, Kitzbühel**. Let's face it, your chances of competing in the actual race are about as slim as Claudia Schiffer. But you can always do a couple of practice runs to test your mettle. The start is at 1665m, the finish at 802m, and the total course

spans 3.3km. You might want to ratchet up your insurance first, though.

● **Bring the hills alive on a Sound of Music tour** Plenty of tours follow in the dance steps of the von Trapp family, but Panorama Tours (Ⓦhttp://en .panoramatours.com/soundofmusic) has the backing of Fräulein Maria herself. Trips centre on the city of Salzburg but also include the palaces of Frohenburg and Leopoldskron. The whole wonderfully (or painfully) kitsch experience is typically tackled with a bus tour that can be arranged anywhere in town.

● **Take a yodelling course** When in the Alps, strike a blow for non-verbal throat noises and make lots of alternative friends at the same time. Just don't use your new-found vocal skills in downtown Vienna. To get a little warm-up, try Ⓦwww.jodelkurs.de.

Costs

Don't be put off by Austria's well-heeled surrounds; it's not as forbiddingly expensive as it seems at first glance. You can eek out an existence on €32 a day, but you may not get much of a feeling for the country that way. Plan to spend closer to €45, which will give you

Average temperatures and rainfall in Austria

Average daily temperatures (maximum and minimum °C) and monthly rainfall (mm)

	Jan	Feb	Mar	Apr	May	June	July	Aug	Sept	Oct	Nov	Dec
Vienna												
max ˚C	2	4	9	14	19	22	25	25	21	14	7	4
min ˚C	-3	-2	2	5	9	13	15	15	12	6	2	-1
rainfall mm	38	42	41	51	61	74	63	58	45	41	50	43

the occasional private room and restaurant meal, especially once you learn to spot the money-magnet cafés that will gladly relieve you of half your daily budget for a Sachertorte and a cup of coffee. Just as in the rest of the Germanic world, cash is king, so avoid embarrassing situations by not relying solely on your credit card.

Accommodation

Paying for a place to stay is likely to be a major post in your budget. For €37–49 you will get a double room in a mid-range pension; an extra €16 will make your temporary home just that little bit nicer. If you're willing to slum it, you can squeeze under €16 for a bed in a hostel.

Eating and drinking

When Jörg Haider's xenophobes ask what immigrants have ever done for Austria, the rest of the country answers, "Cheap food!" All the usual suspects can be found, especially in student areas in the larger cities. You can tank up your gut for around €4. For a hearty Austrian sit-down meal, figure on €16. Coffee is particularly expensive, so make every cup last.

Transport

Austria is as well equipped as any other environment-conscious Western democracy when it comes to public transport. The rail network is not the fastest in Europe, but it is punctual and clean and

the views are often incredible. Where rail services stop, the Bahnbus and Postbus systems will take you farther. The former is run by the ÖBB (who operate the trains as well) and hence they leave from train stations, while the Postbus service departs from post offices. Both are usually cheaper but slower than the train. Their prime functions are delivering mail and shuttling kids to school, though there are a few late-night services that can bring you home after a night on the town.

In Vienna, the Vienna Card is worth looking into. For just under €16, you get 72 hours of unlimited free travel by underground, bus and tram, and discounts to nearly all museums, concerts and restaurants. You can pick up the card in almost any hotel or department store around the city.

By train

Austrianrail Pass Any three days of travel in fifteen days €131 (first class) and €89 (second class). Additional travel days cost €16 (first class) and €12 (second class).

Switzerland 'n Austria Pass Any four days of travel in two months €245 (first class), €171 (youth, second class). Additional travel days cost €29 (first class) and €22 (youth, second class).

European East Pass (also valid in the Czech and Slovak republics, Hungary and Poland) Any five days of travel in one month €184 (first class) and €131 (second class). Additional travel days cost €21 (first class) and €15 (second class).

Eurodomino Austria Pass Ranges from any three days of travel in one month – €172 (first class), €114 (second class) and €88 (youth, second class) – to any eight days of travel in one month – €263 (first class), €184 (second class) and €142 (youth, second class).

For Europe-wide Eurail and InterRail passes, see p.38. For tips and tricks on maximizing your rail pass, see p.71. For internal rail prices, see Ⓦwww.oebb.at.

By bus

Busabout (see p.39) allows some travel in Austria. For internal bus prices, see Ⓦwww.bahnbus.at. For buses to other countries, see Ⓦwww.eurolines.at.

Events

- **The Imperial Ball, Vienna** The Imperial Ball (*Kaiserball*) at the Hofburg on New Year's Eve kicks off the traditional ballroom season in Vienna, and it's not as hard a party to get into as you might think

– just expensive (€50–300). Even if you miss it, there are plenty of other opportunities later in the year to waltz until the end. Dec 31; Ⓦwww.hofburg.com.

- **Salzburg Festival** If classical music floats your boat, try this five-week extravaganza. Mozart is a natural focal point – especially with the 250th anniversary of his birth in 2006 – but there are plenty of international stars performing other works, too. July–Aug; Ⓦwww.salzburgfestival.at.

- **ImPulsTanz, Vienna** Dancing, or something that looks vaguely like it, is nonstop during this month-long celebration of rhythmic movement in Vienna. World-famous choreographers and dance companies perform all over the city, and there are courses and workshops if you want to get in on the action yourself. Early July–early Aug; Ⓦwww.impulstanz.com.

Austria online

Country info Ⓦwww.austria-tourism.at
Rail Ⓦwww.oebb.at
Bus Ⓦwww.bahnbus.at
Vienna info Ⓦwww.aboutvienna.org

The Baltic States

ESTONIA
Capital: Tallinn
Population: 1,341,664
Languages: Estonian (also Finnish, Russian and Ukrainian)
Currency: Estonian kroon (EEK)
GDP per capita: €10,000
Minimum daily budget: €21

LATVIA
Capital: Rīga
Population: 2,306,306
Language: Latvian
Currency: Latvian lat (Ls)
GDP per capita: €8250
Minimum daily budget: €20

LITHUANIA
Capital: Vilnius
Population: 3,607,899
Language: Lithuanian
Currency: Lithuanian litas (Lt)
GDP per capita: €9150
Minimum daily budget: €19

When to go: May–August for the best weather and outdoor café scene
When not to go: September, when rain is heaviest. December–March can be severe, with icy-cold temperatures and few daylight hours

Estonia, Latvia and Lithuania have clearly gone to great lengths to maintain their independence and defined borders after breaking away from the Soviet empire, yet the three of them continue to be grouped under a heading that sounds like a 1970s heavy metal band. There are several nations bordering the Baltic Sea that could have also landed this rather unfortunate moniker, but for these three it stuck.

One of the best reasons to visit this region is precisely because you're not familiar with it. Few are. And that means far fewer tourists and far more cultural insight (and value for money). Estonia's blood sausages aren't the big draw, anyway. Nor are Latvia's bogs. And nor is the Frank Zappa statue in Lithuania.

The people and prices, and the notion of untrampled lands, attract a different breed of traveller – ones who are less interested in a checklist of "must-sees" and more interested in finding a path of their own. That said, the Baltics are booming, at least compared to other former Soviet nations. You'll see designer brands and BMWs everywhere you go, and all three capital cities are vying to become the area's economic and cultural hub.

Main attractions

- **Tallinn's old town** Often compared to Prague, Estonia's capital is an up-and-comer on the budget travel scene. It turns out that Soviet rule was a sort of backward blessing for this old city (except the part when the Soviets bombed the old quarter one day in 1944 and flattened ten percent of it). The economic stagnation kept development to a minimum, so Tallinn's old city has remained largely intact.

Check out the area round Toompea Hill, where the aristocracy and clergy once lived.

● **Rīga Castle** Now home to Latvia's president, Rīga Castle has sat for nearly 700 years on the bank of the Daugava River, though only the Tower of the Holy Ghost remains from the original. Its southern part houses the Museum of

Foreign Art, the Rainis Museum of Literature and Art History, and the Museum of History of Latvia.

● **Toomkirik, Tallinn** Estonia's oldest church was built in 1223 and remains the burial site of German and Swedish noblemen. It was founded by the Danes, and houses the largest organ in the country.

Average daily temperatures (maximum and minimum °C) and monthly rainfall (mm)

Tallinn	Jan	Feb	Mar	Apr	May	June	July	Aug	Sept	Oct	Nov	Dec
max °C	-2	-3	2	7	14	18	20	19	13	8	3	-1
min °C	-6	-7	-4	1	6	10	13	12	8	3	-1	-4
rainfall mm	33	23	25	30	38	51	66	71	71	58	53	43

Average daily temperatures (maximum and minimum °C) and monthly rainfall (mm)

Rīga	Jan	Feb	Mar	Apr	May	June	July	Aug	Sept	Oct	Nov	Dec
max °C	-2	-2	3	9	16	19	21	20	15	10	4	0
min °C	-6	-6	-2	2	7	11	13	13	9	5	1	-4
rainfall mm	33	23	25	36	43	58	71	69	66	53	51	38

Average daily temperatures (maximum and minimum °C) and monthly rainfall (mm)

Vilnius	Jan	Feb	Mar	Apr	May	June	July	Aug	Sept	Oct	Nov	Dec
max °C	-3	-2	2	10	18	21	22	21	16	10	3	-1
min °C	-8	-8	-4	1	7	10	12	11	8	3	-1	-5
rainfall mm	43	33	38	48	51	76	84	69	66	56	51	53

● **Pärnu** You won't find many foreigners taking a beach vacation in Estonia, but this resort is a big draw locally. The white sandy beaches attract thousands, and those who want to get away from the crowds head for the nearby dunes and mud baths.

Alternative activities

● **Explore Lahemaa Park** Estonia's largest national park, Lahemaa combines dense forest, coastal bluffs, lakes, waterfalls and eighteenth-century manor houses. Situated in the north of the country, the park encompasses the Koljaku-Oandu and Laukasoo reserves, a wet-sea forest and – brace yourself – 7000-year-old bog respectively.

● **Visit Hiiumaa** If you're looking for ecotourism, consider this sparsely populated Estonian island 22km west of the mainland. There's a concerted effort underway here to protect the 1000-square-kilometre island's lovely stretches of coast from overdevelopment. There's no shortage of wildlife for viewing: elks, red deer, wild boars, foxes, lynxes, black storks, golden eagles and cranes.

● **Relax in Abruka** This tiny Estonian island offers a summer retreat for naturalists. Horse riding and farmhouse accommodation await visitors, as does the big attraction: a botanical-zoological reservation.

● **Get bogged down in Soomaa National Park** Estonia's famous bogs aren't exactly a playground of fun, but they do have their own particular charm. And bog walking brings out the best in a bog. One of the most popular spots is the Soomaa National Park in the southwest.

● **Canoe Gauja National Park** The Gauja, Salaca and Abava rivers in this Latvian lake region provide some of the best paddling around, and there's plenty of flora and fauna to keep you and your camera occupied. This unique Baltic Sea environment allows northern–southern and western–eastern vegetation to flourish side by side. See Ⓦwww.gnp.lv for information on the park.

Costs

Lithuania is the cheapest of the Baltic States, but within Estonia and Latvia, there's a range from great deals to rip-offs. At the upper end, Latvia and Estonia compare to Western Europe, but on the budget end, it's easier to dig for bargains. If you're using travellers' cheques, remember to change them in the larger towns or you may not get much use out of them.

Accommodation

Outside of Lithuania (where accommodation costs €2–8), this is likely to be your biggest expense. Figure on more than €16 for a shared room with a bathroom down the hall. However, breakfast is often included with the deal. Look for campground cabins, which can be as low as €6.50 a night.

Eating and drinking

It's not difficult to find a nice meal for €25, but dining is where you're likely to save the most. A simple meal, for example, can be found for under €2, even in Latvia and Estonia. Pep yourself up for pork and potatoes, soup and sausage, and smoked fish. In summer, you can skip the blood pancakes if you please, but don't miss the fresh berries. If you want to drink something extra special (and extra revolting) in Latvia, try the Rīga Black Balsam, a brake-fluid-like 45-percent-proof concoction. The syrupy, sweet Vana Tallinn liqueur is also a palate challenger, whether you add it to coffee or champagne.

Transport

Getting around the Baltic States is still quite cheap (and slow). No regional rail passes cover the area, nor do Eurail or InterRail, but there is a local rail service, running two types of train: "passenger" and "fast". Both are slow, but inexpensive. Busabout doesn't operate in the region either, but for buses to other countries, see Ⓦwww.eurolines.ee (Estonia), Ⓦwww.eurolines.lv (Latvia) or Ⓦwww.eurolines.lt (Lithuania).

In the capital cities, there's a comprehensive network of trams, trolleys and buses, but these can get very crowded. Save money by buying a ticket before boarding, or better, buy a ten-ticket pack.

Events

● **Usini** Not for the faint-hearted, the Latvian festival of Usini starts with a sunrise swim for horses and then quickly descends into rooster killing (their blood is daubed across doors to celebrate the arrival of the "summer singing" season). End of April.

● **Ollesummer, Tallinn** The largest beer festival of the Nordic countries, Estonia's Ollesummer has over 100 different brews on hand to lure nearly 100,000 thirsty visitors. Performances and food stalls keep you busy while you drink. Early July; Ⓦwww.ollesummer.ee.

● **Midsummer** People flee to the countryside when the summer solstice arrives. Special foods (cheeses and pies) are made for the occasion, while flower-and-grass wreaths are strung up. Usually June 21.

● **Vilnius Jazz Festival** Jazz junkies turn up in mass for this East–West music fusion. Lithuania's Russian Drama Theatre comes alive for the three days the acts come to town. Mid-Sept; Ⓦwww.vilniusjazz.lt.

● **Jazzkaar, Tallinn** It can't be easy getting the big names to make a trip to the Baltics, but that's exactly what the Jazzkaar festival has managed to do over the years. Acts, which in 2003 included Earth, Wind and Fire, Randy Brecker and John Scofield, perform across the city. April; Ⓦwww.jazzkaar.ee.

Baltic States online

Estonia info Ⓦwww.visitestonia.com
Rail Ⓦwww.edel.ee
Tallinn info Ⓦwww.tallinn.ee

Latvia info Ⓦwww.latviatourism.lv
Rail Ⓦwww.ldz.lv/en/index.html
Rīga info Ⓦwww.rigalatvia.net

Lithuania info Ⓦwww.visitlithuania.net
Rail Ⓦwww.litrail.lt
Vilnius info Ⓦwww.vilnius.lt

Belgium and Luxembourg

BELGIUM
Capital: Brussels
Population: 10,348,276
Languages: Flemish, French and German
Currency: Euro (€)
GDP per capita: €23,500

LUXEMBOURG
Capital: Luxembourg City
Population: 462,690
Languages: Luxembourgish (national language), French and German (administrative languages)

Currency: Euro (€)
GDP per capita: €45,000

When to go: May–September, when the weather's at its warmest. Fortunately, the crowds aren't much of an issue, especially outside of Bruges (Belgium)
When not to go: Overcast skies, raincoats and umbrellas are prevalent year-round, but November–March provides the strongest dose of misery from above
Minimum daily budget: €40

Belgium's cultural diversity belies its reputation among travellers as merely a great country to pass through. The EU's central administrative offices here may have added to the diversity, but the notorious bureaucracy that comes with the influx of Eurocrats has been a difficult image- issue to overcome.

Belgium has three official languages. The French-speaking Walloons in the south make up about forty percent, the Flemish speakers up north account for nearly sixty percent, and there are small pockets of German speakers on the eastern border who barely show up on the lingual radar screen. The effect is a divided country (and incredible gourmet beer and rectangular waffles). Luxembourg, though just barely large enough to be found on a hand-held map of Europe, is a fairy tale of villages and woodlands that, unlike

Belgium, clings fiercely to its identity. In the north of the country, there's skiing, hiking and rock climbing, waterfalls and fast-flowing rivers, and towering castles. The south has a history of wine making, and you can reach just about any spot in the country from the capital within an hour.

Main attractions

● **The Bock casemates, Luxembourg City** In 963 AD, Sigefroid, Count of Ardennes, laid the cornerstone of Luxembourg City on a rocky outcrop now called "the Bock". The most impressive remains of this high fortress are the labyrinthine casemates – built in 1644 – which sheltered 35,000 people when the city was bombed during World War II. There are 17km of this damp maze of subterranean passageways open to the public.

● **Bruges** The most popular tourist attraction in Belgium is this entire town, the best-preserved medieval city in Europe. On some streets you feel as if you're wandering through a museum's thirteenth-century installation.

● **Grand Place, Brussels** The Belgian capital's central square is a popular place to sip a coffee or eat an intimate meal while gazing at some of the finest Baroque guildhalls in the country. The twelfth-century square unfolds like a personal discovery as you enter from one of the many narrow side streets. The Hôtel de Ville is the only building on the square that survived King Louis XIV's bombing in 1695 and is open for tours.

● **Waterloo** In 1815, the Duke of Wellington drafted a message in this town announcing the defeat of Napoleon. The Battle of Waterloo (which was mostly fought in nearby Braine-l'Alleud) is commemorated with the *Butte du Lion* (Lion's Mound) monument and a platinum-selling song by Abba.

● **Manneken Pis, Brussels** This tiny statue of a urinating boy, sculpted in bronze by Jerôme Duquesnoy in 1619, has an undefined history (some say he extinguished a fire with his you-know-what), yet the city has embraced this rather unorthodox landmark, sometimes dressing up the boy in one of his 650 costumes (which allow for simulated urination). And, thanks to the tourist industry, you can take home a "urinating boy" key chain or bottle opener to help re-kindle the feeling you had when you first laid eyes on him.

Alternative activities

● **Play some chess** Head to *Le Greenwich*, an "Old World" café in

Average daily temperatures (maximum and minimum °C) and monthly rainfall (mm)

	Jan	Feb	Mar	Apr	May	June	July	Aug	Sept	Oct	Nov	Dec
Brussels												
max °C	14	14	16	18	22	27	30	30	27	23	18	15
min °C	6	6	8	9	13	17	19	19	17	14	9	7
rainfall mm	53	53	46	36	25	10	3	10	30	58	56	53

Brussels known for its top-notch chess matches, and test your skills against one of the local masters.

● **Try the local brew** Belgian beer must, possibly by law, only be served in the glass that was specifically made for it, such is the level of sophistication (and marketing) in this country. Many of the beers have a higher alcohol content than wine and, if you sink a few of those cute little bottles, you may have a difficult time finding your way back to your hostel. But if you only taste one a day, it'll take about a year to try them all.

● **Visit a spa** Not just any old spa, *the* spa. Since Roman times, the Belgian town of Spa has been known for its curative baths. The rich and famous of the sixteenth century came here, and Victor Hugo was a regular. There are still several spas in this town you can visit: Pouhon Pierre-le-Grand Spa and the Spa Monopole are among the best known.

● **See diamonds being cut** The diamond trade has made its home in Antwerp for centuries. Precious stones may pass through continually, but it's not all that easy for visitors to see what's happening. Each Saturday afternoon at Antwerp's Diamond Museum (Ⓦwww.provant.be/diamant), you can watch a diamond-cutter at work.

Costs

Luxembourg may have the highest GDP per capita in Europe, but it's not as expensive as Norway or Switzerland. Both Luxembourg and Belgium are priced roughly the same as Germany – bargains aren't easy to come by, but they can be found with careful looking and a willingness to wander well off the main routes. Living on €25 a day is possible sleeping in tents and on public-park benches, but €40 a day is going to allow for some cheap restaurant meals, museums and a few lattes to wash down your waffles with.

Accommodation

Hostels are cheap here (€10–15 for a dorm), but there's not an abundance of them and most get booked up over the popular summer months. Campgrounds with cabin rentals can be a good option (there's a free booklet you can pick up in the tourist office listing where they are and what they cost), but you'll want to get in the habit of booking ahead.

Eating and drinking

You can find some sandwiches for under €4, and there's the usual assortment of kebabs and pizzas, but in general you'll have to choose between your wallet and your palate – one is likely to suffer. A decent meal can be found for under €16. The food in the French part of the country is on a par with the best French cuisine. In the Flemish part, it's much like the food in the Netherlands.

Transport

As compact countries, Belgium and Luxembourg are easy to get around, and the short distances make the fares relatively cheap. There are no domestic flights and even the official tourist website recommends the trains over the inter-city buses. In the major cities, trams and buses are available – the only subway is in Brussels, for which five- and ten-journey tickets are good value if you're in town for more than a day. Check out the multi-mode travel cards for longer visits.

Luxembourg has one main rail route with a few lesser lines that branch off. Buses supplement the other areas. Ask at the train station for special one-day travel cards.

By train

Benelux Tourrail Pass (also valid in the Netherlands) Any five days of travel in one month €186 (first class), €133 (second class) and €89 (youth pass). Several more rail deals are available through the Belgian rail website (Ⓦwww.sncb.be).

Germany and Benelux Pass (also valid in Germany and the Netherlands) Ranges from any five days of travel in two months – €268 (first class), €200 (second class) and €162 (youth, second class) – to any ten days of travel in two months – €406 (first class), €305 (second class) and €244 (youth, second class).

Eurodomino Belgium Pass Ranges from any three days of travel in one month – €92 (first class), €63 (second class) and €47 (youth, second class) – to any eight days of travel in one month – €158 (first class), €111 (second class) and €79 (youth, second class). For Europe-wide **Eurail** and **InterRail** passes, see p.38. For tips and tricks on maximizing your rail pass, see p.71.

Weekend Ticket You get fifty percent off rail fares if you leave after 7pm on Friday and return by the Sunday of the same weekend. It's also possible to leave and return the same day. The catch is that it's not transferable, changeable or refundable.

By bus

A Busabout pass (see p.39) allows some travel in Belgium. Because so much of Belgium is accessible by train, buses are only used for short distances and parts of the Ardennes with few rail lines. For internal bus prices, see Ⓦwww.delijn.be. In Luxembourg, domestic buses can be found at Ⓦwww.autobus.lu. For buses from Belgium to other countries, see Ⓦwww.eurolines.be.

Events

● **National Day, Luxembourg** National Day is June 23, but for more action than the traditional cathedral *Te Deum* song and military parade, show up the evening before for a torchlight parade, fireworks and a huge party. Several other towns around the country have celebrations, complete with pyrotechnics. June 22–23.

● **Dancing Procession of St Willibrord, Echternach** There are probably several ways to purge your sins, but, since the death of St Willibrord in 739, pilgrims in Echternach have been shaking a leg while shaking loose the evil spirits. People come from across Europe to dance to the sound of the sixteenth-century bell in the town's abbey. June; Ⓦwww.willibrord.lu.

● **Binche carnival** Binche hosts the famed orange-throwing parade (don't throw them back; they're good luck) when dozens of *Gilles* march with what appears to be John Lennon masks and giant ostrich-feather hats (of course, the hats and masks are not worn at the same time). This multi-day carnival fest is one of the oldest in Europe. Feb 6–8; ⓦwww.carnavaldebinche.be.

● **Ommegang pageant** Brussels' Grand Place gets invaded by 3000 spectators (including the royal family) for the Ommegang, a procession of nobles in period costume as well as craftsmen and soldiers. To view the pageant, book in advance with the tourist office (ⓦwww.visitbelgium.com). Try the town of Mechelen if the one in Brussels is sold out. First Tues of July.

Belgium and Luxembourg online

Belgium info ⓦwww.visitbelgium.com
Rail ⓦwww.sncb.be
Bus ⓦwww.delijn.be
Brussels info ⓦwww .brusselsinternational.be

Luxembourg info ⓦwww.ont.lu
Rail ⓦwww.cfl.lu
Bus ⓦwww.autobus.lu

Britain

Capitals: London (England), Edinburgh (Scotland) and Cardiff (Wales)
Population: 60,270,708
Languages: English (also Welsh and Gaelic, Scottish form)
Currency: British pound (GBP)
GDP per capita: €22,905
When to go: May–September, when the weather should be lovely (if it's not raining and there's no heat wave), but with so much to do inside (museums, pubs, getting lost on the Underground), you can get by just fine if the weather turns miserable
When not to go: July and August are crowded at the best budget accommodations, while October–March is seriously cold and rainy, and makes seeing London by foot rather unpleasant
Minimum daily budget: €37

A famous headline that ran in the British press read: "Fog in the Channel, Continent Cut Off." There's now an underground umbilical cord of sorts, but in the minds of the Brits there's little question who the parent in the relationship is. That is to say, there's a strong sense of cultural independence. The Brits are profoundly British and only European by default. Moreover, the nation has developed the sort of pride one can only acquire as the power centre of a colonial empire. Never mind the state of the empire today; the rich history and left-over architecture seems to be enough (especially if you include a winning rugby team). Yet, with common immigration issues, flourishing trade, and quicker (and cheaper) international transport, Britain finds itself becoming increasingly closer to mainland Europe.

The nations of Wales and Scotland, each with proud cultures and rich histories of their own, are politically connected to England via the central government in London. The names get a bit confusing from here on. The official name of the country is the United Kingdom of Great Britain and Northern Ireland. When people speak about the UK, they're referring to this: the political grouping of England, Scotland, Wales and Northern Ireland. When they say "Great Britain" or "Britain", they're excluding Northern Ireland (but sometimes they don't mean to). That's the confusing part for most visitors. England, Scotland and Wales (and Northern Ireland) each try to qualify a team for the football World Cup and European Championships, but only the United Kingdom sends a team to the Olympics (under the banner of "Great Britain and Northern Ireland"). Go figure.

The hamlets and towns in the countryside resemble scenes out of Frodo's Shire, while the cities are a maze of thriving, bustling commerce and fashion (and near misses, as tourists forget to look right as they cross the street).

There are far more famous sites than your wallet and schedule will allow, but the cheap international air tickets and language combine to make London an excellent starting point for many travellers, so you won't be the only one trying to get your footing on the travel trail.

Main attractions

● **Buckingham Palace, London** The official London residence for blue blood since 1837, Buckingham Palace is still home to the Queen and has fairly recently opened its doors to tourists. You're unlikely to catch Her Majesty in front of an off-track betting screen, but you can see paintings by Rembrandt, Rubens and Vermeer in the Queen's Royal Collection, and rooms fitted with some of the finest furniture and porcelain in the world. See ⓦ www.royal.gov .uk for tour times and prices.

● **Whitehall and Parliament Square (and Big Ben), London** The original building can be traced back to the eleventh century and is today home of the House of Commons (elected) and House of Lords (if you own more than ten polo ponies or a Gulfstream jet). It's mostly known for Big Ben, which is not the clock, but the 13.8-tonne bell inside. For reasonably good entertainment, view the House of Commons from the gallery when the Prime Minister fields (sometimes ruthless) questions. See Ⓦwww.parliament.uk for parliamentary session times.

● **Westminster Abbey, London** Every Coronation since 1066 has taken place in this architectural masterpiece. There are also approximately 3300 people buried here, including Geoffrey Chaucer, Charles Dickens, Charles Darwin, Isaac Newton, Laurence Olivier and Ben Jonson, an Elizabethan poet who was buried standing up.

● **British Museum, London** When a colonial superpower decides to bring home souvenirs, it doesn't mess about. Many of the world's treasures can be found under this one (newly renovated) roof, with free admission. See p.12 for more.

● **Tower of London** The Tower of London isn't much of a tower, but it is the best-preserved medieval castle in any European capital. It's been the royal living quarters, a prison for notorious traitors and even once housed lions and bears. Today, it's best known as the only place you can get nearly as close to the royal jewels as Camilla Parker-Bowles. See Ⓦwww.hrp.org.uk for opening times and prices.

● **Bath** There's the royal crescent, a majestic half-ring of buildings designed by John Wood in 1767. There's Bath Abbey, with arching stained-glass windows and ornate spires. But the big pull (with a price to match) is the Roman Baths (Ⓦwww.romanbaths.co.uk), built approximately 2000 years ago, over a hot spring that spits up over a million litres of 46- degree Celsius water a day.

● **Edinburgh Castle** This castle looks like it's dropped straight out of *Lord of*

the Rings. Occupying the top half of a rocky hill in the centre of the city, this ancient castle gets over one million visitors a year and seems to sell as many postcards. See Ⓦwww .edinburghcastle.biz for tour times and prices.

Alternative activities

● **Join in the Summer Solstice at Stonehenge** The most interesting time to visit this ancient enigma is during the longest day of the year, when about 30,000 people show up. What's the big deal about this pile of rocks? Stonehenge is believed to have been built by the Druids, but how they moved these four-tonne stones from 400km away (in the Prescelly Mountains in Wales) in 2000 BC, a time when hydraulic fork-lift operators were hard to find, is something of an engineering marvel.

● **See Romeo and Juliet at Shakespeare's Globe** A reconstruction of the original open-air playhouse, the Globe Theatre in London is Shakespeare's backyard. The season runs from May to September; see Ⓦwww.shakespeares-globe.org for play schedules and ticket prices.

● **Watch a football match** The singing, cheering, yelling is at a fever pitch when the big teams clash. And even when they don't. Manchester United, Arsenal, Liverpool, Chelsea and other top teams play regularly through-out much of the year. Little tip: make sure you're wearing the right colours for your section of seats.

● **Play golf at St Andrews** The Royal and Ancient Golf Club of St Andrews is unlikely to accept you as a member, but that doesn't mean you can't play a round on the 600-year-old Old Course, the world's first golf course. The bunkers

Average daily temperatures (maximum and minimum °C) and monthly rainfall (mm)

	Jan	Feb	Mar	Apr	May	June	July	Aug	Sept	Oct	Nov	Dec
Edinburgh												
max °C	6	7	8	11	14	17	19	18	16	12	9	7
min °C	1	1	2	3	6	9	11	11	8	5	3	2
rainfall mm	56	41	48	38	51	51	64	69	64	61	64	63
London												
max °C	7	7	9	12	16	19	22	22	18	14	10	7
min °C	3	3	4	5	7	10	12	12	10	8	5	4
rainfall mm	64	51	51	48	56	56	66	76	64	74	69	69

are the size of squash courts, the wind is typically hovering just around gale force and the thick gorse bushes can eat golf balls by the twelve-pack, if the €164 green fee doesn't eat your wallet first. See ⓦ www.standrews.org.uk for course information and bookings.

Costs

Britain's a cheap place to fly to and from, but that's where the bargains start and end. London, in particular, can put a hole in your budget, largely because of all the perceived "must-sees", many with a horrific admission fee. In London, figure on €37 a day as a minimum, more if you plan to see a few things and sample the odd pint of lager. With a full day of sightseeing, a public transport travel card and a pit stop at the pub, don't be surprised if you're closer to €50 a day. There are various museum and tour passes available at ⓦ www.raileurope.com, such as the three-day attraction and museum pass for €70.

Accommodation

In London, there's no such thing as a cheap place to stay unless you're taking a nap in the park and partying all night. There's plenty of budget accommoda-

tion – even in high season – but it's hard to find anything for under €17. A more generous estimate is €21–25. To find a room, ⓦ www.londontown.com can be helpful. You can find a place to pitch a tent outside of town, but it's a long journey back and forth, so you'll likely lose on travel expenses what you save in sleeping on the ground.

Eating and drinking

There are loads of fantastic inexpensive treats, especially the Indian offerings at the local curry house. A package of warm salted chips (French fries) with vinegar is hard to beat (about €1.50). Much of the pub food doesn't seem all that fresh or appetizing, especially since they seem to think it's a selling point to announce that there's blood in some of the items. Black pudding (made with pig's blood and eaten at breakfast), for example, sounds more like something you'd expect to find in Transylvania. Restaurants can be budget killers, but there's plenty of non-*McDonald's* fast food to keep your palate busy.

Transport

Britain has the unique distinction of being home to Europe's most expensive rail service, and without getting any prizes for efficiency, speed or comfort. Neither Eurail nor InterRail passes cover Britain, though numerous regional rail passes do – for all the options, see ⓦwww.britrail.net. The bus is a very popular option in Britain, especially for single trips. It takes a bit longer, but unless you book your train tickets in advance, there are significant savings to be had. A trip from London to Edinburgh, for example, costs €134 on the train and €42 on the bus (the bus is about 2hr slower).

As much fun as London is to traverse by foot, it's somewhat easier and much faster by Underground (aka "The Tube"). The cheapest single ticket costs €2.30; for more than a short trip, a Travel Card (also valid on buses) is the way to go: a one-day pass for travel in Zones One and Two costs €6 (€9 for the weekend), a seven-day pass costs €30. A carnet of ten single tickets is available for Zone One only, at a relative bargain of €17.

By train

BritRail Consecutive Pass Ranges from any four consecutive days of travel – €231 (first class) and €117 (youth, second class) – to a month of travel – €752 (first class) and €375 (youth, second class).

BritRail Flexi Pass Any four days of travel in two months €289 (first class), €198 (second class) and €148 (youth, second class). Any eight days of travel in two months €426 (first class), €285 (second class) and €214 (youth, second class). Any fifteen days of travel in two months €641 (first class), €429 (second class) and €322 (youth, second class).

Freedom of Scotland Pass Any four days of travel in two months €120 (second class). Any eight days of travel in two months €156 (second class).

By bus

A Busabout pass (see p.39) connects London with Paris and mainland Europe. For internal bus prices, see ⓦwww.nationalexpress.com. For buses to other countries, see ⓦwww.eurolines.co.uk.

Events

- **Bonfire Night** On November 5, 1605, the Gunpowder Plot, a conspiracy to blow up the English Parliament and King James I was under way. Someone leaked the plot to Lord Monteagle, word spread, and it failed. The foiling of this rebellious deed has become a national pastime, celebrated nationwide with fireworks and bonfires, during which effigies of the conspirator, Guy Fawkes, are burned.

- **Edinburgh Fringe Festival** August in Edinburgh means one thing: The Fringe. From near and far, high and low, come the world's jugglers, fire eaters, comedians, singers, dingers, dancers, prancers…everyone. Over a million tickets get sold for this eclectic performing-arts bash. Aug; ⓦwww.edfringe.com.

- **Cooper's Hill Cheese Rolling** Double your life insurance and join in this race down a frighteningly steep grassy hill in Gloucester. Participants flip, cartwheel and tumble out of control on their way to the bottom, or hospital, whichever comes first. You can of course just watch. May; ⓦwww.cheese-rolling.co.uk.

- **Notting Hill Carnival, London** Each summer, the streets of Notting Hill in west London fill with technicolour floats, costumed dancers and half a million spectators (Europe's largest street fest) as the spleen-shaking sound systems fill the air. Last weekend in Aug; ⓦwww.thecarnival.tv.

- **Grand National, Aintree** You might call it "the Ironman Triathlon for horses".

It's four and a half miles long and has thirty wicked fences – many riders are happy if they can just hold on until the finish. There's a statue on hand at the Aintree racecourse in Liverpool so you can pay homage to Red Rum, the Grand National's greatest champion. April; Ⓦwww.aintree.co.uk.

● **Chelsea Flower Show, London** Even if you don't have the greenest of fingers, or know a fern from a ficus, the Chelsea Flower Show is likely to impress. At the end of spring, the eleven-acre site at the Royal Hospital becomes a blooming wonderland of colour with more fragrances than an airport duty-free shop. May; Ⓦwww.rhs.org.uk/chelsea.

● **Glastonbury Festival** The open-air music festival of all open-air music festivals (much of it spent under a tent). The perimeter of the Worthy Farm venue stretches for more than 10km, and you'll find more diversity here than Darwin found in the Galapagos Islands, not to mention some of the world's top music acts.

● **Wimbledon Championships, London** The world's greatest tennis tournament is set on a stage that most people associate more with golf. Tennis aficionados, celebrities and long queues of fans turn out to see who will hold the jug trophy (men) and the oversized hors d'oeuvre plate trophy (women) over their head at the end of the two-week contest. End June–beginning July; Ⓦwww.wimbledon.org.

Britain online

Country info Ⓦwww.visitbritain.com
Rail Ⓦwww.nationalrail.co.uk
Bus Ⓦwww.nationalexpress.co.uk
London info Ⓦwww.visitlondon.com
Edinburgh info Ⓦwww.edinburgh.org
Cardiff info Ⓦwww.visitcardiff.info

Bulgaria

Capital: Sofia
Population: 7,517,973
Language: Bulgarian
Currency: Lev (Lv)
GDP per capita: €6200
When to go: Mid-April to mid-September, when the weather is warm. If snowfall is plentiful, you can ski from just before Christmas until April
When not to go: October–February, when there's little relief for non-skiers
Minimum daily budget: €16

Tucked away in the southeastern corner of Europe, Bulgaria calls itself the "Jewel of the Balkans", but that may be overstating things just a tad. It has come a long way since it threw off the choke hold of the Ottoman Empire in 1870, but there are far fewer sights and accommodation choices than most European countries offer – though fewer tourists, less Western influence and lower prices as well. Independent travel isn't common, but the traditional towns, romantic architecture and mountain scenery provide enough to sculpt an interesting itinerary.

There's a strong Russian influence here (Cyrillic alphabet included), partly out of gratitude to the 200,000 Russian casualties suffered while liberating Bulgaria from the Turks in 1878. Today, only 85 percent of the country's inhabitants are Bulgarian. Besides almost a million Turks, there are smaller minorities of Macedonians and Roma (Gypsy).

Finding Bulgaria on the map isn't the only thing that trips up some travellers; nodding up and down means "no" and shaking your head from side to side means "yes".

Main attractions

- **Valley of the Roses** Roses have been grown in the fertile valley east of Sofia since the Phoenicians were the hottest act in town. You won't find a more all-encompassing celebration of their beauty anywhere in the world.

- **The Black Sea Riviera** Arguably Bulgaria's greatest asset, the beaches of the Black Sea rightfully fill up during the summer holidays. The best ones can be found northeast of Varna. If you need a day in the shade, Aladja Monastery is just around the corner.

- **Nesebâr** This former Byzantine trading hub is at least 2500 years old, and you can't swing a cat in it without hitting a medieval church. It's all about adorable little squares, cobbled streets and a crumbling city wall – impressively jammed together on a tiny peninsula shooting out into the Black Sea.

Alternative activities

- **Ski on the cheap** The alpine skiing World Cup hasn't raced in Bulgaria for twenty years, but there's good skiing to be had if you're not too picky about amenities. Aim for Borovets, Bansko or the Rhodope mountains. See ⓦwww.bulgariaski.com for resort information.

● **Take a holy hike** Over the ages, God-fearing Bulgarians have built monasteries with a vengeance (many of them well and truly off the beaten track), so there are plenty of pleasant, calorie-burning vistas for the visitor. Rila Monastery, 120km south of Sofia, is where Bulgarian culture was nursed during the five centuries of Turkish rule, and it can be reached after a few days on foot from Borovets.

● **Sip some water** Mineral water, that is. The Bulgarian stuff has been world famous in the Balkans since the pre-tap-water days. There are 1600 wells to choose from, but if you only have time to fill your water bottle in one or two spots, try Hissar (ⓦwww.hissar.org) in the middle of the country, and Pomorie (ⓦwww.pomorie.com) outside Burgas. If you've previously been abusing your liver, get the stuff with sulphate in it, said to get that organ back into shape.

Costs

Bulgaria is about as cheap as Europe gets. You can probably find ways to scrape by on pocket change, but allow for €16 per day at the very least. Double that to rub some comfort on it.

Accommodation

This is the one area where the Bulgarian tourist industry slaps you with special tourist prices, so don't expect accommodation to be as comparatively cheap as other Bulgarian prices. Upper-end

Average daily temperatures (maximum and minimum °C) and monthly rainfall (mm)

	Jan	Feb	Mar	Apr	May	June	July	Aug	Sept	Oct	Nov	Dec
Sofia												
max °C	2	4	9	14	19	23	26	26	22	16	8	3
min °C	-4	-3	1	5	9	12	14	14	11	6	1	-2
rainfall mm	33	36	38	53	69	79	56	43	41	36	51	43

hotels charge €35, but if you shop around, you can find a bed with a roof over it for under €8.

Eating and drinking

Bulgarians keep full with meals of meat, potatoes, beans and salads. These, plus the precarious liquors (*rakia* and *mastika*) used to toss it back, are going to be your cheapest feed. Breakfast is a nice bread-based snack on the run picked up at most hole-in-the-wall kiosks and washed down with *boza*, a gluggy millet drink loved by those who've managed to acquire a taste for it. Lunch is the main meal of the day and offers the best value. A late dinner – which you should be able to find for less than €5 – signals the switch from aperi-tifs to serious drinking.

Transport

Due to the Balkan mountain range, trav-elling east–west is going to be faster and easier than any north–south routes. You can get across the country by train in first class for about €8 (worth it, if you have long legs). The buses are slow, but the trains are even slower.

Sofia has a well-organized public transport system of buses, trams and trolleybuses. And the sixteen-cent fare is extremely reasonable. The trick is getting good information, as the signs (some-times just a rusted pole) leave a good deal to the imagination. Don't forget to buy an extra ticket for your rucksack and punch both tickets when you get on – or face a stiff €2 fine.

By train

Bulgarian Flexi Pass Any three days of travel in one month €57 (first class). **Balkans Flexi Pass** (also valid in Greece, Romania and Turkey) Any five days of travel in one month €156 (first class) and €93 (youth, first class). Any ten days of travel in one month €273 (first class) and €162 (youth, first class). Any fifteen days of travel in one month €328 (first class) and €197 (youth, first class).

For Europe-wide **InterRail** passes (**Eurail** doesn't cover Bulgaria), see p.38. For tips and tricks on maximizing your rail pass, see p.71.

By bus

Busabout doesn't operate in Bulgaria. For internal bus prices, see Ⓦwww.busbg.com. For buses to other countries, see Ⓦwww.eurolines.bg.

Events

● **Trifon Zarezan** This wine festival takes place on "Vinegrowers' Day" and is a blessing of the grape harvest. Its roots (no pun intended) go all the way back to the Thracians, an illiterate group of ancients who nevertheless enjoyed the odd cup of *tinto*. Feb 14.

● **Ladouvane** The name means "Singing to Rings", but this festival is all about unmarried women looking for husbands. Confusingly enough, it's celebrated on opposite ends of the year in different parts of the country – either New Year's Eve or Midsummer's Day – so if you're a lovelorn man, make sure you're in the right place at the right time.

● **Fake Christmas** Under communism, Bulgarians weren't allowed to celebrate Christmas. Solution: make up a new, non-religious holiday the day after. And guess what? It looks an awful lot like Christmas. Today, they celebrate both. Dec 26.

● **Festival of Roses, Kazanlük** With over seventy percent of the world's production, Bulgaria has long cornered the market on rose oil. Not as lucrative as petroleum, alas, but still a matter of some national pride. In early summer, homage is paid to this symbol of youth and beauty. Late May–early June.

Bulgaria online

Country info ⓦwww.bulgariatravel.org
Rail ⓦwww.bdz.bg
Bus ⓦwww.busbg.com

Croatia

Name: Croatia
Capital: Zagreb
Population: 4,497,000
Language: Croatian
Currency: Kuna (Kn)
GDP per capita: €8848
When to go: May–June and September are good for beating crowds on the Adriatic

When not to go: July and August are hot, expensive and jam-packed with tourists. Best avoided unless you're going for the classical music of Zagreb's Summer Festival, in which case you have no choice
Minimum daily budget: €29

The Croatians managed to keep their glorious coastline from the limelight thanks to Communism and the Yugoslav Wars. Now that it's safe to go, travellers have realized that just across the water from the overdeveloped Italian coast is the even nicer Croatian one. And it's cheaper. Cities such as Solin, Rab, Rovinj and Pula, and islands like Korčula and Mljet, have become the new playgrounds of those who appreciate the pristine. Well, comparatively pristine. The best way to enjoy it is from the deck of a yacht, but if you can afford one of those, chances are you won't be holding this book.

Many rock climbers come to Croatia, and there are even a few inland ski resorts – though the Croatians themselves go to neighbouring Slovenia or Austria to ski. Only a few areas, in eastern Croatia, are still not yet cleared of landmines from the wars, but regular tourism won't take you anywhere near them; all the attractions are either in the capital or along the coast.

Main attractions

● **Dubrovnik** The 1991 shelling of Dubrovnik, near the southern border with Serbia, should have secured prison sentences for all those responsible. Fortunately, this 1300-year-old architectural gem has been lovingly rebuilt, stone by stone, and is looking better than ever.

● **Diocletian's Palace, Split** You'd think that Italy would have all the best Roman ruins in the world, but these rock piles in the southern city of Split must make it into the Top 10 least. The ruins are what are left of the retirement home of the Roman Emperor Diocletian.

● **Lotrščak Tower, Zagreb** The medieval centre of Croatia's capital Zagreb is a treat for the eyes, and no place will give you a better view than this old watchtower at the southern gate of the inner city. Among the sights is the Cathedral of the Assumption of the Blessed Virgin Mary.

● **Korčula** This Dalmatian island south of Split claims to be the birthplace of Marco Polo. Whether or not it's true, it's captivating enough to merit a visit – imagine the Greek islands before tourists started outnumbering locals and you've got Korčula. If you can, try and catch the Moreška, a twelfth-century sword dance.

Alternative activities

● **Skinny-dip in the Adriatic Sea**
Croatia has a claim to fame as the first
European country to open its arms to
nude bathers – or naturists, to use the
rather eco-sounding euphemism. Rab
Island is where the bare-bum tradition
started back in the 1930s, but the sites
to head for today are Valalta outside
Rovinj, Koversada near Vrsar, and Poreč
on the Istrian peninsula. Note: single
men aren't welcome without a member
card from the International Naturist
Federation (Ⓦ www.inffni.org). Not to
worry – there are plenty of non-official
nudie beaches, too. Just to be on the
safe side, make sure you're not the first
naked person on the beach.

● **Dive off Mljet Island** Even though
the cool Adriatic offers less exotic diving
than tropical waters, French scuba-gear
inventor Jacques Cousteau called the
waters around Mljet Island (near
Dubrovnik) "one of the most beautiful
diving locations in the world". It may be
just a matter of time before the place fills
up with divers and you have to float in
line to get a glimpse of the corals.

● **Climb Anica Kuk** The innards of
Croatia are as rocky as the coast is flat,
making it great for climbing. Good
routes are accessible from big cities
such as Zagreb and Split, but for the
truly hair-raising stuff, head for Paklenica
near Zadar (between Rijeka and Split),
and take on the 350-metre-high face of
Anica Kuk. See Ⓦ www.climb-croatia
.com for route information.

Average temperatures and rainfall in Croatia

Average daily temperatures (maximum and minimum °C) and monthly rainfall (mm)

	Jan	Feb	Mar	Apr	May	June	July	Aug	Sept	Oct	Nov	Dec
Zagreb												
max °C	3	5	11	16	21	24	27	26	22	16	8	4
min °C	-4	-3	1	5	9	13	14	14	11	6	2	-1
rainfall mm	52	48	56	68	83	95	79	79	79	93	86	66

Costs

Communist Yugoslavia was cheap for Western travellers, but those days are all but gone. Things have gotten more expensive in recent years even though Croatia is by no means challenging Switzerland or Norway. Be prepared to spend €29 a day as a minimum. Add an extra €20 to sweeten the deal. By the time you reach €66 a day, you're living in style. As always, big cities and tourist spots will charge you more for just about everything.

You'll notice most tourist prices will be displayed in euros but rejigged to kunas according to the day's rate when it comes time to pay.

Accommodation

It's not as cheap as it used to be, but with a smart eye and some patience you can squeeze by on €12–16 a day in living expenses. Ask the tourist office about private rooms in Croatian homes – abundant, reasonably priced and even fun if you're lucky. There are also scores of inexpensive campgrounds along the coast.

Eating and drinking

Figure on at least €8 a day to ward off undernourishment and scurvy. You can save money by grabbing at least one meal a day from a street vendor. Inexpensive cheese-stuffed pastries (*burek*) will keep you going for a few hours. Supermarkets can set you up with the basics, but if you aim for a market instead, like the Dolac market in Zagreb, you'll get a cultural experience thrown in for free.

Transport

Trains are a good deal if you can actually find one to take you where you're headed. The rail lines are quite limited, and your Eurail pass won't work here (although an InterRail pass that includes Zone D will). The buses are more common transport (and thus should be booked in advance in the summer for popular routes along the coast). Busabout doesn't cover Croatia but Eurolines (ⓦ www.autotrans.hr) does; however, if you're coast-hopping and not in a hurry, ferries offer a nice alternative.

In Zagreb, bus and tram tickets cost €1 if bought from the driver; ninety cents at newsstands. And a day pass is €18. In Dubrovnik, a city bus ticket costs €1.35 from the driver and €1 at newsstands.

For Europe-wide **InterRail** passes (**Eurail** does'nt cover Croatia), see p.38. For tips and tricks on maximizing your rail pass, see p.71.

Events

● **Rijeka Carnival** The advent of spring (well, at least the thought of it getting nearer) has been turning things upside down here for over a hundred years. Costumed inhabitants parade through the streets, scare off evil spirits, celebrate their escape from Turkish invasion and generally have a blast. Jan–Feb; ⓦwww.ri-karneval .com.hr.

● **Split Summer Festival** The Croatian National Theatre has been putting on a big show since 1954, and every summer season sees a variety of concerts, dance shows, operas and exhibitions from both Croatian and international performers. Mid-July to mid-Aug; ⓦwww.splitsko-ljeto.hr.

● **International Puppet Festival, Zagreb** Either you love 'em or they freak you out. Puppets are all the rage

in Zagreb as summer winds down. When you're not taking in a show, you can check out a puppet exhibition or learn how to make your own puppet. All performances are judged by two juries – one made up of experts and one of kids. If you're not a fan, at least be glad the shows are no longer performed in Esperanto. Aug–Sept; ⓦhttp://public.srce.hr/pif-festival.

Croatia online

Country info ⓦwww.croatia.hr
Rail ⓦwww.hznet.hr
Zagreb info ⓦwww.zagreb.hr
Dubrovnik info ⓦwww.dubrovnik-online .com

The Czech and Slovak republics

CZECH REPUBLIC
Capital: Prague
Population: 10,246,178
Language: Czech
Currency: Czech crown (CZk)
GDP per capita: €12,800

SLOVAK REPUBLIC
Capital: Bratislava
Population: 5,423,567
Languages: Slovak (also Hungarian)
Currency: Slovak crown (Sk)
GDP per capita: €10,850

When to go: May–June and
September–October, when the
sightseeing is at its best (good
climate, fewer visitors).
May–October for hiking
When not to go: July and August
(for Prague), when it can be hard to
see the cobblestones for all the
tourists standing on them. Outside
of Prague, many castles and
museums close down
October–April
Minimum daily budget: €25

In 1989, Czechoslovakia divided itself into
the Czech Republic and the Slovak
Republic (Slovakia) without a shot being
fired. This impressive separation, a testa-
ment to the liberal, global-minded citizens
on both sides, became known as the
"Velvet Revolution". The Czech Republic
has emerged as one of the star economic
engines and tourist attractions of Eastern
Europe and keeps raising the bar for its
neighbours, though it's no doubt experi-
encing the growing pains of a young
nation. The most famous Czechs fall into
two categories: in one, there's Franz
Kafka, Milan Kundera and playwright-
turned-dissident-turned-president Václav
Havel. And on the other side of the rink,
Jaromir Jagr and Dominik Hasek. But
when you arrive, the literary and ice-
hockey powers are overshadowed by the
country's wealth of architects. Situated in

the middle of Europe, the Czech Republic
has been a natural trading centre for centuries, a geographic advantage that has
worked against it as well, since more
powerful nations have been anxious to
march in and take the country for themselves when the opportunity presented
itself. Miraculously, *Maticka Praha* ("little
mother Prague") emerged largely
unscathed from World War II.

The modern travel hippies making
jewellery and playing *Stairway to
Heaven* may be limited to the streets of
Prague, but the knock-your-socks-off
architecture isn't. Several towns, such
as Cheb, Kutná Hora and Loket, can
boast striking Renaissance and Baroque
facades. With hiking, spas and mountain biking, there's also plenty to do
once your neck tires of staring at all the
soaring spires.

Slovakia was left holding the less glamorous end of the stick (but the better skiing facilities) when the countries separated and is attempting to rebuild without the magnetic draw of a city such as Prague. What that means is there are fewer tourists, cheaper prices and the folk traditions are more intact. There are plenty of castles and rugged terrain to keep cultural buffs and hiking enthusiasts busy, as well.

Main attractions

● **Staroměstské náměstí (Old Town Square), Prague** You can probably count on one hand the number of people who've visited Prague and never seen the Old Town Square. This 17,000-square-kilometre centrepiece is the heart of the city, and has been since the tenth century. Today, cafés, buskers and horse-drawn carriages compete for your attention, but this commercial circus still can't hide the beauty of the square. If you follow the flow of human traffic, you'll make the short, cobblestoned stroll to the 600-year-old Charles Bridge.

● **Prague Castle** On the other side of the river from the Old Town Square, the 1000-year-old walled-in Prague Castle peers down on the city from its cliff-top perch. There's plenty of room in the compound for visitors (it's the most popular attraction in Prague) to view the seat of the Czech government since Prince Borivoj.

● **Josefov (Jewish Quarter), Prague** Prague's Jewish cemetery, plus a half-dozen old synagogues and a ceremonial hall, were disturbingly saved by Nazi leaders as an "Exotic Museum of an Extinct Race". Instead, this former Jewish ghetto has survived as a memorial to hundreds of years of oppression.

● **Bratislava** Old City torture chambers, a museum of wine, and the Primate's

Palace can all be found in the Old Town centre. The castle hovering above the River Danube was part of the Roman Empire for 400 years and offers great views of the city plus a folk museum.

Alternative activities

● **Cleanse your soul at Karlovy Vary** World-famous (in certain circles, anyway) for its regenerative waters, Karlovy Vary is the oldest of the Bohemian spas. The Victorian atmosphere of elegant colonnades may aid the healing process. If not, the surrounding parks with wooded hills should. See Ⓦ www.karlovyvary.cz for spa price info.

● **Enjoy "Prague" without the crowds** Český Krumlov is one of Bohemia's most striking towns, and is deservingly on UNESCO's World Heritage list. The charming city centre is car-free and – as if it's been built by a postcard company – the city's castle (the second largest in the country) rests on a hill overlooking a bend in the Vltava River.

● **Go canyoning and caving around the Moravský kras** The heavily wooded and hilly region of the Moravský kras (Moravian Karst) is home to caves and canyons, several with evidence of prehistoric human remains. You can boat on the underground river or abseil through waterfalls in Rudice. See Ⓦ www.cavemk .cz for more info on the region.

● **Hike the Vysoké Tatry** The narrow peaks of the Vysoké Tatry (High Tatras) tower over glacial valleys with dizzying cliff faces and, down at lower elevation, thick forests cover the hillsides. With a hundred glacial lakes and gurgling streams neatly packed into a small area with trails, it couldn't be better suited for hiking. The end of August is a good time to go, and Starý Smokovec is perhaps the best starting point.

Average daily temperatures (maximum and minimum °C) and monthly rainfall (mm)

	Jan	Feb	Mar	Apr	May	June	July	Aug	Sept	Oct	Nov	Dec
Prague												
max °C	1	2	8	12	18	21	22	23	18	12	5	3
min °C	-4	-4	0	2	7	11	12	12	9	4	0	-2
rainfall mm	20	18	25	36	58	69	66	64	41	30	28	23

Average temperatures and rainfall in Slovakia

Average daily temperatures (maximum and minimum °C) and monthly rainfall (mm)

	Jan	Feb	Mar	Apr	May	June	July	Aug	Sept	Oct	Nov	Dec
Bratislava												
max °C	2	4	11	16	21	24	26	26	22	15	7	3
min °C	-3	-2	2	4	9	13	14	14	11	6	1	-1
rainfall mm	36	41	38	36	56	71	63	61	38	41	53	-1

Costs

Outside of Prague and the famous spas, costs can easily be kept to a minimum. The problem for most is that Prague is unmissable and Prague's prices, at least for accommodation, are on a par with those found in Europe's biggest cities. With stand-up dining and hostel dorms, you can survive on around €16 a day, but €25 will give you some breathing room. If you share a decent double room with bath in a mid-range hotel or pension and eat out at inexpensive restaurants, figure on €33 a day. In Slovakia, things remain a bit cheaper; perhaps €4 cheaper per day, slightly more if you're comparing to Prague. ATMs aren't common outside major towns.

Accommodation

This is the most expensive part of travelling here. Private rooms, which a decade ago cost a pittance, are already competitively priced in some areas and, in Prague, exceed the bargains long associated with Eastern Europe. Campgrounds aren't as fancy as some of the multi-star complexes in Western Europe, but there are "chalets" for rent, and a shared double may very well beat whatever deals you can find in the city centre. Around Slovakia, you should be able to find accommodation for less than €12.

Eating and drinking

Normally you can't count beer as a meal, but in this part of the world some travellers seem to be doing just that. And with beer this good (and cheap), it's hard to fault them. Plus, all that Communist isolation didn't do much for the development of the cuisine, other than get people used to not paying that much for it. Check out some of the "wine cellars" outside of Prague for a stylish meal. And expect lots of soups, pork and beef, with the occasional goose or wild boar. A nice meal can be found for under €10.

Transport

The region has a comprehensive rail network that's reasonably cheap, clean and mostly dependable. There are some internal flights, but the short distances don't allow you to shave many minutes off the journey. Bus connections for longer routes are often more frequent than the trains (even if a bit slower), and can be especially useful for visiting more remote locations.

By train

Czech Flexi Pass Any three days of travel in fifteen days €55 (first class) and €39 (second class). Additional travel days cost €7 (first class) and €5 (second class).

European East Pass (also valid in Austria, Hungary and Poland) Any five days of travel in one month €184 (first class) and €131 (second class). Additional travel days cost €21 (first class) and €15 (second class).

Eurodomino Czech Pass Ranges from any three days of travel in one month – €77 (first class), €51 (second class) and €28 (youth, second class) – to any eight days of travel in one month – €170 (first class), €111 (second class) and €88 (youth, second class).

Prague Excursion Pass A seven-day pass – €45 (first class), €33 (second class) and €37/€29 (youth, first class/second class) – from the Czech border to Prague and back (the return trip does not have to be to the same border town), allowing day-stops in both directions.

For Europe-wide **InterRail** passes (**Eurail** doesn't cover the Czech and Slovak republics), see p.38. For tips and tricks on maximizing your rail pass, see p.71.

By bus

A Busabout pass (see p.39) allows some travel in the Czech Republic but does not operate in Slovakia. For internal bus prices, see ⓦwww.vlak-bus.cz (Czech Republic) and ⓦwww.cp.sk (Slovakia). For buses to other countries, see ⓦwww.eurolines.cz (Czech Republic) and ⓦwww.eurolines.sk (Slovakia).

Events

● **Burning of the Witches, Prague** This pre-Christian festival for warding off evil has been politically corrected with the burning of bonfires in Prague, mostly at all-night parties. April 30.

● **Prague Spring International Music Festival** Early summer brings great musicians from around the world to Prague, the international stars complemented by impressive home-grown soloists and orchestras. Venues include the recently refurbished Smetana Hall and Rudolfinum, as well as Prague Cathedral. Mid-May to beginning of June; ⓦwww.festival.cz.

● **Khamoro World Gypsy Festival** The itinerant Roms (Gypsies) steer their show on the road into Prague for a gathering to showcase their classical music, jazz, film, theatre, dance, painting and photography. May; ⓦwww.khamoro.cz.

● **Bratislava Jazz Days** The first international star appeared here in 1982. Since then, the likes of Bill Evans, Herbie Hancock, Bobby McFerrin and Wynton Marsalis have played this thirty-year-old festival. Sept; ⓦwww.bjd.sk.

Czech and Slovak republics online

Czech Republic country info ⓦwww.czechtourism.com
Czech Republic rail ⓦwww.cdrail.cz
Czech Republic bus ⓦwww.vlak-bus .cz
Prague info ⓦwww.prague.cz

Slovakia country info ⓦwww.slovakia .org
Slovakia rail ⓦwww.zsr.sk
Slovakia bus ⓦwww.cp.sk
Bratislava info ⓦwww.bratislava.sk

Denmark

Capital: Copenhagen
Population: 5,413,392
Languages: Danish (also Faroese and Greenlandic)
Currency: Danish krone (DKK)
GDP per capita: €25,798
When to go: May–August, when the days are long enough to enjoy the frequent spurts of good weather that come your way
When not to go: Mid-October to March the gloom is filled with far more freezing drizzle than snow
Minimum daily budget: €34

Denmark is full of surprises. An unaccomplished singer and ballet dancer who goes on to become one of the world's great storytellers (Hans Christian Andersen), for example. Or the north of the country being home to Europe's largest desert. Denmark may be the smallest Scandinavian nation, but it's no easier to pin down than a Greco-Roman wrestler. It shares social policies with Sweden and Norway and alcohol prices and perceptions with the rest of Europe. And, as such, neatly bridges the gap between its northern neighbours and the centre of the EU.

The three landmasses that comprise the bulk of the country (Sjælland, Fyn and Jylland, the peninsula that's connected to Germany) each have their own sensibilities. Jylland is perhaps the most distinct, with green hills and undulating heathlands. The northwest part of the peninsula has incredible beaches, some of which are wide and compact enough to drive and bike on.

Copenhagen, Scandinavia's largest and most affordable capital, is, like the rest of the country, best conquered by bike. The only thing more stunning than the architecture is the people. As Bill Bryson said in *Neither Here Nor There*, "Everyone, without exception, is youthful, fresh-scrubbed, healthy, blond and immensely good-looking. You could cast a Pepsi commercial in Copenhagen in fifteen seconds."

Main attractions

● **Legoland** The little plastic snap-together blocks have gotten a good deal more sophisticated than they once were, but their simplicity is still their strength and a visit to their Danish birthplace should cap off any lingering childhood fantasies about an entire Lilliputian Lego city.

● **Ribe** You don't need to be a history buff to be charmed by the oldest town in Scandinavia. The 700 AD market town almost looks its age, partially because it was spared from modernization due to economic decline. If the town itself doesn't feel enough like a museum, try Ribes Vikinger (Viking Centre) just south of town.

● **Kronberg Castle, Helsingor** This castle was made famous by Shakespeare when he penned *Hamlet* and set his play in Elsinore (*Helsingor* in Danish). Never mind that the real Hamlet was the son of a Jylland pirate and lived on the island of

Mors; the story makes for better tourism. And the castle, situated on a promontory jutting into the sea, is impressive enough.

● **The Little Mermaid, Copenhagen** Perhaps the most petite of Denmark's attractions, the statue sitting atop a small rock a few metres from shore at the entrance to Copenhagen's harbour attracts an astounding number of visitors (and graces possibly even more postcards). The mermaid was made famous as Hans Christian Andersen's heroine, but the statue, despite losing its head on a number of occasions, has taken on a following of her own.

Alternative activities

● **Dip your feet in the "Marriage of the Waters"** On the northernmost part of Denmark – in the artist community of Skagen – you can rent a bike and pedal 4km north to the Grenen lighthouse and stand on the very tip of the country, with one foot in the Kattegat Sea and the other in the Skagerrak Sea, and peer out at a faintly visible line where the two seas meet.

● **Take a bike tour around Fyn** Stay in farmhouses and castles and, after a long day in the saddle (and if

Average temperatures and rainfall in Denmark

Average daily temperatures (maximum and minimum °C) and monthly rainfall (mm)

	Jan	Feb	Mar	Apr	May	June	July	Aug	Sept	Oct	Nov	Dec
Copenhagen												
max ˚C	3	2	5	9	16	19	21	21	16	12	7	4
min ˚C	-1	-2	0	2	7	11	13	12	10	7	3	0
rainfall mm	43	25	36	41	43	53	66	74	51	53	53	52

your budget allows), sample one or more of the famous gourmet restaurants in the area.

● **Windsurf Denmark** Few tourists get blown away by Denmark's wind, but there's good reason to take advantage of it. Just ask Danish World Champion windsurfer Bjorn Dunkerbeck. The sheltered coastal inlets are perfect for beginners and the open sea offers ideal conditions for advanced surfers. And, with over 7300km of coastline, there are plenty of locations to choose from.

Costs

Copenhagen may be the cheapest of the Scandinavian countries, but that's not saying much, especially since free camping is common in Sweden and Norway, which typically cuts costs by sixty percent. What is inexpensive, compared to its Nordic neighbours, is alcohol. If you're camping (often for free) and preparing your own food, you might squeak by on €17–21 a day. Figure on a minimum of €34 a day with hostel dorms, and €50–65 with cheap rooms and inexpensive restaurants.

Accommodation

Hostels are a few euros cheaper, on average, than Sweden, but that mainly applies to dorm rooms, which cost around €19. A private room for two in a hostel with your own bathroom costs

€75! Looking for rooms (*rum* or *zimmer*) on the side of the road may be your best bet. You can also find cosy farmhouses that charge less.

Eating and drinking

You'll find most places you stay will set you up with a filling breakfast, included with the accommodation. If not, it's probably available for a relative bargain. Lunch deals for under €8 can be found easily. For dinner, your hostel may provide the best option, even if that's just a kitchen where you can make it yourself. A decent meal in a restaurant isn't going to cost less than €17.

Transport

Denmark is covered by trains, and the few parts that aren't have good bus services. In Copenhagen, you can rent a bike for a small fee at your hostel. If you're going to use public transport a lot, a Copenhagen Card will save you money, which also gets you into museums for free.

By train

ScanRail Pass (also valid in Finland, Norway and Sweden) Any five days of travel in two months €241 (second class) and €168 (youth, second class). Any ten days of travel in two months €323 (second class) and €226 (youth, second class). Any 21 consecutive days of travel €375 (second class), €261 (youth, second class).

For Europe-wide **Eurail** and **InterRail** passes, see p.38. For tips and tricks on maximizing this rail pass, see p.71.

By bus

Busabout doesn't operate in Denmark. For internal bus prices, see ⓦwww.xbus.dk. For buses to other countries, see ⓦwww.eurolines.dk.

Events

● **Roskilde festival** Every year, Denmark (and northern Europe's) biggest rock concert (30min from Copenhagen) ignites a pilgrimage stretching to all corners of the continent. The week-long festival kicks off with a bang and doesn't stop no matter how much it rains. Free camping (and mud-pit sliding) included with ticket. Late June or early July; ⓦwww.roskilde -festival.dk.

● **Copenhagen Jazz Festival** For ten days every summer, many of the world's greatest jazz musicians congregate in the nation's capital and turn it on its head. Early July; ⓦhttp://festival.jazz.dk.

● **Århus festival** Jesters, jugglers, archers, thespians, jousters and thousands of visitors invade Århus for nine days of Viking-like cheer and tomfoolery. First Sat in Sept; ⓦwww .aarhusfestuge.dk.

Denmark online

Country info ⓦwww.visitdenmark.com
Rail ⓦwww.dsb.dk
Bus ⓦwww.xbus.dk
Copenhagen info ⓦwww .visitcopenhagen.dk

Finland

Capital: Helsinki
Population: 5,214,512
Languages: Finnish (also Swedish)
Currency: Euro (€)
GDP per capita: €22,574
When to go: July–August for the warmest weather and midnight sun; late January–May for world-class cross-country skiing
When not to go: November–March, unless you love skiing or plunging into a hole in the ice after a sauna
Minimum daily budget: €37

Once Finland was able to get the occupying Swedes and Russians out of their hair (independence gained in 1917), they could get back to their national pastime: sitting in a sauna and coaxing the vodka out of their systems with a birch branch. Skiing and hiking in Europe's largest preserved wilderness is also popular. This unique combination may explain why Finns believe that 75° C in a sauna is chilly, but 25° C outside is hot. For those who'd rather take a more cosmopolitan approach to this Nordic climate, Helsinki offers art and architecture in abundance. The former capital, Turku, is the country's oldest city.

Many travellers use Finland as a gateway to Russia – it's just a short train or ferry ride from Helsinki to St Petersburg – but be careful you don't zip by too quickly. The country is worthy of a trip all its own.

Main attractions

● **Kiasma Museum of Contemporary Art, Helsinki** This building in downtown Helsinki is so striking (with its gleaming steel exoskeleton) it will surely lure you inside. The high-tech interior alone may be worth the price of admission, even if the experiential installations sometimes aren't.

● **The North Pole** Rovaniemi may be a few thousand kilometres from the North Pole, but don't tell Santa, who has set up shop in the North Pole Shopping Centre (where else!) and has a team of elves that take photos and answer children's letters. With European flights dropping off passengers all winter for an intimate chat with the multilingual Santa, this is as close as you'll get to the real thing. See ⓦwww.santaclauslive.com to find out about getting some face time with St Nick.

● **Stockmann Department Store, Helsinki** You can't miss it. It's Europe's largest department store, selling everything you need and even more that you don't.

● **Helsinki Train Station** This 1914 industrial-looking terminal is believed by many to be architect Eliel Saarinen's finest work.

● **Uspenski Cathedral, Helsinki** The green turnip domes of this Russian Orthodox cathedral create the most striking of sights when approaching Helsinki from the water. Inside, there's a cornucopia of icons and incense, and Slavonic choirs set the mood.

Alternative activities

• **Try an ice dive** If you like to dive, you might like this: cutting a hole in the ice and slipping below the bluish surface into the freezing water (with excellent visibility). When it's really cold (by Finnish standards, that's around minus 20° C), you need to have a sauna nearby. Not so much to warm up, but to get your scuba gear off in. It will literally freeze to your body. See ⓦwww.happydivers.net for sub-zero arrangements.

• **Take a walk in Lemmenjoki National Park** This Finnish national park deserves

more than a day's stroll. Some of the best trekking in Lapland – rivers, Arctic landscapes, waterfalls – awaits, though getting there may take more effort than the walking. A postbus leaving from Inari will suffice, or grab a river taxi from Kultala.

• **Watch a reindeer race** Fearless Finns don't actually drive reindeer to the North Pole, but they do race them chariot style. Standing on downhill skis just behind the reindeer with short reins, they shout and whip them into a sprint and compete side by side in an Arctic Ben Hur. In winter, races are held all over Finland, often through the closed-off streets of small towns.

Average temperatures and rainfall in Finland

Average daily temperatures (maximum and minimum °C) and monthly rainfall (mm)

	Jan	Feb	Mar	Apr	May	June	July	Aug	Sept	Oct	Nov	Dec
Helsinki												
max °C	-3	-3	1	2	7	15	21	19	13	8	2	1
min °C	-9	-9	-5	-1	5	9	12	11	6	2	2	7
rainfall mm	46	36	36	38	43	46	61	74	66	69	66	56

● **Take a snowshoe or snowmobile safari through Lapland** If you're heading to Finland in wintertime, you might as well embrace it. Strap some high-tech tennis rackets to your feet, or hold on tight as you speed over frozen rivers and through snow-covered woods on a snowmobile. See Ⓦwww.arcticsafaris.fi or Ⓦwww.laplandsafaris.com for information on tours.

Costs

Nothing in the Nordic lands is cheap, and Finland is no exception. If you're arriving from Russia, there may be some sticker shock. Otherwise, you'll be used to it by the time you pass through Denmark and Sweden. The one thing that may catch you off guard is that accommodation prices buck the trend and can actually go *up* out of season, which can make that €37 daily budget even more challenging.

Accommodation

Finding a cheap place to stay can be a challenge. The Finncheque programme (Ⓦwww.visitfinland.com) allows you to purchase vouchers – €43 per person in a double room, breakfast included (category I) or €35 per person in a double room, breakfast included (category II) – and use them to stay in 110 participating hotels. There's a €25 surcharge for single occupancy. Also, you need to buy these Finncheques before arriving, and you can't make reservations more than three months in advance. There are 150 hostels in Finland, most starting at more than €17 for a dorm. There are plenty of campgrounds (two people sharing a spot €8), but to take advantage of them, you'll need an International Camping Card or National Camping Card (available at every ground), which costs less than €4.

Eating and drinking

You'll need to figure on €5–7 for fast food, €12–21 for a decent meal and over €40 for fine dining. As in the rest of Scandinavia, sticking to falafels, pizza, hot dogs and supermarket food is a matter of budget survival.

Transport

Regular train travel is quite reasonable and covers the country particularly well on north–south routes. And if you can find two or more other travellers heading to the same place, you can book a group ticket at the train station and get about twenty percent off. Buses take care of east–west travel and connect well with the trains.

Helsinki transport isn't exactly a bargain. A single ride on the metro costs €1.60, so you're better off buying a ten-trip pass for €12 or a Helsinki Card – one day (€15), two days (€20) or three days (€25) days – which allows unlimited travel on all public transportation as well as free entry to several museums and some discounted theatre tickets. You even get a free sightseeing tour thrown in.

By train

Finnrail Pass Any three days of travel in one month €177 (first class), €118 (second class). Any five days of travel in one month €237 (first class), €158 (second class). Any ten days of travel in one month €320 (first class), €214 (second class). Add-ons available for the train to St Petersburg (€120 second-class round-trip) and the day-trip ferry to Tallinn, Estonia (€65 second class).

ScanRail Pass (also valid in Denmark, Norway and Sweden) Any five days of travel in two months €241 (second class) and €168 (youth, second class). Any ten days of travel in two months €323 (second class) and €226 (youth, second class). Any 21 consecutive days of travel €375 (second class), €261 (youth, second class).

For Europe-wide **Eurail** and **InterRail** passes, see p.38 and ⓦwww .raileurope.com. For tips and tricks on maximizing your rail pass, see p.71.

By bus

Busabout doesn't operate in Finland. For buses to other countries, see ⓦwww.expressbus.com.

Events

- **Midsummer Day** The biggest event

of the year is a private one, and to truly experience it you need to meet a Finn and get invited along. Most flee the cities for summer cottages, welcoming the longest day with bonfires and overzealous alcohol consumption. Mid-June.

- **Pori Jazz Festival** This annual festival attracts top-end acts to the old factory buildings that line the banks of the Kokemäenjoki River. There are over 100 concerts at this week-long jam, and you'll have to vie for a spot among the 130,000 revellers. Late July; ⓦwww .porijazz.fi.

- **Savonlinna Opera Festival** Finland's most famous festival is held at the ambience-rich medieval Olavinlinna Castle. The operatic blowout lasts a month. Early July; ⓦwww .operafestival.fi.

- **Wife-Carrying Championships, Sonkajärvi** Finland's most media-savvy event is the annual wife-carrying championships. Strapping Finns carry their wives over a 250-metre obstacle course, competing for the fastest time. The winner receives his wife's weight in beer. New rules state that "cohabitants living in a marriage-like relationship" may also compete. Early July; ⓦwww .sonkajarvi.fi.

Finland online

Country info ⓦwww.visitfinland.com
Rail ⓦwww.vr.fi
Helsinki info ⓦwww.hel.fi

France

Capital: Paris
Population: 60,424,213
Languages: French (also Alsatian, Basque, Breton, Catalan, Corsican, Flemish and Provençal)
Currency: Euro (€)
GDP per capita: €21,499
When to go: March–May and September–October, when the weather is great and the tourists are fewer; June–August for the Mediterranean (but also the time when it's busiest); November –March, when it's ski season in the Alps and Pyrenees
When not to go: Mid-July to August, when most of the French take their holidays – everything closes and the transport system feels the strain
Minimum daily budget: €33

France still carries a certain mystique, preserved in part by the wickedly decadent pastries served up in *boulangeries*, the tiny shops that regularly stock no less than twenty types of goat's cheese, doctors who still prescribe red wine for common ailments, small doggies with couture outfits that leave even smaller landmines on the sidewalk for you to navigate, and zippy cars that take on roundabouts at Mach 3. In other words, France is still French enough to fulfil the high expectations of most travellers. But brace yourself for *McDonald's* and 7-Elevens and neighbourhoods with far more North African cuisine than baguettes and liver pâté. As long as you don't expect an artisan crêpe maker with a beret juggling Grand Marnier on every street corner, France will not disappoint. The country that brought the world the Yellow Leader's jersey, the croissant, Debussy and Champagne still has much to offer. In Paris, you'll have a hard time walking ten minutes without bumping into a building you've seen on a postcard. In Chamonix, you'll pull a neck muscle taking in all the vistas. In Lyon, you can find enough Michelin-starred chefs to fill a rugby team, with plenty left over to cheer. There's a good reason France is the world's most popular tourist destination.

Main attractions

● **The Louvre, Paris** This museum could eat most sports stadiums for breakfast and still have space left over to confuse the most directionally gifted art connoisseur. It first opened in 1793 and was immediately stuffed full of stolen goods pillaged by Napoleon's armies. Courtesy of architect I.M. Pei, it now sports a snazzy glass-pyramid entryway with a reflective pool that helps calm the impatiently waiting crowds. The world record for seeing the *Mona Lisa*, *Winged Victory* and *Venus de Milo* and getting back out the front door is something like two hours.

● **Palace of Versailles** Louis Quatorze certainly knew how to live. Or so it would seem. There's the grand

Amsterdam   Hamburg

0   150 km

BRITAIN   Dover
Portsmouth   Newhaven   Calais   BELGIUM
Plymouth   Boulogne   Dunkerque   BRUSSELS   Cologne
Lille   Liège   GERMANY
ENGLISH CHANNEL
Dieppe   Amiens   LUXEM-
Cherbourg   BOURG
Le Havre   LUXEMBOURG CITY
Rouen   Reims   Metz
Caen
Roscoff   Versailles   PARIS   Strasbourg
Brest   St Malo   Mont-   Chartres   Nancy
St-Michel
Quimper   Rennes
Le Mans
Orléans   Dijon   Basel
Tours
N   Nantes   Bourges   BERN
Nevers
Poitiers   SWITZERLAND
Lausanne
La Rochelle   A   L   P   S
Geneva
Limoges   Clermont-   Chamonix
Ferrand   Lyon   Savoie
ATLANTIC   St-Etienne   Turin
OCEAN   Périgueux   Grenoble
Bordeaux   Briançon   ITALY

Avignon   Ventimiglia
Nîmes   Nice
Bastia   Biarritz   Toulouse   Grasse   MONACO
Bayonne   Béziers   Montpellier
Corte   Lourdes
Corsica   Irun   Narbonne   Marseille
Ajaccio   Perpignan   MEDITERRANEAN SEA
SPAIN   Portbou

Berlin & Prague   Munich   Zürich   Milan   Genoa   Corsica

Madrid   Barcelona

entrance, room enough to properly house an entire class of illegitimate children, endless gardens that require an army of trimmers and pruners, and a hall with more mirrors than a Las Vegas magic act. It's good to be king.

● **Eiffel Tower, Paris** Built for the International Exhibition of Paris in 1889, this giant phallic radio antenna has become not just the urban icon for Paris but for all Europe. It didn't win over the French right away: several petitioned to have it torn down. You can still ride the elevator or you could make the world's most famous stair climb and earn the spectacular view.

● **Mont Saint-Michel** This outcropping town on the north coast of France looks like a sandcastle come to life. That the tide comes in and turns it into an island periodically just adds to this visual effect.

● **The Alps** In the winter, it's a skiers', snowboarders' and ice -climbers' paradise. In the summer, the hikers, mountain bikers and rock climbers take over. Either way, you can't lose. The soaring jagged peaks seem fresh off the pages of a fairy tale.

● **Notre-Dame, Paris** The lady with the stone flying buttresses sits on the Île de la Cité in the epicentre of Paris. In fact, stand out in front of the main entrance and you'll find a spot in the cobblestones that marks the very centre of the city.

Alternative activities

● **Skate through Paris** At 10pm on Friday, at the base of the Montparnasse tower, about 15,000 in-line skaters congregate to commence their three-hour (30km) tour of Paris. In 1994, the Paris Roller Club turned the once ragtag gathering into an established event that now consumes the city with skaters. It runs all year long, unless it's raining or the streets are wet.

● **Taste wine in Bordeaux** Even if you fancy yourself as a beerophile, a tasting tour of the greatest vineyards on the planet is a remarkable experience. The hardest part may be spitting the wine out (on a long day of tasting, the idea is to keep yourself from slipping under the table).

● **Cycle in Corsica** Corsica lives up to its billing as the *île de beauté* (the island of beauty); roads wind by cliffs and beaches as they circle this unlikely piece of French property off the southeastern coast. The capital, Ajaccio, is as well-known for its cuisine as it is for being the birthplace of its most famous son, Napoleon.

● **Shop at the Clignancourt Market, Paris** It doesn't really matter what you're looking for, or even if you buy anything, the market will keep your eyes and nostrils on full alert. There are elaborate antiques – and mass-produced fakes that will fool people back home for a fraction of the price – and every street food vendor worth his salt (and cayenne pepper) seems to have a stall.

● **Barge through Bordeaux** Thomas Jefferson wrote of barging, "Of all the methods of travelling I have ever tried,

this is the pleasantest", and you can actually float all the way from the Atlantic coast to the Mediterranean. Just head up the Garonne to the Dordogne – which will bring you to Toulouse – then take the Canal Lateral to the Canal du Midi. Travellers tend to pony up for week-long rides on lavishly renovated models with full catering and scheduled pit stops at wineries.

● **Sample cheese in the Savoie** Each region of France is famous for its own particular type of cheese and you'd fare well following your own taste buds. However, if you're not sure which of the 265 kinds to try, head to the Savoie, the region that packs in the most cheese diversity.

● **Watch the Tour de France go by** Join the 15 million people who line the roads each year to watch the 189 riders and 1600 support vehicles zip by in a few eye-blinks. In some of the more popular spots along the big climbs in the Alps and Pyrénées, you may have to camp out to get a good view; in other places, five minutes ahead of time will suffice. The route changes each year. To find out when it's passing by, see Ⓦ www.letour.fr.

● **Take a crêpe** Walk into a supermarket in Normandy and you'll find as many different kinds of crêpes as types of bread, possibly more. But the best ones are home-made or fresh off the crêpe-maker's grill. Try banana-chocolate, lemon-sugar, chocolate-Grand Marnier… heck, try them all.

● **Browse for perfume in Grasse** Centuries of gardening and perfume mixing in Grasse have seen it blossom into the olfactory epicentre of Europe. Master sniffers (called *nez*, or "noses") train for years to recognize thousands of scents. If you're not interested in a tour of the perfumeries, a garden stroll will still delight the senses.

Average temperatures and rainfall in France

Average daily temperatures (maximum and minimum °C) and monthly rainfall (mm)

	Jan	Feb	Mar	Apr	May	June	July	Aug	Sept	Oct	Nov	Dec
Paris												
max °C	6	7	11	14	18	21	24	24	21	15	9	7
min °C	1	1	3	6	9	12	14	14	11	8	4	2
rainfall mm	54	46	54	46	63	58	54	52	54	56	56	56
Marseille												
max °C	11	12	14	17	21	26	29	28	25	20	14	12
min °C	3	3	6	8	12	16	19	18	16	11	7	3
rainfall mm	48	41	46	46	46	25	15	25	64	94	76	58

Costs

France is one of the most expensive countries in Europe for the budget traveller, mostly because the low-end accommodation is comparatively high. On the tightest budget, €33 a day can be a challenge. In addition to the expense of Paris, be particularly wary when heading to the Riviera. The haves and have-yachts aren't anxious to see scores of budget travellers marching their streets and have priced things accordingly to keep them at bay.

Accommodation

Even the cheapest rooms come with sticker shock. A dorm bed in a Parisian hostel costs between €21 and €29; a single room will set you back €40–70 – about the same as a hotel if you book ahead on the Web. A double room is €58–75. Outside the capital, prices drop, though not as much as you'd expect.

Eating and drinking

In most towns, you'll be able to find restaurants offering a basic three-course meal for €10, and it won't cost you more than €1 to pick up a warm baguette. Wine is cheap (even more so if you buy it at a store). If you're whipping up your own meal, any wine vendor can recommend the vintage that best accompanies your food – and it shouldn't cost more than €5.

Transport

France has the world's fastest train – the expensive, double-decker TGV – and one of the best rail networks on the planet. The bus system isn't quite so comprehensive. The cheapest way of getting round Paris is to buy a Paris Visit Ticket (Ⓦwww.ratp.fr), which is valid on the metro, bus, RER and the Montmartre funicular. Prices range from €8.50 for a one-day ticket covering Zones 1–3 to €53.50 for a five-day ticket covering Zones 1–8.

By train

Francerail Pass Any four days of travel in one month €208 (first class), €189 (second class) and €156/136 (youth, first class/second class). Additional travel days (maximum of six) €27 (first class), €23 (second class) and €20/17 (youth, first class/second class).
France'n Italy Pass Any four days of travel in two months €247 (first class), €214 (second class) and €165 (youth, second class). Additional travel days (maximum of six) €25 per day (first

class), €22 per day (second class) and €17 per day (youth, second class).

France'n Spain Pass Any four days of travel in two months €244 (first class), €211 (second class) and €162 (youth, second class). Additional travel days (maximum of six) €27 per day (first class), €24 per day (second class) and €18 per day (youth, second class).

France'n Switzerland Pass Any four days of travel in two months €247 (first class) and €173 (second class and youth, second class). Additional travel days (maximum of six) €30 per day (first class) and €22 per day (second class and youth, second class).

Eurodomino France Pass Ranges from any three days of travel in one month – €273 (first class), €206 (second class) and €149 (youth, second class) – to any eight days of travel in one month – €509 (first class), €387 (second class) and €292 (youth, second class).

For Europe-wide **Eurail** and **InterRail** passes, see p.38. For tips and tricks on maximizing your rail pass, see p.71.

By Bus

A Busabout pass (see p.39) allows you to travel throughout France. For buses to other countries, see ⓦwww.eurolines.fr.

Events

● **Nice Carnival** A million spectators take in the parade, music and fireworks, while papier mâché figures are danced down the street on giant floats. "Fat Tuesday" following Lent; ⓦwww.nicecarnival.com.

● **Monaco Grand Prix** The glam stop on the Formula One circuit, with cars racing through the pretzelled roads that comprise James Bond's stomping ground. May; ⓦwww.visitmonaco.com.

● **International Kite Festival, Dieppe** The world's best gather to show their piloting skills at Europe's biggest kite festival. Sept 11–19; ⓦwww .dieppe-cerf-volant.org.

● **Le Mans 24-Hour Race** Endurance, skill and auto mechanics come together in this gruelling, legendary car race. June 12–13; ⓦwww.lemans.org.

● **French Open Tennis Championships, Paris**. The world's elite players duke it out on the famously unforgiving red-clay courts of Stade Roland Garros. Last week in May to first week in June; ⓦwww.rolandgarros.com.

● **Paris Grand Steeplechase** The most prominent horseracing event on the French calendar. Watch fantastic leaps over the Hippodrome d'Auteuil's carefully clipped hedges and precariously placed ditches. May 30; ⓦwww .france-galop.com.

● **Biarritz Surf Festival** Dude, it's not just one of Europe's biggest surfing events. As world-class riders rip up the waves, Biarritz gets inundated with surfing enthusiasts who jump-start the beach party. July 10–18; ⓦwww .aspeurope.com.

France online

France info ⓦwww.franceguide.com
French rail ⓦwww.sncf.fr
Paris info ⓦwww.paris-touristoffice.com
Public transport in Paris
ⓦwww.ratp.fr/index_eng.htm

Germany

Capital: Berlin
Population: 82,424,609
Language: German
Currency: Euro (€)
GDP per capita: €22,822
When to go: The weather's at its finest March–September, while March–May and September–October provide the best combination: nice climate, few tourists
When not to go: The Dark Rainy Miserable Season (possibly the actual name) is November–February. If you're heading to popular attractions, July and August are packed with people trying to do exactly the same thing
Minimum daily budget: €31

You can leave your stereotypes (that Germany is a robotic industrial powerhouse that favours rules over creativity and hockey haircuts over fashion) behind with your 2000-watt hairdryer. OK, maybe there's a dash of truth in there, but Germany today is a modern, multicultural patchwork of regional and international identities that are as diverse as its open fields, thick forests and mountain terrain. Its large cities are throbbing with *haute couture* shops, and its beer gardens continue to serve up some of the world's best brew.

The shadow of World War II still lingers for many who visit, but new generations of Germans have moved beyond carrying this heavy ancestral burden with them 24/7. The more recent reunification of the country in 1990 has been a far greater issue, and bridging the forty-year divide is a work in progress.

For the traveller, Europe's largest and most populous nation is extremely accessible. Smaller festivals can be found almost year-round and getting to them with public transport couldn't be easier (unless you speak German).

Main attractions

● **Heidelberg** A picturesque town featuring picturesque Heidelberg Castle and picturesque postcards. It couldn't be more … well, scenic. Visitors rarely miss a stroll along the Hauptstrasse through the old town.

● **Reichstag, Berlin** Germany's past and future are represented in no other building quite like this one. Construction started in 1884, and a decade later it was the parliament for Bismarck's German Empire. After the collapse of the Berlin Wall in 1989, British architect Sir Norman Foster's glass dome has capped off the Hitler-tainted building's rebirth as a united democracy. Visitors can walk right up to the dome and even have a meal there.

● **Cologne Cathedral** The *dom* is a positively enormous thirteenth-century Gothic cathedral in the centre of the city (a few steps from the central train station) that makes a trip to Cologne worthwhile on its own.

● **The Marienplatz glockenspiel, Munich** This hyperactive cuckoo clock in central Munich forms part of the town hall's Gothic facade. Time your visit for 11am, noon or 5pm and you'll get to see the re-enactment of Duke William V's wedding to Renata von Lothringen.

● **Neuschwanstein** If you're one of those picky travellers who'd rather see the original than be satisfied with the Disney replication, you'll need to brave the crowds and make a pilgrimage to this famous "Sleeping Beauty" castle. (Extra kitsch bonus: there's now also the

Musical Theatre Neuschwanstein, a nightly performance based on King Ludwig II's tragic life.)

● **Dachau concentration camp** No matter what you've read or how many movies you've seen on the subject, it's hard to appreciate what happened under Hitler's regime without a trip to a concentration camp memorial. Dachau wasn't the largest such death machine but it was the first to be built, and a few

Average temperatures and rainfall in Germany

Average daily temperatures (maximum and minimum °C) and monthly rainfall (mm)

	Jan	Feb	Mar	Apr	May	June	July	Aug	Sept	Oct	Nov	Dec
Berlin												
max °C	2	4	8	12	18	21	23	23	19	13	7	3
min °C	-3	-3	1	3	7	12	13	13	10	6	2	-1
rainfall mm	43	37	38	42	55	71	53	65	46	36	50	55

hours of wandering the grounds will likely leave a powerful imprint on your soul.

Alternative activities

● **Soak in a spa at Baden-Baden** Germany's most famous spa lies in the heart of the Black Forest. Its famed curative mineral waters bubble up from thermal springs at temperatures over 68° C. The Therme of Caracalla is popular with families, but for a more upscale (and less clothed) experience, try Friedrichsbad.

● **Cycle along the Danube** The cycle path that runs along the Danube River passes monasteries, castles, meadows and forests on a route that is littered with UNESCO World Heritage Sites. If you get hooked, you can continue all the way down to Vienna and Bratislava.

● **Windsurf Lake Constance** Near the Swiss border, the winds of Lake Constance lure German windsurfers by the dozen. Rent a board at Strandbad Eichwald. If your arms get tired, you can also fish the lake (with a permit) for pike, perch and eel. Or head to Lindau, rent a bike, and circle the water on two wheels. Or just take a dip; the mountains surrounding the lake provide a magical backdrop for a swim.

● **Mountain bike the Black Forest** The Black Forest Bike Park has the largest network of mountain-bike trails in the world – about 1400km worth, and with

routes for all levels. There are several places to access the trails: the Elz and Simonswälder valleys, Triberg, Schonach, Schönwald, Furtwangen, St Georgen, Hardt, Lauterbach, Schramberg and Tennenbronn.

Costs

Germany's prices are just about the average for all of Europe, which means stretching your budget in Germany isn't that easy, but it won't be as fiscally painful as the northern countries or around the French Riviera.

Accommodation

You'll see plenty of *Zimmer* signs advertising rooms in private homes, which go for about €12 for a single and €21 for a double (more in cities). The prolific HI hostels are clean but often booked with giant school groups, so check the Web for bookings as far in advance as possible. Prices are around €10–12 at the low end, and €3 for a campground spot.

Eating and drinking

German cuisine doesn't get the sort of fanfare that welcomes Italian and French culinary arts, and for good reason. It is, however, nice and filling in a meat-and-potatoes and deep-fried-anything sort of way. The bread is excellent and you'll find plenty of puffy pastries, but these German street snacks aren't especially cheap. For the very tightly budgeted, supermarket shopping and Turkish food (Germany has a large Turkish population) is the key. The beer isn't ridiculously priced for the amount you get. The problem, budget wise, is that this delicious swill comes in sizes you could use to put out a fire.

Transport

German transport is clean, fast, comfortable and reliable, but not particularly cheap; figure on about €12 per 100km in slow trains and €24 per 100km on fast ICE (InterCityExpress) trains. The buses are mostly owned by Deutsche Bahn and run in conjunction with the trains, which makes for convenient connections, but monopoly pricing. Within the larger cities, you'll mostly likely want a strip card (multiple use) or day card if you plan to hop on the city transit subways (U-Bahns and S-Bahns) for more than three rides.

By train

Germanyrail Pass Any four days of travel in one month €215 (first class), €149 (second class) and €117 (youth pass, second class). Additional days (maximum of six) €28 (first class), €20 (second class) and €11 (youth pass, second class).

Germany and Benelux Pass (also valid in Belgium, the Netherlands and Luxembourg) Ranges from any five days of travel in two months – €268 (first class), €200 (second class) and €162 (youth, second class) – to any ten days of travel in two months – €406 (first class), €305 (second class) and €244 (youth, second class).

Eurodomino Germany Pass Ranges from any three days of travel in one month – €302 (first class), €205 (second class) and €155 (youth, second class) – to any eight days of travel in one month – €447 (first class),

€316 (second class) and €238 (youth, second class).

For Europe-wide **Eurail** and **InterRail** passes, see p.38. For tips and tricks on maximizing your rail pass, see p.71.

Bahn Card 25 Receive fifty percent off all rail travel €100 (first-class card) and €50 (second-class card). If you plan to spend more than €200 (roughly the cost of a return ticket from Frankfurt to Munich), this is a good way to save.

By bus

Busabout barely operates in Germany, merely serving Berlin, Dresden and Munich. For internal bus prices, see Ⓦwww.berlinlinienbus.de. For buses to other countries, see Ⓦwww.eurolines.de.

Events

● **The Berlin Love Parade** and **Munich's Oktoberfest**, Germany's two largest events, are covered on p.17. One is the biggest street party in the Western world, the other is the biggest beer party in the Western world. Both encourage participation and get wonderfully out of hand. (The Love Parade was cancelled in 2004 due to financial difficulties, but organizers expect a big comeback.)

● **Cologne Carnival** Germany's biggest pre-Ash Wednesday blowout bash is in Cologne, where the 178-year-old event is called *Fasnacht*. The second of the three-day event is Rose Monday, and if you're there, it's hard to miss the giant parade through town, with political-themed floats and a bizarre collection of costumes. If you want to dress up, the only guideline they use is "brighter is better".

● **Rhineland in Flames** On five selected dates between spring and autumn, pyrotechnics from decorated barges fill the night sky with colour, while blue flares (known as "Bengal fires") light up the castles and palaces. May–Sept; ⓦwww.germany-tourism.co.uk.

● **World Cup 2006** The country is already bracing itself for when football's greatest show rolls into town. Fans of the world's top football teams will bring a frenzied atmosphere to German cities as they erupt with parties and – in all likelihood – beer-fuelled brawls. June–July 2006; ⓦwww.fifaworldcup.com.

Germany online

Country info ⓦwww.germany-tourism.de
Rail ⓦwww.bahn.de
Bus ⓦwww.berlinlinienbus.de
Berlin info ⓦwww.berlin.de
Munich info ⓦwww.muenchen.de

Greece

Capital: Athens
Population: 10,647,529
Language: Greek
Currency: Euro (€)
GDP per capita: €16,250
When to go: Mid-April to mid-June and September to mid-October, when the attractions are less crowded, the temperature is pleasant, and accommodation easy to find
When not to go: In the heart of summer (mid-June to August), when the heat is searing, and the winter months (November–February), when the tourist infrastructure goes into lock-down mode
Minimum daily budget: €29

For the backpacker, Greece has traditionally been about island hopping, ouzo drinking and plate smashing. But this country has far more to offer than most ever realize. The land that gave the world the Olympics, Socrates, drama, democracy, an enormous chunk of our vocabulary and the inspiration for toga parties deserves more than a cursory glance. From the recently renovated Athens with its Acropolis views to riding a mule up the cliffs of Santorini to farmers that are happy to have you taste their just-pressed olive oil, the Greek gods seem to have blessed the country with ample sights and activities.

Before heading out to explore the country's 2000-island archipelago, where you can easily lose yourself for years, you might head up the mainland or down to the Peloponnesian peninsula, where many of the most outstanding archeological sites and monuments can be found.

Main attractions

● **Acropolis** You may not get above the *nefos* (smog), but the views are still stunning from this ancient site, often called the "Sacred Rock" of Athens. Four masterpieces are assembled on this rocky hill: the Parthenon, the Propylaea, the Erechtheum and the Temple of Athena Nike.

● **Medieval city of Rhodes** Perched at the northern tip of the island of the same name, this is one of the most festive UNESCO World Heritage Sites you'll come across. Bustling bars and restaurants now occupy this walled city that was previously run by the Order of St John of Jerusalem (1309 to 1523), Turks and Italians. You can sit on the beach just outside the walls and look out to the Turkish coast.

● **Delphi** One of Greece's greatest cultural treasures, Delphi lies just 150km northwest of Athens, harbouring the Temple of Apollo, Castalian Spring and Corycian Cave in its hillside complex. It's not just another collection of ruins, though; according to mythology, Delphi was the "navel of the Earth" (centre of the world).

● **Olympia** The site of the first Olympic Games (776 BC), Olympia still houses some of Greece's most important monuments: the Temple of Zeus, the Temple of Hera, the Stadium, the Bouleuterion, the Gymnasium and the Prytaneion (site of the eternal flame).

● **Knossos' Royal Palace, Crete**
According to legend, King Minos's wife give birth to the half-bull, half-man Minotaur at Knossos on the island of Crete. The labyrinth-like West Court is where the Minotaur caught his victims, and where Daedalus and his son, Icarus, were imprisoned and created wings of wax for their ill-fated escape.

Alternative activities

● **Row into the Melissáni Cave** "Cave" may be a loose definition for this geo-

logical wonder on the island of Kefalloniá, since part of the roof collapsed thousands of years ago, leaving most of the football-pitch-sized submersed area in daylight. What you won't be able to see from a rowboat is that a series of subterranean passages connect the cave to the other side of the island, 28km away.

● **Climb the cliff-top monasteries of Metéora** James Bond climbed the walls to one of these monasteries using only his shoelaces in *For Your Eyes Only*, but it was a favourite spot among travellers long before that. The agile ninth-century hermits who first settled in the caves and rock fissures would descend every Sunday for Mass.

Average daily temperatures (maximum and minimum °C) and monthly rainfall (mm)

	Jan	Feb	Mar	Apr	May	June	July	Aug	Sept	Oct	Nov	Dec
Athens												
max °C	13	13	16	19	23	28	32	31	28	23	18	14
min °C	7	7	8	11	15	19	23	22	19	15	12	8
rainfall mm	48	41	41	23	18	8	5	8	10	53	56	63

● **Visit the gods of Mount Olympus**
Mount Olympus, Greece's highest peak, served as a sort of Melrose Place for the Greek gods. Today, it's Greece's oldest and most carefully protected national park. Staying at refuges along the way, visitors can trek among the peaks, stopping at the Plateau of the Muses to see the peak of Stefani (the throne of Zeus), and look down on the world like the gods once did.

● **Kayak around the Ionian Islands** In the waters between Greece and Italy, you'll find a calm and clear passageway, sheltered from the prevailing northeastern winds. Kayak between famous islands and uninhabited little jewels. Sightings of loggerhead turtles, monk seals and dolphins are common.

● **Attend a show at Epidaurus**
Throughout the summer (on Fridays and Saturdays), the well-preserved Ancient Theatre of Epidaurus takes a step back in time to put on classical Greek dramas. The acoustics are excellent but the tickets are hard to get (ⓦhttp://groups.msn.com /ancientepidavrosgreece).

Costs

Greece is one of those countries that was dirt cheap not so long ago, and if you run into an ageing budget traveller, you'll get an earful of how great it all was before you arrived. Figure on €29 per day for a bare-bones budget, with hitching, supermarket food and minimal island hopping. For ferries, eating out at a few restaurants, it rises to €40–50.

Accommodation
Travel out of peak season (mid-June through August) and you'll save a small fortune on hotels, which typically drop their rate by over 25 percent.

Eating and drinking
A nice restaurant meal costs about €12, but you can snack your way to a full meal for less than that. Small kebabs and cheese pies are delicious and cheap. You can find oven-baked *mousaka* and *tzatziki* (yoghurt, garlic and cucumber dip) everywhere.

Transport
Mainland Greece is an easy place to travel around by a combination of buses and trains. The rail lines are cheap (€12 for a 6hr journey) but somewhat limited, while the buses reach even the smallest villages. Eleven ferry companies serve the islands domestically, but are not terribly punctual, and erratic visits to some islands make scheduling difficult. High-speed ferries go twice as fast for twice the price. For three times the price, you can fly. One of the most charming ways to island hop is by tagging a lift on a private yacht or by taking one of the colourful wooden skiffs, called *kaikia* or *caiques*. On the islands, bikes and

scooters are popular to rent, but be warned: Greece has the second highest traffic fatality rate (after Portugal) in Europe.

By train

Greek Flexi Pass Rail'n Fly Any three days of travel in one month, plus two flight coupons €208 (first class) and €202 (youth, first class).

Balkans Flexi Pass (also valid in Bulgaria, Romania and Turkey) Any five days of travel in one month €156 (first class) and €93 (youth, first class). Any ten days of travel in one month €273 (first class) and €162 (youth, first class). Any fifteen days of travel in one month €328 (first class) and €197 (youth, first class).
For Europe-wide **InterRail** passes (**Eurail** doesn't cover Greece), see p.38. For tips and tricks on maximizing your rail pass, see p.71.

By bus

Busabout doesn't operate in Greece. For internal bus prices, see Ⓦwww.ktel.org.

Events

● **Easter** Easter is the biggest holiday in Greece, with celebrations across the country. In central Macedonia, villagers walk barefoot across hot coals. In Lerissos, there's line dancing. In Agios Nikolaos, you'll see the Burning of Judas. In Corfu, jar smashing. Greek Orthodox Easter, however, does not always fall on the same Sunday as the Catholic and Protestant Easter, since it is calculated with a different calendar.

● **Rockwave, Athens** The capital's premier rock concert brings in headliners such as Peter Gabriel and Judas Priest to keep the 50,000-plus visitors entertained for three days of live music. June; Ⓦwww.didimusic.gr.

Greece online

Country info Ⓦwww.gnto.gr
Rail Ⓦwww.ose.gr
Bus Ⓦwww.ktel.org
Ferry Ⓦwww.ferries.gr
Athens info Ⓦwww.cityofathens.gr

Hungary

Capital: Budapest
Population: 10,032,375
Language: Hungarian
Currency: Forint (HUF)
GDP per capita: €11,341
When to go: March–May is ideal, but be prepared for spring showers; June–August is warm and sunny, but can be crowded in parts around July and August; September and October are also pleasant
When not to go: November is cold rain, and after that it's just cold; August is called "the cucumber-growing season" because there's not much else happening with so many Hungarians on holiday
Minimum daily budget: €21

When most travellers head to Hungary, they bring few of the preconceptions that typically get carted along with them to France, Italy and England. And, for many, Hungary feels like one of those surprise foreign films that you never realized you'd enjoy so much. Make no mistake, Budapest doesn't pack the architectural punch of Paris, but there's plenty of Magyar magic in this town, and without any of that Parisian pretence. The country's history reads like a James Clavell novel. As recently as 1999, the country joined NATO. Before that, János Kádár's 1970s reforms, a "goulash communism" that was slightly more consumer-oriented, helped make Hungary the richest, most liberal country in the region. When the fence along its border with Austria came down in 1989, the country held its first free elections in forty years. So be careful when you lump this land together with the rest of the Balkans – you might get an earful from a local. Keep in mind the ballpoint pen, match, Rubik's cube and helicopter were all invented by Hungarians.

If you want the charm, luxury and tree-lined walkways of Western Europe and the prices of Eastern Europe,

Hungary offers a nice compromise. The language may be an enigma, but there's no mystery about the rich wines and elegant thermal spas. The lakes are lined with resorts and there's a lively, though not frenetic, café scene. Budapest straddles the River Danube with Buda to the west, rising dramatically from the banks, and Pest sitting on the edge of the eastern Great Plain.

Main attractions

● **Castle Hill, Budapest** Castle Hill beckons to travellers when they arrive. It's the "What's that?!" up on the hill that holds Budapest's most important museums and monuments. Make the trip over the river and up and you'll find both the Old Town and Royal Palace within this walled area. Plus, some of the best views in town.

● **Lake Balaton** Just 100km outside Budapest, this lake is one of Europe's largest. The south shore has most of the glitz and hotels (specifically the town of Siófok), while the north shore has the hiking trails and historical sights. Balantonfüred, once a writers' colony and political retreat, seems to bridge the gap.

● **Gellért Hill, Budapest** When your legs recharge after Castle Hill, the next panoramic climb is to the Citadella, a fortress atop Gellért Hill that also serves as Budapest's unofficial symbol. On the way down, stop at the *Gellért Hotel*, an old-world lodging with a remarkable spa that feels as if you're swimming in a half-submerged church.

● **Royal Palace, Budapest** The Royal Palace has been rebuilt more times than Michael Schumacher's car. It now houses the Hungarian National Gallery, the National Széchényi Library and the Budapest History Museum; allow plenty of time.

Alternative activities

● **Take a bath** Taking a dip in the warm thermal and cool mineral springs that bubble under Budapest is the perfect antidote to the tired legs and traveller grime you get from sightseeing, though some of the baths are architectural wonders themselves. Two baths (Palatinus and Hajos) are located on Margaret Island, just between Buda and Pest. The Király baths – sitting just on the Buda side, with four pools and a sixteenth-century sky-lit dome – are flanked by the Lukács baths to the north and the Rác and Rudas and Gellért baths to the south.

● **Row down the Danube** Rowing and kayaking are possible on the Danube. In Budapest, you can hire boats, kayaks or canoes on Margaret Island or along the Romai River Bank.

● **Head underground** The Mátyás Caves can be found right under Budapest, formed by thermal waters gushing through thousands of years ago. The tiny passageways don't make for a leisurely stroll; you may spend more time on your belly than your feet. Helmets, overalls and head-lamps are the way to go. Trips can be arranged though several of the hostels in town, such as *Backpackers* Ⓦ www.backpackers.hu.

Average daily temperatures (maximum and minimum °C) and monthly rainfall (mm)

	Jan	Feb	Mar	Apr	May	June	July	Aug	Sept	Oct	Nov	Dec
Budapest												
max °C	2	4	11	16	21	24	26	26	22	15	7	3
min °C	-4	-3	2	5	11	13	15	15	11	1	1	-2
rainfall mm	41	38	34	41	61	68	45	55	39	34	59	48

• **Take a day-trip to Veszprém** A few hours by bus or train out of Budapest is one of Hungary's most impressive sights: the walled-in castle district of Veszprém resting atop a plateau. Formerly a royal residence, it now serves as a museum of Baroque art and architecture.

Costs

The relatively low costs are one of Hungary's biggest draws, but it's not exactly dirt cheap. Figure on €17, with some real scrimping, or €21 with basic frugality. You can live well for under €45, but as you move up in quality the tipping also goes up – Hungary is tip-conscious and ten percent is the norm.

Accommodation

Hostels and, in the summer, university dormitories are less than €12. But don't rule out B&B-style private homes, which can be arranged through the tourist office for €8–18. For a three-star hotel, rates start around €45. Campground bungalows will be your cheapest roofed option in many parts of the country, and the quality of the bungalows ranges from "fully operational kitchen" to "at least the roof isn't leaking too much".

Eating and drinking

There are slim pickings for vegetarians in this farmhouse-style meat-and-potatoes-based cuisine. Goulash soup doesn't get everyone excited, but it's worth a try while you're here. A traditional three-course meal can be had for less than €8, and a simple, filling meal for less than €3. A beer in a trendy bar is under €1 and in a regular bar just sixty cents. Which all means it's a fine place to treat yourself.

Transport

You won't break any speed records on the Hungarian public transport, but it'll get you around. The toughest part might just be getting information without access to the Web at every train and bus stop. The trains are dependable, although also dependably late. You'll probably have better luck buying tickets at a MAV office than the train station. (A reservation is cheap and avoids standing for hours on the train.) Eurail and InterRail passes cover Hungary, but buses can be quicker between many of the destinations, and cost just €2–4 per 100km.

In Budapest, a block of ten single tickets costs €4, a one-day travel card is €3 and a three-day card is €6. A two-day Budapest Card costs €15 and gets you into museums, gives you discounts on restaurants and spas, and entitles you to free transport. (Don't forget to punch each metro ticket you use in the machines provided on every bus, tram, trolleybus and at each metro station entrance, however.)

By train

Hungarian Flexi Pass Any five days of travel in fifteen days €62 (first class). Any ten days of travel in one month €78 (first class).

Eurail Romania-Hungary Pass Ranges from any five days of travel in two months – €163 (first class) and €114 (youth, second class) – to any ten days of travel in two months – €245 (first class) and €171 (youth, second class).

European East Pass (also valid in Austria, the Czech and Slovak republics and Poland) Any five days of travel in one month €184 (first class) and €131 (second class). Additional travel days cost €21 (first class) and €15 (second class).

For Europe-wide **Eurail** and **InterRail** passes, see p.38. For tips and tricks on maximizing your rail pass, see p.71.

By bus

Busabout (see p.39) doesn't operate in Hungary, but a "link" with Vienna in Austria can be bought for an additional €69. For internal bus prices, see ⓦwww.volanbusz.hu. For buses to other countries, see ⓦwww.eurolines.com.

Events

● **Budapest Spring Festival** The onset of spring signals the start of Hungary's biggest annual cultural event. There are chamber concerts, opera, jazz, dance, film screenings and more scattered at venues throughout Budapest. You'll see the best Hungarian performers, in addition to international artists. Third Thurs in March; ⓦwww.fesztivalvaros.hu.

● **Danube Water Carnival** The Danube Water Carnival is one of the most stunning sights in Budapest. It includes stunt-plane flying, parachuting, a rowing regatta, a parade of illuminated yachts and a water show by fire-service boats. Plus a fireworks display from the Chain Bridge. Third Sat in June; ⓦwww.karneval.hu.

● **Budapest Parade** Over fifty carnival floats prance across Budapest from Roosevelt Square to Hero's Square. Wild costumes and revelling accompany the floats until the fireworks kick off to signal the start of the "real" party, as clubs open their doors for the post-parade bashes. Don't forget to wear something that looks good when completely covered in foam. Fourth Sat in Aug; ⓦwww.sziget.hu /budapestparade.

● **Vizimozi Cinetrip, Budapest** Here's a seriously cool pool party. Every couple of months, the normally men-only Rudas Bath House opens its doors to anyone in a swimsuit, and features silent films viewed from the main pool. There's belly dancing, drinking and a host of DJs. ⓦwww.cinetrip.net.

Hungary online

Country info ⓦwww.hungary.com
Rail ⓦwww.elvira.hu
Bus ⓦwww.volanbusz.hu
Budapest info ⓦwww.budapestinfo.hu

Ireland

THE REPUBLIC OF IRELAND
Capital: Dublin
Population: 3,969,558
Languages: English (also Gaelic, spoken mainly on the western seaboard)
Currency: Euro (€)
GDP per capita: €24,200
Minimum daily budget: €32

NORTHERN IRELAND
Capital: Belfast
Population: 1,685,267
Language: English

Currency: Pound sterling (GBP)
GDP per capita: €18,800
Minimum daily budget: €34

When to go: April–May and September are ideal. June–August is, with a bit of Irish luck, lovely, even if crowded
When not to go: Prices go up in the summer and the miserable winter weather chases so many away that many small hotels and restaurants outside the main cities shut from October to the end of March

The Irish landscape has an enchanting and mystical nature that's nearly as disarming as the Irish themselves. Despite the hypersaturated weather conditions ("horizontal rain" is common in some parts) and lack of leprechauns, few leave without being touched by the country's green charm.

For all the years of strife between the Republic and Northern Ireland, we've thrust them together for the sake of the traveller, who is not confined by boundaries or history. Both countries share the same landmass, and even many of the same bus and rail connections. They also share green, rolling hills; wild, rugged coastlines; and people with an uncanny ability to strike up conversation. As the expression goes in Ireland, "It never rains inside a pub." And they're not just a shelter from the elements; the pub is a social engine that powers the country, whether you're tasting traditional Irish stew, listening to folk tunes on the fiddle, or getting a long, almost-coherent Guinness-fuelled tale from a pub regular. In *Ulysses*, Joyce noted: "A good puzzle would be to cross Dublin without passing a pub."

Ireland has been riding an economic swell of late. The ebb of Irish seeking fortune abroad has turned into a flow of tourists – Ireland has become one of the top destinations in Europe. Things may seem a bit grey at times, the urban architecture less impressive than in Europe's other marquee cities, but if it's the personal connections that make the strongest memories, you'll be hard-pressed to find more welcoming citizens over on the continent.

Main attractions

● **Guinness Storehouse, Dublin**
Guinness may look like discarded

Cairnryan & Troon

Stranraer & Troon

Liverpool

Liverpool, Holyhead & Mostyn

Fishguard

Pembroke

brake fluid, but this thick stout with a scientifically measured head of foam is worshipped like a minor deity. And the Guinness Storehouse in Dublin is the high altar. Naturally, you have to suffer a marketing blitz to get to the liquid lunch at the end of the tour. See ⓦ www.guinness-storehouse.com for tour details.

• **Dublin Castle** One of the best parts of Dublin Castle, built in the thirteenth century by order of King John, is the bit beneath it. Recent flooding has led to

excavations, which revealed new finds: the old city walls and a moat.

• **Blarney Stone** Blarney Castle in southwest Ireland holds the famous Blarney Stone – given to Cormac McCarthy by Robert the Bruce in 1314, a time when stones were appropriate gifts – high up in its battlements. To kiss it (and give yourself the gift of the gab – that is, an eternity of yapping) you have to lie down, tilt your head back, get lowered in upside down by a helper and plant your pucker on the stone.

Average daily temperatures (maximum and minimum °C) and monthly rainfall (mm)

	Jan	Feb	Mar	Apr	May	June	July	Aug	Sept	Oct	Nov	Dec
Belfast												
max °C	7	7	9	11	14	16	17	17	15	11	8	7
min °C	4	5	6	7	9	12	13	13	11	8	6	6
rainfall mm	86	58	67	53	60	63	64	80	85	88	78	78
Dublin												
max °C	8	8	9	11	14	17	19	18	16	13	10	6
min °C	3	3	4	5	7	10	12	12	10	8	5	4
rainfall mm	15	10	10	8	15	36	48	46	25	20	18	20

● **Giant's Causeway** The only World Heritage Site in Northern Ireland is a geological phenomenon on the North Antrim coast. Caused by a volcanic eruption sixty million years ago, the rock formations look something like a ceramic plate warehouse, or perhaps the world's largest collection of petrified tortoise shells.

Alternative activities

● **Watch Gaelic games** Croke Park in Dublin plays host to the All-Ireland Hurling finals; something between lacrosse and field hockey, this uniquely Irish sport is not for the timid. While you're there, you might check out the Gaelic football finals. It's just like regular football, except there's none of that off-side nonsense. And you can use your hands, provided you alternate using your feet as well. And if the ball sails over the goal, you still get a point (if it goes in, you get three). Other than that, just like football.

● **Go fishing** Ireland is famous for its fishing, and it's not uncommon for people to show up at the airport with a rod and reel. Permits are mandatory, as is a state national licence, if you're going after salmon or sea trout. There's over 5000km of coastline to cast in for the big one.

● **Take a walk in the country** Believe it or not, walking is one of Ireland's biggest draws. There are several designated walks, such as the Wicklow, Kerry and Beara Ways, to help you reach some of the most beautiful sections of the country. Or you can head underground for a walk in the Burren, a series of caverns, springs and chasms just outside Limerick and Galway.

● **Dive the Irish Sea** Ireland is unlikely to be the first place that comes to mind when you want to go scuba diving, but it has some of Europe's best conditions. At Dunmanus Bay near Cork, Bantry Bay around Hook Head and Galway Bay near Wexford, you'll find plenty of dive sites. For a wreck dive, there's the HMS *Drake* off Rathlin Island on the northeast coast.

Costs

Ireland isn't a cheap place to visit. In fact, for most shopping it can be downright expensive. Accommodation is one beacon of budget hope, with reasonable prices by European standards.

Accommodation

Regular rain can make the camping experience fairly unpleasant, but many tough it out. There are plenty of hostels to keep you dry if you prefer to stay indoors. Independent hostels in larger city centres are reasonable (€10–16) and the Irish Youth Hostel Association and Hostelling International Northern Ireland can help find even cheaper digs, provided you have Hostelling International membership (ⓦwww.hiayh.org). B&Bs are a good option as well. For about €20, you can find a charming place to spend the night.

Eating and drinking

There are more hearty, inexpensive dishes in this country than you can shake a shamrock at. Most can be bought in a pub and few are fit for vegetarians. There's less high-end, gourmet fare, so a typical meal is unlikely to break your budget – €4–12 is standard for a small feast. For a real treat, try the oysters, one of Ireland's most celebrated catches.

Transport

Rail fares aren't cheap, so many travellers without a rail pass go by bus, bike or thumb.

By train

Irish Explorer Any five days of travel in fifteen days €143. Any eight days of travel in fifteen days (valid in Ireland only; allows travel on Bus Éireann as well) €176. Any fifteen days of travel in thirty days (valid in Ireland and Northern Ireland; allows travel on Bus Éireann as well) €341.
For Europe-wide **Eurail** and **InterRail** passes (which cover Ireland but not Northern Ireland), see p.38. For tips and tricks on maximizing your rail pass, see

p.71. For internal rail prices, see ⓦwww.irishrail.ie (Ireland) and ⓦwww.nirailways.co.uk (Northern Ireland).

Translink Student Discount Card

Full-time students can buy a discount card (€10) that gives fifteen percent discounts on buses and 33 percent discounts on rail travel in Northern Ireland and cross-border services to Ireland. You should be able to make up the cost of the card with just a few trips. See ⓦwww.translink.co.uk.

By bus

Irish Explorer Any three days of travel in eight days €53. Any eight days of travel in fifteen days (valid in Ireland only; allows travel on Irish Rail as well) €176. Any fifteen days of travel in thirty days (valid in Ireland and Northern Ireland; allows travel on Irish Rail as well) €341.

Busabout doesn't operate in Ireland nor Northern Ireland. For internal bus prices, see ⓦwww.buseireann.ie. For buses to the UK (from Ireland only), see ⓦwww.eurolines.ie.

Events

● **St Patrick's Day**, the largest festival, is your chance to dress in green and drink yourself green on the same day. There's far more than a parade for this multi-day event. See p.16 for more.

● **Irish Derby** Each summer, this enormous equestrian event takes place at the Curragh (one of the oldest sporting venues in Europe), and most of the country tunes in to watch the top horses speed around this ancient racecourse. June; ⓦwww.curragh.ie.

● **Bloomsday, Dublin** Every June, the work of author James Joyce is celebrated on the day his masterpiece,

Ulysses, is set, and the literati retrace the steps of the book's famous character, Leopold Bloom. June 16; ⓦwww.rejoycedublin2004.com.

● **Banks of the Foyle Halloween Carnival, Derry** At the end of October, Ireland's best Halloween carnival gets cranked up in Derry as over 35,000 witches, ghouls and other Harry Potter-types take to the streets. Fireworks, ghost tours and the like can be found in this spooktacular fest. Oct 31; ⓦwww.derrycity.gov.uk/halloween.

Ireland online

Ireland info ⓦwww.ireland.travel.ie
Ireland rail ⓦwww.irishrail.ie
Ireland (and Northern Ireland) bus info ⓦwww.buseireann.ie
Dublin info ⓦwww.visitdublin.com

Northern Ireland info ⓦwww
.discovernorthernireland.com
Northern Ireland rail ⓦwww
.nirailways.co.uk
Belfast info ⓦwww.belfast.net

Italy

Capital: Rome
Population: 58,057,477
Language: Italian
Currency: Euro (€)
GDP per capita: €22,160
When to go: April–May and October–November, when the landscape colours are at their best, the temperatures are more moderate and there are relatively few crowds
When not to go: August. Italians take their vacations then, so many shops and businesses are shut, and the tourists are the only ones walking the searing streets
Minimum daily budget: €33

From frescoes to Ferraris, Venice to Versace, and the Pope to pasta, there's something in this boot-shaped nation for every sort of traveller. You can take a chilly dip in the Med at one end of the country or go skiing at the other. There's fashion on the streets of Milan and fish in the street markets of the little villages dotted around Sicily. The rich textile town of Treviso, just north of Venice, couldn't be more different to the rougher areas of Naples. At times, the country seems so diverse, the only thing holding it together is the national football team. In other words, a short visit to Venice, Florence or Rome will provide little more than a snapshot of this culturally overflowing land.

Main attractions

● **The Vatican, Rome** OK, technically this is a city-state, not an attraction within Italy, but guidebooks have been guilty of pairing them for decades with less justification than this. Let your jaw drop when you enter St Peter's Cathedral, considered Christianity's most magnificent Renaissance church. And get ready to queue for Michelangelo's Sistine Chapel (or book ahead), though many find the maps and frescoes on the way to the Chapel even more compelling than the main draw.

● **Assisi** Perched halfway up Mount Subasio, overlooking the town of Perugia, this walled city with a four-teenth-century fortress (Rocca Maggiore) is the birthplace of St Francis (1182). Work began on his basilica in 1228, two years after his death, and if you can get past all the religious pil-grims, it's one of the most enchanting towns in the country.

● **The Colosseum, Rome** Long before *Gladiator* was made into a movie and David Beckham put on body armour for Pepsi, the Colosseum in Rome (com-pleted in 80 AD) was the ultimate arena for public games.

● **Venice** It's sinking (possibly under the weight of all the tourists), and there's a chance the water may be knee-deep in St Mark's Square by the time you visit, but to stroll Venice without crowds (off season, or at sunrise) may top your European visual highlights. There's a reason so many use it for comparison (Stockholm says it's the "Venice of the North", the Okavango Delta calls itself the "Venice of Africa"). There's little need for an overpriced gondola ride. A cheap city bus-boat will do just fine. Do yourself a favour while visiting, and get lost; put away your map and wander the narrow back-alleys until you need to ask a local for directions.

● **Florence** This city offers more art history per square metre than any other place outside the Louvre. You could spend a year here and not see it all. In fact, several guidebooks far thicker than this book are devoted entirely to Florence.

This Renaissance wonderland boasts the Uffizi Gallery, Ponte Vecchio, the Duomo, Michelangelo's *David*, and the Basilica di San Lorenzo, to name but a few.

Alternative activities

● **Walk the Cinque Terre** The five post-card-perfect fishing villages of the Cinque Terre (Riomaggiore, Manarola, Monterosso, Vernazza and Corniglia) along the northwest coast are con-

Average temperatures and rainfall in Italy

Average daily temperatures (maximum and minimum °C) and monthly rainfall (mm)

	Jan	Feb	Mar	Apr	May	June	July	Aug	Sept	Oct	Nov	Dec
Venice												
max °C	6	8	12	16	21	24	27	27	23	18	11	7
min °C	-1	1	4	8	13	16	18	18	15	10	4	0
rainfall mm	56	53	61	74	69	79	69	79	66	76	89	62
Rome												
max °C	13	13	15	17	22	25	28	28	26	22	17	14
min °C	4	4	6	8	12	16	19	19	17	13	8	6
rainfall mm	81	71	69	66	51	33	15	25	69	114	112	97

nected by a cliff-side hiking trail that can be completed in one long day or divided up into a few days with hotel stays and good meals.

● **Climb the vie ferrate in the Dolomites** The *vie ferrate* (iron ways) are a magnificent system of steel ladders and fixed cables, originally built during World War I to help Alpine troops move through the mountains. With only modest modifications, they now allow beginner climbers to clip in and safely ascend to incredible heights.

● **Take a wine tour** Brunello di Montalcino is the Rolls-Royce of Italian wines. You can tour Montalcino, Chianti, or try the Cabernet Sauvignon of the Tuscan coast. The choice is limitless; you can taste some of the world's top wines almost everywhere you go.

● **Watch a volcano blow** Check your insurance coverage (see p.113 for more details), then take a ferry from Naples or the north of Sicily to the island of Stromboli, hike a few hours up to the top of its volcano (you can't miss it), watch the sunset and then stick around for Mother Nature's fireworks as small eruptions send orange molten lava 50–100m up into the air.

● **Take in a football match** The bigger clubs like AC Milan, Juventus and

Roma are among the best in the world, but you might find it more culturally enlightening to watch a game at a smaller stadium. Just make sure you're wearing the right colours. Rather, make sure you're not wearing the wrong colours. If you're not sure, bring a bag with a few options so you can adapt to your surroundings.

Costs

Italy may be cheaper than Switzerland and Scandinavia, but between the beckoning *gelato*, coffee and museums, there's a load more tempting "necessities" you're likely to spend your money on. Prudent backpackers might manage on €33 a day, but cutting costs is extrapainful in this country, even if the museum visits are minimized. Comfortable hotels and restaurants with table service will up this to over €65 per day.

Accommodation
Lodging can be found for €12 a night, but it's typically over €17 and, as soon as you get into the genuine hotel range, prices soar. There are a number of luxury campgrounds just outside of cities that provide budget relief (and a pool).

Eating and drinking

Italy may be famous for its cuisine, but if you want to *mangiare* on the cheap, especially in the tourist areas, you'll likely be underwhelmed by what you get. Pasta may be difficult to mess up, but it's not always easy to find the truly divine dishes. Pizzas come in one size, taste better than average (occasionally amazing), and are relatively cheap. Prices vary around Italy, but generally it's high prices up north and better deals down south. There's a reason you'll see so many people standing at cafes and bars – prices are higher if you grab a seat.

Transport

Major train and bus lines are quick and reliable (when not on strike); even the small village buses are surprisingly timely. And, aside from the high-speed rail, it's quite cheap. Always check the local prices before you use your rail or bus pass; it's better value to pay €8–17 for a short ride than waste a day of your pass. The Rome public transport system (Metrebus) sells a daily transport pass ticket for €4, a three-day pass for €11 and a seven-day pass for €16. Tickets can be bought at newsstands, hotels and vending machines. For more information, see Ⓦwww.atac.roma.it.

By train

Trenitalia Pass (includes ferry to Sicily) Any four days of travel in two months €198 (first class), €158 (second class) and €132 (youth). Additional days (maximum of six) €20 (first class), €16 (second class) and €13 (youth).

France'n Italy Pass Any four days of travel in two months €247 (first class), €214 (second class) and €165 (youth, second class) Additional days (maximum of six) €25 (first class), €22 (second class) and €17 (youth, second class).

Eurodomino Italian Pass Ranges from any three days of travel in one month – €221 (first class), €188 (second class) and €142 (youth, second class) – to any eight days of travel in one month – €351 (first class), €197 (second class) and €222 (youth, second class).

For Europe-wide **Eurail** and **InterRail** passes, see p.38. For tips and tricks on maximizing your rail pass, see p.71.

By bus

A Busabout pass (see p.39) allows you to travel throughout Italy. For internal bus prices, see the Italian-language-only site Ⓦwww.sita-on-line.it. For buses to other countries, see Ⓦwww.eurolines.it.

Events

● **Alba Truffle Auction** You can call them fungi if you like. Or *Turber magnatum pico*, if you want to impress. But in Alba, the home of the delicacy found in the ground by trained dogs, they're known as *tartufo bianco* – white truffles. More prized than France's black truffles, top chefs shell out over €1620 per kilo for these "white diamonds," most popular on omelettes, fresh pasta and risotto. Some truffle oils even fall within the price range of normal people. Mid-Sept to Nov.

● **The Italian Job** If you've seen *The Italian Job*, you might want to catch this film-inspired sponsored rally. A train of Mini Coopers speed across the Alps, pick up a load of local wine and then head back to the UK to auction it off for charity. Late Oct–Nov; Ⓦwww.wordserf.co.uk/italianjob.

● **Carnevale, Venice** Perhaps the only thing better than seeing St Mark's Square without tourists is seeing it during Carnevale, which comes alive with theatrical, dance and acrobatic performances. The most famous and traditional aspect of the festival are the traditional masked balls, which feature elaborate eighteenth-century costumes. Feb–March; ⓦ www.venice-carnival.com.

● **Verona Opera Festival** Even if you don't like opera, seeing grand performances in Verona's exquisite Roman amphitheatre will stir your heart. All classes of society come together for this highlight of Italy's summer calendar. June–Aug; ⓦ www.arena.it.

● **Il Palio, Siena** This madcap medieval horse race in Siena's town square is surrounded by days of rituals and pageantry – nearly all of it just as much fun for visitors as the race itself. See p.17 for more.

● **Regata Storica, Venice** A trial of strength and skill for the city's gondo-

liers, this floating parade of antique boats and rowers in period dress could-n't be any more photo-friendly if it had been invented by a team of Fuji film executives. Spectators are expected to support the contestants and may even get issued with the appropriate colours. First Sun in Sept.

Italy online

Country info ⓦ www.italiantourism.com
Rail ⓦ www.trenitalia.com
Bus ⓦ www.sita-on-line.it
Rome info ⓦ www.romaturismo.com
Florence info ⓦ www.comune.firenze.it
Milan info ⓦ www.turismo.comune .milano.it
Venice info ⓦ www.veniceonline.it

The Netherlands

Capital: Amsterdam
Population: 16,318,199
Languages: Dutch (also Frisian)
Currency: Euro (€)
GDP per capita: €23,250
When to go: Mid-march to mid-May, when the tulips and daffodils are in bloom and when you'll get the best views of the country, while missing the crowds
When not to go: Late October and November, when there's freezing rain, and December–February, unless you're happy to ice-skate your way around the country.
Minimum daily budget: €30

The preconceived images of windmills and wooden clogs and tulips have given way in recent decades to sex, drugs and tulips. Sure, you can buy small amounts of marijuana in coffee shops. And yes, prostitution is legal and regulated. But it's a shame to visit and leave without learning more about the Netherlands than this.

The country is one of Europe's most developed and densely populated, yet the Dutch maintain a charming balance between the fun-loving attitude found along the Mediterranean and the more reserved and regulated philosophy of the Scandinavian countries. Among the many misconceptions is the country's name. It's often called Holland – even by the tourist board, who believe this is an easier name for foreign visitors to remember – but this is technically incorrect. Holland is one of the most populated regions, and the one where many of this once-great colonial power's sailors came from, but "the Netherlands" is the official name.

Nearly half of this nation is below sea level, and much of it has been physically reclaimed from the sea. The part that does rise above the water-mark looks, at least on a topographical profile map, like the chart of a patient who just flatlined. Which is why the country is so popularly navigated by bike. Or by canal, either on the barges in the summer or by ice skates in the winter; it's no accident the Dutch bring home Olympic speed-skating medals by the crate. The capital, Amsterdam, is centrally located and rarely missed by those trying to conquer Europe in a summer. You may be lured in by the famous vices and a reputation for budget travel, but you'll often find this visually stunning city serves only as a gateway to a very accessible country largely overlooked by most travellers.

Main attractions

● **Van Gogh Museum, Amsterdam**
The drawings, notebooks and letters of this one-eared Dutch Master come with a chronologically displayed collection of his paintings. Famous works such as the *Potato Eaters* and *Sunflowers* series and the tortured *Wheatfield with Crows* can all be found here. See Ⓦwww.vangoghmuseum.nl.

- **Anne Frank House, Amsterdam** In
July 1942, Otto and Edith Frank and
their daughters, Margo and Anne, went
into hiding in this building on
Prnsengracht in Amsterdam. Along with
a few others, they hid for two years
before they were betrayed and deported
to Auschwitz. Both sisters died just
weeks before their concentration camp
was liberated, but Anne's diary survived,
and has since been published in more

than 55 languages. The house is now a
popular museum. See Ⓦwww.annefrank
.nl for exhibition info.

- **Amsterdam's Red Light District**
Started as a place to "comfort" the
returning sailors after long voyages,
the District is now mostly a strange
sight: bored women in ornate lingerie
beckoning passers-by (often tourist
families with grandmothers in tow) to
come a little closer to their door-sized

Average daily temperatures (maximum and minimum °C) and monthly rainfall (mm)

	Jan	Feb	Mar	Apr	May	June	July	Aug	Sept	Oct	Nov	Dec
Amsterdam												
max °C	8	6	8	12	17	19	21	21	18	14	9	7
min °C	5	0	3	4	8	12	13	13	11	8	4	3
rainfall mm	78	45	94	37	51	62	73	61	81	106	76	69

windows. Innocently snap a picture and you'll likely find the entire roll of film forcefully removed from your camera and tossed in the canal by a human tank in a leather jacket. For all its famed erotica, this area is one of the least arousing places you'll stumble across.

● **Tulips** It will take some time to tiptoe through them all, but you can rent a bicycle and pedal through fields of them extending to the horizon. Or you can pay to enter the tourist-friendly Keukenhof Gardens (⊛www.keukenhof .nl), where they've been impressively arranged in every conceivable manner. The tulips are in bloom from mid-March to mid-May.

Alternative activities

● **Sample some cheese** Cheese is no laughing matter in the Netherlands, where it's been made for over 1600 years and can still be found in round chunks the size of wagon wheels. Gouda, Edam and Leiden are the best-known varieties. At a traditional cheese market, like the one in Alkmaar (April–Sept, every Friday from 10am), you can see porters in white uniforms carrying sleds of heavy cheese.

● **Go kite skating** With exceptional winds and long stretches of firm beach, kite skating (racing along the beach on a special skateboard and a powerful kite)

is perfect for this environment. In IJmuiden, Renesse, Oostvoorne and the Drunen Dunes area, you'll find the best conditions to try this unique sport.

● **In-line skate along the coast** The Netherlands is considered one of the best in-line skating countries in the world. Strap on a daypack and go. Routes have been mapped out to take you along the most beautiful spots on the coast, past dunes, dykes and even along sections of the famed "Eleven-City Skating Tour".

● **Tour the Heineken brewery** The old Heineken brewery, just a stone's throw from the Van Gogh Museum in Amsterdam, may not be churning out beer any more, but it's still serving it at least to the hoards of tourists who pay up to €9 for the tour. Free beer is included on this walk-through infomercial. See ⊛www.heinekenexperience .com for tour times.

● **Walk the mud flats** Wadden Sea is the largest continuous nature reserve in Europe and, when the tide is low, it's possible to walk the uncovered mud flats. These are actually sandbanks crisscrossed by channels, leaving a soft footing that makes for a low-impact but strenuous hike.

● **Cycle across the Netherlands** You can easily rent a bike and find your way around Amsterdam, but there's really no reason to stop there. Dedicated signed trails lead you from town to town. You don't need a dual-suspension mountain bike, either. A simple three-speeder should do the trick.

Costs

The Netherlands is slightly more expensive than your typical European country but, with so many budget travellers hanging out there, it's easy to slip into the frugal lifestyle. You can scrape by on just over €30 a day, but €45 is a more reasonable target for the first few days in Amsterdam, when you're paying admission fees to the various attractions. To live in backpacker budget comfort, figure on €60 a day.

Accommodation

Some of the classic budget digs, like *Bob's Youth Hostel* in Amsterdam, are still up and running. However, they're not the bargains they once were, so for real budget accommodation, you'll need to check into a campground, where you can probably split a cabin with a few others for just €7 each. The cheapest hotels start at round €50, then jump to €70 for a room at a three-star hotel.

Eating and drinking

The Dutch aren't famous for their food and, even though you can certainly find excellent top-tier restaurants, this may not be the best place for a big splurge. Fast-food street snacks, especially around the Red Light District and other nightspots, offer filling cheap eats. There's plenty of Indonesian culinary influence (a former colony), and the noodle dishes are excellent and a good way to keep your batteries charged. If you eat at hostels, you can find a good meal for under €7, but you should be able to do better than that out on the town or at a supermarket.

Transport

There aren't many places in this country you can't reach by rail, whether it's on the quiet city trams that catch wandering tourists off guard or the high-speed rail links to Brussels and Paris. Dutch Railway has reasonable fares and frequent and modern trains that welcome Eurail- and other pass-holders.

For the inner-city trams, you'll want to pick up a Strippen Card (valid throughout the country on buses, trams and subways), which can be purchased anywhere, though it's more expensive to actually buy it on the tram or bus. A basic fifteen-strip card costs about €6 and will get you a few rides, depending on how far you go (each strip buys you a zone). The other way to go is the Amsterdam Pass, which gives you unlimited transport (even on canal cruises) and free entry to the top museums for about €25 (one day), €33 (two days) and €40 (three days). Or there's a pure transport version that costs around €16 for a day.

By train

Hollandrail Pass Any three days of travel in one month €98 (first class), €65 (second class) and €49 (youth, second class). Any five days of travel in one month €140 (first class), €100 (second class) and €78 (youth, second class).
Benelux Tourrail Pass (also valid in Belgium and Luxembourg) Any five days of travel in one month €186 (first class), €133 (second class) and €89 (youth pass).
Germany and Benelux Pass (also valid in Belgium, Germany and Luxembourg) Ranges from any five days of travel in two months – €268 (first class), €200 (second class) and €162 (youth, second class) – to any ten days of travel in two months – €406 (first class), €305 (second class) and €244 (youth, second class).

Eurodomino Netherlands Pass

Ranges from any three days of travel in one month – €95 (first class), €83 (second class) and €47 (youth, second class) – to any eight days of travel in one month – €241 (first class), €159 (second class) and €123 (youth, second class).

For Europe-wide **Eurail** and **InterRail** passes, see p.38. For tips and tricks on maximizing your rail pass, see p.71.

By bus

Busabout (see p.39) only serves Amsterdam, connecting it with Bruges in Belgium and Berlin in Germany. For internal bus prices, call the contact at ⓦwww.connexxion.nl (the website is Dutch-only). For buses to other countries, see ⓦwww.eurolines.nl.

Events

● **Queen's Day, Amsterdam** About a million people descend on Amsterdam for this annual street party on behalf of the previous queen's birthday. On this day, all street trade is unregulated so there's a citywide (and nationwide) rummage sale to the delight of secondhand shoppers. Many are out for more laughs than profit. April 30.

● **The Elfstedentocht** The "Eleven-City Skating Tour" is the most anticipated sporting event in the country. Only every few years does it get cold enough to hold the 200km circular race that starts and ends in Leeuwarden, To receive the coveted finisher's cross, the 16,000-plus entrants need to get their cards stamped in each of the eleven cities (plus at a few spots in between), and all by midnight the following day. There's now a summer bike race along the route as well, though you might prefer to start out with the four-day version. ⓦwww.elfstedentocht.nl.

● **Amsterdam Pride Parade** The Amsterdam Pride Parade isn't just one of the biggest gay carnivals in the world, it's also the only one with floats that actually float. The spectacular show moves down Amsterdam's main canals with costumed dancers and probably a few things you (or the other 250,000 visitors) never thought you'd see. Find a spot on a bridge for the best views. Aug; ⓦwww.amsterdampride.nl.

The Netherlands online

Country info ⓦwww.holland.com
Rail ⓦwww.ns.nl
Bus ⓦwww.connexxion.nl
Amsterdam info ⓦwww
.visitamsterdam.nl

Norway

Capital: Oslo
Population: 4,574,560
Languages: Bokmal Norwegian and Nynorsk Norwegian
Currency: Norwegian krone (NOK)
GDP per capita: €30,760
When to go: January–April for some of the world's best cross-country skiing, June–September for hiking, biking and sightseeing
When not to go: November–December, when it's dark and freezing cold. January and February aren't much better, but at least winter activities are under way by then
Minimum daily budget: €38

Norway offers the most spectacular landscape in Europe and as such is a country best enjoyed outdoors. The weather isn't always that accommodating, but that doesn't stop the Norwegians. "There's no such thing as bad weather, only bad clothing", goes the popular saying. And if you don't let the occasional rain shower (or freezing rain shower, or blizzard) get in your way, Norway is like a giant playground for the outdoor enthusiast. To Norwegians, fjords and their surrounding mountains are meant to be hiked and biked and skied, not viewed from a cruise-ship deckchair, and the fact that this is how most of the world chooses to see their nature continues to baffle them (possibly just as much as their determination to continue hunting whales in the face of international bans baffles most of the world).

Norwegians' oil reserves have made them one of the richest countries in Europe. The oil has also made Norwegians less worried about trade, which is one of the reasons they voted to stay out of the EU. Besides, as Sweden voted to enter the EU, they had a slight obligation to do the opposite.

The Norwegians have been explorers since the Viking ages. Thor Heyerdahl was the twentieth-century hero of the high seas, conquering them on a boat that looked to the untrained eye like a big bail of hay. Many of today's heroes, however, are cross-country skiers and biathlon competitors – if you see a crowd of burly men hovering around a bar TV in the winter, chances are they're watching one of these two events.

For the traveller, Norway is one of the most expensive countries in Europe and, with the exception of seafood, has one of the least appealing regional cuisines. A few days in the fjords, however, and this is easily forgotten – in part because of the natural beauty and in part because, if you're camping, you're actually spending less than you would be staying in hostels in Spain.

Main attractions

• **Kon-Tiki Museum, Oslo** In 1947, Thor Heyerdahl crossed the Pacific on a balsawood raft to prove that the first Polynesian settlers could have sailed from pre-Inca Peru. This adventure – and the rest of his research – are celebrated in this excellent museum.

• **National Gallery, Oslo** In theory, no one's meant to be able to walk in and rip paintings off the walls during opening hours at the National Gallery, but with less security than your average pet-food store, a pair of crooks did just that with *The Scream*, Edvard Munch's masterpiece. Hopefully, there will still be a few famous paintings left by the time you arrive.

● **"Norway in a Nutshell" Tour** This tour of Sognefjord by train, boat and bus is an extremely popular (and expensive) day-trip from Oslo and Bergen. As one Norwegian called it, "Fjords for people who can't be bothered to do them". See Ⓦwww.norwaynutshell.com for tour times and prices.

● **Coastal Steamer** In 1893, the Vesteraalens Dampskibsselskap steam-ship company opened an express shipping route between Trondheim and Hammerfest along the same rocky and treacherous route that was rejected by the larger shipping companies. Today, they carry passengers as well, and the Hurtigruten (Ⓦwww.hurtigruten.com) is now called – at least in all of the tourist propaganda – "the world's most beautiful voyage".

Alternative activities

● **See the Northern Lights** You don't need to head up to Hammerfest as Bill Bryson did in his book *Neither Here Nor There*; this celestial show can be viewed

Average temperatures and rainfall in Norway

Average daily temperatures (maximum and minimum °C) and monthly rainfall (mm)

	Jan	Feb	Mar	Apr	May	June	July	Aug	Sept	Oct	Nov	Dec
Oslo												
max °C	-1	-2	4	9	17	20	22	21	16	9	4	0
min °C	-7	-7	-3	1	7	11	13	12	7	3	-2	-6
rainfall mm	49	36	47	41	53	65	81	89	90	84	73	55

across the country. There's no magic winter date to see the psychedelic display, but, if you leave the big cities and find some large stretch of flat terrain for a wide-open view (or take a quick drive out of town on a clear night) and give yourself at least a few days, chances are you won't miss it.

● **Hike a glacier** Norway is home to the largest glacier on continental Europe (the Jostedalsbreen), and several tour companies arrange for hikes on the glaciers. One of the better-known spots to try your hand at scaling the slippery slopes is Briksdalsbreen. ⓦwww.briksdalsbreen.com.

● **Kayak the fjords** One of the best ways to view the fjords is from a sea kayak. The waters are calm, it's hard to get lost, there are small towns along the way with guest rooms and food, and the kayaks can be rented all across Norway.

● **Raft the mountain rivers** In addition to the spectacular scenery, Norway boasts excellent rafting. This can be done in several spots, including the Trysilelva River in Hedmark, and Dagali River in Voss.

● **Fish for salmon in a fjord** You can go fishing just about everywhere, but the best spots require a guide (or a good tip) and, more importantly, a licence, which you can pick up around the country. Many local deep-sea angling associations and tourist information offices organize fishing

trips. Typically, the best time for salmon fishing is from mid-July to mid-August, but this can vary a lot from region to region.

Costs

Because of the costs (and logistics), few budget travellers spend much time (or any time at all) in this Nordic land. This means there aren't the typical gaggles of backpackers – even in high season – but few places to save money, either. Tightening the budget belt is a necessity here, no matter which bracket you plan to travel in. Even though it's more expensive in general, there are fewer "must-see" museums and attractions with fees. It's more about the natural beauty of the country, which is free, so you can sneak by on €38 a day. A more realistic goal for budget travel is €50, though you can get by on €20 or less if you bike, camp and cook yourself.

Accommodation

Youth hostels go for around €20 for a dorm, €60 for a double room, and that's just for starters. For a single room in an "inexpensive" hotel, paying €80 is not unheard of. Prices go as high as you like once you start looking for luxury.

Eating and drinking

Alcohol is prohibitively expensive and, if you're trying to save money, this is a decent place to cut back on consumption. Even *McDonald's* and the average petrol station hot dog are shockingly pricey, so it's a case of bulk cooking with items at the supermarket if you want to squeak by on a budget. A decent meal isn't going to cost less than €16.

Transport

Norway has relatively few train lines compared to the rest of Europe. A number of them – Oslo to Bergen, Oslo to the airport and Oslo to Lillehammer – are modern and quick. The rest can be painfully slow. This can also be said for the roads – often single lanes with minimal passing opportunities and low speed limits – and the buses that travel on them. The railways have some excellent scenic routes, but the bus network is more extensive and there are plenty of picturesque passages to be viewed from the road. All transport is extremely pricey, so this is *the* place to use a rail or bus pass.

By train

Norway Rail Pass Any three days of travel in one month €171 (second class) and €123 (youth). Additional travel days €29 (second class) and €20 (youth) per day.

ScanRail Pass (also valid in Denmark, Finland and Sweden) Any five days of travel in two months €241 (second class) and €168 (youth, second class). Any ten days of travel in two months €323 (second class) and €226 (youth, second class). Any 21 consecutive days of travel €375 (second class), €261 (youth, second class).

For Europe-wide **Eurail** and **InterRail** passes, see p.38. For tips and tricks on maximizing your rail pass, see p.71.

By bus

Nor-Way Bus Pass Any 21 consecutive days of travel on any of the fifty bus companies that cover Norway (€272). See ⓦwww.nor-way.no for more info.

Busabout doesn't operate in Norway. For buses to other countries, see ⓦwww.eurolines.no.

Events

● **Independence Day** On May 17, 1814, Norway declared independence from Denmark and established its own constitutional government. To celebrate this day, many Norwegians dress up in traditional costume of regionally decorated and handmade colourful *bunad* to march down the street of their local town. Some of the more sports-oriented take to the high-elevation glacial tracks on skis.

● **Pagan bonfires** On the longest day of the year in Norway (*Sankt Hans*), the sun doesn't set in many parts of the country. Even in the south, it barely dips below the horizon. To celebrate the ancient Pagan ritual of the summer solstice, huge bonfires are lit all over Norway.

● **The Mobil Bislett Games, Oslo** One of the biggest track and field meets of the year takes place at this classic old stadium in the centre of Oslo. The track is notoriously fast, so many top athletes time their peak condition with this event to go after world records. See ⓦwww.bislettgames.com for info on the Games.

Norway online

Country info ⓦwww.visitnorway.com
Rail ⓦwww.nsb.no
Bus ⓦwww.nor-way.no
Oslo info ⓦwww.visitoslo.com

Poland

Capital: Warsaw
Population: 38,626,349
Language: Polish
Currency: Zloty (zl)
GDP per capita: €8975
When to go: Mid-May to June and September to mid-October, when the weather's decent and you'll miss the (relative) crowds
When not to go: July and August, when the walking trails, lakes and beaches get swamped with people, and November–February, when it's cold and dark, and many hostels are closed
Minimum daily budget: €19

Long tucked away in the economic doldrums between the Soviet Union and Western Europe, Poland has been sliced up by conquering nations in more ways than a bag of onions. Today, however, Poland is emerging as a diverse and vibrant state. The exciting part is that Poland is still in its capitalist infancy trying to figure out the road ahead, with Coke billboards and chic cafés in the cities and horse-drawn wagons still kicking up dust on country roads.

Poland offers a slightly more rugged experience than countries in Western Europe, but it's far easier on the wallet. You can find the luxury living, but there's also all the sports and outdoor pursuits you're likely to ever want, from horse-back riding to sailing to scuba diving; the challenge is just carving out enough time to do them. There are beaches on the Baltic, craggy mountains in the south, lakes and green rolling hills. Plus, a long tradition of Slavic hospitality, with feast-like meals for even casual visitors. As the Polish saying goes: "a guest in the house is God in the house." The trick of course is how to get invited through the front door.

Main attractions

● **Kraków** This southern city emerged from World War II relatively unscathed, making it one of UNESCO's twelve greatest historic cities in the world and an architectural trove for city strolls. The church spires are old, cobbled square provide the ideal backdrop for lounging in cafés and people-watching; it may look like a history lesson, but the city is very much alive and buzzing.

● **Oświęcim** Most know this industrial town 60km west of Kraków by its German name: Auschwitz. The largest of the concentration camps, much of it was destroyed as the Nazis retreated in 1945, but there's still plenty to get a sense of the magnitude of this death factory. Four million people were killed here (and at the nearby linked camp Birkenau) during the Holocaust. It's hard to forget a trip to this haunting memorial.

● **Royal Castle, Warsaw** Like much of Warsaw, the Royal Castle has been rebuilt (1971–77). The Baroque lines seen at a distance give way to Gothic traits once inside – tapestries, paintings, even the furniture, is crafted into place in each room, and makes for an inspiring visit.

Alternative activities

● **Pay homage to Copernicus** Nicolaus Copernicus, the famous astronomer who "stopped the sun and moved the earth", was born in Toruń. The town itself, with soaring Gothic buildings, is worth a visit anyway, but Torun's planetarium packs extra meaning to the journey.

● **Hike the Tatras** Poland's outdoor life is often overlooked by visitors, but head into the Tatras mountains and you'll get a taste of the Poland the locals enjoy. The Pieniny, Bieszczady and Karkonosze mountains will all do as well. The highest peak in Poland is Rysy, 2499m.

● **Sail across the Mazurian lakes** Few would put "Poland" and "sailing" in the same sentence, but the Mazurian lakes are packed with hundreds of boats in summer. Sailors also head for Jeziorak lake near Ilawa. In winter, the sailing continues on ice, with championships held in the Mazurian region.

● **Head underground** Caving is common near Kraków and in the Tatra mountains. There are literally thousands to choose from, but just a handful ready for commercial visitors without experience. The most famous are the Bear's Cave near Klodzko and the Paradise Cave near Kielce.

	Jan	Feb	Mar	Apr	May	June	July	Aug	Sept	Oct	Nov	Dec
Warsaw												
max °C	1	1	7	12	18	21	23	23	18	12	6	2
min °C	-4	-4	0	3	8	11	13	12	8	4	1	-6
rainfall mm	28	25	30	38	51	66	76	71	46	41	38	30

Costs

At the upper end, you can certainly spend in Warsaw what you would in most of the world's big cities. If you're travelling cheap, though, this is an excellent place to do it. You can get a hotel room, restaurant meal with drinks, entry to a museum, and a latte for the price of a dorm-room bed and super-market snacks in the more expensive European countries.

Accommodation

You shouldn't need to pay more than €16 for budget accommodation any-where in Poland. In some places, like university hostels in the summer, you might be able to survive on less than €5 a night, but figure on €8 to be safe. Even private rooms – that is, a room in a private home – shouldn't be more than €12 outside of Warsaw and Kraków. Camping doesn't offer the same sort of savings it does elsewhere, though.

Eating and drinking

The best place to fill up is a "Milk Bar", which is open from early morning until 6pm and offers traditional Polish snacks for prices well under the syllable count on the items you're ordering. Soups are an integral part of the meal, or even a meal unto themselves. The main dishes often don't look *haute cuisine* (there's only so much you can do with stewed cabbage), but you'll find several that

agree with your palate and even more that are at least wallet-friendly. A decent restaurant meal will cost about €4 and a good one can be had for €8.

Transport

Trains are moderately efficient (provided you're not stuck on a "normal service" train that stops at every third mound of dirt) and well priced – it's difficult to pay more than €20 for a single-day trip. A second-class sleeper for a long journey is under €16. In rural areas, the bus is probably faster than the train. The national bus carrier, PKS, specializes in cramped and slow service. Polski Express, a private company, is better, but most useful out of Warsaw.

In Warsaw, a 24-hour transport ticket costs just €1.60 (€0.80 with student card), and a three-day ticket is €2.45 (€1.20 with student card). Kraków is very accessible on foot, but if you're hit-ting loads of museums and want to save energy by taking buses and trams in between, try the Kraków Tourist card. The two-day (€10) or three-day (€15) card entitles the holder to free travel on city buses and trams and to free entry in up to 32 museums.

By train

Polrail Pass Ranges from any eight days of travel – €174 (first class), €120 (second class) and €125/€85 (youth, first class/second class) – to one month of travel – €298 (first class), €199 (second class) and €210/€140 (youth, first class/second class).

European East Pass (also valid in Austria, the Czech and Slovak republics and Hungary) Any five days of travel in one month €184 (first class) and €131 (second class). Additional travel days cost €21 (first class) and €15 (second class).

For Europe-wide **InterRail** passes (**Eurail** doesn't cover Poland), see p.38. For tips and tricks on maximizing your rail pass, see p.71.

By bus

Busabout doesn't operate in Poland. For internal bus prices, see ⓦwww.pks .poznan.pl and ⓦwww.polskiexpress.pl. For buses to other countries, see ⓦwww.eurolinespolska.pl.

Events

● **Music in Old Kraków Festival**
Established by the early-music ensemble Capella Cracoviensis in the 1970s, this annual event continues to grow. It's now a seventeen-day happening with concerts filling venues across the city. Aug; ⓦwww.krakow.pl.

● **Wratislavia Cantans, Wroclaw**
Every year, 2000 performers and 25,000 spectators flood into the thousand-year-old city of Wroclaw for a cultural jamboree: classical concerts, ballet performances, films and art exhibitions. Sept; ⓦwww.wratislavia.art.pl.

● **Warsaw Autumn Festival**
Organizers pack twenty concerts into nine days in this premier event, which was started in 1956. The audience can expect to hear Schönberg and Webern, as well as avant-garde, experimental performances. Third week Sept.

Poland online

Country info ⓦwww.polandtour.org
Rail ⓦwww.polrail.com
Bus ⓦwww.pks.poznan.pl and ⓦwww.polskiexpress.pl
Warsaw info ⓦwww.warsawtour.pl
Kraków info ⓦwww.krakow.pl

Portugal

Capital: Lisbon
Population: 10,524,145
Languages: Portuguese (also Mirandese)
Currency: Euro (€)
GDP per capita: €14,687
When to go: March–October for the south, May–September for

Lisbon and the north
When not to go: November–February, when the weather's chilly, even in the Algarve. June–August is best avoided if you're not partial to crowds
Minimum daily budget: €22

Neatly tucked away on the "other" side of Spain, this century-long gateway to Africa and the Americas is often missed by travellers who start heading west across Europe, then get caught up in Spain's attractions and run out of time. Those who do make it to the far end of Iberia typically make a pit stop in Lisbon before beelining it to the Algarve for a glimpse of the poster-pin-up beaches, leaving the many small-town and countryside gems largely undiscovered.

The Portuguese take life slowly (unless behind the wheel of a car) and savour the little things: folk festivals, fish, fruit, flowers, and food drenched in olive oil. The ethos of the nation is very much tied to the sea. Vasco da Gama is more than a historical seafarer in Portugal; he embodies the spirit of the country.

The nation is cut tidily in half by the River Tagus. To the south, where the Moors and Romans once had strongholds, you'll find darker-skinned people and a more Mediterranean lifestyle. To the north, you'll find a more Celtic and Germanic sort.

Main attractions

● **Lagos** The spectacular combination of cliffs and white beaches in Lagos sells plenty of film and even more beer; the beach scene in this Algarve town is a party stop on the travel circuit, though it's steadily pricing itself out of most people's range. Renting a bike, moped or even a horse will make beach exploration all the more easier.

● **Évora** This walled town has seemingly been dropped into a field of vineyards, olive trees and flowers. The cathedral and Roman temple provide popular focal points, but the ossuary chapel, made from thousands of human skulls and bones, is too bizarre to miss.

● **The Rossio, Lisbon** The actual name of this plaza is Praça D. Pedro IV, but if you want to sound like a local (or just want to be able to pronounce it), go with "Rossio". With a new face-lift, the plaza looks better than ever, and it still acts as the heart of Lisbon.

● **The ruins of St George's Castle, Lisbon** Used to defeat the Moorish invaders, St George's offers *the* classic panoramic overlook of Lisbon, with a great view of Santuario do Cristo Rei, the 34-metre replica of Rio de Janeiro's Christ the Redeemer statue, and the remains of a cathedral destroyed in the 1755 earthquake.

Alternative activities

● **Hike Madeira** The volcanic island of Madeira is a little over 50km wide, but it has been providing shelter to transatlantic travellers since 1420. Mountain trails make for azure panoramas, while wild flowers and lush landscape take care of the rest.

● **Test some port** With its low lighting, squidgy sofas and soft music, the Institute of Port Wine in Lisbon (a short tram-ride uphill from Praca dos

Restauradores), is a great place to while away the hours with friends. A glass of the national snifter costs anywhere between €1 and €25 and goes best with Serra – a viscous cheese scooped up with crackers.

● **Eat a meal to the sound of Fado** Fado is the traditional music of Portugal and in a Fado-themed restaurant, classic Portuguese food is served while guitar players and singers perform their lament. For a list of Fado restaurants in Lisbon, see ⓦwww.visitlisboa.com.

Average temperatures and rainfall in Portugal

Average daily temperatures (maximum and minimum °C) and monthly rainfall (mm)

	Jan	Feb	Mar	Apr	May	June	July	Aug	Sept	Oct	Nov	Dec
Lisbon												
max °C	14	15	17	18	21	25	28	28	27	21	17	14
min °C	7	8	9	11	12	15	17	18	17	14	11	9
rainfall mm	110	111	69	64	39	21	5	6	26	80	114	108

● **Surf the Atlantic coast** Portugal's waves aren't in the same league as Hawaii's, but there are enough break-ers around the country to keep most beginner and intermediate surfers happy. Peniche, just outside of Lisbon, is one of the top spots. Surfing's also popular in Lagos and Sagres on the Algarve, and Sines, just between Lisbon and the Algarve.

● **Pick up a bargain at the Alfama market, Lisbon** Originally named Fiera da Ladra, or "Thief"s Market", the Alfama market has been selling *tschoskes* to bargain hunters for over a hundred years. Hand-painted pottery and lace are among the most popular items, but you can find loads of deals on rugs, glassware, jewellery, books, old sailing gear and art. Sat and Tues 5am–1pm.

● **See fish get tanked** When Lisbon hosted the World Expo in 1998, this modern aquarium served as a centre-piece. Located, appropriately enough, right next to the harbour, the Oceanário de Lisboa offers environmental sound-scapes and interactive media, in addi-tion to a vibrant array of sea life.

Costs

Portugal is one of the cheaper countries in Europe, but not so cheap that you can comfortably release the grip on your wallet. But with a bit of restraint you can stretch your funds a long way.

Accommodation

There are plenty of cheap hostels around Portugal, but far fewer in the resort towns along the Algarve, where you're more likely to pay the sort of rates you would in Paris or Barcelona. If you feel like a bit of a splurge, you might try a *pousada* (Ⓦwww.pousadas.pt), which are converted castles, fortresses or historical sites.

Eating and drinking

You'll find some of Europe's best seafood in Portugal, and it's decently priced. Add to this some *vinho verde* (green wine) and you've got one of the best meals you'll find on your trip for under €12.

Transport

Train prices are reasonable (about €8 per 100km), so any journey less than two hours is not going to be worth using a day of your Eurail pass. Buses cover many of the same routes as trains, in less time, and for competitive prices. Since many also leave from the central station, it's easy to compare if you're buying tickets individually. If you're thinking of renting a car or scooter, be warned: Portugal has the highest traffic fatality rate in Europe.

Look into a Lisbon Card (Ⓦwww .atl-turismolisboa.pt) if you're just in the capital for a day or two and are trying to hit every attraction. For less than €20, you get 48 hours of free transport and up to fifty percent off entry to museums and monuments.

By train
Portugal Pass Any four days of travel in fifteen days €86 (first class).
Iberic Pass (also valid in Spain) Any three days of travel in two months €203 (first class). Additional travel days €29 per day.
For Europe-wide **Eurail** and **InterRail** passes, see p.38. For tips and tricks on maximizing your rail pass, see p.71.

By bus
A Busabout pass (see p.39) connects Lisbon with Lagos and major cities in Spain. For internal bus prices, see ⓦwww.rede-expressos.pt, ⓦwww.setubalense.pt and ⓦwww.eva-bus.com.

Events

● **Funchal Carnival** If you're in Portugal during Carnival, consider heading to the island of Madeira to celebrate this pre-Lenten event. The capital, Funchal, is overrun with party-goers as a parade of floats takes the place of traffic. Even samba troupes take to the streets. Late Feb.

● **Festa do Colete Encarnado, Vila Franca de Xira** Portugal's answer to the running of the bulls. The macho and the mad dodge bulls let loose on the streets. During the daily Portuguese-style bullfights, the bull is wrestled, but not killed, which is more impressive and less gruesome than the Spanish version. First Fri of July.

● **Alta Estremadura Jazz Festival** Four towns two hours north of Lisbon (Pombal, Leiria, Marinha Grande and São Pedro de Muel) host this talent-heavy jazz festival. Sept–Oct; ⓦwww.jazzportugal.net.

Portugal online

Country info ⓦwww.portugalinsite.pt
Rail ⓦwww.cp.pt
Bus ⓦwww.rede-expressos.pt
Lisbon info ⓦwww.atl-turismolisboa.pt

Romania

Capital: Bucharest
Population: 22,355,551
Languages: Romanian (also Hungarian and German)
Currency: Leu (L)
GDP per capita: €5630
When to go: May–August, when the weather's best (crowds aren't much of an issue). September and October have decent weather as well
When not to go: July and August, when it's crowded along the Black Sea and at the Painted Monasteries of southern Bucovina. November–February is normally too cold for sightseeing
Minimum daily budget: €18

Romania's main export, other than Olympic gymnasts, seems to be Dracula. And neither of these are large income-producers, especially with Hollywood reluctant to cough up name-use fees. So the country has to rely on an industry of textiles, auto assembly, mining, timber, food processing, petroleum refining and football stars. The problem is that these don't bring in much income, either (except Gheorghe Hagi). But big change is under way as Romania pulls itself into the capitalist arena with Ceauşescu out of the way. You might call it the "Wild West of the Eastern Bloc"; the dichotomy shows itself in several forms: horse-drawn carts passed by drivers with one hand on the wheel and the other on their mobile phone, a traditional craftsman beside a businessman in the latest Hugo Boss suit. It's no secret that the new money is leaving many behind on the journey towards development, but other nations in the region share a similar path.

One of the old-style customs that's still found in abundance, though, is hospitality. Romanians welcome you into their unassuming homes and feed you to bursting capacity. Then they sink their sharp teeth into your neck, or so the tourist bureau would have you believe with all the Dracula hype. Medieval towns, stately castles and excellent hiking trails await, and for about half the price (and a fraction of the tourists) of Western Europe's marquee cities.

Main attractions

● **Bran Castle** Also known as "Dracula's Castle", the popular castle actually has no ties to Vlad Tepeş, the medieval prince associated with the vampire extraordinaire. It doesn't look so ominous either, but what did they expect, with white walls and Disney-style towers? None of this seems to prevent the tourists from coming.

● **Sighişoara** This atmospheric Saxon medieval town in Transylvania is another destination on the Dracula trail. Vlad Tepeş was born within the citadel's walls, in the "Dracula House", which is now – surprise! surprise! – a bar and restaurant.

● **Palace of Parliament, Bucharest** It's the second largest building in the world (after the Pentagon), but Ceauşescu ploughed over 7000 homes and 26 churches to build it in the 1980s, so there's understandably less pride in this engineering achievement than there otherwise might be.

● **Painted Monasteries of southern Bucovina** These frescoed monasteries near Suceava in Romania's northeast corner are UNESCO treasures – the Voronet church is known as the "Sistine Chapel of the East". Despite their remote location, the sites do get crowded in high season.

Alternative activities

● **Twitch for birds in the Danube Delta** From late spring to mid-autumn, the Danube Delta is home to hundreds of species of birds. Binoculars are a good idea, but you don't need a licence or any other equipment. If you'd rather not bird-watch on your own, tour operators will happily guide you to the best spots. With a bit of luck, you might even see a Black Pelican colony.

● **Go skiing** Romania may not be the first place that comes to mind when you plan a ski trip, but don't rule out this bargain vacation. Cross-country skiing, snowboarding and tubing are also possible, with peaks around 3000m. The major ski resorts are Poiana Brasov, Sinaia and Predeal. See ⓦwww .skiresorts.ro for season info and lift-pass prices.

● **Track wolves in the Carpathian mountains** The forested slopes of Romania's Carpathian mountains help shelter the grey wolf, and Zărneşti, at the southern tip, makes the best base for setting out on their trail. See ⓦwww.cntours.de for details of guided trips.

Average temperatures and rainfall in Romania

Average daily temperatures (maximum and minimum °C) and monthly rainfall (mm)

	Jan	Feb	Mar	Apr	May	June	July	Aug	Sept	Oct	Nov	Dec
Bucharest												
max °C	2	4	10	17	22	26	28	28	24	17	8	3
min °C	-5	-4	1	6	11	14	16	15	11	6	1	-3
rainfall mm	43	38	36	46	66	86	56	56	36	28	46	43

Costs

Even though Romania may be the cheapest country in Europe, not everything is priced for the budget traveller and there aren't always great savings where you might expect them. But with a bit of looking (and limiting your time in Bucharest), there are plenty of insanely cheap deals reminiscent of the prices grey-haired backpackers still wax on about. ATMs are increasingly common, as well as vendors who accept credit cards.

Accommodation

The best deals are private accommodation outside Bucharest (for guesthouses in rural areas, see ⓦ www.antrec.ro), where you can get a room and breakfast for under €8. In the capital, things can cost fifty percent more, though you can get a double for €20 if you find another traveller to split the cost. For under €40, you can stay in a nice hotel.

Eating and drinking

Because most Romanians can't afford to eat out, many restaurants cater to wealthy foreign visitors and up their prices accordingly. Finding a local hangout with local rates may take some looking, especially around Bucharest and the more touristy areas. Outside of these places, you can easily dine for less than €4 and pick up a bottle of

Romanian wine for under €2 to wash it down with. However, this is beer country and the swill is as cheap as any you'll find in Europe.

Transport

Romania has an impressive railway infrastructure that covers the entire country. The trains are the best way to get around; they offer cheap transport and tend to arrive on time. Local trains are a bargain but stop at every other telephone pole. The Express trains only sound fast – with €2 taking you approximately 100km, they're inexpensive. The fastest Inter-city trains cost a bit more. There are several bus companies offering connections between Romania's main cities, but they typically aren't as cheap or quick as the trains. Several bus companies provide daily service to Istanbul (700km) for about €10.

Bucharest's trolleybuses and trams cost eighteen cents per ride, and tickets can be purchased from almost any street kiosk. Day passes are fifty cents and week passes cost €1.80. The city's "express buses" are roughly double the standard fare.

By train

Romanian Pass Any three days of travel in fifteen days €81 (first class only).

Eurail Romania-Hungary Pass Ranges from any five days of travel in two months – €163 (first class) and €114

(youth, second class) – to any ten days of travel in two months – €245 (first class) and €171 (youth, second class). **Balkans Flexi Pass** (also valid in Bulgaria, Greece and Turkey) Any five days of travel in one month €156 (first class) and €93 (youth, first class). Any ten days of travel in one month €273 (first class) and €162 (youth, first class). Any fifteen days of travel in one month €328 (first class) and €197 (youth, first class).

For Europe-wide **InterRail** passes (**Eurail** doesn't cover Romania), see p.38 but, because of the low train fares, they aren't nearly as essential here as they are in other European countries. For tips and tricks on maximizing your rail pass, see p.71.

By bus

Busabout (see p.39) doesn't operate in Romania. For buses to other countries, see Ⓦwww.eurolines.ro.

Events

● **Whit Sunday Szekely Pilgrimage** A Franciscan monastery 2km northeast of Miercurea Ciuc, in the eastern Szekely Land, hosts the year's biggest traditional folk and religious festival. Held in thanks for the Szekely victory at

Marasszentimre, black-clad pilgrims still assemble in the yard and church interior of the city to sing hymns and touch the wooden Madonna in the sanctuary.

● **Medieval Days** The last three days of July, Sighişoara hosts this festival of arts, crafts and music. People dress in traditional costume and stage music and theatrical performances.

● **Halloween in Transylvania** What better place to be for Halloween? Celebrations, shows and tours follow in the footsteps of Bram Stoker's infamous character, Count Dracula. Oct 31.

● **Pageant of the Juni, Braşov** To commemorate the only day of the year when Romanians could freely enter this Saxon city, the town's youth dress up in costumes – some over 150 years old – and ride through the old quarter on horseback. First Sunday in May.

● **Sambra Oilor** This festival in Bran celebrates the sheep herds' annual return from the high mountains (Hurray!). Sept.

Romania online

Country info Ⓦwww .romaniatourism.com
Rail Ⓦwww.cfr.ro

Russia

Capital: Moscow
Population: 143,782,338
Language: Russian
Currency: Ruble (RUR)
GDP per capita: €7262
When to go: May–June and September–October, when you'll avoid the rain and summer tourist crowds
When not to go: April is slushy, July and August wet, yet popular with tourists, and November–February is bitterly cold
Minimum daily budget: €29

Perhaps one of the strangest things about Russia is its very presence in a European guidebook. How can a land that stretches all the way across the northern Chinese border up to the Bering Strait be part of Europe? Look closer at a map and you'll see Europe's eastern borders are shaped, in part, by the Ural mountains. Both St Petersburg and Moscow lie on the European side.

It's hard to keep up with Russia. Twenty years ago, the Soviets were pointing fingers, missiles and world-class shot-putters at America. Now the nation has splintered into a batch of republics with more syllables than a championship Scrabble game; there's a new market economy, largely employing the bodyguard and bulletproof car industry (plus the Chelsea football team); and the protesters that make the news are the ones who want communism back. Despite that, it's not as dangerous as it sounds on TV and, if you take basic precautions (see p.184), you'll almost certainly be fine.

Churchill's famous 1939 description of the Soviet Union still applies to Russia. It is "a riddle wrapped in a mystery inside an enigma". Few on the outside can begin to understand or decipher its cultural complexities. As a traveller, though, you'll get a chance to chip away at Russia's mystifying facade, even if you're just obtaining a visa, hitting the sights, getting lost in the subway system or trying to buy some chocolate biscuits from a street vendor. The national character reveals itself with enough time and interaction.

Main attractions

● **The Kremlin, Moscow** Still the seat of power for Russia, much of this walled-in triangular city of churches, armouries and palaces on Borovitsky Hill is open to the public. You can pace the grounds where Khrushchev engaged in the Cold War, Stalin unleashed his raids of terror, and Lenin orchestrated his radical vision of government. See box on p.12 for more details.

● **Hermitage Museum, St Petersburg** The only museum in the world that you might put in the ring against the Louvre, this colossal structure houses particularly impressive collections of Italian Renaissance and French Impressionist paintings, as well as works by Rembrandt, Picasso and

WHITE SEA

● Arkhangel'sk

N

Gulf of Bothnia

FINLAND

HELSINKI

Lake
Ladoga

Gulf of Finland

● TALLINN

St Petersburg

ESTONIA

● Novgorod

RĪGA

● Yaroslavl'

River Volga

LATVIA

Tver

LITHU-
ANIA

● MOSCOW

VILNIUS

Smolensk

● Brest

MINSK

BELARUS

Yekaterinburg, Omsk & Vladivostok

0   200 km

Note: This map shows only the western
parts of Russia, corresponding to the
area covered by this country profile.

Kiev & Kharkov ▼   Rostov & the ▼ Caucasus mountains   ▼ Samara

Matisse. What started as the private art collection of Peter the Great (and expanded by Catherine the Great) finally opened its doors to the public in 1917. It would take years to see it all, even if you wanted to. See box on p.12 for more details.

● **Red Square, Moscow** Perhaps the world's most spectacular city centre, this enormous cobbled square is big enough to land a Cessna in (which 19-year-old German-born Mathias Rust did in 1987, just before taxiing to a Soviet labour camp for 432 days while his plane doubled in value and got sold to a Japanese collector). It housed enormous military parades in the Soviet era

and is framed by the GUM department store (which sold consumer goods at a time when they weren't easily found), St Basil's Cathedral (the one with the multi-coloured turnip spires that find their way onto every postcard) and the Kremlin. You'll also find the entrance to Lenin's Mausoleum, where the waxy, embalmed body of the former leader rests Snow White-style under a glass box.

● **Moscow and St Petersburg subways** Head under-ground for a real architectural and engineering wonder. After a long ride down the escalator, it's hard to tell if you've entered a museum or a five-star hotel lobby. The last thing it feels like is a subway sta-

Average temperatures and rainfall in Russia

Average daily temperatures (maximum and minimum °C) and monthly rainfall (mm)

	Jan	Feb	Mar	Apr	May	June	July	Aug	Sept	Oct	Nov	Dec
Moscow												
max °C	-6	-1	1	9	17	21	22	20	14	7	0	-4
min °C	-12	-11	-6	1	7	11	13	11	6	1	-4	-9
rainfall mm	36	28	33	38	51	66	81	71	58	51	43	43
St Petersburg												
max °C	-4	-4	1	8	16	19	21	19	13	7	2	-2
min °C	-9	-9	-4	1	7	11	13	12	7	3	-2	-7
rainfall mm	28	25	25	30	43	56	66	76	61	51	41	36

tion. The marble, sculptures and exquisite lighting make it hard to believe – in the case of Moscow, anyway – that it's the busiest system in the world, carrying eight million passengers a day.

● **The Peter and Paul Fortress, St Petersburg** Or, if you care to try your hand at Russian, Petropavlovskaya Krepost. This military fortress is as strategic as it is stunning. It was built under Peter the Great in the first half of the eighteenth century and was subsequently turned into a bestselling postcard for the Russian tourist bureau. The main spire sticks up like a lance ready to do battle with the clouds and the "irregular hexagon" shape of the fort looks more like a symmetrical snowflake when viewed from above.

● **The Church of Our Saviour on Spilled Blood, St Petersburg** Emperor Alexander II was assassinated in 1881 in St Petersburg. Without conspiracy theorists or Oliver Stone around, the only thing left to do was build a church to honour his memory. This dazzling onion-domed edifice, completed in 1907, now sits on the very spot and contains – hold on to your paintbrush – 7000 square metres of mosaics.

Alternative activities

● **Skate a Russian river** To make the most of Russia's arctic winter, buy a cheap pair of skates and join the locals for some free frozen fun on nearby lakes and rivers.

● **Ski the Caucasus** Done the Alps and want something new? Limited skiing can be found in Dombay, in the western Caucasus mountains, and Tcheget, close to Mount Elbrus. Heli-skiing is possible, but make sure you don't pay up until the helicopter comes – they're notorious for skipping out with your advance payment.

● **Experience space** If you arrive in Russia loaded with cash and don't mind spending it in a hurry, swing by the Yuri Gagarin Cosmonaut Training Centre at Star City and take a low-orbit flight in a MIG-29 aircraft at twice the speed of sound or go weightless on a space-training flight.

● **Take an icy dip** Join the St Petersburg Walrus Club for a plunge in the Neva River. Of course, you'll have to cut a hole in the ice first. This extraordinary winter custom occurs by the Peter and Paul Fortress, near the Lenin Stadium and at several other locations.

Costs

Outside of Moscow and St Petersburg, and not including any pre-booked fancy hotels, Western restaurants or luxury shopping, Russia is quite affordable and a clever budget traveller can stretch out their finances like an old T-shirt. The biggest single expense outside your €29 daily budget is probably going to be the tourist visa that got you into the country in the first place (see p.110).

Accommodation

Technically, if you're travelling on a tourist visa (see p.110), you've pre-booked all your accommodation. There is a way around this, however – the hotel/hostel you're spending the first night with can offer invitations for any length of time, provided you spend one night with them (see box on p.110). Hotels in Moscow and St Petersburg are expensive. St Petersburg has a campground, but that's about it. Hostels are the way to go, but you should make reservations as far in advance as you can. Private accommodation is catching on, and some offers are even affordable.

Eating and drinking

The good news is that you don't have to tip. The bad news is that a tip has already been added, and the bill isn't as cheap as you might hope. For most people, traditional fare is too bland or palate-challenging to make eating particularly enjoyable. And if you look in the places that have familiar food, you won't find the sort of prices you're hoping for. Fortunately, the vodka is cheap. And it almost counts as a meal.

Transport

Neither Eurail or InterRail passes cover Russia, but the slow trains are cheap and there are plenty of travel agencies around to help you avoid waiting in queues at the station. Train prices seem to vary like the weather. Don't be surprised if two ticket agents at the same train station quote different prices for the same train.

Local buses are also cheap and can be an excellent option. The catch is you need to figure them out; there are long, confusing queues and few English–speakers. If you're heading there from Eastern Europe, you can get some great deals. Tallinn to St Petersburg, for example, costs about €8 for a one-way ticket.

In both Moscow and St Petersburg, you'll find a range of metros (over 150 stations in Moscow alone), buses, trams and trolleybuses. Tickets are subsidized and cheap, but the prices still fluctuate. Roughly 15–30 cents will get you where you want to go around the city.

By bus

Busabout doesn't operate in Russia, but you can take the Beetroot Bus (ⓦwww.beetroot.org) around the country; ten days of touring costs €714, including room and board. For buses into and out of Russia, see ⓦwww.berlinlinienbus.de and ⓦwww.eurolines.ru.

Events

● **Stars of the White Nights Festival** St Petersburg's renowned Mariinsky Theatre jump-starts summer with this taxing schedule of performances, launched by Valery Gergiev, the indefatigable conductor of the Kirov Opera's orchestra. May–June; ⓦwww.mariinsky.ru.

● **Easter in Moscow** The holy day of the Russian Orthodox Church is most notably observed in Moscow's spectacular Kolomenskoe Church, with its flower-like domes soaring 70m into the air.

● **Russian Winter Festival** This twelve-days-of-Christmas-timed festival is celebrated in cities across Russia. Singers and musicians from around the world perform in the largest cities, including in Moscow's Izmailovo Park. If you get the chance, try some Russian pancakes with caviar.

Russia online

Country info ⓦwww.russiatourism.ru
Rail ⓦwww.poezda.net
Moscow info ⓦwww.moscow-guide.ru
St Petersburg info ⓦwww.spb.ru

Slovenia

Capital: Ljubljana
Population: 2,011,473
Languages: Slovenian, Serbo-Croatian
Currency: Tolar (SIT)
GDP per capita: €14,930
When to go: September, when the weather's ideal for outdoor pursuits, or December–March for skiing
When not to go: July–August, when the coast gets crowded, and November–February, when it's too chilly for sightseeing
Minimum daily budget: €29

Sandwiched between Italy, Croatia, Austria and Hungry, Slovenia will likely be on the route of many travellers. The ones that stop for a look around will find an uncrowded gem with Habsburg and Venetian architecture and a ubiquitous assortment of impressive European churches, castles, monasteries, medieval cities and mansions from the Renaissance. Located on the south-western side (the tourist bureau prefers "the sunny side") of the Alps, Slovenia offers incredible mountain vistas and perhaps the most affordable (and undis-covered) skiing in Europe. Think Switzerland at seventy percent off.

After the breakup of the former Yugoslavia, while Bosnia-Herzegovina, Croatia and Kosovo were enmeshed in fighting, Slovenia mostly waited on the sidelines. That is, holding free elections and voting for independence (in 1991), then fending off Milosevic and his Yugoslav army during a ten-day war before a truce was called and Milosevic backed down. The Slovenians were relatively quick to cotton on to capitalism and have already proven themselves an eco-nomic power of Eastern Europe.

Main attractions

● **Ljubljana** Narrow streets snake through the Old Town while cafés buzz with 35,000 university students. This charming, once-Roman town may not have the architectural magnificence of Prague, but it doesn't have the gaggles of tourists either.

● **The Adriatic Coast** Every country cherishes its coastline, and Slovenia is no exception. The small stretch along the Adriatic (just 100km across the water from Venice) is the home to Piran, with its Venetian Gothic architecture and narrow streets, and Fiesa, with its clean sandy beach and tranquil boat-restricted waters.

● **Bled** This town has three draws: a medieval castle that served as a summer residence to the Yugoslav royal family and before that South Tyrolian bishops; a fifteenth-century belfry with a "bell of wishes" (anyone who rings it will get what they wish for); and the Alps hanging like curtains in the background, which any Slovenian will gladly sell you if you believe the thing about the bell.

Alternative activities

● **Climb Mount Triglav** Action junkies and outdoor enthusiasts in Slovenia head for the triple-crested Mount Triglav (2864m), the country's highest peak. Slavs once believed the mountain to be the lair of a three-headed deity who ruled the sky, the earth and the underworld. Today, the pilgrimage up Triglav has become a confirmation of Slovenian identity. The best routes start near Bled, at Savica waterfall and Stara Fužina.

● **Visit the Škozjan Caves** When the area was covered by the sea millions of years ago, limestone deposits were left on the bottom. A tunnel now passes through them and into an underground canyon that stretches 500m, a jungle of stalactites and stalagmites that's home to 250 types of plant and five types of bat.

● **Go wine tasting** Slovenia has supposedly been making wine since the time of the Romans, so it's not surprising that they figured out how to do it well over the years. There are fourteen distinct wine-growing regions to explore, but if you want to concentrate your palate on a specific area that doesn't require driving, make base camp in Ptuj and sample the Haloze Hills and the Jeruzalem-Ljutomer districts. A bike will get you from one tasting to the next if you can't find someone willing to drive.

● **Soak in a spa** Rogaška Slatina is not just an objectionable Scrabble word, it's also Slovenia's oldest and largest spa town, with a mind-boggling assortment of cures. Everything from the rather

Average temperatures and rainfall in Slovenia

Average daily temperatures (maximum and minimum °C) and monthly rainfall (mm)

	Jan	Feb	Mar	Apr	May	June	July	Aug	Sept	Oct	Nov	Dec
Ljubijana												
max °C	2	4	9	14	19	23	26	26	22	16	8	3
min °C	-4	-3	1	5	9	12	14	14	11	6	1	-2
rainfall mm	33	36	38	53	69	79	56	43	41	36	51	43

uncomfortable-sounding "lymph drainage pressotherapy" to the scary "elecktro-acupuncture" and the mysterious "surprise bath". (Surprise! Here's your bath!) See ⓦwww.terme-rogaska.si for more treatment information.

● **Ride the rapids** Take your pick of kayaks, canoes, rafts or hydrospeed boards for the white water of the Soča and Savinja rivers.

Costs

Slovenia's still much cheaper than neighbouring Italy or Austria, though prices are increasing. To travel in comfort and style, expect to spend around €80 a day; those happy to stay at guesthouses and eat at medium-priced restaurants should get by on €55 a day. Those putting up at hostels and eating at self-serve restaurants can cut costs to around €29. Nearly all prices are in tolars, but some hotels, guesthouses and campgrounds quote rates in euros. It's simple to change cash and travellers' cheques at banks, post offices, travel agencies and any *menjalnica*, the ubiquitous private exchange offices.

Accommodation

Hostels aren't plentiful, but there are some. Figure on about €13–18 for bare-bones accommodation and €35 for a decent double. For €25 each, you and a travel partner can find a very comfortable three-star hotel double room.

Eating and drinking

Fresh fruit and vegetables at outdoor markets are a bargain, as are breakfast pastries and street snacks. Liver and brains (fried or grilled to your disliking) are common dishes, but the strudel desserts with apple and rhubarb or home-made cheesecake are delicious, and the Italian influence means plenty of inexpensive pasta as well. A full meal, even without brains, can be found for under €6.

Transport

Slovenia scores poorly in the rail and bus pass department – only InterRail covers the country (see p.38 for Europe-wide **InterRail** passes). Eurail isn't valid here, Busabout doesn't operate in Slovenia and nor is there a Slovenian Eurolines website. But you can find the transport info you need (if you speak Slovenian or want to make a stab at using the simple departure format) for the bus (ⓦwww.ap-ljubljana.si) or train (ⓦwww.slo-zeleznice.si) lines. The trains are smooth and efficient and local bus companies fill up on popular routes in the summer, so book ahead if you're heading to the coast.

Ljubljana is easily explored on foot, or by bike, but public transport is easily affordable. A single ticket on the city's bus system costs 75 cents, while passes are available for one day (€3) and one week (€13).

Events

● **Festival Ljubijana** The premier cultural event in Ljubljana sees dance, theatre and international music performances inundate the capital for six weeks of the summer. Past performers include José Carreras, Wynton Marsalis and Slide Hampton, and attendance for the combined events reaches 50,000. Second week of July; ⓦwww.festival-lj.si.

● **The Cows' Ball** It's not a bovine dance ritual; just an excuse for drinking and merrymaking when the cows return to the valleys around Lake Bohinj from their high-altitude pastures. Mid-Sept.

● **Kurentovanje, Ptuj** The biggest Mardi Gras celebration in Slovenia; for ten days leading up to Shrove Tuesday, there are masked balls, oodles of free-flowing wine and street performances. Mid-Feb; ⓦwww .kurentovanje.net.

Slovenia online

Country info ⓦwww.slovenia-tourism.si
Rail info ⓦwww.slo-zeleznice.si
Bus info ⓦwww.ap-ljubljana.si
Ljubljana info ⓦwww.ljubljana-tourism.si
Bled info ⓦwww.bled.si

Spain

Capital: Madrid
Population: 40,280,780
Languages: Castilian (also Catalan, Basque and Gallegan)
Currency: Euro (€)
GDP per capita: €17,950
When to go: One of the reasons Spain is so popular is that it's good for travel all year round. The south is ideal April–June and September–October, and quite mild November–February. The north is best May–June and September
When not to go: July and August can mean tortilla-frying heat and a crush of tourists. In the north, November–February can be chilly
Minimum daily budget: €20

Someplace between the bullfights, crowded beaches and pitchers of sangria, you'll find the swirl of propaganda surrounding post-Franco Spain. To move beyond that, you need simply set foot in the country. There's more to Spain than most ever anticipate, and every little town seems to maintain its own architectural treasures, from the mind-blowing works of Gaudí in Barcelona to the ornate *Hostal Dos Reis Catolicos*, the world's oldest hotel, in Santiago de Compostela. The wealth of variety alone is perplexing. The far south still has Moroccan remnants of Moorish invaders, while the rolling green hills and Celtic music in the north (regional instrument: the bagpipe) seem to have more in common with Ireland and Scotland. Roman aqueducts and Gothic cathedrals come together, with a few medieval castles thrown in to boot.

You can retrace the painting grounds of the famous artists (the museums are stuffed with Picasso, Velázquez, Dali and El Greco) or watch flamenco dancers clatter the cobblestones with the hope of collecting your loose change. And if an icy gazpacho can't cool you off on a hot Andalucian day, your only choice is to make for the ocean, which is rarely far off.

With all this, plus a kind sky that rarely rains for more than a day or two at a time, it's not surprising that Spain is the world's second most popular destination (after France). With comparatively cheaper prices, it's an even bigger draw for the budget-minded crowd.

Main attractions

● **Temple Expiatori de La Sagrada Familia, Barcelona** This Gaudí masterpiece has been under construction since 1882. You read right. And it's not expected to be completed until roughly 2080. So, even if you're with someone who has seen it before, remind them that things will have changed. You can bring your camera, but picking your favourite angle might take a few hours and nearly all two million of last year's visitors will tell you that pictures just don't do this towering structure justice.

● **Plaza Mayor, Madrid** This old-town-enclosed square in Madrid is the perfect place to buy (and pay too much for) a good coffee while you soak up the ambience. Kings have been crowned here; trials of the Inquisition held; bulls fought. Not only is it the most important historical landmark in the city, it has been beautifully preserved.

● **Beaches** The Canary Islands (a few chunks of Spain located off the coast of Morocco), Balearic Islands (southeast of Barcelona, in the Med) and the entire Costa del Sol pull in the majority of Spain's tourists who aren't looking for much more culture than they can find with a beach towel and some sun block. The sun gods willingly oblige with a blanket of warm, clear weather.

● **Prado Museum, Madrid** Even at the time it opened in 1819, the Prado was one of the most important art collections in Europe. There's far too much to see without a few weeks of museum-dedicated time, so most confine their browsing to the famous Spaniards – and even then it's a daunting pursuit.

● **Alhambra, Granada** Resting majestically atop an enormous citadel in the centre of Granada, the Alhambra is almost a visual overload. The Alcazaba, Generalife gardens and Palacios Nazaries take nearly a day to explore. Started by Ibn al-Ahmar, the structure's Moorish columns and domes and light-reflecting water basins inspire even the weariest traveller.

Alternative activities

● **Walk the Camino de Santiago** Completing the entire journey to the city of Santiago de Compostela on foot takes most people 35–45 days, though no one says you have to do the entire thing. Some attempt this northern route across Spain on bike. See ⓦwww.caminosantiago.com for details of the route.

Average temperatures and rainfall in Spain

Average daily temperatures (maximum and minimum °C) and monthly rainfall (mm)

	Jan	Feb	Mar	Apr	May	June	July	Aug	Sept	Oct	Nov	Dec
Madrid												
max °C	11	12	16	17	22	28	32	32	28	20	14	11
min °C	0	2	3	6	9	13	16	16	13	8	4	2
rainfall mm	46	43	38	46	41	25	10	10	30	64	64	48
Seville												
max °C	16	17	21	22	26	31	35	35	32	26	21	17
min °C	6	7	8	10	13	17	19	19	18	13	9	7
rainfall mm	84	72	55	60	30	20	2	7	21	62	102	92

● **Watch Real Madrid** Perhaps never before have so many football stars been collected on one team. Or so much money spent on them. Zinedine Zidane, David Beckham, Ronaldo, Roberto Carlos, Luis Figo, Raul, Michael Owen – see them on their home turf at the Santiago Bernabéu Stadium and there's a good chance you'll be seeing them stroll to victory. See ⓦwww.realmadrid.com for ticket information.

● **Go canyoning in the Pyrenees** Slip into a wetsuit, strap on a helmet and drop into the Barranco de Lapazosa. Near the Ordesa y Monte Perdido National Park, this is one of the most spectacular spots to splash, jump and rappel downstream in a ravine.

● **See the Guggenheim, Bilbao** Frank Gehry's gleaming metallic creation isn't on the main tourist route; if you want to catch a glimpse of this modern architectural treat, it'll take a good eight hours on a bus to get there from Madrid. See ⓦwww.guggenheim-bilbao .es for info on current exhibitions.

● **Visit Dalí's House** Salvador Dalí's surreal melting clocks and bent views can be found in many places but, if you want to step into his universe, try the Dali House museum in Portlligat,

just outside Barcelona. ⓦwww.salvadordalimuseum.org.

● **Ski the Sierra Nevada mountains** In late spring, you can ski all morning on 1300 vertical metres of slopes, then hop in a car or bus and head to the beach for a lazy afternoon of sunbathing. It's just 150km from Europe's southernmost ski resort to the Costa del Sol.

Costs

Away from the most touristy areas, Spain can be downright affordable. If you avoid museums, bars and restaurants, you can scrape by on €20 a day with dorm living, but who wants to do that all the time? On €33–40 a day, you can live pretty well.

Accommodation

Spain has some of the cheapest accommodation, with dorm rooms ranging between €13 and €18. Pensions are particularly common and often involve speaking into an intercom outside the front door of an unmarked apartment building and waiting for an elderly Spanish-speaking lady to buzz you in so you can hike up five flights and find out she doesn't have any room left. But often her neighbour or a friend down the street will, so don't despair. Out of season, you can (and should) try to bargain a bit for room rates.

Eating and drinking

Tapas in hip bars (€1–3) may be tasty, but they're far from the best way to fill up. A *tortilla de patatas* (potato omelette) will get you much further for your money. Don't miss out on the local wines (ask for the regional speciality), and buy them in a shop, not a restaurant, when you do your taste-testing. Also, be wary of low-priced seafood anywhere where you can't actually see the open ocean from the place you're ordering.

Transport

Spain is fairly well covered by a simple network of rail lines, with a complicated pricing system. The luxury high-speed trains work well for those who can afford them, with an increasing number of them departing from Madrid; budget travellers may need to hop between regional trains to get around cheaply. All this switching can be tricky and may involve an alternative route. If the local ticket sellers are reluctant to work this out (and if you speak Spanish), ring RENFE (☎902 240 202), or try playing around with the schedules on their web-site (ⓦwww.renfe.com).

Bus services are comfortable and dependable and often faster than the slower trains.

In Madrid, you can pick up a Madrid Card (one day €28; two days €42; three days €55), which is good for getting around on public transport and gets you admission to forty museums.

By train

Spain Flexi Pass Any three days of travel in two months €184 (first class), €143 (second class). Additional travel days €29 (first class) and €24 (second class).

Iberic Rail Pass (also valid in Portugal) Any three days of travel in two months €203 (first class). Additional travel days €29.
France'n Spain Pass Any four days of travel in two months €244 (first class), €211 (second class) and €162 (youth, second class). Additional travel days (maximum of six) €27 per day (first class), €24 per day (second class) and €18 per day (youth, second class).
Tarjeta Explorerail Pass Seven (€115), fifteen (€140) or thirty days (€180) of travel.
Eurodomino Spain Pass Ranges from any three days of travel in one month – €160 (first class), €123 (second class) and €104 (youth, second class) – to any eight days of travel in one month – €351 (first class), €285 (second class) and €238 (youth, second class). For Europe-wide **Eurail** and **InterRail** passes, see p.38. For tips and tricks on maximizing your rail pass, see p.71.

By Bus

A Busabout pass (see p.39) allows you to travel throughout Spain. For internal bus prices, see ⓦwww.secorbus.es (Spanish only). For buses to other countries, see ⓦwww.eurolines.es.

Events

● **The Running of the Bulls, Pamplona** The town may look like it's been invaded by pizza delivery men, but the white outfits with red scarves are the traditional dress for running alongside a stampeding herd of bulls though a series of narrow passageways. The one-kilometre-long, early-morning *encierro* (bull run) has almost become secondary to the night-long fiesta preceding each day's run and bullfight. See p.17 for more details.

- **La Tomatina, Buñol** If you've never been trapped inside a pasta sauce factory during an explosion, here's your chance to get the next best thing: a free-for-all tomato fight in the square of this tiny Spanish town. Participants travel from around the globe to freely fling ripe tomatoes at strangers. See p.17 for more details.

- **Las Fallas, Valencia** Spectacular floats (*ninots*) of wood, wax and papier mâché are marched through the town during this six-day fiesta. Only one *ninot*, by popular vote, is saved, while the others are burned in the final night of celebrations. See p.16 for more details.

- **Carnaval, Sitges** For a wild dose of Carnaval (which can be celebrated virtually anywhere in Spain), try Sitges, near Barcelona. Expect little sleep, ample beer, and a pulsing mass of vibrant costumes. Mid-Feb; ⓦwww.sitges.com/carnaval.

- **Feria de Abril, Seville** This end-of-April festival in Seville is a week-long party, with flamenco dancing, a horse fair and (you'll never guess), bullfights which has become *the* place for Spain's socialites to mingle. Mid-April; ⓦwww.turismo.sevilla.org.

Spain online

Country info ⓦwww.tourspain.es
Rail ⓦwww.renfe.es
Bus ⓦwww.secorbus.es, ⓦwww.tgcomes.es or ⓦwww.alsa.es
Madrid info ⓦwww.descubremadrid.com
Barcelona info ⓦwww.bcn.es
Seville info ⓦwww.sevilla.org

Sweden

Capital: Stockholm
Population: 9,000,000
Language: Swedish
Currency: Swedish kronor (SEK)
GDP per capita: €21,210
When to go: June–August, when days are generally mild, lovely and long. May and September require a bit more luck for good weather

When not to go: November and December. There are nice Christmas markets in December, but it's hard to count on a white Christmas. You may just get the dark, freezing rainy part. January and February aren't much better, but at least winter activities are under way
Minimum daily budget: €37

If this Nordic land conjures up images of Abba's disco outfits, Ikea's stylish discount furniture, boxy Volvos or Björn Borg's tennis headband, there's little of Sweden that will disappoint. The Cardigans and Hives may grab more headlines, but Abba's music is still more popular than the national anthem. The Swedish countryside sprouts up more giant blue Ikea boxes than berries. Volvo is softening the corners on their boxes, but still subscribes to a basic design the shape of a sauna. And Björn Borg, in addition to the headband, now has a popular underwear line.

For those slightly more tuned in to Swedish culture, there's idyllic archipelago living, the trendy glass-blowers of the Småland region, herring in the summer, and *glögg* (a spicy warm wine) around Christmas.

There are also 96,000 lakes, some of the best beaches in Europe and, up north, an inexhaustible supply of pristine hiking trails where there's a good chance you won't encounter another soul. Stockholm is the big urban attraction, and deservingly so, but the bicycle-inundated university towns of Lund and Uppsala clamour for a visit. And don't forget to try the meatballs.

Main attractions

● **Vasa Museum, Stockholm**
Sweden's most popular museum has just one exhibit, a mighty wooden warship that was launched from that very spot in 1628. Moments after it touched the water on its inaugural journey, the flawed, top-heavy ship tipped over and sank, where it was preserved in the mud of Stockholm's harbour. In an ironic twist, this failure has earned more money for Sweden than if the ship had been built correctly in the first place.

● **Glass Kingdom** Hidden within the thickly forested region of Småland, several boutique glass factories can be found churning out trendy transparent glasses, bowls and sculptures. You can see the glass-blowers in action, pulling glowing orbs out of the white-hot furnaces, before buying some of their creations in the attached shop. Orrefors and Kosta Boda are the most popular, and many of the glass artists are as well-known as pop stars around Sweden.

● **Gamla Stan, Stockholm**
Stockholm's Old Town, or Gamla
Stan as it's known, rests on just one
of the capital's fourteen islands.
From above, it looks like a maze of
tiny streets surrounding the Royal
Palace (which looks like Buckingham
Palace, yet, in a feat of architectural
one-upmanship, was built with one
more room). The Old Town is packed
with tourists, but there are narrow
enough sidestreets (several not much
wider than your shoulders) to allow for
some exploration.

● **Visby** This medieval port on the island
of Gotland (accessible by plane and just

a few hours by ferry from east coast
cities) is perched on a hill, lined with
cobblestones and ringed by a high
stone wall. It's probably the most picturesque and charming town in Sweden,
with more than forty towers and scores
of church ruins remaining from the
Hanseatic period.

● **Skansen, Stockholm** A vast
open-air museum packed with recre-
ated farms, windmills and 150 buildings from Sweden's past. There's a
zoo with monkeys, snakes, moose
and bears, plus a petting area for kids
who want to get a little closer to goats
and kittens.

Average daily temperatures (maximum and minimum °C) and monthly rainfall (mm)

	Jan	Feb	Mar	Apr	May	June	July	Aug	Sept	Oct	Nov	Dec
Stockholm												
max °C	-1	-2	3	8	16	19	21	20	14	9	4	0
min °C	-6	-7	-3	-1	5	9	12	12	7	3	-1	-5
rainfall mm	39	27	26	30	30	45	72	66	55	50	53	46

Alternative activities

● **Hike Sarek National Park** The glaciers, peaks, valleys and lakes of this remote northern park cover 2000 square kilometres. The trails are demanding and best suited for advanced hikers who can pack and carry what they need (there are few huts or bridges), so those who make the effort will have a vast wilderness all to themselves.

● **Kayak the archipelago** Stockholm's archipelago has 24,000 islands, and if you don't have access to a sailboat – or the ability to sail one – a kayak is the best way to get around. Bring a tent, a good map and even a mobile phone (there's coverage over most of the islands) and book inexpensive cabins along the way.

● **Skate on thin ice** One of the most popular recreational sports in Sweden is long-distance ice-skating. You do need some special equipment, including 55-centimetre-long blades, but that can be easily purchased or rented for a tour. More important is that you know where you're going and take safety precautions, just as the locals do.

● **Run the Stockholm Marathon** Held on the first Saturday of June, this 43.5-kilometre race through Stockholm is one of the world's most beautiful marathons. There are other ways to get the same vistas, but few that will earn the same sort of respect from the locals. See ⓦ www.marathon.se /stockholm for entry details.

Costs

Sweden is hardly a cheap destination, especially for the mid-range traveller who may like to dine out. If you're camping (often for free) and cooking your own food, you might squeak by on €16–20 a day. Figure on €37 a day at a minimum with hostel dorms, and €49–61 with cheap rooms and inexpensive restaurants.

Accommodation

Legally, you can camp in the woods for free, and even on private property (as long as it's unfenced land and more than 100m from the nearest dwelling, and, even then, etiquette stipulates that you ask permission from the landowner). Getting around this way will save you a fortune and turn Sweden into one of the cheapest destinations. Otherwise, expect to pay around €20–29 for a cheap dorm bed and €50–80 for mid-range accommodation.

Eating and drinking

Falafels and pizza are the cheapest easily found fillers but, if you plan to eat out, do so during lunch. Most restaurants offer lunch specials for about €5–8 that include a salad bar, warm meal, cold drink and coffee. Order the same food in the same restaurant at dinner time and you'll pay about €25–37 for it. Alcohol is particularly expensive, but picking up your beer or wine from one of the government-run *Systembolagets* will make a significant saving.

Transport

Getting around in Sweden is comfortable and often quick, but never cheap. Rail and bus passes are an especially good way to get around in these parts. And that goes for inner-city transport as well (it's possible to pay €6.50 for a fifteen-minute subway ride in Stockholm if you buy a single ticket). The capital's transit authority offers clipcards for €16, which should give you about seven to ten rides, depending on distance. There's also a Stockholm Card (24hr card €28, 48hr card €43, 72hr card €59) that allows unlimited public transport, museum admission and boat sightseeing. For more details, visit Ⓦwww.sl.se or Ⓦwww.stockholmtown.com.

By train

ScanRail Pass (also valid in Denmark, Finland and Norway) Any five days of travel in two months €241 (second class) and €168 (youth, second class). Any ten days of travel in two months €323 (second class) and €226 (youth, second class). Any 21 consecutive days of travel €375 (second class), €261 (youth, second class).

For Europe-wide **Eurail** and **InterRail** passes, see p.38. For tips and tricks on maximizing your rail pass, see p.71.

By bus

Busabout doesn't operate in Sweden. For internal bus prices, see Ⓦwww .swebusexpress.se. For buses to other countries, see Ⓦwww.eurolines.se.

Events

● **Crayfish party** It's a national event without a national party or fixed date. The idea is to make friends with a local and get invited to a private bash. Swedes don silly hats as they sing drinking songs and wash down minuscule amounts of crayfish meat with schnapps (spiced vodka) and beer. Late July or Aug.

● **Midsummer's Day** The longest day of the year (at least, the closest Friday and Saturday to the longest day) is celebrated with the pagan rite of maypole dancing and schnapps drinking. There are decorations around towns, but it's essentially a family holiday. Mid-June.

● **Sankta Lucia Day** If you're in Sweden in early December, don't forget to head to church and witness a parade of white-gowned young women with candle crowns. The singing is excellent, and the traditional saffron buns and ginger snaps aren't too bad either. Dec 13.

Sweden online

Country info Ⓦwww.visit-sweden.com
Rail Ⓦwww.sl.se
Bus Ⓦwww.swebusexpress.se
Stockholm info Ⓦwww.stockholmtown .com

Switzerland

Capital: Bern
Population: 7,450,867
Languages: German, French, Italian and Romansch
Currency: Swiss franc (CHF)
GDP per capita: €26,760
When to go: Any time. June–August is excellent for exploring nature, November–March sees the country turn into a mountain playground and April–May and late September–October bring comfortable weather, without the crowds. Skiing in the Alps lasts from the end of November until April
When not to go: November–February in the cities and around the lakes is icy-cold and not an ideal time for wandering
Minimum daily budget: €37

The best-known art in Switzerland may very well be the panoramic postcards for sale on racks throughout the country. When you look around, it seems the only thing missing are frames around the mountains. The best way to see the peaks, of course, is to put down your camera and strap on a pair of skis or hiking boots. Switzerland is also famous for its political neutrality, milk chocolate, yodellers, timepieces that cost more than small aeroplanes and an army equipped with tiny folding knives. What many don't know is that this teeny, wealthy, mountainous country is a potpourri of cultures speaking four languages: French, German (Switzerdeutsch is the dialect), Italian and the little-known and little-used Romansch. Together, this motley confederacy of cantons has picked up more Nobel prizes (per capita) than any other country. And you can bet your last cowbell that the sombre gaggle of bankers is going to keep the country's finances secure.

Main attractions

● **Zermatt** A glam skiing and mountaineering resort tied to the fame of per-haps the most visually stunning Alp: the Matterhorn (4478m). The car-free town is best explored on foot, and there's a cog railway that will lift you up to Gornergrat for even more impressive vistas.

● **Château de Chillon** Perched on the shore of Lake Geneva, the most visited historical building in Switzerland was started in the eleventh century and has been modified ever since. Dungeons, courtyards and towers make it a fairy-tale castle and 360-degree photo op. Not surprisingly, the dreamy home found its way into the writings of Lord Byron.

● **Zürich** Geneva may have the Red Cross, but Zürich has had an explosion of trendy cafés, bars and shops. The Old Town offers a cultural afternoon of wandering. You don't need to open a numbered bank account to visit, but it certainly helps.

● **Lake Thun** Welcome to *Schloss* (castle) country. There's Schloss Thun, Schloss Oberhofen, and Schloss Hunegg (which mixes in Art Nouveau renovations). You can visit all three on a one-day boat trip on Lake Thun and still have time to try the nearby 100-metre bungee jump.

Alternative activities

● **Explore the Franches Montagnes** If you're going to head up into the mountains, you may as well avoid a superhighway of tourists gasping for oxygen. This range offers fewer visitors, cross-country skiing and gentle horses. Saignelégier is a good place to start your exploring.

● **Munch on fine chocolate** The world-famous Lindt chocolate factory is located just outside Zürich and offers an all-you-can-eat tasting treat at the end of their tour. The factory is a mesh of metal pipes labelled "cocoa butter" and "chocolate", but you'll have to sit through a rather long infomercial about the company before you're allowed access to the choco-binge room. See ⓦwww.lindt.com for tour times.

● **Fly a glider in the Alps** Take advantage of the updraughts with a ride (or lesson) in a glider. Soar over cliffs and ride thermals as high as they'll take you (and your pilot). Switzerland is one country that deserves a bird's-eye view. To find a local listing of flight centres, try ⓦwww.landings.com.

● **Go luging** The most famous luge course in the world is the Cresta Run, built in St Moritz for the 1884–85 season. It's now a private club, but you can try your head at it (you go head first, skeleton-style) on the ice track. Travelling 1200m at 90kmph isn't impressive for a bullet, but it's not bad for a sledge. For five runs with some instruction, you pay a small fortune (€285). Book ahead for a spot at ⓦwww.cresta-run .com/html/booking_view.cfm.

● **Cycle around Switzerland** Nine national cycle routes (3300km in total) crisscross the country, most of them well away from traffic; route maps and information in English are available from tourist offices. Eurotrek can rent you a bike, book hotels along your route and transport your gear from hotel to hotel. See ⓦwww.eurotrek.ch for tour information.

Costs

The Swiss franc may be stable and more visually compelling than the euro but, when you look at the prices, you'll

Average temperatures and rainfall in Switzerland

Average daily temperatures (maximum and minimum °C) and monthly rainfall (mm)

	Jan	Feb	Mar	Apr	May	June	July	Aug	Sept	Oct	Nov	Dec
Zürich												
max °C	2	3	8	12	17	19	23	22	18	13	6	3
min °C	-2	-2	2	4	9	12	14	14	11	7	2	0
rainfall mm	61	61	69	84	102	127	127	124	99	84	71	71

wonder if you've been cheated into a bad exchange rate. Squeaking by for under €37 will be a challenge. For nightlife, restaurants and foamy lattes, you'll have to nearly triple that.

Accommodation

There's enough accommodation to find a room almost anywhere on the same day, but to get your choice of the cheapest digs in town in summer, try to book a few days or weeks in advance. Geneva Hostels, for example, charges about €19 for a dorm room and €58 for a double. Wherever you check in, always ask for a free guest card (*gästekarte*, *carte des visiteurs*, *tessera di soggiorno*). This bonus for overnight visitors gives reasonable discounts for local attractions and transport. At higher altitudes, the season is shorter and more popular (snow may not melt on those high passes until mid-June), so huts and mountain refuges should be booked well in advance.

Eating and drinking

In the south, there's an Italian influence; in the west, French cuisine; while it's German dishes everywhere else. The food is excellent – fondues, polenta, chocolates and a collection of famous cheeses await visitors – but the question is if you can afford it. The country with the world's most expensive *McDonald's* prices doesn't welcome budget diners with open arms. Kebabs

and falafels are among the most popular survival meals for the traveller. Younger travellers can also head for a nearby university cafeteria and find something filling for under €6.

Transport

Switzerland offers some of the most scenic routes in the world on funiculars, cable cars, cog railways, trains, buses and boats. All are clean, expensive and arrive and depart with the accuracy of a Swiss watch. There are several unique rail passes (see Ⓦwww.rail.ch), each with their own advantages; the Swiss Pass, for example, lets children under 16 travel for free and allows free bus travel on some routes. The 9 O'clock Pass (€13) provides discounted transport after 9am on Saturdays and Sundays.

In Zürich, a 24-hour pass (€5) is good for travel on all public transport, but a better deal might be the Zürich Card (€10 for a 24hr pass, €20 for a 72hr pass), which also allows free admission to museums and a complimentary drink at 24 restaurants.

By train

Swiss Pass Ranges from any four consecutive days of travel – €212 (first class) and €139 (second class) – to one month of travel – €457 (first class), €306 (second class).
Swiss Flexi Pass Ranges from any three days of travel in one month –

€204 (first class) and €135 (second class) – to any eight days of travel in one month – € 367 (first class) and €245 (second class).

France'n Switzerland Pass Any four days of travel in two months €247 (first class) and €173 (second class and youth, second class). Additional days (maximum of six) €30 per day (first class) and €22 per day (second class and youth, second class).

Switzerland'n Austria Pass Any four days of travel in two months €245 (first class), €171 (youth, second class). Additional days €29 per day (first class), €22 per day (youth, second class).

Eurodomino Switzerland Pass Ranges from any three days of travel in one month – €172 (first class), €115 (second class) and €88 (youth, second class) – to any eight days of travel in one month – €263 (first class), €180 (second class) and €136 (youth, second class).

Swiss Half-fare Card Fifty percent off all trains, buses, boats and most city trams for a month for €117.

For Europe-wide **Eurail** and **InterRail** passes, see p.38. For tips and tricks on maximizing your rail pass, see p.71.

By bus

A Busabout pass (see p.39) allows some travel within Switzerland. PTT Post Buses (Ⓦwww.post.ch) permit some travel with a non-Eurail Swiss pass. For buses to other countries, see Ⓦwww.eurolines.ch.

Events

● **Yehudi Menuhin Festival, Gstaad** Yehudi Menuhin founded this festival in 1956 to bring chamber music to the swanky Swiss Alps resort of Gstaad. Well, it seemed like reason enough at the time. The event has grown and the concerts are held in the churches and surrounding villages. World-renown

soloists also perform. July–Sept; Ⓦwww.menuhinfestivalgstaad.com.

● **Santa Claus World Championship, Samnaun** St Nick gets to show his competitive edge in this odd but colourful contest in Samnaun. There's no milk and cookie eating, but previous years have seen reindeer rodeo, sledging and skiing on primitive skis. Nov 27; Ⓦwww.clauwau.com.

● **Red Bull Vertigo, Villeneuve** Watch for falling psychopaths! The world's best hang-gliders and paragliders descend on Villeneuve for a few days as part of the Acrobatics World Cup. The pros land on a tiny floating platform in the middle of a lake, where over 20,000 spectators wait for an embarrassing face plant. Late Aug; Ⓦwww.redbull-vertigo.com.

● **St Moritz Christmas Market** If you haven't finished your Christmas shopping come the beginning of December, this is the place to go. Tree decorations, woodcraft, dolls and snacks – nothing you actually need – are hyperinflated and put on display for purchase. Dec 3; Ⓦwww.stmoritz.ch.

● **Montreux Jazz Festival** Europe's most famous jazzfest is like a tractor beam for the world's top musicians. Performers from B.B. King to Phil Collins to Bobby McFerrin to the Black Eyed Peas – and nearly anyone you can think of in between – have played this event in Montreux, a town delightfully sandwiched between the edge of Lake Geneva and the Alps.

Switerland online

Country info Ⓦwww.myswitzerland.com
Rail Ⓦwww.rail.ch
Bus Ⓦwww.post.ch
Bern info Ⓦww.berne.ch
Zürich info Ⓦwww.zuerich.com
Geneva info Ⓦwww.geneve-tourisme.ch

Turkey

Capital: Ankara
Population: 68,893,918
Language: Turkish
Currency: Turkish lira (TL)
GDP per capita: €5465
When to go: May and October are ideal – great weather, few tourists. June and September have the best weather, but they also have the crowds
When not to go: December–March is rainy and cold (though Febuary –March are fine on the southeast coast). July and August are hot and crowded, the southeast especially so
Minimum daily budget: €20

No other country provides as spectacular a bridge between East and West as Turkey, and nowhere more tangible as in the capital, İstanbul. On one side of İstanbul is Europe. On the other, Asia. This quickly modernizing city (still hoping to lead the country into the EU) has retained its magical frenetic energy, mixing luxury hotels and clubs with minarets, churches and smooth-talking carpet salesmen who speak eight languages and can guess which town you're from by your dialect. With the range of poverty and wealth, European and Asian influences, Ottoman and Byzantine styles, religious and secular peoples, it seems like the country has an identity crisis. And it just may. But this fusion, combined with an outpouring of hospitality and food to die for, makes it an enormously rewarding place for the traveller.

Outside of İstanbul, there are spectacular ruins, several of the finest beaches on the Aegean Sea and some of the wildest geological formations on the planet, from Pamukkale to Cappadocia.

Main attractions

● **Kapalī Çarşī (Covered Bazaar)**

İstanbul is worth visiting for the shopping alone. And the Kapali Çarşī, or "Covered Bazaar", in the old city is the logical place to start. This labyrinth of streets and passages houses more than 4000 shops. The names recall the days when each trade had its own quarter: "Goldsmiths' Street", "Carpet Sellers' Street", "The Sreet of the Skullcap Makers". Sit down for tea with some of the sellers and let them charm you into buying a few souvenirs you never realized you wanted.

● **Pamukkale** Chances are you'll catch your first glimpse of Pamukkale (translated as "Cotton Castle") on a postcard. Calcium-oxide-rich waters paint this Caldag hillside white, creating a series of Gaudí-like dripping terraces. Try to view this stunning geological formation early without thousands of people crawling all over it and turning the white surface dark with foot scum.

● **Topkapī Palace, İstanbul** One of İstanbul's big draws, this expansive fifteenth-century estate served as the centre for the Ottoman empire for four centuries and is difficult for most travellers to miss. Among the maze of rooms, you'll find inner courtyards, a throne room, a circumcision room and a harem.

Note: This map shows only the western parts of Turkey, corresponding to the area covered by this country profile.

- **Dolmabahçe Palace, İstanbul** When the Ottomans moved on from Topkapı Palace in 1853, they decided to build on the Asian side of the Bosphorus. It doesn't look as magnificent from the outside, but the opulence within will put even the most overdecorated Las Vegas lobby to shame. It's also where Kemal Atatürk (Turkey's first president) died on November 10, 1938 – if you want to know when, just look at the clocks, which have been set to his exact time of death (9.05am).

- **Blue Mosque, İstanbul** If you're look-ing for a Smurf-coloured mosque, forget it – it's the blue tilework on the insides that gives this mosque its name. If you want to walk barefoot across countless handwoven rugs while marvelling at the serenity and architecture, you won't be disappointed by this seventeenth-century Mehmet Aga creation, known locally as the "Sultanahmet Camii".

- **Ephesus** Walking around the dry stacks of cut stone of Ephesus, it's hard to imagine that it once sat on the Aegean coast, now 8km away. And even harder to imagine the Temple of Artemis in full glory, when it was once a Wonder of the World. The site as a whole, however, has been impressively preserved.

Alternative activities

- **Take a Turkish bath** Nothing scrapes off the travel grime quite like a trip to a *hammam*. These enormous marble steam rooms, often fitted with hot baths, showers and cooling-down chambers, can be found all over Turkey. Let a masseuse scrub you with an abrasive mitt and you'll see chewing-gum-sized wads of dead skin tumbling off your body. Then he'll pound your muscles to a pulp, crack your joints, and you'll emerge feeling like a boneless chicken. In a good way, of course.

- **Explore İstanbul's sewer** Literally translated, Yerebatan Saray is the

First-Time **Europe** | **WHERE TO GO**

Average daily temperatures (maximum and minimum °C) and monthly rainfall (mm)

	Jan	Feb	Mar	Apr	May	June	July	Aug	Sept	Oct	Nov	Dec
Istanbul												
max °C	6	7	11	14	18	21	24	24	21	15	9	7
min °C	1	1	3	6	9	12	14	14	11	8	4	2
rainfall mm	54	46	54	46	63	58	54	52	54	56	56	56

"Sunken Palace". It's İstanbul's largest underground cistern, naturally air condi-tioned and renovated for public access. This one-time plumber's nightmare has been atmospherically spruced up – the water dripping from the ceiling is now accompanied by pulsing lights and creepy music.

● **Sleep in a cave** Head into the Swiss-cheese-like region of Cappadocia and you'll find a mind-boggling assortment of caves. Some of these Hittite dwellings (often called "Fairy Chimneys") have been converted into damp youth hostels that offer a nice respite from the heat. You'll also find underground cities and rock churches.

● **Pick out an "Evil Eye"** Nazar Boncuk, or "Evil Eye" charms as they're commonly known, are cheap and come in many shapes and sizes: earrings, necklaces, hatpins and so on. The little blue eye is an old superstition to ward off misfortune. Wear one and you'll likely get a smile from the locals. It's a nice way to let them know you're interested in more than snapping pictures of old ladies making carpets. Something they'll enjoy pointing out while they sell you a teaset, anyway.

Costs

You can go a long way on a minimal budget in Turkey. In the more popular spots on the traveller's trail, you can squeak by for under €20 a day; in less-visited spots, under €16. If you want to stay in slightly nicer hotels and eat some decent restaurant meals, €40 a day should do the trick. Remember to bargain for all souvenirs (see p.79) – it's part of the shopping experience and the only way to make sure you get a decent price.

Accommodation

Rooms are cheap (figure on €6.50–12 for a cheap room in a hostel), and campgrounds, when available, are even cheaper. Outside of summer, try bar-gaining for your room. Start by asking for a twenty percent off-season discount and see what they say.

Eating and drinking

In no other country listed in this book can you eat so well for so little. The street snacks and "fast food" around Turkey are to die for: Turkish pizzas, baklava, salted cucumber on a stick, Turkish delight, pistachio nuts, yoghurt – you won't go hungry or break your budget. Leave a bit of pocket change for a tip (five percent) and that will be fine. Offer it again (twice if necessary) if they decline the first time.

Transport

Most people travel by bus in Turkey. How much you spend depends in part on your haggling and in part on what type of bus you take, from the slightly run-down to the incredibly modern. There are some express train services, but these are mostly between İstanbul and Ankara (and most are still slower than the bus). You may save some time by taking a ferry, say, from İstanbul to the south, but the buses are hard to beat.

By train

Balkans Flexi Pass (also valid in Bulgaria, Greece and Romania) Any five days of travel in one month €156 (first class) and €93 (youth, first class). Any ten days of travel in one month €273 (first class) and €162 (youth, first class). Any fifteen days of travel in one month €328 (first class) and €197 (youth, first class).

Eurodomino Turkey Pass Ranges from any three days of travel in one month – €64 (first class), €42 (second class) and €34 (youth, second class) – to any eight days of travel in one month – €156 (first class), €102 (second class) and €76 (youth, second class).

For Europe-wide **InterRail** passes (**Eurail** doesn't cover Turkey), see p.38. For tips and tricks on maximizing your rail pass, see p.71.

By bus

Busabout doesn't operate in Turkey. For internal bus prices, see ⓦwww.varan.com.tr. For buses to other countries, see ⓦwww.eurolines.com.

Events

● **Oiled-wrestling Festival, Edirne** Every summer, the large stadium near Edirne on the Greek-Turkish border erupts into wrestlemania. The week-long "sudden-death" format narrows the 1000-plus field of olive-oil-covered competitors down to a few slick champions. ⓦwww.kirkpinar.com.

● **Mevlana Whirling Dervishes Festival, Konya** Spin your way over to Konya (with over a million others) for this religious spectacle in the ancient Seljuk capital. The Dervishes (Sufi members of the Mevlevi Order) whirl to achieve mystical union with God. Dec; ⓦwww.mevlana.net.

● **İstanbul Music Festival** In early summer, İstanbul's Hagia Eirene Museum and Ataturk Cultural Centre welcome an international cast of performers playing traditional Turkish music, classical numbers and everything in between, from *West Side Story* to Venetian masters of Baroque. June; ⓦwww.istfest.org.

Turkey online

Country info ⓦwww.tourismturkey.org
Rail ⓦwww.tcdd.gov.tr (see ⓦwww.turkeytravelplanner.com/Transportation/Train/tcdd_website.html for how to translate the timetable)
Bus ⓦwww.varan.com.tr
İstanbul info ⓦwww.istanbul.com

First-Time Europe

Basics

Transport

Flight booking engines

Ⓦ **www.expedia.com** Microsoft's online travel agency

Ⓦ **www.opodo.com** A major European flight-booking engine

Ⓦ **www.orbitz.com** The airlines' own group booking engine, with fares from 450 airlines

Ⓦ **www.travelocity.com** A leading Sabre-powered booking site

Budget travel agents

Ⓦ **www.adventureworld.com.au** Based in Australia with an office in New Zealand

Ⓦ **www.airbrokers.com** International consolidator

Ⓦ **www.airtreks.com** Multi-stop international specialist based in the US

Ⓦ **www.flightcentre.com** Offices in Australia, Britain, Canada, New Zealand and the US

Ⓦ **www.moments-notice.com** Discount travel club based in the US

Ⓦ **www.sta.com** Britain-based agent with hundreds of offices in the US, plus offices in Australia, Canada and New Zealand

Ⓦ **www.studentuniverse.com** US-based student site

Ⓦ **www.trailfinders.co.uk** Britain-based with offices in Australia

Ⓦ **www.travelcuts.com** Canada-based, with offices in the US

Ⓦ **www.yha.com.au** Offices around Australia

Cheap flights within Europe

Ⓦ **www.airhitch.org** A budget-minded way to fill last-minute seats for travellers with flexible schedules

Ⓦ **www.airtech.org** Standby flight-pass service for travellers with flexible schedules

Ⓦ **www.attitudetravel.com /lowcostairlines** Gives the lowdown on which budget carrier flies where, so you know the websites to check

Ⓦ **www.cheapflights.co.uk** Scours the Web for the best deals offered by other discount brokers and consolidators, and then points you there

Ⓦ **www.lastminute.com** Last-second deals mostly for charter flights and holiday spots, but with destinations around the continent

Ⓦ **www.priceline.com** Name-your-own-price bidding system

Airlines and airports

Ⓦ **http://flightview.com/traveltools** Allows you to check the status of any flight with a real-time display of the plane in the air

Ⓦ **www.airlineandairportlinks.com** Links to all airports

Ⓦ **www.sleepinginairports.net** A guide to sleeping in airports

Ⓦ **www.travel-watch.com/airlink .htm** Links to every airline worldwide

Trains

Ⓦ **http://railplus.raileurope.com** Europe rail passes for Australians

Ⓦ **www.interrail.co.uk** European fare and timetable information

Ⓦ **www.raileurope.co.uk** Europe rail passes for Europeans

Ⓦ **www.raileurope.com** Europe rail passes for North Americans

ⓦ **www.railplus.co.nz** Europe rail passes for Kiwis

ⓦ **www.railserve.com** Links to rail services across Europe

Cars and motorcycles

ⓦ **www.theaa.com** The UK's Automobile Association for all things automotive

ⓦ **www.aaa.com** America's Automobile Association

ⓦ **www.caa.ca** Canadian Automobile Association – offers carnet info for Americans as well

ⓦ **www.rac.co.uk** Royal Automobile Club – offers similar services to the AA

ⓦ **www.horizonsunlimited.com** Tips and tales on motorcycling around Europe

ⓦ **www.viamichelin.com** Driving directions throughout Europe

Ferries and freighters

ⓦ **http://members.aol.com /cruiseaz/freighters.htm** UK-based freighter bookers

ⓦ **http://routesinternational.com /ships.htm** Links to ferry services across Europe

ⓦ **www.freighterworld.com** Will help book passage on freighters worldwide

ⓦ **www.tcpltd.com/tcpltd1.htm** Canada-based freighter bookers

ⓦ **www.traveltips.com /freighterdirectory.html** Directory providing a sample of the freighters on the move; will also help with booking

Red tape

Travel insurance

ⓦ **www.eglobalhealth.com** eGlobalHealth Insurers

ⓦ **www.roughguides.com** Rough Guide insurance

ⓦ **www.sosinternational.com** SOS International

ⓦ **www.specialtyrisk.com** Specialty Risk International

ⓦ **www.travelinsure.com** Travel insurance services

ⓦ **www.worldtravelcenter.com** An excellent starting spot for finding a policy

Embassies

ⓦ **www.escapeartist.com /embassy1/embassy1.htm** Find an embassy anywhere in the world

Money

ATM locators

ⓦ **www.mastercard.com /cardholderservices/atm** For MasterCard users

ⓦ **www.visa.com/pd/atm/main .html** For Visa card owners

American Express travel offices

ⓦ **http://travel.americanexpress .com/travel/personal/resources /tso** Access to a list of their European offices

Currency exchange rates

Ⓦ **www.oanda.com** Quick conversions with 164 currencies

Discount cards

Ⓦ **www.hiayh.org** Hostelling International cards

Ⓦ **www.isecard.com** International Exchange Student Cards

Ⓦ **www.isic.org** International Student Identity Cards, Teacher Cards, Youth Cards

Ⓦ **www.vipbackpackers.com** Discounts for select private hostels

Money transfer

Ⓦ **www.moneygram.com** Affiliated with Thomas Cook, American Express and various banks and post offices – for sending money and paying bills urgently

Ⓦ **www.westernunion.com** Western Union – for sending money to an overseas Western Union office

Travel tools

Conversions

Ⓦ **www.digitaldutch.com /unitconverter** Converts weights, measurements, distances, etc as quick as you can type in the numbers

Events

Ⓦ **www.festivals.com** Find out when and where the party is on, no matter where you go

Ⓦ **www.holidayfestival.com** A calendar of European holidays

Global adaptors

Ⓦ **www.kropla.com/electric.htm** The lowdown on what adaptors you'll need if you're bringing electrical appliances with you, and where to buy them

Ⓦ **www.kropla.com/phones.htm** Like above, but for phone adaptors and line checkers; all the tools you'll need, and some you won't

Language

Ⓦ **www.travlang.com** Downloadable online phrasebooks and dictionaries for 23 languages

Online maps

Ⓦ **www.map24.com** Award-winning map-viewing site with great zooming technology

Ⓦ **www.mapblast.com** Good graphics, and shows things such as hotels and petrol stations on the map as well

Ⓦ **www.maporama.com** Another solid online map site that allows you to zoom into nearly any spot in Europe

Ⓦ **www.randmcnally.com** More of a map store, with gadgets and atlases for sale as well

Times and dates

Ⓦ **www.timeanddate.com**

Ⓦ **www.worldtimeserver.com**

Weather

Ⓦ **www.intellicast.com/Travel /World** Global five-day forecasts

Ⓦ **www.worldclimate.com** Lists average temperature and rainfall everywhere

Health and safety

Health

ⓦ **www.cdc.gov** The US Centers for Disease Control has the latest updated information on vaccinations and outbreaks

ⓦ **www.who.org** The World Health Organization site has a country-by-country health profile

Travel warnings

ⓦ **http://travel.state.gov/travel /warnings.html** The US State Department's warnings can be vague – if one spot is potentially dangerous, they put the whole country on the list

ⓦ **www.fco.gov.uk** The UK's Foreign office (click on "travel") is a good starting point

ⓦ **www.smartraveller.gov.au /zw-cgi/view/Advice/Index** Australia's consular advice

ⓦ **www.voyage.gc.ca/dest/sos /warnings-en.asp** Canada's warning page

Working abroad

English teaching certificates

ⓦ **www.cambridge-efl.org** Home of Cambridge TESOL programmes; allows you to find nearest location

ⓦ **www.eslcafe.com** Dave's ESL Café is a TEFL forum with general job searching and classroom teaching tips and lessons

ⓦ **www.teflinternational.com** Info on getting cheaper TEFL degrees in Thailand or Egypt

ⓦ **www.windsorschools.co.uk** For the CELTA programme certificates

Internships and programmes

ⓦ **www.amscan.org** Two- to three-month summer placements for Americans aged 21 and over; particularly for those studying engineering, chemistry, business and computer science

ⓦ **www.bunac.org** Exactly what the name says (except, perhaps, the "Bunac" part); European programmes are only offered in Britain and Ireland

ⓦ **www.cdsintl.org** Programmes in Germany and Switzerland aimed at young professionals seeking international experience

ⓦ **www.ciee.org** Offers programmes in Germany, France and Ireland

ⓦ **www.interexchange.org** Programmes in Belgium and Norway for Americans and Canadians aged 18 and older

Job searches

ⓦ **www.anyworkanywhere.com** Find work, and get help with visa information

ⓦ **www.escapeartist.com/jobs /overseas1.htm** Overseas jobs by region and profession

Ⓦ**www.iagora.com** Online community featuring entry-level jobs and
internships around Europe

Ⓦ**www.jobsabroad.com** Allows
searching by country or job type;
also links to study and volunteer
programmes

Ⓦ**www.jobs-in-europe.net** A solid
starting point for a job search

Ⓦ**www.jobmonkey.com** Search by
job type, from skiing to teaching

Ⓦ**www.liveworkplay.com.au** A
Down Under guide with useful
"Working Holiday" information,
complete with visa permits

Ⓦ**www.michaelpage.com**
Professional work placement
agency

Ⓦ**www.monster.com** Helps with
available positions for skilled
workers

Ⓦ**www.payaway.co.uk** A resource
for jobs abroad with advice and listings. They also have a magazine,
the *Working Traveller*

Ⓦ**www.pickingjobs.com** Advice on
finding seasonal work abroad

Ⓦ**www.transitionsabroad.com**
A good resource, with specific tips
and leads for working abroad

Ⓦ**www.work4travel.co.uk** Lists
short-term work opportunities, such
as fruit harvest, carpentry and bar-
tending

Volunteering

Ⓦ**www.idealist.org** "Action Without
Borders" works to connect people,
organizations and resources with
the aim of free and dignified lives
for all

Ⓦ**www.takingitglobal.org** Online
community with information on
issues and opportunities to take
action

Ⓦ**www.vfp.org** "Volunteers for
Peace" is a US-based organization
with inexpensive international programmes

Ⓦ**www.volunteerabroad.com** Huge
directory of international volunteer
programmes, so you can search by
location

Ⓦ**www.volunteerinternational.org**
An updated list of volunteer opportunities

Ⓦ**www.wwoof.org** WWOOF
("Willing Workers on Organic
Farms") will help connect you with
farms in the region you want to be;
room and food exchange for work

Reading resources

Online-only travel
publications

Ⓦ**www.bootsnall.com** A great travel resource with many "how to do it"
and "what it was like" pieces

Ⓦ**www.connectedtraveler.com**
Offers a refreshing perspective on
cultural travel

Ⓦ**www.igougo.com** Swap photos

and travel writing, with mileage-
type points accrued for your
contributions

Ⓦ**www.journeywoman.com**
Highlights the female perspective
and offers tips and tales

Ⓦ**www.kinetictravel.net** Tales of
adventure combining mayhem and
meditation

Ⓦ **www.literarytraveler.com** Tracing steps of famous authors and learning about their inspirations is just part of the literary journey

Ⓦ **www.responsible-travel.org** Points out the impact of tourism and how to minimize yours while you're on the road

Ⓦ **www.worldhum.com** A travel version of *Arts and Letters Daily,* with interesting links plus original articles, interviews and reviews

Rough Guides advertiser

Rough Guides travel...

ROUGH GUIDES ADVERTISER

Rough Guides are available from good bookstores worldwide. New titles are published every month. Check www.roughguides.com for the latest news.

...music & reference

Trinidad & Tobago

Africa & Middle East
Cape Town
Egypt
The Gambia
Jordan
Kenya
Marrakesh
  DIRECTIONS
Morocco
South Africa, Lesotho
  & Swaziland
Syria
Tanzania
Tunisia
West Africa
Zanzibar
Zimbabwe

Travel Theme guides
First-Time Around the
  World
First-Time Asia
First-Time Europe
First-Time Latin
  America
Skiing & Snowboarding
  in North America
Travel Online
Travel Health
Walks in London & SE
  England
Women Travel

Restaurant guides
French Hotels &
  Restaurants
London
New York
San Francisco

Maps
Algarve
Amsterdam
Andalucia & Costa del Sol
Argentina

Athens
Australia
Baja California
Barcelona
Berlin
Boston
Brittany
Brussels
Chicago
Crete
Croatia
Cuba
Cyprus
Czech Republic
Dominican Republic
Dubai & UAE
Dublin
Egypt
Florence & Siena
Frankfurt
Greece
Guatemala & Belize
Iceland
Ireland
Kenya
Lisbon
London
Los Angeles
Madrid
Mexico
Miami & Key West
Morocco
New York City
New Zealand
Northern Spain
Paris
Peru
Portugal
Prague
Rome
San Francisco
Sicily
South Africa
South India
Sri Lanka
Tenerife
Thailand

Toronto
Trinidad & Tobago
Tuscany
Venice
Washington DC
Yucatán Peninsula

**Dictionary
Phrasebooks**
Czech
Dutch
Egyptian Arabic
EuropeanLanguages
  (Czech, French, German,
  Greek, Italian,
  Portuguese, Spanish)
French
German
Greek
Hindi & Urdu
Hungarian
Indonesian
Italian
Japanese
Mandarin Chinese
Mexican Spanish
Polish
Portuguese
Russian
Spanish
Swahili
Thai
Turkish
Vietnamese

Music Guides
The Beatles
Bob Dylan
Cult Pop
Classical Music
Country Music
Elvis
Hip Hop
House
Irish Music
Jazz
Music USA

Opera
Reggae
Rock
Techno
World Music (2 vols)

History Guides
China
Egypt
England
France
India
Islam
Italy
Spain
USA

Reference Guides
Books for Teenagers
Children's Books, 0–5
Children's Books, 5–11
Cult Fiction
Cult Football
Cult Movies
Cult TV
Ethical Shopping
Formula 1
The iPod, iTunes &
  Music Online
The Internet
Internet Radio
James Bond
Kids' Movies
Lord of the Rings
Muhammad Ali
Man Utd
Personal Computers
Pregnancy & Birth
Shakespeare
Superheroes
Unexplained
  Phenomena
The Universe
Videogaming
Weather
Website Directory

ROUGH GUIDES ADVERTISER

Also! More than 120 Rough Guide music CDs are available from all good book
and record stores. Listen in at www.worldmusic.net

ROUGH GUIDES ADVERTISER

NOTES

369

small print and
Index

A Rough Guide to Rough Guides

In the summer of 1981, Mark Ellingham, a recent graduate from Bristol University, was travelling round Greece and couldn't find a guidebook that really met his needs. On the one hand there were the student guides, insistent on saving every last cent, and on the other the heavyweight cultural tomes whose authors seemed to have spent more time in a research library than lounging away the afternoon at a taverna or on the beach.

In a bid to avoid getting a job, Mark and a small group of writers set about creating their own guidebook. It was a guide to Greece that aimed to combine a journalistic approach to description with a thoroughly practical approach to travellers' needs – a guide that would incorporate culture, history and contemporary insights with a critical edge, together with up-to-date, value-for-money listings. Back in London, Mark and the team finished their Rough Guide, as they called it, and talked Routledge into publishing the book.

That first *Rough Guide to Greece*, published in 1982, was a student scheme that became a publishing phenomenon. The immediate success of the book – with numerous reprints and a Thomas Cook prize shortlisting – spawned a series that rapidly covered dozens of destinations. Rough Guides had a ready market among low-budget backpackers, but soon also acquired a much broader and older readership that relished Rough Guides' wit and inquisitiveness as much as their enthusiastic, critical approach. Everyone wants value for money, but not at any price.

Rough Guides soon began supplementing the "rougher" information about hostels and low-budget listings with the kind of detail on restaurants and quality hotels that independent-minded visitors on any budget might expect, whether on business in New York or trekking in Thailand.

These days the guides – distributed worldwide by the Penguin group – offer recommendations from shoestring to luxury and cover more than 200 destinations around the globe, including almost every country in the Americas and Europe, more than half of Africa and most of Asia and Australasia. Our ever-growing team of authors and photographers is spread all over the world, particularly in Europe, the USA and Australia.

In 1994, we published the *Rough Guide to World Music* and *Rough Guide to Classical Music*; and a year later the *Rough Guide to the Internet*. All three books have become benchmark titles in their fields – which encouraged us to expand into other areas of publishing, mainly around popular culture. Rough Guides now publish:

- Travel guides to more than 200 worldwide destinations
- Dictionary phrasebooks to 22 major languages
- History guides ranging from Ireland to Islam
- Maps printed on rip-proof and waterproof Polyart™ paper
- Music guides running the gamut from Opera to Elvis
- Restaurant guides to London, New York and San Francisco
- Reference books on topics as diverse as the Weather and Shakespeare
- Sports guides from Formula 1 to Man Utd
- Pop culture books from Lord of the Rings to Cult TV
- World Music CDs in association with World Music Network

Visit **www.roughguides.com** to see our latest publications.

Rough Guide credits

Text editor: Keith Drew
Layout: Ajay Verma
Cartography: Ed Wright
Picture research: Karin Andreasson
Proofreader: Nikky Twyman
Editorial: **London** Martin Dunford,
Kate Berens, Helena Smith, Claire Saunders,
Geoff Howard, Ruth Blackmore, Gavin
Thomas, Polly Thomas, Richard Lim, Clifton
Wilkinson, Alison Murchie, Sally Schafer,
Karoline Densley, Andy Turner, Ella
O'Donnell, Edward Aves, Andrew Lockett,
Joe Staines, Duncan Clark, Peter Buckley,
Matthew Milton, Daniel Crewe; **New York**
Andrew Rosenberg, Richard Koss, Chris
Barsanti, Steven Horak, AnneLise Sorensen,
Amy Hegarty
Design & Pictures: London Simon
Bracken, Dan May, Diana Jarvis, Mark
Thomas, Jj Luck, Harriet Mills, Chloë
Roberts; **Delhi** Madhulita Mohapatra,
Umesh Aggarwal, Jessica Subramanian,
Amit Verma

Production: Julia Bovis, Sophie Hewat,
Katherine Owers
Cartography: **London** Maxine Repath,
Katie Lloyd-Jones, Miles Irving;
Delhi Manish Chandra, Rajesh Chhibber,
Jai Prakash Mishra, Ashutosh Bharti,
Rajesh Mishra, Animesh Pathak,
Jasbir Sandhu, Karobi Gogoi
Online: **New York** Jennifer Gold, Suzanne
Welles, Benjamin Ross; **Delhi** Manik
Chauhan, Narender Kumar, Manish Shekhar
Jha, Lalit K. Sharma, Rakesh Kumar
Marketing & Publicity: **London** Richard
Trillo, Niki Hanmer, David Wearn, Chloë
Roberts, Demelza Dallow; **New York** Geoff
Colquitt, Megan Kennedy, Milena Perez;
Delhi Reem Khokhar
Custom publishing and foreign rights:
Philippa Hopkins
Finance: Gary Singh
Manager India: Punita Singh
Series editor: Mark Ellingham
PA to Managing Director: Megan McIntyre
Managing Director: Kevin Fitzgerald

Publishing information

This edition published April 2005 by
Rough Guides Ltd,
80 Strand, London WC2R 0RL.
345 Hudson St, 4th Floor,
New York, NY 10014, USA.
Distributed by the Penguin Group
Penguin Books Ltd,
80 Strand, London WC2R 0RL
Penguin Putnam, Inc.
375 Hudson St, NY 10014, USA
Penguin Group (Australia)
250 Camberwell Rd, Camberwell,
Victoria 3124, Australia
Penguin Books Canada Ltd,
10 Alcorn Ave, Toronto, Ontario,
Canada M4V 1E4
Penguin Group (New Zealand)
Corner Rosedale and Airborne roads
Albany, Auckland, New Zealand
Typeset in Bembo and Helvetica to an
original design by Henry Iles.
Printed in Italy by LegoPrint S.p.A

384pp includes index

A catalogue record for this book is available
from the British Library

ISBN 1-84353-407-X

The publishers and authors have done their
best to ensure the accuracy and currency of
all the information in **The Rough Guide to
First-Time Europe**, however, they can
accept no responsibility for any loss, injury,
or inconvenience sustained by any traveller
as a result of information or advice contained
in the guide.

10   9   8   7   6   5   4   3   2   1

Help us update

We've gone to a lot of effort to ensure that **The Rough Guide to First-Time Europe** is accurate and up-to-date. However, things change, and if we've got it wrong or left something out, we'd like to know.

We'll credit all contributions, and send a copy of the next edition (or any other Rough Guide if you prefer) for the best letters. Everyone who writes to us and isn't already a subscriber will receive a copy of our full-colour thrice-yearly newsletter. Please mark letters: "**Rough Guide First-Time Europe Update**" and send to: Rough Guides, 80 Strand, London WC2R 0RL, or Rough Guides, 4th Floor, 345 Hudson St, New York, NY 10014. Or send an email to **mail@roughguides.com**

Have your questions answered and tell others about your trip at **www.roughguides.atinfopop.com**

Acknowledgements

There are two people who played a particularly large role in the completion of this book. One is my editor, Keith Drew, who went over every word with the sort of care and consideration you hope your beloved grandmother would get in a nursing home. He was a joy to work with, though I sometimes wondered if his kind editorial comments – only because all-caps letters read like someone is shouting – were actually REFLECTING SOME SORT OF EDITORIAL FRUSTRATION. The other person, Henrik Harr, is the senior editor at Scandinavian Airlines' *Scanorama* magazine. While holding down a full-time job and planning his wedding, he willingly volunteered help (without me having to threaten to print a particularly embarrassing photo of him in this book) with the most demanding research portions within these pages.

I'd also like to thank the rest of the Rough Guides family – Kevin Fitzgerald, Martin Dunford, Kate Berens, Richard Trillo, Demelza Dallow and Claire Saunders in London, and Geoff Colquitt, Megan Kennedy and Milena Perez in New York – for all the editorial support, marketing, and the large box of paper clips I took on my last visit to the office.

I'm grateful to those writers and travellers kind enough to share their wisdom in this book's sidebar sections. As you may have noticed, several of them have written excellent books conveniently available at your favourite bookstore.

And finally, enormous praise for my agent, Michael Bourret, who somehow convinced Rough Guides to pay me to write this book when I would have gladly done it for a warm meal and pack of subway tokens.

Photo credits

Cover credits

Main front picture Colosseum, Rome © Alamy
Front (left image) Matterhorn, Switzerland © Imagestate
Front (right image) Arc de Triomphe, Paris © Alamy
Back (top) Casa Mila, Barcelona © Alamy
Back (lower) Pyrenees © Alamy

Colour introduction

Espresso machine © Getty/Stewart Cohen
Neuschwanstein Castle © Werner H. Müller/CORBIS

Eastern European beer bottles © Robert Harding
Vegetable seller in Madrid © Corbis/Paul Almasy
Paragliding with the Matterhorn in the background © Valais Tourism
Café society © Alamy/Alex Segre
Goreme Valley, Anatolia, Turkey © Corbis/Jonathan Blair
Trevi Fountain © Alamy/Travel-Shots

Things to enrich your journey

1   Mont Blanc, France © Alamy/Agence Images
2   Chestnut seller, Turkey © Alamy/Pat Behnke

Black and white photos

Author picture

Doug Lansky © Ulla Montan

Index

Map entries are in colour.

U

V

V

W